GOING POSTAL

1,200.99

361 - 9/3

39.82 9/1

2,023.74

488.25 - 9/1

1,461.14

583 - 9/2

1,928.53

311.00 - 9/3

943 - 9/3

984.95 9/3

252 -

342.95 9/1

GOING POSTAL

Rage, Murder, and Rebellion

From Reagan's Workplaces
to Clinton's Columbine and Beyond

Mark Ames

Design by Gary Fogelson
Cover photo by Jacqueline DiMilia

Published by Soft Skull Press
55 Washington Street, 804
Brooklyn, NY 11201
www.softskull.com

Distributed by Publishers Group West
800.488.3123 | www.pgw.com

Printed in Canada

Library of Congress Cataloging-in-Publication Data

Ames, Mark, 1965–
  Going postal : rage, murder, and rebellion : from Reagan's workplaces to
Clinton's Columbine and beyond / by Mark Ames.
    p. cm.
  ISBN 1-932360-82-4
  1. Murder—United States. 2. Violent crimes—United States. 3. United
States—Social conditions—1980– I. Title.

HV6529.A52 2005
364.152'3'0973—dc22

CONTENTS

"The chimps are infected! They're highly contagious!"
"Infected with what?"
"Rage ..."

—*28 Days Later*

Part IV: Wage Rage

Part V: More Rage. More Rage.

Part VI: Welcome to the Dollhouse

PART I

If He'd Just Got the Right People

1

"I told them I'd be back."

ON SEPTEMBER 14, 1989, Joseph Wesbecker, known as "Rocky" to his co-workers, inadvertently helped spark a bloody rebellion.

At just around 8:30 AM, he pulled up to the Standard Gravure building in downtown Louisville, a 1920s-era printing press attached to the *Louisville Courier-Journal*. The severe rectangular building took up an entire block of Sixth Street between Broadway and Chestnut in the rundown city center. Wesbecker parked his red Chevy Monza hatchback at a meter just in front of Standard Gravure's main entrance. He wore jeans and a tan jacket and his trademark tinted steel-framed glasses.

One witness who saw Wesbecker emerge from his car said that he was "acting weird," in part because parking on that block of Sixth Street is prohibited until 9 AM. She also said she saw him handle what looked like a package under a blanket in the back of his hatchback.

"I was going to hold the elevator for him," she told the *Courier-Journal*, but Wesbecker stayed at his car so she rode up alone.

The street-level entrance that Wesbecker parked in front of led to the third floor executive offices of Standard Gravure. The main door to the elevator was left unlocked during work hours—only the stairwell door remained locked. The entrance at one time had a mounted security camera above the door, but it was removed over the summer after having been repeatedly vandalized. In many of America's midsized cities, downtowns have become like South Vietnamese hamlets: "ours" during the day, "theirs" at night.

The elevator went straight up to the executive reception area on the third floor. The other entrance, around the block on Broadway, led straight to the printing presses. That was the blue-collar entrance, the one "Rocky" would normally take. But on this day he didn't plan to work the printing press folder.

Wesbecker rode the elevator up, brandishing a Chinese-made AK-47 semiautomatic at his hip and packing a German-made SIG-Sauer 9mm pistol in his pants. Strapped around his shoulder was a gym bag (within a few years, the gym/duffel bag would be recognized as a standard-issue rage murder accessory), packed with two MAC-11 semiautomatic pistols, a .38-caliber Smith & Wesson revolver, and several rounds of ammunition, including five loaded clips for the AK.

The elevator door opened and Wesbecker immediately opened fire. His first two victims were receptionists Sharon Needy, who later died, and Angela Bowman, who was shot in the back and paralyzed from the waist down. Needy usually reported to work at 9 AM, but on this day she showed up a half hour early so that she could take an extended lunch break. Bowman had given birth a few months earlier and had just returned to Standard Gravure from maternity leave.

Wesbecker rounded the corner to the hallway of offices where the executive and managerial staff worked. Payroll administrator JoAnne Self, whose office was near the reception, heard the first two shots and stuck her head out the door. There she saw Wesbecker standing outside the office of Mike Shea, Standard Gravure's new owner and president. Shea just happened to be away that day.

Wesbecker fired; Self didn't see where. She fled.

"[Wesbecker] wasn't running," Self told the *Courier-Journal*. "He was walking very slowly. But I ran. I ran and fell and crawled the rest of the way."

Self and three other employees hid at the end of the hallway in the office of data processing manager Mike Delph, who had managed to call 911.

Wesbecker walked slowly, firing deliberately. Police major Ed Mercer told reporters that day that Wesbecker showed "extreme shooting discipline," firing directly at his human targets and taking few random shots.

Systems operator Kathy Johnson was at work in the computer room, around the corner from the reception area, when she heard a "loud bang." She poked her head out to see what was happening when a co-worker sprinted by in a panic. Johnson closed her door and stayed in the computer room.

"I was going to get in the closet, but it was locked," Johnson said. "So I stooped behind the computer." She heard four shots—then silence. Johnson quietly called the other offices in the hallway. One person answered, Paula Warman, the assistant to the vice president of human resources (the VP was gone that day along with Shea and the company's number-two man).

Warman, who had been shot in the legs, answered, "Some of us have been shot. Some of us have been shot." As it turns out, Warman figured as one of the key players in a management-worker dispute that helped push Wesbecker over the edge.

Wesbecker moved from the white-collar office area down a long narrow hallway and into the third floor bindery. He opened the door and shot John Stein, a maintenance supervisor, in the head and abdomen. Two other maintenance workers in the bindery were also shot, Forrest Conrad, shot in the legs, and James G. "Buck" Husband, who was killed. When two female employees happened into the bindery a few minutes later, not realizing what was happening, they saw Stein bleeding from the head, leaning against the door.

One woman lifted Stein's head and tried to put a shirt under it to comfort him. "He grabbed the shirt out of my hand," the woman later told reporters before breaking down in tears.

From the third floor Wesbecker headed down a metal stairwell into the pounding dissonance of the pressroom. It was more crowded with workers than usual because of the shift change at 9 AM. Wesbecker shot and wounded two men in the bindery basement and killed another, Paul Sallee, who was found on the floor with a bullet wound in his chest.

Wesbecker crossed a tunnel to the basement of the pressroom. It was a large room cluttered with giant paper rolls, which look like huge rolling pins without the handles. Large aluminum ducts, ladders, and other printing equipment were cluttered together to form a kind of mid-twentieth-century industrial labyrinth. The bottom halves of the three printing press machines, which operated on the ground floor above, extended down into the basement.

Wesbecker entered the basement room just as John Tingle, a pressman who'd heard a "loud noise that sounded like a steel plate hitting the floor," rounded the corner to see what was happening.

Tingle knew Wesbecker and greeted him as if it was just another day, despite the smoking AK and the ominous duffel bag packed with guns and ordinance.

"Hey, Rock, what's happening?" Tingle asked, using the friendly shortened version of Wesbecker's menacing-sounding nickname.

Wesbecker, who had always been on friendly terms with Tingle, replied, "Hi John . . . I told them I'd be back. Get away from me."

"I said, 'What are you doing, Rocky?'" Tingle later told reporters. "I started to walk toward him, and he said, 'Get away.'" Wesbecker repeated himself, this time telling Tingle to get the fuck away. Tingle obeyed and motioned to the others nearby to move away.

Rocky headed toward a stairwell between two presses, firing as he approached. The body of Richard O. Barger, who was shot in the back, lay at the bottom of the stairwell—head cocked back onto a conveyor belt, arms splayed on the rubber belt as if crucified, and with blood splattered on the floor around him. That image—a now famous page one *Courier-Journal* photo—led to a lawsuit filed by Barger's family and a Supreme Court ruling on press freedoms versus the privacy of the bereaved. It seems that Wesbecker didn't intend to kill Barger. He was coming down the metal stairwell, and Wesbecker probably didn't see who it was before he fired. According to witnesses, after killing him, Wesbecker walked over to Barger's body, apologized, then turned around and continued his rampage.

Wesbecker fired three times as he walked up the stairwell and about another dozen times when he reached the top. He walked down the long row between press one and press two, shooting at anyone who hadn't scrambled out of his way— Lloyd White and James Wible Sr. were both murdered on the press floor. The shots and screams were drowned out by the din of the printing presses.

At the far end of the pressroom was the break room, with vending machines, an eating area, and an adjacent locker room. Wesbecker pushed open the door with his shoulder and sprayed the seven workers inside, emptying his clip. All seven were shot; one, William Ganote, was killed immediately with a bullet to the head. Wesbecker popped out the empty clip, loaded a fresh one, lifted the AK, and fired into the group a second time. A second man also died, while the other five all received multiple bullet wounds.

The presses churned, moans and cries were muffled. Bodies lay strewn from the white-collar elevator entrance on one end of the building all the way to the opposite end, the break room. The company was destroyed. His mission accomplished, Wesbecker stepped out of the press room, pulled out his German SIG-Sauer 9mm semiautomatic, put it up to his face, and pulled the trigger.

After nearly thirty minutes, the first modern private workplace massacre in American history, the rage murder that would spawn so many, had ended. Seven were killed, twenty wounded.

And everyone was left asking why. The same question they still ask today after each workplace rage massacre.

2

Pow! Pow! Pow!

MICHAEL CAMPBELL is a squat, vigorous, always-smiling retiree with tinted steel-framed glasses and a thick black mustache. He walks with a sinking limp. One of his stubby arms is so disfigured at the elbow from gunshot wounds that it looks as though he got stuck while trying to demonstrate a double-jointed quirk, and never was able to pop the bones back in. He was shot six times by Wesbecker.

Campbell struck me as almost pathologically cheerful, laughing while he recounted the most horrible details of the murder spree, not because he found them funny, but because he wanted to make sure that the listener was at ease by demonstrating his own ability to laugh at his pain.

When my friend Allie, my Louisville connection, called him to help arrange an interview about Wesbecker, she told him that my angle would be unusual: I was trying to figure out if Wesbecker was in any way "justified." That is to say, did former employees and victims think that he simply snapped, as the popular conception tells us, or did they think he was driven to desperation by circumstances within the company. I'd expected that Campbell, as a disfigured victim who barely escaped with his life, would have recoiled at the very suggestion. But according to Allie, his first response was, "Hell, everybody supported him, everybody understood where he was coming from. His only problem was that he shot the wrong people."

Campbell was a little more guarded with me than he was over the phone with Allie. He spoke of how Wesbecker suffered from manic depression, emphasizing that he was on antidepressants in the years leading up to the massacre. Campbell and other victims had sued the drug company Eli Lilly and settled out of court, alleging that Prozac had led Wesbecker to violence. He wouldn't say much more about the lawsuit, but the results were clear: Campbell and his wife lived in a spacious split-level home in a gated community, with its own golf course, in the lush rolling hills just southwest of Louisville. Not exactly your typical blue-collar pensioner's fate, at least not in post-Reagan America.

Michael Campbell was one of the seven men in the break room—Wesbecker's last stop on his rampage spree. Here is how he described the experience to me:

"There were two presses running, and evidently, the workers were all in between the units working and didn't see him. There's three presses in a row. He walked this way [between press two and press three] saw a guy here and shot him. At this point a bunch of them, when they heard the shots, took off. Now this is a room where you can rub your foot and the static from the electricity will set this thing off. The fumes in there are so strong, you know. A lot of times we'd pull paper through and the little thing would arc off and the ink would catch fire. He's firing a gun in there and it's not doing anything! We found out later he put a fire suppressor on there. So he kills one guy—he's looking for the foreman, there's two offices at the end of the hall."

"Was it Wesbecker's foreman?" I asked.

"Yes. Well, it wasn't his regular foreman. His regular foreman was on a different shift . . . but Wesbecker knew that the superintendent would be there. And he knew that the people who were part of his problem were there."

That was an interesting line I didn't catch until I played the tape back afterward: "He knew that the people who were part of his problem were there."

"So just as he was coming up, the foreman was just walking out his door. Luckiest man alive. He walked right past Wesbecker and said, 'I saw him.' And all of a sudden somebody said something to [Wesbecker] and he shot him. Another guy went past him and slammed against the wall and he was banging on the door [to the locker room], like a garage door, asking people to let him. . . . There were some two dozen workers in the locker room. They scattered through another door to the other side when the one they let in yelled, 'Wesbecker's shootin' everybody!' Some were in the showers; they hid against the wall and waited.

"We're sitting inside the break room, right by the door to the pressroom, and I heard the pop! pop! pop! And I thought, 'Oh God, that sounded like a gun.'" In an earlier interview, Campbell had described it as sounding "like a balloon popping, not like a gun."

". . . I was readin' the paper, and the door's back behind me. And I'm thinking, 'Damn, that's soundin' like a gun, doesn't sound like anything that I've ever heard here.' And before I could do anything I look around and here he comes through this door, pushing the door open. And I just went, 'Oh boy!' And it went Pow! Pow! Pow! and hit me three times. All three times."

"Where?"

Campbell's scars were conspicuous, like deep, long flesh dents. He wore shorts and a polo shirt on the day of our interview, so he could show me his scars, which he did obligingly, even enthusiastically. It was as if Campbell was describing what had happened to someone else, as if he'd researched some other victim's story so well he could recite it by heart without feeling the victim's fear or pain.

"Right through the knee. And these, you can't even believe. It went right through here and through the bone." He showed me his right arm, the dent now smooth, like erosion on stone. "It shattered my elbow. And then he went on around the room. We were sitting around a round table. So the guy at this table dunked the table over and hit the ground. The only bullet that they ever found in anybody went into his head and stayed in his head. He only got shot once, and he died. The rest of us in the room got shot many times.

"One guy stood up. I thought he said, 'Oh no,' but he said, 'Oh, Joe,' and he just shot him—pow! pow! pow!"

Later, I thought about this as further proof of Wesbecker's clearheaded resolve. Tingle said, "Hey Rock, what's happening?" and Wesbecker responded amicably at first, and spared him; in the last target area, the break room where the supervisor should have been, a friendly, "Oh, Joe," was answered with bullets.

"[Wesbecker] turned to me and shot me. Went around the room and shot everybody. And stepped outside—we didn't know this but he stepped outside, pulled the banana clip out, turned it over, popped it back in, went back in and went Pop! Pop! Pop! Pop! Going around the room. And he got me six more times.

"I fell over on the table trying to act like I was dead, like this—" Campbell excitedly demonstrates for me: slumped forward, arms limply outstretched, eyes closed; then he lifts his head up, beaming with a smile, and continues recounting: "I was tryin' not to breathe, cuz I didn't know where he was. You know, all these things are runnin' through your mind when you're sittin' there and seconds, milliseconds, and I thought, 'God, so he's just gonna walk up behind me and just shoot me!' And you know, why would you shoot somebody in the room if you didn't kill them, you know. And I was tryin' not to breathe, and I was thinkin', 'What in the hell is goin' on?' There was this long pause where he stepped outside and changed the clip.

"One guy got up and ran out of the room. 'Course, I couldn't see him, I could hear somebody rustlin' around. And all of a sudden—POW! . . . POW! POW! I can feel my body jerk, but I couldn't feel anything at that point. The first [bullet] just numbed me completely. I didn't feel anything after that, but I could feel my body jerking around. He hit me six times, in the legs, arms.

"And then there's a long pause again, and one guy's laying on the floor and he said, 'Can you get up?' And I said, 'Where in the hell is he?' You know. 'What the hell's going on?'" Campbell laughed. "And he said, 'He just went outside the door.' And I said, 'I can't get up.' I could feel my leg, when it was hit it went out sideways, and my arm was just dangling down this way. I said, 'I can't get outta this chair, I don't think.' And he said, 'We gotta get out of here.' One of the bullets punctured a water line, and water just whooo was sprayin' around the room. And we had this much [several inches] of water on the floor. He said, 'We gotta get out of here.' He said, 'I got shot in the chest.' It collapsed his lungs and he was bleedin'. Of course I didn't know I was bleedin', but I knew he shot me in the arm, I mean I could tell cuz the arm was just hanging at an awkward angle.

"So I scooted a chair over and tried to get down. 'Course—ha!—my arm collapsed and I hit the floor. And I'm thinking, 'Oh gawd, I'm gonna bleed to death.' And there was water everywhere. He said, 'We gotta go and get help.' And I said, 'I can't go anywhere, you know, I can't move.' So he said, 'Well I can, I can crawl.' So he crawled over the top of me and went out the door . . .

"So when this guy crawled over the top of me, he left. He didn't come back. I thought, 'Oh god, I'm in here and I'm bleedin' on this floor and I don't know where the hell this guy is.' I could see this guy layin' outside the door in this great big pool of blood. . . . He had like either a pale green or tan jacket on, and sort of reddish colored hair. I didn't know who it was until the next day. I thought, 'I gotta get out of here.' So I started crawlin—now this is funny!" Campbell smiled and laughed. "It's not funny, but—I started crawlin', laying on my back, and I was crawling this way, pushing with my right leg . . . and thought, 'God, you gotta pull this door'. I couldn't get out in the hallway cuz you gotta pull it. And I thought, 'Oh god.' So I lay there for a few minutes and I thought, 'You know, if I can get my head into the damn thing, I can get it open.' So I got my arm over here, and I couldn't get this one, and I reached back here—" Campbell demonstrated how, back to the floor, head first, he maneuvered his way through the door. "I pulled the door just a little bit, got my head in there, then got my shoulders in, then I got into the hallway that runs right into the pressroom.

"I started whistlin' and yellin'. I said, 'Somebody help us. Guy's in here with a gun.' A guy at the end of the hallway, about thirty feet away, said, 'I know he's in there, but we don't know where he is. And we can't get in there.' And I said, 'He just killed himself.'" Campbell laughed. "I knew in my mind that he'd killed himself. I said, 'He just shot himself.' And he said, 'Is he dead?' And I said, 'I don't know, he's layin' in a big pool of blood.' So this guy runs down the hallway, goes through those doors, and goes up and looks at this person laying on the floor, and came back and said, 'Yep, that's him.' And broadcasts it over his radio."

"So this was a cop?" I asked.

"It was an EMS guy. He put his life on the line. The cops were all over the place but they wouldn't go in. And this guy did."

"The cops wouldn't go in?"

"They knew he was loaded with guns and they didn't know where he was, and there's a building where he knows all the openings. They were in the building, but they were behind him all the way."

The cops were still in the basement when another EMS worker—an African American woman, her first day on the job—came and helped set Campbell on a gurney. It turned out that she served in the same National Guard medical unit as Campbell's daughter.

When she started cutting his clothes off, she couldn't hide her fear and revulsion. "I said to her, 'Dammit, stop, you're scarin' the hell out of me,'" Campbell said, laughing. "Every time she'd tear it up, she'd go, 'Oh-ho!' It wasn't funny, but later on it was. And she laughed about it later on and said, 'I'm sorry, I've never seen anything like that.' Things were just blown away. Although it wasn't that bad. I had a big flap of skin just hanging down here that was pretty bad—" He pointed to the three-inch-long, inch-deep dent on his right arm. "There was blood all over. My glasses were full of blood, my everything's full of blood. But, uh, I didn't know it at the time. I had on a uniform and she's just cuttin' it off of me. And she'd go, 'Heww!'"

3

Little Doughboy

IN THE FIRST PART of my interview with Michael Campbell his description of Wesbecker pretty much fit the ready-to-snap kook portrait that the press had drawn. He was troubled, from a broken home, the damaged survivor of two broken marriages, he blamed others for his problems . . . He was "tormented by mental illness," according to the *Courier-Journal*. Wesbecker's mother was in a mental institution and his father abandoned them early in life. He was convinced that he wasn't being paid properly—supposedly another sign of his "persecution complex," but as I was to learn, in the eyes of government arbitrators, Wesbecker was indeed persecuted, and he wasn't the only one not being "paid properly." This narrow portrait of a mentally-ill nut who snapped not only helped bracket Wesbecker as a loon, but it also strengthened the survivors' class-action suit against Eli Lilly, the makers of Prozac.

Another picture of Wesbecker also emerged: that of a desperately ambitious striver crushed by the brutal new corporate culture that started to dominate under Reaganomics.

And another image: Wesbecker was a pathetic nerd whose every attempt to reinvent himself only brought him greater humiliation.

He never quite fit in with the other workers at Standard Gravure because he came from a different working-class district of Louisville—the West End, now predominately African American—than most of the other pressmen. A job at Standard Gravure was something of a territorial right. The plant had been operating since the 1920s and was a mainstay of downtown Louisville's old industrial heyday. Wesbecker's first job as a pressman was at the old Fawcett-Dearing Printing Company, also in downtown Louisville. In 1971, he switched to Standard Gravure because the money was better.

Joseph Wesbecker was a workaholic. He regularly put in twenty-five to thirty hours of overtime a week. He even worked the folder, an operating machine featuring a panel full of buttons that controls such final quality factors as color registry and correct fold. The folder was the command center of the printing line—and the most stressful job on the floor. The operator of the machine was called "the man in charge," which suited Wesbecker fine when he was still at the top of his game. If you worked the folder, you operated it in thirty-minute shifts because the fumes and solvents, as well as the stress, made longer shifts impossible.

"He was obsessed with money," Campbell said. "He'd work two shifts in a row. He was manic about it."

He bought an expensive sports car and a nice house in a good neighborhood just west of Iroquois Park, a lush well-to-do residential district east of downtown. "It was as if he had something to prove. He really overcompensated with everything," Campbell said.

Wesbecker reportedly had a couple hundred thousand dollars saved up in the bank, quite a lot of money in Kentucky, where property is cheap. All that hard work and relative wealth didn't convert itself into the respect and satisfaction he was hoping for: Wesbecker's second marriage was an even greater disaster than his first. He accused his second wife of sleeping around with his co-workers from the plant. Some former colleagues implied that Wesbecker's fears were justified.

Wesbecker was short, around five feet eight inches, and "chubby," particularly around his face and belly. He had red curly hair and wore large tinted glasses. His first nickname at Standard Gravure was "Little Doughboy"—Campbell couldn't help but chuckle when he revealed this first nickname. "It was funny to those who knew him." Campbell added, "He wasn't a ladies' man."

The nickname "Rocky"—used by the press to imply a pugnacious and violent man—appeared later.

Wesbecker tried to play the ladies' man in spite of his disadvantages. He'd always party after work, was always up for a beer at the bar. Hard-working, hard-playin' hard hat kinda guy. Never afraid to hit on women, though rarely successful, he kept going for more, never down for the count. To some of his co-workers, the latest story about Wesbecker's sexual misadventures was a running comedy skit; to others, it was painful to hear.

And then came the Rocky incident. Wesbecker was sitting at a bar popping off to a woman, a former YMCA instructor, for the benefit of the guys, when she transformed his blue-collar banter into every nerd's nightmare: she beat the living shit out of Joe Wesbecker. Right in front of his friends. After that, everyone at the plant started calling Wesbecker "Rocky." Not because he was a violent person by nature, but rather because he got stomped by a woman whom he'd tried to hit on. Thus the nickname "Rocky" was so cruelly ironic, on a playground scale, that for the media to have explained where it really came from would have been confusing, since it cannot help but arouse some pathos, some sympathy.

Wesbecker joined Standard Gravure's workforce in 1971 at the age of twenty-nine. In 1978, Wesbecker divorced his wife of seventeen years. One son suffered from scoliosis; the other son was busted for exposing himself in public. In 1980, Wesbecker started complaining about the stress from his job and asked his supervisor if he could stop working the folder. He complained that the fumes from the solvents were harming his health, physically and mentally—he even blamed the chemicals for his son's defects. Most Standard Gravure workers agree that the fumes and solvents were harmful. Two former employees told me they'd often get dizzy.

Incredibly enough, the company refused to take Wesbecker off the folder. He continued complaining and asking to be moved—but for several more years, management refused. His union, which had been decimated during the eighties due to both local economic conditions and a general anti-union trend at the national level under Reagan, failed to help. No other co-worker wanted to take the folder off of his hands. By all accounts, it was the worst job in the plant. Wesbecker, as the outsider and laughingstock, was low on the pecking order.

Meanwhile, conditions at the printing plant were deteriorating. During the seventies, the Standard Gravure plant was prosperous, and the workers there, whose union was strong (in an era when unions still mattered), had good, comfortable lives. The salad days came to an abrupt halt in the eighties, in part due to technological changes in the printing industry, in part due to the new corporate culture ushered in by the Reagan Revolution—specifically, an era in which the power of unions wilted under a new morality that prioritized competition and shareholder value over the increasingly "quaint" notion that companies should take care of their workforce first. Campbell told me that the Bingham family, old-money Kentucky aristocrats who had owned the Standard Gravure plant since the early twenties, engaged in a combination of brutal downsizing, union-crushing, and what President Bush would now call "corporate malfeasance."

It all started in the early eighties, when the Binghams threatened to close the plant if the union didn't cave in to their downsizing demands. According to Campbell, a new plant was built in Tennessee without the union's knowledge. When the workers found out, they confronted the Binghams, who threatened the union, telling them they had a choice: bend to their demands or face closure at the Louisville site. Their Tennessee plant would be union-free. The Standard Gravure union caved. Cuts were made. And more cuts. In 1982, employees agreed to a wage freeze that continued for six years. Then the Binghams offered a raise if the union agreed to lay off another thirty-five of their fellow workers. The workers were fired, but once again the Binghams pled poverty and the promised raise never materialized. Unionized staff dropped from three hundred to sixty-eight, according to Campbell. Employees were working up to five shifts in a row. Divorce shot through the roof. The workers didn't get a single raise for eight straight years and had been working without a contract for eighteen months.

"Tensions within the plant grew," Campbell said. "Stress doesn't unite people."

Don Frazier, president of the Graphic Communications International Union Local 19 said, "As soon as we found out the Binghams were going to bust up the empire, that's when the anxiety started to build."

In 1986, the Binghams put their communications empire up for sale, which included Standard Gravure and the *Louisville Courier-Journal*. To sweeten the offer, the employees' retirement fund, to the tune of ten million dollars, was raided in the sale and division of assets: Gannett, publisher of *USA Today*, took the *Courier-Journal*, and a young corporate raider from Atlanta named Michael Shea took Standard Gravure. Sometime after taking over Standard Gravure, Shea took a page out of the Bingham family's corporate management handbook: he announced plans to build a new printing press plant in Pennsylvania, further pressuring Louisville's workers.

In spite of this, Shea told reporters on the day of the rage massacre that he did not consider the company a stressful place to work.

Campbell sharply disagreed: "Most people were bitter at the company," he said. Relations were so bad that Campbell's wife wouldn't even let Standard Gravure's management visit him in the hospital after the shooting.

The day after the shooting, Tom Gosling, a Standard Gravure pressman, described the atmosphere at the plant to the *Courier-Journal*: "It's miserable."

Wesbecker started seeing a psychiatrist in the early eighties. He married for a second time in 1981. "Wesbecker was whipped," Campbell quipped. He suspected his wife was cheating on him—and Campbell hinted it was true, even with friends of his from the plant. As the stress compounded, Wesbecker asked that he be taken off the folder. His supervisor refused. Wesbecker complained. He even had a doctor write a letter to the company urging them to take him off the folder—and they still refused. In 1987 Wesbecker filed a discrimination complaint with the Louisville and Jefferson County Human Relations Commission against Standard Gravure. In the complaint he said that he was a manic depressive and he charged the plant with discrimination by assigning him to stressful jobs that worsened his condition and made it more difficult to perform his duties.

As an object of mockery, as the socially awkward outsider, "Rocky" or "Little Doughboy" Wesbecker wasn't likely to get much sympathy from the other employees, all of whom were stressed out as well, none of whom wanted the awful folder job. After all, they hadn't received a wage increase since 1982; what was the point of killing yourself for a company that clearly didn't care about you anyway? Wesbecker was squeezed between the schoolyard cruelty of his co-workers and the management culture now ruling the company. Clearly management wanted to get rid of him, or if not, to squeeze him for everything they could until he finally withered and dropped off the vine by himself.

Wesbecker finally came to a settlement with Standard Gravure. Officially they denied they'd violated his rights but agreed to "make accommodation for any mental handicap he may continue to suffer" and return him to work as soon as he was better. He stopped working in August 1988, taking medical leave for psychological stress. On February 2, 1989, rather than compromise by moving him to a position in the plant that was less stressful, the company put Wesbecker on long-term disability and slashed his pay. He asked to be allowed to work again full-time, but they offered him only part-time work at best.

"There was no full-time work left," Campbell said.

The company planned to slash Wesbecker's disability pension in October 1989, cutting his pay to just sixty percent of what he'd made before. Take it or leave it. He didn't wait for October's paycheck cut to arrive.

Wesbecker had worked harder than any other employee, even by some of his victims' own admission, for nearly two decades. And for all that not only did they freeze his pay, but when he started to suffer from the effects of overwork, the company refused to help him by lightening his load. In the pro-management book *New Arenas For Violence*, a workplace violence-prevention study that offers various "management techniques" to deal with the growing problem, author Michael Kelleher commented on Wesbecker: "This tragedy should have been avoided by the corporate management. Wesbecker was a local employee who had performed well for two decades. When he was faced with a crisis in his life and approached his employer for assistance, the organization abandoned him. By their actions in ignoring Wesbecker's plea for help, those in charge at the Standard Gravure Corporation helped set the stage for murder. With nothing left in his life but his job, and with obvious ties and commitments to his employer, Wesbecker felt he had no option but to take revenge." This is partly true, but the author failed to see that the management's attitude towards Wesbecker wasn't a localized case of mismanagement, but rather a broader cultural effect of the top-down revolution emanating straight out of the cold mouth of Ronald Reagan, who used his bully pulpit to persuade middle America that unions were the cause of economic stagnation and at were essentially anti-American.

In the months leading up to the massacre, Wesbecker became fascinated with Patrick Sherrill. Sherrill was responsible for the first major post office massacre in America, the 1986 murder rampage in Edmond, Oklahoma, which left fourteen people dead and six injured and spawned a new mass-murder phenomenon that became known as "going postal." Until Wesbecker's massacre at Standard Gravure, those "postal" rampages were confined to post offices. To most of America it seemed to be a bizarre, darkly comic yet localized problem that had something to do with this one particular government agency, rather than the early signs of a new trend set to spread through the nation's workplaces. Wesbecker saw these postal rampages differently. He was desperate, cornered, cracked, and humiliated. In this frame of mind, the post office massacres of the previous few years provided a kind of script that had never existed before, a language of direct vengeance, if not empowerment. It is strange, in fact, to think that before Wesbecker, before 1989, there had been no popular history of employees snapping and massacring their companies by shooting everyone inside. But that is because, as I will show, until the eighties America's corporate culture was much different.

Indeed, Wesbecker, though he makes an unlikely revolutionary, represents the bridge between the post office massacres and office massacres in general. He broke the taboo. Before Standard Gravure, no one could have imagined that the workplace—any workplace—could be the setting of a massacre initiated by one of the company's own. After Wesbecker, the language of office massacres had entered America's lexicon. Anyone, anywhere might "go postal" at anytime.

Employees later recalled that Wesbecker bragged about his weapons collection and spoke of going into Standard Gravure and "showing them." At the time it was seen as empty bluster—there was no precedent, no context for a workplace massacre carried out by a company employee. There had been no private office massacre to prepare people, to catalogue and value-grade events which had previously seemed literally unimaginable.

After the massacre, news reports told of Wesbecker's "random choice of victims" in their general portrait of a psycho who'd snapped, thereby lending quiet support to the company president's claim that Standard Gravure wasn't a stressful place to work.

But others have since sharply disagreed. "He had an exact route. He did have a purpose," Campbell said.

Today, it's hard to find anyone who is angry with Wesbecker, but easy to find people, even victims, who will tell you that Wesbecker was pushed to do what he did.

Earl Gardner, a fellow pressman at Standard Gravure who retired a couple of years before Wesbecker's massacre (he took an early retirement package after watching how the plant's owners were stripping his retirement and health benefits, as well as company assets), told me, "Oh, Joe? He was pushed into it! Lotta folks will tell you that. They pushed him! If he'd just got the right people, he'd've had a lot more sympathy. Still does, as it is!" Gardner, a devout Christian who has traveled on evangelical missions to Eastern Europe and Israel, is still disgusted with the way the company was sold off and stripped, leaving the workers' lives destroyed.

In a locally made documentary, "A Pain in the Innards," another former Standard Gravure pressman, in words carefully chosen before the video camera, said of Wesbecker's murder rampage, "It's not impossible to imagine how you could be pressed to that place."

A police officer who was on the scene of the massacre said, in the same documentary, "The amazing thing to me was that when I talked to the employees they named three or four other workers before Wesbecker who they thought might have been capable of doing that."

Even Larry VonderHaar, vice president of labor relations for the *Courier-Journal*, conceded in an interview a few years after the massacre that management's decision to put Wesbecker on long-term disability rather than take him off the folder was wrong and "that would obviously not be the case today."

In other words, Wesbecker's "rebellion" had some positive effect *ex post facto*: management started listening.

And Standard Gravure is closed. It no longer exists today. Which is one of the goals of these rage massacres—the perpetrators are attacking the entire company, the workplace as an institution, the corporate culture, at least as much as the individuals whom they shoot. That's why there are no "random" victims—everyone in the targeted company is guilty by association, or they're collateral damage. The goal is to destroy the company itself, the source of the pain.

VonderHaar had no doubt that Wesbecker wasn't merely murdering at random: "I think he was looking for the supervisor. The supervisor's office was right there and, obviously, the supervisor was the focal point of his unhappiness about the assignment to the folder. And the guess of many of us is that that's who he intended to get revenge on." Both the CEO and the supervisor just happened to be out when Joe Wesbecker's revenge came.

4

Just Tough It Out

IN A DEPOSITION taken a few years after the massacre, Daniel Mattingly, a compliance officer with the Louisville and Jefferson County Human Relations Commission who handled Wesbecker's job discrimination complaint, gave testimony that reveals what I believe to be the true underlying cause of the massacre: an unprecedented corporate cold-bloodedness that has overtaken America over the past several decades. Here is Mattingly's account of Wesbecker's last eighteen months, as he desperately fought against Standard Gravure's callous and cruel management, exhausting every legal, nonviolent tool he could.

A. Well, he came in complaining that he was being discriminated against on the job by the company that he worked for. His complaint revolved around his assertion that his supervisors were forcing him to work on a machine at work called the folder, and that when they did not force him to work on that machine they were threatening to make him work on that machine. . . . [H]e had a statement from the company psychologist saying that he should not be made to work on this folder, which was a stressful machine, unless absolutely necessary. But that even though he had this statement from the psychologist, the company officials were making him work the folder and, more than that, threatening to make him work the folder. [. . .] He was maintaining that the company would make exceptions for people with physical ailments and not make them work the folder, but they would not make an exception for him, who had an emotional problem, and therefore discrimination. And that was his basic argument.

Q. With regard to his statements on that date, sir, did he give you any names of people at work or discuss any specifics of foremen or supervisors?

A. Yes. He mentioned that Donald Cox was his general foreman and there were two immediate supervisors, Popham and McKeown. He gave examples. I think he said that Mr. Popham kept insisting that there was really nothing wrong with him and that, "If we need to put you on the folder, we will." And that Mr. McKeown said things like, "All you need to do is just tough it out and do your job." You see, he maintained that they were using his handicap against him, because if they threatened him he would go home and worry about that and stew and fret over it. And so it became a problem even when he was away from the job because he was afraid when he went back in they were going to make him do that.

Q. Did he discuss the work environment at Standard Gravure with you, sir?

A. Well, he had a theory about what caused his—his problem, and that was related to the work environment at Standard Gravure.

Q. How so?

A. He told me that for the last fifteen, seventeen years, whatever it is he had worked there, that he had been exposed to a chemical called toluene, and he brought with him copies of pages from a magazine that discussed the effects of being exposed to toluene, and they indicated that extended exposure can destroy the central nervous system, and his theory was this is why I am the way I am and he handed me this article for me to read. Toluene, as I understand, is a solvent. I'm not sure what they used it for and I don't think that it had anything to do with the folder, it was just if you worked at Standard Gravure you were exposed to this.

According to the Web site of the Agency for Toxic Substances and Disease Registry, an agency of the U.S. Department of Health and Human Services: "Toluene may affect the nervous system. Low to moderate levels can cause tiredness, confusion, weakness, drunken-type actions, memory loss, nausea, loss of appetite, and hearing and color vision loss."

Canada's National Occupational Health & Safety Resource Web site cautions that some studies on toluene's long-term effect on the nervous system include "changes such as memory loss, sleep disturbances, loss of ability to concentrate, or incoordination . . ."

Q. Did he make any statements to you or did you make any observations about him as to what his attitude generally was towards his employer in that first meeting?

A. He had a lot of hostility toward his supervisors and toward the company. Because of what I described earlier, he thought the supervisors were using his handicap against him, and he saw the company as they are—these supervisors are representatives of the company. The company is doing nothing to stop them from harassing me and, therefore, the company, too, is at fault. That was his attitude.

Apart from the familiar, relentless harassment and petty corporate malice revealed in Mattlingly's testimony, the last part, where Wesbecker blames not only individual supervisors for his suffering but more importantly the company with a capital C—that is, the abstract, the symbol, the institution—explains, in the most explicit, clear language possible, the logic of his tactics on the day of his murder rampage. Wesbecker was out not just to get vengeance on a cold-blooded supervisor or two. He was out to destroy the Company. In this context, it is impossible to say that a single one of Wesbecker's shots was fired "at random." Each worker was a tangible part of the intangible Company that had crushed him—unless that worker was, like John Tingle, a recognizable friend of Wesbecker's, in which case he was consciously spared. Tingle was not seen as part of the system that crushed him.

Wesbecker didn't start firing until the elevator opened to the reception room—until the he came face to face with *The Company*—and he only stopped once he'd made his way through the entire company building, sweeping from the management's toner-ink penthouse on the third floor all the way down to the solvent-stench of the working-class basement and locker room on the other end. By destroying the Company's physical manifestations—its employees being the Company's concrete pillars—he attacked the sum of the Company's parts more than simply its parts.

The *Courier-Journal*'s VondorHaar believed that Wesbecker was looking to get revenge on a supervisor. He was at least partly right, in that the murder rampage wasn't simply a psycho gone berserk shooting anyone or anything in his path. But even VondorHaar misunderstood how deliberately the crime was executed. Wesbecker sought revenge on the entire institution that mistreated, abused and injured, insulted, and eventually threw him away when there was nothing left to squeeze. Nothing could be more contrary to the general view of the violent, unbalanced, murdering-at-random nut-case who goes postal—the freak who snaps.

Yet this is the common portrait we are given. And it is the wrong portrait. Not only was this rage murder spree an example of targeted vengeance, but its details and circumstances are strikingly similar to other rage murders in offices, workplaces, post offices, and even in the most recent setting of this crime, schoolyards. Moreover, the details and circumstances are also remarkably similar to doomed rebellions we have seen throughout American history—in their goriness, in the way they are totally misrepresented at the time of the uprising, in the mentally unbalanced psychology of the rebel (Wesbecker was not entirely "healthy," as he admits, but then again neither were John Brown or Nat Turner—one who murders is by definition not "healthy"), and in the grisly, often tragi-comic results.

5

"Your request is . . . irrelevant"

MATTINGLY SET UP A MEETING a month later with Paula Warman, the human resources VP whom Wesbecker subsequently shot in the legs in her office, and who cried into the telephone, "Some of us are shot! Some of us are shot!"

Here is Mattingly's account of his dealings with Warman, starting with their first meeting in June, 1987. I am reprinting much of his deposition testimony in full because Mattingly's flat account perfectly captures the bland, easily recognizable nastiness of contemporary corporate America. You can sense the pressure cooker intensifying, the frustration and battened-down stress—you start to understand how Wesbecker, an already troubled buffoon whose vulnerability seemed to invite more abuse, had to conceal it all in a culture that only allows smiles, back slapping, and toughing it out.

Mattingly: Well, the clearest memory that I have of that meeting [with Paula Warman] is something I said and then something that she responded. In the course of the meeting I told her that, "I'm sure you're not going to want to hear what I'm about to say and I know the company is not going to want to hear it, but in my opinion, before you put Mr. Wesbecker on the folder you ought to shut it down, because putting him on the folder is endangering—could be endangering his life and the lives of the people around him." Her response was she agreed with the first part. She said, you know, "The company is not going to want to hear that, and we cannot make an exception for Mr. Wesbecker because his job—because we have a union contract, and the union contract says this is his job description, and we cannot make an exception . . ."

Q. When you said, "I'm sure you're not going to want to hear this or the company is not going to want to hear this," and then said, "Before you put Mr. Wesbecker on the folder you ought to shut it down," did I state that correctly as you just did, sir?

A. Yes, sir.

Q. Shut what down, sir?

A. Well, the folder, and if the folder meant shutting the plant down, shut the plant down, too. But in my opinion, it would have been—it was—it would be creating a dangerous situation to put him in that stress, in that stressful condition.

Stress: the word comes up often in the study of rage murders. The problem is that even in spite of the awful effects of stress—from mental and physical health ailments to provoking massacres—we, the ones who suffer stress, are ourselves loath to describe our own stressed condition with language that might match the suffering it produces, for fear of sounding melodramatic, whiny—of not being able to tough it out. A little light goes off in most "normal" people's heads warning them not to complain about cracking under stress and risk being marked as a loser.

As Wesbecker and his discrimination handler pursued the case, Standard Gravure resisted. Nearly a year before Wesbecker's rampage murder, Paula Warman wrote in a letter to Mattingly, "It is the company's contention that manic depression is a condition rather than a handicap; therefore, your request for a workforce breakdown indicating those who are handicapped is irrelevant. . . . [W]e cannot in good conscience exempt him from this duty permanently."

Mattingly replied to Warman's letter by telling her that his position represents the government's position, and that Standard Gravure is not authorized to decide when it is or isn't violating discrimination codes:

> Pursuant to your letter of August the 7th, 1987, I think I should point out that Mr. Wesbecker's, quote, condition, unquote, as you call it, is not the issue here. The local ordinance forbidding discrimination in the workplace clearly applies to handicaps, both physical and mental. The only question at issue is to what extent, if any, does Standard Gravure make accommodations for its handicapped employees. The commission is not in the habit of letting complainants or respondents decide what information in an investigation is relevant or irrelevant. The respondent who refuses to cooperate in an investigation leaves us only two resources to draw an adverse inference as directed by EEOC and to require needed documentation through court-ordered subpoena. In an effort to avoid both these extreme actions, we once again request the following information and items.

To which Warman replied:

> We have never exempted employees from working a particular function on a permanent basis. We will continue to accommodate Doctor David Moore's request to, quote, if possible, unquote, allow Mr. Wesbecker to work at places other than the folder, but we cannot totally exempt him from this duty permanently.

Mattingly and the commission decided that it was useless trying to reason with Warman and Standard Gravure. For one thing, Warman was simply lying. The plant's union president, Don Frazier, admitted to Mattingly that there were indeed three employees he could name off the top of his head who had been permanently removed from working the folder, thus confirming Wesbecker's supposedly paranoid sense that he was being persecuted. I mention his persecution paranoia because in nearly every account I have read on this case, and in my personal interviews with former employees, everyone seems to agree that Wesbecker suffered from an irrational persecution complex. Indeed "persecution mania" is one of the supposed signs to look for in an employee ready to snap, according to more than one profiling attempt. Yet when pressed, most people close to this case will admit that Wesbecker was indeed badly mistreated, singled out, and pushed too far. But somehow what struck all of these people, even those sympathetic, was the fact that Wesbecker would show his sense of persecution rather than "tough it out." It was as if that admission, that focus on what was wrong and terrible at the plant, was a violation of the social code—and it made him therefore seem, after the fact, like a wacko. Either he was right, in which case all the other workers who didn't protest seem like cowards or suckers, or he was paranoid and weird, in which case they were the normal ones and he the lone freak.

Mattingly gave up negotiating with Warman and sent Wesbecker's case before an antidiscrimination panel. The panel agreed with Mattingly that there was probable cause for action—that "discrimination had occurred"—and gave him what he thought would be powerful leverage in negotiations with Standard Gravure. Incredibly enough, seven months later, Warman continued to stonewall him, as if merely out of spite. Or out of the sense that since she represented the business side, she couldn't possibly lose.

Negotiations failed. One year and two months after Wesbecker brought the complaint—which itself was preceded by years of frustrating and devastating attempts to reason with Standard Gravure while it was being stripped and downsized—Mattingly ended the fruitless negotiations and passed the case on to his supervisor, Elizabeth Shipley, an attorney.

6

Rocky's Best Friends

AFTER THE STANDARD GRAVURE MURDER RAMPAGE, the media drew a portrait of a pugnacious psycho nicknamed "Rocky" who snapped, thereby framing the rage murder in terms of Wesbecker's fragile mental health. And indeed Wesbecker was not a smiley All-American winner. Wesbecker suffered from manic depression (as do one in six Americans at some point in their lives), he was on medications, he'd been through two failed marriages, and one of his sons had been busted for exposing himself. This characterization allowed people to safely frame the murder rampage as a freak occurrence committed by a freak.

But the truth is that Wesbecker was a very common type, or at least he was seen as such before the murders. Think about any office you've worked at or the school you went to. Every workplace, school, or grouping of humans not brought together through friendship includes a percentage that the majority consider to be weird, not normal, strange, or even psycho. There's always someone who seems "like the type who would snap," although in case after case, it's never the type who would snap who actually snaps. It's the type who "no one could imagine he would ever do such a thing" who explodes in rage murder. Everyone's family has at least a few "freaks" or "weirdos" who make their appearance at holiday functions. As a policeman at the Standard Gravure crime scene said, he spoke with employees who "named three or four other workers before Wesbecker who they thought might have been capable of doing that." Even Wesbecker's mental illnesses, his complexes and quirks, and his dysfunctional family are not at all uncommon in America, as is evidenced by the number of antidepressant prescriptions, the popularity of self-help books and depression-battle memoirs, or the numerous dysfunctional family memoirs, sitcoms, movies, and so on. Few are honest about this once the credits roll, but everyone knows how utterly ordinary these dysfunctions are.

As an example of Wesbecker's ordinariness, Mattingly observed, "Joe Wesbecker had a wonderful sense of humor, and he would come into my office oftentimes agitated or even angry, but invariably before he left he would be laughing or he would have me laughing."

This is one of the most painful revelations in the testimony. A "cheerful attitude" and laughing are tactics employed by all Americans, at an unconscious, even genetic level. Though many Americans privately know that one's own smile is an attempt to put the other party at ease rather than a reflection of one's own inner happiness, publicly, this is rarely admitted. Thus few of us know how many other Americans also force this desperate smile—we all think we're the only ones faking it. These smiles are more like mammal calls used to identify the individual with the herd, to keep from being expelled. These calls that have to be repeated and repeated: you can't just recite the backslapping platitudes once and you're off the hook—as mammals, the office herd requires you to send out the correct marking signals every single day, every hour. It can be exhausting and humiliating. Yet the consequences of not constantly reminding everyone how normal you are range from getting placed on the slow-track to being first on the plank when the next downsizing diktat arrives from headquarters. In my own experience, this cheerfulness, this desperate smile, is one of the most corrosive features to daily life in America, one of the great alienators—a key toxic ingredient in the cultural poison.

> No employer would ever admit to passing her over because she was missing that radiant, tooth-filled smile that Americans have been taught to prize as highly as their right to vote. Caroline had learned to smile with her whole face, a sweet look that didn't show her gums, yet it came across as wistful, something less than the thousand-watt beam of friendly delight that the culture requires. Where showing teeth was an unwritten part of the job description, she did not excel.
> —**David Shipler**, *The Working Poor: Invisible in America*

The cheerful attitude must be employed if one does not want to be pushed farther from the herd, or expelled altogether. The optimism and laughter may or may not indicate that the person is enjoying himself, but they do always mean the person is trying to curry the favor of the collective, and trying to keep people from asking questions. As Mildred Higgins, Wesbecker's aunt, said in an interview the day after the murders, "He seemed like he was happy."

The lie of the smile, this smile-as-cloaking-potion, is revealed at the end of the Shea Communications attorney's cross-deposition of Mattingly:

[Mattingly]: Mr. Ganote had been involved in an accident at work and had had to have reconstructive surgery on his hand or his arm, and the company had exempted him from going back on the folder until he thought he was ready. And Mr. Wesbecker saw that as someone that he could compare himself to. You know, "They did it for Bill Ganote, they can do it for me." At some point I said, "Why don't you have Mr. Ganote give me a call so that I can get from the horse's mouth exactly what happened to him and what the company agreed to do." So he agreed to ask Mr. Ganote to call me, but that telephone call never occurred.

Q. Did you take it that Mr. Wesbecker and Mr. Ganote were friends or on a friendly basis or that Mr. Ganote was going to cooperate with him in that regard?

A. Yes.

Q. That they were friends?

A. Yes.

Q. Did you know that Bill Ganote was one of the people that Joe Wesbecker shot and killed?

A. Yes.

Q. That's all I have.

The questioning attorney was trying to show here that if Wesbecker murdered a "friend," it proved that he murdered at random, and therefore he was a freak, rather than a victim of the company's brutality. But what neither the attorney nor even Mattingly could grasp—indeed what Wesbecker himself may not have been consciously aware of—is that a friend in that environment needn't be a friend even in the casual sense of the word. A friend can be just another humiliation, a desperate, ongoing, failed attempt to connect with the herd. A friend could be a worker who doesn't make your life hell, or a friend could be one of the workers who does make your life hell but slaps your back after every jibe and tells you that "it's all in fun" and "don't take things too seriously" because "we're all just having a good time here." Or it could be the person with whom you have to maintain good relations in order to keep everything from getting worse.

Wesbecker very clearly spared one man during his shooting spree. I would bet that that man, John Tingle, was spared precisely because he never gave Wesbecker any grief, which is the most Wesbecker could have hoped for. Tingle told the *Courier-Journal*, "He didn't fire at me, I guess because he liked me." Then he added, "The guys he had shot in the pressroom were friends too." Were they?

In the post-Reagan era, where no one's job is safe, where no one's salaries or benefits are safe, and where the workforce is constantly subjected to downsizing, intra-worker pressures, and a top-down culture of fear, there is no such thing as a friend.

To add to all of these pressures, Wesbecker had to put up with the kind of toxic bullying which is common in the workplace, yet until recently, rarely considered. Sometimes Wesbecker would come to Mattingly's office "very agitated at what had happened at work."

Here he describes one telling incident: "[S]omeone put something up on the bulletin board and it said, 'If you need help in this regard, call Joe Wesbecker at 585-NUTS.' He was not only upset, his feelings were hurt. And it wasn't just that this was on the bulletin board, but that . . . no one in authority had taken it down." The tough-it-outers might snicker and roll their eyes at the significance of this kind of harassment or of Wesbecker's feelings being hurt. But as Mattingly noted, "He told me that he had attempted suicide more than once."

On March 29, 1988, Wesbecker told Mattingly that he would have his "friend" Bill Ganote call him and support Wesbecker's case against the company. A year and a half later, on September 14, 1989, Ganote still had not called to defend his friend. Either Wesbecker had never asked him to call, for fear of providing further proof that he was a whining troublemaker, or Wesbecker asked Ganote to make the call, but Ganote saw no advantage for himself in doing so.

PART II

The Banality of Slavery

"Our slave population is not only a happy one, but it is a contented, peaceful and harmless one."

—James H. Gholson, 1832

1

The Heart of Submissiveness

OUR IDEA of what a revolution is like, how it is carried out, and who it is carried out by has been warped by our own cultural propaganda, and by the romantic Marxist propaganda of the twentieth century. We have this idea that revolutions are led by rational-minded, tea-sipping men in three-pointed hats who discuss the rights of man while burning the candle at both ends. Or we're warped by the Marxist ideal of revolution: a rational, inevitable historical process in which the most enlightened, most sympathetic, least overdressed human beings team up with the Historical Trend itself to effect a glorious, clean revolution. In fact, revolutions are messy, ugly, gory affairs. Nowhere in our popular notion of revolutions are such factors as stupidity, bad luck, unintended comedy, and revolting madness allowed in. Yet most of the time revolutions are "led" by people we would call nutcases and who indeed were considered nutcases during their time (and in all likelihood were nutcases). While time and distance provide a romantic vew of revolutions, when they actually occur, they usually seem bizarre, uncalled-for, frightening, and evil to their contemporaries, which is why they almost always are snuffed out at their inception.

To illustrate this point, look no further than America's rare examples of domestic rebellion. We tend to think that all rebellions or domestic uprisings were as well understood in their time as we understand them now, but the fact is that most rebellions took place in a kind of contextual vacuum, rendering them little more than outbreaks of seemingly senseless, crazed violence. This is how they were viewed until later, when an intellectual or ideological frame was provided to explain or ground them and to give them a sense of dramatic order. Today's rage murders fit the pattern of rebellions before they have been contextualized.

Domestic uprisings in this country are extremely rare. Nowhere is this more painfully obvious than in slave uprisings. The number of documented slave rebellions in the United States, from the mid-1500s up through the end of the Civil War, number under a dozen. Yet slavery was perhaps the most savage, gruesome policy ever carried out by white Americans, a remarkable honor given our encyclopedia of genocides. Over a period of four centuries, it is conservatively estimated that more than fifteen million Africans were forced into slavery by the colonial powers and in the process some thirty or forty million more died as a result of slave raids, coffles, and barracoons or slave warehouses. While not all of that is directly attributable to colonial white Americans, the numbers are staggering nonetheless. Yet it only produced a few rebellions in American territory, mostly minor rebellions at that, a few of which are being contested today by historians as possible outbreaks of white paranoia rather than genuine black rebellion.

The low number of slave revolts might strike many Americans as shocking and disheartening. It would seem that slaves should have rebelled far more often. For one thing, they had the numbers. In 1800, the United States population was five million, and of that one million were blacks, ninety percent of whom were slaves. According to the census taken in 1820, 40 percent of the South's population was black, and in some areas they made up 70 to 90 percent of the inhabitants.

Given those demographics, why didn't they rise up more? Why didn't they kill their masters and restore their dignity, the way we'd like to imagine we would ourselves? The most obvious answer is that the slaves knew they would be slaughtered trying. Unlike, say, slaveholding regions of the Caribbean, the United States was sufficiently militarized and its methods of domestic repression so well-refined that it was totally assured of crushing any domestic revolt, slave, peasant, proletarian, or otherwise. If the Confederates, fielding a great army with the best officers and weapons in the world, could get crushed and destroyed by the United States, think of the odds a band of slaves, with no chance of blending in with the dominant population, had! Instilling fear is one of the most effective ways of creating a docile, obedient slave population. Today, for example, TV shows like *Cops*, which show that lower-class criminals have no chance of outfoxing the omnipotent state, combined with terrifying stories about U.S. prisons, are two highly effective tools in keeping the population docile and workfocused. This is something Michael Moore missed in *Bowling for Columbine*: fear works not only on the dominant middleclass to emotionally separate them from the criminal underclass, but also on the underclass, the TV show's target audience, to remind them that if they dare step out of line, they will lose.

For a slave considering rebellion as an option, the eighteenth-century Americans offered up their own version of *Cops* programs to effectively scare the insurrection right out of him, as described here in *White Over Black*:

> Whenever slaves offered violent resistance to the authority of white persons, the reaction was likely to be swift and often vicious even by eighteenth century standards. The bodies of offenders were sometimes hanged in chains, or the severed head impaled upon a pole in some public place as a gruesome reminder to all passers-by that black hands must never be raised against white.

Not exactly the image of rational humanists that we normally associate with our pious, liberal forefathers, but a far truer glimpse into the way this country was founded and conquered than those Crown films they used to show in public school civics courses.

But the broader reason why there weren't more slave rebellions is simpler: most slaves didn't want to rebel. This depressing fact is not limited to African slaves in America, but rather is a product of human nature and our ability to adapt, to be conditioned out of fear, and to serve. Frederick Douglass explained that slaves chose not to rebel out of a fear of the unknown, which, he wrote, quoting *Hamlet*, had made slaves "rather bear those ills we had/than fly to others, that we knew not of."

Indeed the only time America's slaves stirred in large numbers was when they were bribed and lured into rebellion by the whites, and even then their response was relatively feeble. During the Revolutionary War, the British, hoping to incite behind-the-lines slave rebellions against the colonials, offered freedom to any slave who rebelled against his white master or sided with the Crown. Remarkably, as a puzzled Winthrop Jordan noted in *White Over Black*, "During the Revolution, British armies provided opportunities for escape to freedom, but, almost surprisingly, no important slave uprisings took place."

However, many slaves escaped to the British side and some even fought for them, including Lord Dunmore's Ethiopian regiment (estimated at between three hundred and eight hundred ex-slaves, most of whom died of fever) and Colonel Tye's Black Brigades, a Loyalist detachment that terrorized New York and New Jersey in 1779–80. On the other hand, blacks served on the pro-slavery American side from the outset of hostilities, taking casualties in the battles of Lexington and Bunker Hill. Yet their further enlistment in the rebel army was blocked by none other than George Washington, a slaveholder as intent on defending slavery as in achieving independence. In 1775, at the outbreak of hostilities, Washington, fearing that arming blacks could incite a wider slave insurrection, barred the further recruitment of blacks in the Continental Army. He only relented after the 1777–78 winter had almost wiped out his army, and after three years of warfare proved that he didn't have to worry about rebellious slaves. In all, some five thousand blacks fought on the side of the Americans, about one-sixth of the total military. An officer of the French army at the decisive battle of Yorktown wrote, "A quarter of them [the American army] are Negroes, merry, confident, and sturdy." Anywhere from one thousand to ten thousand fought on the side of the British, but the figure is not known.

Why did most slaves fail to rise up against the American slaveholders? It can't be explained simply by hindsight, that the British eventually lost anyway. Throughout most of the Revolutionary War, the smart money was on the British winning, and battle by battle, the smart money looked pretty smart. The Brits generally were able to march up and down the colonies almost with impunity. They just didn't have the troops and supply lines to hold and pacify what they'd conquered, nor did they have the will to exterminate the colonials the way they did so many other peoples, largely because the colonials were racially and culturally the same people. The Brits couldn't break the Americans, so eventually they threw in the towel.

Given our current propaganda and what we believe about ourselves, and considering how much slaves stood to gain if they took up the British offer—in other words, how favorable the risk/reward ratio seemed—it is still surprising and disheartening to know that in roughly eight years of war, few blacks took up arms against their masters and so many sided with them, even firing against escaped slaves on the British side.

Their behavior may not conform to our demand for historical heroism, but it sure made sense given the context. Stuck between two violent predators, the British and the Americans, the slaves must have felt that they were doomed no matter what they did. And that's pretty much what happened. There are stories of British agents infecting runaway slaves with smallpox and then forcibly returning them to their anti-British masters, one of the earliest known uses of human WMDs (a biowarfare trick derived from the British-American tactic of giving smallpox-infested blankets to Indian tribes as gifts in hopes of exterminating them and taking their land). The British promised freedom for escaped slaves, but after the surrender at Yorktown, the British abandoned many of the escaped slaves whom they'd promised to protect. As historian Margaret Washington explained, "Many thousands of African Americans who aided the British lost their freedom anyway. Many of them ended up in slavery in the Caribbean. Others, when they attempted to leave with the British, in places like Charleston and Savannah, were prevented. And there are incredible letters written by southerners of Africans after the siege of Charleston, swimming out to boats, and the British hacking away at their arms with cutlasses to keep them from following them."

In Washington's Virginia, where chronic manpower shortages had finally forced the whites to offer freedom to slaves who joined local militias during the war, the problem of slaveholders reneging on their promises and re-enslaving blacks who had served as substitute soldiers in their place was so widespread that the Virginia legislature was moved to condemn it.

Black slaves were far more unresponsive in the South during the Civil War. Even after the Emancipation Proclamation in 1863, there were no known slave rebellions heeding the North's call to rise up against their masters and go free. Some slaves escaped, and some of those who escaped eventually served in the Union forces, but none rose up to form a counterinsurgency behind Confederate lines. Indeed, most remained on plantations throughout the war and large numbers were pressed into support duty for the Confederate Army to bridge the manpower gap with the North and allow the Confederate cause to last longer than it would have without slaves. As historian Melville Jean Herskovits noted, "Naturally, many slaves did remain with their masters during [the Civil War], and this suggests that the range of variation in human temperament to be found everywhere existed in the large Negro population of the time."

This range of black temperament was geographically based. There were numerous African slave revolts throughout Latin America and the Caribbean during the same period that America's slaves were so comparatively passive. The most famous of these was the successful slave revolution in Haiti (or Hispaniola) in 1797. What the paucity of slave rebellions in the United States really points to is the efficiency of white Americans in pacifying and molding their African slave population as compared to other colonial powers in the hemisphere, notably the Spanish and the French, who were at least as brutal but not nearly as effective in their means of repression. As we know today, brutality alone is no guarantee in keeping a population docile—in fact, it often has the opposite effect.

The average slave was docile before his master. It's the nature of the business, and of the beast. The experience of white European slaves in the hands of North African and West African masters was little different from black slaves in white hands. It is estimated that up to one million Europeans were enslaved by North African Arabs and West Africans between 1530 and 1780 and they behaved no more or less valiantly than slaves elsewhere. As John Blassingame observed in his book *The Slave Community: Plantation Life in the Antebellum South*, "Within a few years after their capture, the world the white bondsmen had known began to recede from their minds, and the degradation of slavery forced them to adopt new behavioral patterns."

These new behavioral patterns were similar to the "lowly" behavior that whites associated with black slaves. North Africans in particular saw white European slaves as subhuman, congenitally prone to petty thievery and drunkenness.

"Occasionally," Blassingame notes of the white slaves, "old slaves made fun of new captives, the strong exploited the weak, and many informed on their fellows to curry favor with their masters."

Mass escapes and rebellions among European slaves were rare. Instead, most were tamed and conditioned by their Arab and African masters, successfully retrained to behave as essentially docile and obedient creatures. It all depended on the master's managerial technique. White slaves became increasingly obedient and many even adopted Islam as their faith, depending on "length of enslavement, treatment while in bondage, age, association with other slaves from their country, and the proselytizing zeal of their masters." Some white slaves were so acculturated that they refused to be ransomed.

Medieval European peasants, whose lives in many ways were as wretched as America's slaves, were generally looked upon as stupid and cunning, cheerful and docile—much like slaves' reputations among the master class. It was assumed that the reason serfs didn't revolt was because they were where they wanted to be in life.

> A peasant only knoweth how to do his labor, but cannot give a reason why . . . more than the instruction of his parents or the custom of the country.
> —**Gervase Markhane**, seventeenth century

Even going back to Greek and Roman times, slave revolts were extremely rare, and no one thought that was strange. Historian K. R. Bradley, author of *Slaves and Masters*, counted only three revolts between 140 BC and 70 BC, including the famous one led by Spartacus. Moreover, no one in the slaveholding population seemed to care much for the slaves' plight. As Richard Donkin notes, "Slavery was such a fact of life it was deemed hardly worth mentioning by some of the greatest philosophers of their age."

To put it in a modern context, why is it that in the roughly twenty years of Soviet gulags we know of only one serious uprising, which took place just before the system was dismantled, in spite of the millions who perished? Why did so many Russians "willingly" go to the camps and "let themselves" be brutalized and murdered without a fight? Varlam Shalamov's *Kolyma Tales* is perhaps the greatest, most wrenching account of how men adapt to the most degrading conditions. It describes how they adjust to the new "normal" life as brutalized slaves, how the word "normal" has no fixed meaning, and how every one of us is hard wired to be a slave, given the right conditions. It's not something we want to think about too much, which is why Solzhenitsyn's version of the gulags, with its focus on evil Communist oppressors and the few heroes who resisted, is infinitely more popular in America than Shalamov's version, which avoids facile divisions between the good guys and bad guys, heroes and oppressors, and instead digs into our inner slave.

We don't hear much about this inner slave from authors and artists, though it is far more common, and manifests itself far more regularly, than the allegedly dangerous, primal "heart of darkness" of which we are warned. The slave psychology is too familiar. It appears in the most banal of settings: in the workplace, in relationships, at home or at school. While Joseph Conrad is to be applauded for his literary entrepreneurship, his *Heart of Darkness* pitch, compared to Shalamov, is an exotic getaway vacation designed to make the reader feel a more profound sense of self. No one wants to travel up the other African river, the one that reveals man's heart of submissiveness.

For contemporary Americans, slavery is acceptable material only if framed as a vice imposed by evildoers, an obstacle to be overcome by heroes, rather than as an ordinary and highly adaptive condition that releases an entirely unheroic side of our psychology. Slavery can only be deployed in the arts as a source of pathos, or as an evil that tests its characters' courage and determination. In other words, slavery is used as a source of contrast to who we are today, a device to define characters and reinforce our false sense of individuality, to make us feel better about ourselves by emphasizing our moral progress—rather than depicted properly as an enduring and recognizable psychological tendency.

Through time slavery has mutated and adapted itself to our modern condition. It is by examining this process that we will ultimately have answers to what creates the rampage murders of today.

2

Inanimate African Cargo

African slaves were most likely to rebel at the beginning of their transatlantic voyages. According to *Black Cargoes*, there are written accounts of 155 mutinies on slave ships between 1699 and 1845—it is unclear, however, how many of those mutinies may have involved the white deck hands, who were often horribly mistreated themselves, though not as appallingly as the African slave cargo. Indeed many slave mutinies occurred in the first hours of the voyage from Africa, sparked by rumors among the captives that they were being taken away by the white devils to be cooked and eaten. Oftentimes the captives would leap from the ship to certain death, drowning with their chains fastened rather than allowing themselves to be eaten. When they finally were convinced that they were to be enslaved rather than consumed, it must have come as almost a relief. But not for long.

On average, one-sixth of the slaves died horrible deaths on these voyages. They were packed and chained below deck, literally stacked side by side, head to toe, in order to maximize space efficiency, for the entire duration. By the time the survivors were let out to be auctioned off at the ports and slave markets, much of their rebellious spirit—indeed, much of their human spirit—was gone.

Woodcuts from this era depict the slaves in the cargo bay laying cramped together side by side, without expression or color, with no emotion in the eyes or mouths. There is no fear, no sickness, no crying or anger. They are represented literally as cargo, as inanimate as container goods, reflecting the generally-held view of African slaves at that time. That the woodcut artist denied these slaves the pathos they deserved is what makes viewing their representations so disturbing today. Did the artist intentionally strip his subject of all of its innate horror? Or was he unable to see it? Did the artist, or the audience, view the slave voyage atrocities in the same way as we generally view farm animal life—stripped of the horrors of the slaughterhouse, the bio-feed, the fetid overcrowding, the stench of waste and rot and decomposure, and the squeals and cries, as a hard fact of life that ultimately benefits society? The white colonials had to view black slaves as something like farm animals in order to avoid empathizing.

The reality of the slave-ship cargo bay, the screams, the stench of vomit and human waste and decomposing flesh, the despair, the heat, and the endless days—these are the details that any modern American artist would emphasize. But the eighteenth-century woodcut artist may not have been able to see this pathos. He may not have found their suffering interesting or marketable. I point this out because in order to understand the nature of slave rebellions, as well as the nature of our present-day rage murders, we need to remember how the concept of "normal" is always in flux. Certainly there are many cruel things in contemporary life whose pathos we are incapable of grasping, but which will seem obvious in a hundred years.

3

Slave Management

AS A CHILD OF THE SEVENTIES, growing up in the San Francisco Bay Area, I was shocked to discover later that the majority of slaves' lives were largely uneventful and unremarkable. The way I saw it, the Holocaust and slavery were the two great horrors which all of us had to face if we were to become truly progressive, modern humanists—the two tragedies lived in my mind as equals. And yet the comparison is totally misleading, to the detriment of both tragedies. Far more Africans died than Jews, with far more devastating long-term effects, as the slavery holocaust lasted centuries. Yet the life of the average African slave in America was quite familiar and comparatively tolerable, while the life of a concentration camp intern was brief and ghastly. The average black slave's life in the antebellum South was nothing like the life of gulag slave laborers or concentration camp victims, who were intentionally worked to death or outright murdered and tossed into mass graves.

Most slaves lived by a dull schedule of work, recreation, and sleep. Slaves generally weren't kept behind barbed-wire or cuffed to a ball and chain (except as punishment in the rare case that they tried to escape). Instead, many slaves were allowed to walk into town (they had to carry their identity papers with them), permitted to visit slaves at other plantations, and given leisure time, so long as it did not affect the slave's work habits. Many slaves were even paid cash or allowed to sell excess crops like serfs or sharecroppers. They used the money to buy clothes and goods, to court a spouse, to raise a family, or in some cases to buy their own freedom.

> One of the most frequent reasons for the slave's industriousness was the feeling that he had a stake in the successful completion of his work. Many slaves developed this feeling because the planters promised them money, gifts, dinners, and dances if they labored faithfully.
> —**Blassingame**, *The Slave Community*

For a good number of slaves it was a life that, on the surface, resembled the life of many working poor at the time, with the obvious exception that they were owned like property and that they were viewed as racially subhuman. But this ownership wasn't an issue that came up everyday or every minute in the average slave's mind—with conditioning, man can get used to anything. As Lunsford Lane wrote in his 1842 slave memoir, "[M]y condition as a slave was comparatively a happy, indeed a highly favored one. . . ." Ownership was certainly in the back of every slave's mind, but he still lived, relaxed, visited his friends and lovers, married and had children, shopped, went to church, and enjoyed whatever entertainment was allowed or available. Just so long as he got his work done and didn't break any laws.

As Blassingame notes, "The planters generally had little concern about the recreational activities in the quarters. They did not, however, want their slaves carousing all over the country and wearing themselves out before the day's labor commenced." The slaves' owners generally weren't worried about their slaves running away. True, runaways were far more common than rebellions, but they were still rare, still fraught with the unknown and the overwhelming chance of failure (as opposed to the certain chance of failure in an uprising). Instead, masters were worried that their slaves might wear themselves out if they were having too much fun off the plantation. As Elijah Marrs, in *Life and History*, notes, [Our master] allowed us generally to do as we pleased after his own work was done, and we enjoyed the privilege granted to us."

As slavery and the slave economy in America became more refined, so did the slaveholders' treatment of their slaves. A whole industry of slave management grew up around the practice. Slaves were generally treated much better than white indentured servants because they were property, whereas indentured servants could only be squeezed for a limited period. It was in the master's interest to stretch out his slave's work efficiency as long a period as possible, either to get a full life's work out of him or her, or to keep the resale value high. That meant keeping the slave relatively healthy and happy. Many masters developed a genuine affection for their slaves, however patronizing, and this affection was often reciprocated. Masters saw it as their moral duty to treat their slaves well and to civilize them, as grotesque as that seems today. As a rule, mainstream slave management theory didn't advocate that slaves had "unlimited juice to squeeze" as former General Electric CEO Jack Welch said of his workers, or that "fear is the best motivator" as Intel's Andy Grove once boasted. Slaves weren't driven by stress or viewed by their masters as having a half-life of "only a few years" as Intel CEO Craig Barrett said of his engineers (although indentured servants were viewed as such, and were truly squeezed for all they were worth). Indeed usually it was the overseers who posed the greatest threat to slaves, not their owners. The overseer had no direct economic incentive to keep the slaves content; his only concern was output.

Mainstream slave management theory of the nineteenth century taught masters that the best way to get the most out of their slaves was to provide them with incentives in order to make the slaves believe that their interests coincide with their master's. In this sense, slave management theory had more in common with mid-twentieth-century corporate management theory than with the kind of sadistic evil we normally associated with slaveholding.

Blassingame writes, "In order to obtain the maximum labor at the cheapest cost, the planter had to construct healthy cabins, provide adequate, wholesome food and proper clothing, permit recreation, and provide medical attention for his slaves [. . .] He also had to maintain a great degree of social distance between himself and his slaves. A Virginia planter asserted: '[The slave] ought to be made to feel that you are his superior, but that you respect his feelings and wants.'"

Substitute "employer" for "planter" and "employee" for "slave" and see how the above passage reads: "In order to obtain the maximum labor at the cheapest cost, the employer had to construct healthy cabins, provide adequate, wholesome food and proper clothing, permit recreation, and provide medical attention for his employees [. . .] He also had to maintain a great degree of social distance between himself and his employees. An AT&T executive asserted: 'The employee ought to be made to feel that you are his superior, but that you respect his feelings and wants.'" It's difficult to say which is more disturbing—how eerily recognizable yesterday's slaveholders are to us today, how oddly pseudo-humane they appear to be in theory, or indeed, how much crueler today's benefits-slashing employers are to their employees compared, at least rhetorically, to slaveholders.

This familiar-sounding slave management theory isn't confined to our fore-fathers. As far back as Roman times, in the first century AD, the agricultural writer Columella's *De Re Rustica* offered guidelines to slaveholders on how best to manage their slaves. Essentially he argued that a slave will work better if he is treated with more respect, or at least *the appearance of respect*: "Such justice and consideration on the part of the owner contributes greatly to the increase of his estate," he wrote. Among Columella's recommendations were that the master should see to it that there was proper lighting in slaves' quarters and enough space in their workspaces, and that they should be provided with sufficient clothing. Columella also suggested that the master should sometimes consult his slave, since this would give the slave the impression that his master cared about him and would thus inspire the slave to please his master by working harder. As *Financial Times* writer Richard Donkin wrote, "Is this what many hundreds of years later would be described as enlightened self-interest? Such thinking would not be out of place in the 'family friendly' employment policies of today's companies. Should we, therefore, identify Columella as the father of human resources as we know it?"

Donkin is too fond of his subject—work—to go that far. He answers his own question with a noncommittal, "Maybe not." Yet even he could not avoid noticing the awful similarities. After his "maybe not," Donkin cites Bradley's book, *Slaves and Masters*: "It is quite clear that Columella's recommendations on the treatment of slaves were designed to promote servile efficiency as the key to economic pro-ductivity in a situation where the owner's profit from the agricultural production was a dominating principle. . . . [T]heir social contentment had to be secured as a prelude to work efficiency and general loyalty." Bradley also showed how the Roman ruling class viewed slaves as "idle and feckless," much like North African masters or American masters viewed their slaves. Donkin comments, "[T]his has parallels in some of the entrenched attitudes among those twentieth-century employers who allowed their labor relations to be conducted in an atmosphere of mutual distrust." This is a startling admission for a mainstream business writer like Donkin to make, and unfortunately he drops it.

The similarities between the antebellum "workplace" and the modern workplace go even deeper, to an interpersonal relationship level. American slave-holders developed the kinds of expectations from their African slaves that again read oddly similar to what many corporations expect from their employees: "The institutionally defined role of the slave required him to identify with his master's interest, to be healthy, clean, humble, honest, sober, cheerful, industrious, even-tempered, patient, respectful, trustworthy, and hard-working. This was the kind of slave the master wanted: a laborer who identified so closely with his master's interest that he would repair a broken fence rail without being ordered to do so."

The master should make it his business to show his slaves, that the advancement of his individual interest, is at the same time an advancement of theirs. Once they feel this, it will require little compulsion to make them act as becomes them.
—*Southern Agriculturalist IX* (1836)

Compare this slave management theory to the 1941 AT&T employee handbook, a handbook that represented the very best of employer-employee relations in America: "By means of this [pension plan] and other welfare practices, the Company endeavors to 'take care' of its employees throughout their working careers, and beyond. In return, it naturally expects employees to be genuinely concerned with the welfare of the business and to feel personally responsible for its reputation and continuing success."

Obviously there is a massive difference between an AT&T employee during the postwar golden age of labor-executive relations and that of an antebellum slave. But expectations were also vastly different; what was considered "normal" was different. Moreover, one cannot deny the fact that the semantics used in both cases are almost identical. This alone is evidence of some systemic parallels. The slaveholders could have used far crueler language and advocated far crueler techniques. But they didn't because it wouldn't have been effective. The slave owner wanted profits, just like today's shareholders. To use a different example, Hitler's plan to enslave the *untermenschen* Slavs used language, and techniques, that were openly cruel. It was a conscious effort at superiority, racism, and exploitation. Southern slaveholders, on the other hand, operated by many of the same platitudes and principles as most employers do today. They could be pious and normal because they didn't see themselves as evil, any more than today's executives, investment bankers, or mutual fund managers see themselves or their work as evil. Your average slave masters, like most employers today, wanted their slaves to increase their profit, but they also wanted them to reinforce their basic moral structure. They wanted their slaves to be both hardworking and well-behaved, because both reflected the master's overall worth. And most tellingly, they wanted their slaves to be cheerful, in keeping with the great American tradition of oppression-with-a-happy-face.

On a certain level these semantic and philosophical parallels shouldn't be too surprising. After all, America's wealth was essentially created by slavery and the slave trade. Scholars have traced how the Industrial Revolution was funded directly by capital accumulated in the slave industry. Malachi Postlethway, an eighteenth-century economist, described the slave trade as "the first principle and foundation of all the rest, mainspring of the machine which sets every wheel in motion." There are numerous examples of this. James Watt's first steam engine was subsidized by wealthy slave-trade merchants, as were the slate industry in Wales and Britain's Great Western Railway. The American corporate magnates of today aren't derived from a different species than their slave-trading ancestors—they have merely evolved by adapting to different conditions and altering their metaphors with the times. Slavery declined as it segued into the Industrial Revolution it had financed, primarily because slavery's workforce was less profitable than the so-called "free" workforce. A "free" employee didn't have to be fed, clothed, and sheltered by the shareholders; he had a greater incentive—the fear of death or starvation—to work hard and keep his job; and he would constantly compete with other "free" workers, keeping a lid on their wage demands. Slavery, and the Confederate culture, was destroyed not by a shift in morality but by economic progress. The Confederate culture was bad for business. It was nothing personal, it just had to go.

Thus, the modern American work culture derives from the same sources that defined slavery's official work culture. When the master managed his slaves correctly, they often responded by fulfilling his expectations, with cheerful, boss-pleasin' initiative. In the same way, most AT&T employees responded positively to their company's treatment of them, just as the company expected. The overwhelming majority identified their own best interests with the Company's, a relationship that only soured as the Reagan Revolution redefined the corporate culture's priorities by giving executives the opportunity to squeeze as much profit out of their employees as quickly as possible for as little expenditure as possible, a tendency that has only accelerated, particularly under George W. Bush's presidency. Similarly, a large number of slaves saw their interests and their master's as one, provided that the master upheld his end of this bargain.

This irrational yet perhaps instinctual mammalian tendency for a subordinate human to identify his interests with the master's/boss's/company's, in spite of the huge difference in profit that each side gains in this relationship, is identified by historian Kenneth Stampp as one of the six key slaveholder tactics for creating a good slave. Those six were:

1. Strict discipline to develop "unconditional submission"
2. Develop a sense of personal inferiority
3. Development of raw fear
4. Establish notion that the master's interests are the same as the slave's
5. Make slaves accept master's standards of conduct as his own
6. Develop "habit of perfect dependence"

When I read that list, I can pretty much imagine myself back in the mid-1990s, when I worked for an investment fund in Moscow, putting in eighteen-hour work days, seven days a week. Many of those hours I spent getting screamed at and sent running around Moscow like a headless chicken. The dependence comes from the salary; the strict discipline from working ungodly hours and being exposed to constant ego-bruising screaming; the fear from fear of losing your job, falling off the career ladder, or a host of other ways that modern corporate theory consciously instills fear.

The identifying of interests between master and employee is the most significant of all. It was an emotion powerful enough among slaves that they usually did act on their own initiative—not only by painting fences without being told in order to please their master, but also by exposing rebellion plots by other slaves in order to protect their masters and curry their favor. There are numerous painful examples of loyal slaves taking up arms against rebellious slaves in order to protect their masters, including the Nat Turner uprising, on which I will expand in a later section.

The instinct to identify with one's superiors and one's company is so strong that even in the current corporate squeeze, even when employers have done all they can to exploit their power over employees, workers at all levels still manage to remain loyal to the companies that treated them like old coffee grinds. As Charles Heckscher observes in *White Collar Blues*, "Middle managers in general— the overwhelming majority in my sample—want to be loyal. They want a community that goes beyond short-term performance and reward, that nurtures and supports, to which they can devote themselves. Though I myself, like many researchers before me, often felt the demands of the corporation on the individual to be excessive, I have rarely heard this complaint from the managers themselves."

Numerous tales of slaves and by slaves revealed the same kind of willingness to fulfill their end of the shared-interests contract if they perceived that their master was upholding his end of the deal by appearing to respect his slave. As one former slave, Lucius H. Holsey, wrote in his 1898 *Autobiography, Sermons, Addresses and Essays*, his master "had great confidence in me and trusted me with money and other valuables. In all things I was honest and true to him and his interests. Though young, I felt as much interest in his well-being as I have felt since in my own. . . . I made a special point never to lie to him or deceive him in any way."

This tendency is not confined to slaves. The inclination to submit is built into our operating system, easily adapting itself to the current corporate culture, operating along the same functions as in slave times. A person's ability to adapt and grovel as much as required is almost the definition of normal. It is normal to accept these conditions and try to thrive within them; it is abnormal to rise up against them. Just think about all the jobs you've taken, especially the ones where you succeeded most—you didn't get promoted by being a maverick and standing up for yourself. You succeeded where you followed orders and pleased the higher-ups. In our own way, we moderns are just as slavish and painfully docile as African slaves. We simply lack the distance to acknowledge it or a proper excuse to explain it.

4

A Normal and Inevitable Aspect of Their Affairs

SO THE REASON THERE were so few slave rebellions in the United States wasn't because African slaves were actually content, as racist whites contended, or even because of brutal repression. It had to do with human nature and effective management technique.

Another reason why there were so few slave rebellions was that until the 1800s, there wasn't even a context to frame a slave uprising. Until then, a slave insurrection was seen as an act of random evil or sheer insanity by the ruling class.

So if the insurrection failed, it would have no resonance, politically, culturally, or otherwise. Slave uprisings weren't framed by the ruling whites as an inevitable consequence of slavery, but rather as random acts of violence by sick, ungrateful Africans. Until the 1800s, it was difficult, if not impossible, for Americans to even imagine why a slave would rebel. As historian Louis Filler wrote in *The Crusade Against Slavery*, "Throughout the colonial period and after the American Revolution, slavery was accepted by most Americans as a normal and inevitable aspect of their affairs."

They knew and feared that slaves might rebel, but they couldn't understand why, except that there was something inherently barbarous (and ungrateful) in the Africans' nature—there were a few bad apples out there. The effective propaganda of the time said that the white man was doing a great humanitarian deed for his African slaves: civilizing them, giving them clothes and comforts that they would be denied in Africa, and teaching them the Word of Christ, thereby saving their souls and giving them a chance to win a spot in Heaven. Whites gave blacks a better life in the here and in the hereafter. What crazy fool could argue with that logic? What kind of madman would take up arms against this?

Christianity played a powerful role both in reinforcing the whites' sense of moral righteousness in enslaving the Africans, and in convincing blacks to accept their slave status as part of Jesus' plan. Church leaders went to great lengths to convince the slaveowning class to allow them to preach to their slaves, including the explicit promise to make the slaves more docile. It wasn't easy. Church leaders literally had to make a pact with the Devil in order to persuade slaveholders that Christianity was exactly the kind of lithium necessary to keep their slaves happy and docile right where they were. Preachers preached humility, orderliness, and resignation to their slave laity, convincing them to accept their earthly ordeals in exchange for Heavenly rewards. They even went out of their way to persuade slaveholders that Christianity could be a positive force in molding the slave's mind and soul. In 1725, Dean George Berkeley wrote that the Christians' problem was to convince American planters "that it would be of Advantage to their Affairs, to have slaves who should obey in all Things their Masters according to the Flesh, not with Eye-service as Men-pleasers, but in Singleness of Heart, as fearing God: that Gospel Liberty consists with Temporal Servitude; and that their slaves would only become better slaves by being Christians." In the same year, Reverend Hugh Jones of Virginia wrote, "Christianity encourages and orders [slaves] to become more humble and better servants, and not worse, than when they were heathens." Thanks to these efforts, Christianity was retooled to fit their needs—the needs of the ruling class, that is. And it succeeded in its pro-slavery task, just as it helped to keep the peasantry docile in medieval times, or as in our time affects similiar situations in Latin America, Ireland, and elsewhere.

When employed successfully by the ruling classes, propaganda convinces the ruled that their condition is entirely normal, inevitable, and even somehow privileged. You may know that you are miserable and unjustly treated, but without a context to frame it, you will be far less likely to act on your sense of injustice. Indeed, you may even feel that somehow you are the sick one for questioning what society says is "normal" and "inevitable."

Today, the inherent injustice of slavery is obvious to everyone, but this was not the case when the Declaration of Independence was composed. More devastating was the fact that radical abolitionism, which today we accept as the only sane view on slavery, was at the time ignored and pushed into the "wacko" margins along with all the other crank ideas of the time. This is how it always works with new and dangerous truths that confront injustice. Arguments against globalization were considered bizarre, quaint, or even insane by mainstream pundits like Thomas Friedman, and when the anti-WTO riots exploded in Seattle in 1999, most Americans were totally perplexed over why such a seemingly innocuous and dull organization would incite so much sixties-esque rage. Only the financial catastrophes in Asia, Latin America, and Russia, along with the increasing size and frequency of the protests, validated the antiglobalization movement, pushing its arguments into mainstream discourse.

> When Parliament met in the early months of 1766 to discuss the Stamp Act rebellion in the colonies, its members focused first on the "strange language" of American arguments against the tax. Most British politicians could not even understand what the colonists were talking about.
> —**Thomas P. Slaughter**, *The Whiskey Rebellion*

The point is that real-time injustice, even of the most epic sort, is often simply not recognized as such at the time, no matter how obvious the injustice later appears. Man is hard wired to submit (adapt) to any condition and then consider it normal. Our acceptance of an injustice is reinforced by the going ideology. With African slaves in America, it was Christianity that helped convince them and the white population that slavery was God's work. Well-funded, sophisticated, and multidimensional PR campaigns have always been employed to sway the general public to accept even the most counterintuitive policies, convincing people that such policies work in their own interests, and are inevitable and morally good. One example noted in the book *Black Cargoes* reveals how "West Indian planters and Liverpool merchants raised a campaign fund of £10,000 to fight the anti-slave trade bill in Parliament. Witnesses were rushed to London from the West Indies and Africa prepared to swear that the trade was a benevolent institution dedicated solely to civilizing the primitive Africans."

We are always slow to recognize injustices to which we have not previously admitted—indeed the normal and natural instinct is to resist reconsidering what one had once taken for granted as grossly unjust. In the United States Congress's 1967 Riot Commission report, issued following a series of violent African-American urban riots, the authors noted that officials in Cincinnati couldn't understand why riots spread to their city—despite the fact that there was only one black councilman in a city whose population was 27 percent black and only one black school board member in a district where blacks comprised 40 percent of the student population. "Mayor Walton H. Bachrach declared that he was 'quite surprised' by the disturbance because the council had 'worked like hell' to help Negroes," the report stated.

It may be—in fact, it is certainly the case—that in one hundred years, historians will look at how we live today and what we accept as normal, and condemn us as a nation of savages, a half-civilization incapable or unwilling to face its own injustices. They will likely shudder in horror at how we could inflict such pain and how we could possibly endure it. Our problem is that we don't even know yet what pain and injustice they are talking about. We may never even find out.

5

Realists and Madmen

THIS ISN'T TO SAY that everyone accepted the slavery paradigm as a fact of life. There was widespread disgruntlement among slaves, some of it internalized, some of it expressed. When there was violence or rebellion, it was nearly always unfocused and appeared to be random, gory, and crazed. The slaves didn't have a context to justify their rebellion against the institution that oppressed them; therefore, their rebellions were carried out in an almost half-conscious state. Similarly, whites, even the best-intentioned whites, even the nicest ones who would never harm a flea and who genuinely cared about their slaves, simply could not understand why the rebellions or violence took place. They were shocked and horrified. Like the reactions to today's rage murders, whites were simply flabbergasted, shocked and even hurt by slave uprisings.

A doctor reporting on a slave insurrection in Rhode Island on the slave ship *Hope*, in which thirty-six slaves died, wrote in 1776: "The only reason we can give for their attempting any thing of the kind, is, [sic] their being wearied at staying so long on board the ship."

Southern whites considered the whole phenomenon of slave runaways as a "disease—a monomania, to which the negro race is peculiarly subject" rather than a rational reaction against slavery. They even had a term for one recurring form of this disease: "To take to the swamp" described those slaves who ran away; discovered that the fugitive life presented its own set of even crueler problems and needs, such as money, food, shelter, clothing, and so on; and returned to the plantation to resume the life of a slave, an all-too-common conclusion which only further reinforced the whites' belief in the virtue of slavery. By completely misrepresenting the cycle of symptoms, they were able to reposition the source of the symptoms from slavery to something endemic to black psychology.

Contemporaries' blindness to the evils and injustices of their times, and their penchant for always rationalizing away or outright ignoring those injustices, is a constant of all times, including our own. Take post office massacres, for example. No one ever imagined that life in an American post office was anything but dull, relaxed, secure work, staffed with easy-going employees, free of the vicious stress and bullying of the corporate world. Then suddenly, seemingly out of nowhere, post offices became the setting for some of the most gruesome murders of the past twenty years. At first, few considered that the culture of the U.S. Post Office was unbearable and unjust. Conventional wisdom held that the reason why so many USPS employees were blasting apart their post offices had to be because of the type of person who works in a post offices, that it must attract some weirdos and freaks. A USPS media relations spokesperson helped reinforce this received idea, commenting on the unusually high rate of post office massacres, "It's not a postal problem. It's everywhere. With 800,000 people, you are going to have a percentage of irrational people."

That may seem an entirely reasonable explanation to us today, if we don't-know anything about the USPS culture (and most don't). Yet that statement is as callous and inflammatory as it is wrong, and the murders alone were proof of something wrong within the USPS culture. Congressional studies, ordered after a spate of murders, criticized the USPS's culture of authoritarianism, "harassment, intimidation, [and] cruelty."

Now compare the USPS spokesperson's quote above to an account in 1755, in which a Maryland slaveholder whose slave James escaped from his plantation wrote, "That this slave should run away and attempt getting his liberty, is very alarming, as he has always been too kindly used, if any thing, by his Master, and one in whom his Master has put great Confidence, and depended on him to over-look the rest of the slaves, and he had no kind of provocation to go off." In *There is a River*, Harding wrote, "The flight of one woman from Tuscaloosa, Alabama, sur-prised her owner, who said the fugitive was 'very pious' and 'prays a great deal and was, as supposed, contented and happy.'"

These accounts are reminiscent of those rage killers who were described as "quiet" and "not at all the type," such as the Standard Gravure shooting in Louisville, in which a policeman on the scene said that employees there had named three other workers whom they thought might be the killer before they got around to identifying Wesbecker.

> He was not somebody you would say, "Tom's going to go off the deep end someday and start killing people."
> —**Acquaintance of Thomas McIlvane**, postal employee who killed four at the Royal Oak, Michigan, post office

School shooters particularly have been described as "polite" and "respectful" by those teachers and administrators who were shocked that the student-killer hid so much rage and violence.

> I still cannot believe that Mitchell Johnson did that, because he was . . . the most polite student I've ever had. "Yes ma'am, No ma'am, May I help you do this?" And it wasn't like he was trying to be fake. It was like he wanted to fit in and he wanted to be helpful."
> —**Westside Middle School teacher** on schoolyard shooter Mitchell Johnson

A plot by slaves to march on Richmond, Virginia, in 1800, the so-called Gabriel Uprising named after its lead slave, was described by then-governor James Monroe as "strange" and blamed on the French Revolution and the Hispaniola slave uprising from a few years earlier. In other words, the future president and creator of the Monroe Doctrine, which vowed to fight against outsiders trying to meddle in our hemisphere, suddenly found these outsiders useful to explain slave unrest in his own state. Blaming the French Revolution and the slave rebellion in Hispaniola is Monroe's version of blaming Marilyn Manson and violent video games. The Gabriel Uprising was finally "put down" when twenty-seven slaves were publicly hanged. The awful truth about the Gabriel Uprising is that no one even knows if a real plot existed. In fact, it probably didn't. But fear of an uprising was real, particularly among a population that refused to face the real cause. Indeed, the intense fear of insurrection seems to match the intensity of the collective denial about its cause. This is reminiscent of the countless school shooting plots "uncovered" over the past few years. While the culture continues to blame everything but schools for schoolyard massacres, paranoia increases, zero tolerance policies are applied oftentimes irrationally, and many kids' lives are destroyed due to rumor, fear, snitching, or childish boasting of the sort that was once ignored.

Much like today's mainstream rush to blame Hollywood, the NRA, or other fuzzy outsiders for causing rage massacres that occur in offices and schoolyards, Americans, particularly Southerners right up to the late 1850s, blamed any slave unrest or rebellion on "outside agitators," whether on Northern abolitionist extremists or alien Jacobins. And they sincerely believed it. They couldn't even imagine that domestic conditions, that the very institution of slavery, caused slaves to rebel. It didn't make sense to them and those who suggested such a thing simply "didn't understand." To suggest that slavery as an institution and the South's culture caused black insurrection and violence was dangerous lunacy; an abolitionist was as shunned and marginalized as today's Earth Liberation Front activists. Indeed, as Harding notes, white Northern abolitionists, as late as the 1830s, were a "despised minority . . . [marked by] deep divisions among themselves." That's Northern abolitionists, not Southern abolitionists. In 1843, at a convention in Buffalo, Henry Garnet, the popular black abolitionist of the time, called on slaves in the South to rise up in armed rebellion against their white masters. He warned the slaves:

> You are not certain of heaven, because you suffer yourselves to remain in a state of slavery, where you cannot obey the commandments of the Sovereign in the universe. . . . In the name of the merciful God, and by all that life is worth, let it no longer be a debatable question whether it is better to choose liberty or death. . . . Brethren, arise, arise! Strike for your lives and liberties. Now is the day and the hour. Let every slave throughout the land do this and the days of slavery are numbered. You cannot be more oppressed than you have been—you cannot suffer greater cruelties than you have already. Rather die freemen than live to be slaves.

Remember that you are four millions! It is in your power so to torment the
God-cursed slaveholders that they will be glad to let you go free.
His call went unheeded. Not a single slave rebellion is recorded in the aftermath of
Garnet's speech.

William Lloyd Garrison, the Northern abolitionist leader, was considered a
"madman" compared to the moderate abolitionists, who were called "practical
reformers" or "realists." Louis Filler, in his abolitionist study *The Crusade Against
Slavery*, gives examples of the divisions between moderates and radical abolitionists in the North that are infuriating to read today. The moderates charged that
radical reformers "preferred to deal with problems which were 'remote' like slavery and 'speculative' like sex equality, while they 'realistically' grappled with—Van
Buren's sub-treasury plan."

In such an atmosphere of realism toward slavery, it's easier to understand why
there were so few organized slave insurrections. Instead, nearly all acts of rebellion
by slaves appeared to be random crimes. They were treated at the time as random
criminal acts carried out by unhinged evildoers who were either mentally deranged
or just plain evil, just as modern rampage murderers are viewed today as wackos
who simply snapped, or worse. The nature of these slaves' random crimes, and the
way they were treated at the time, are remarkably similar to our rage murders.

As Winthrop Jordan wrote in his seminal slavery work, *White Over Black*:

It now seems clear that there were many more rumors than revolts and
that the number of actual revolts was small; if it takes a score of persons
to make a 'revolt' the number all-told before 1860 was probably not
more than a dozen . . . Slave resistance rarely involved large numbers,
though this fact can scarcely be taken as indicating that slaves were
docile and contented. Indeed, slaves struck frequently at the oppressive
white world around them, but in more instances violence involved spontaneous outbursts on the part of individuals or small groups. . . . *Though
in most cases the violence perpetrated by slaves could not have been
rationally regarded, by either the slaves or their masters, as attempts at
freedom, one suspects these incidents must often have involved very little in the way of rationality on either side."* [Italics mine]

In other words, a rebellion doesn't need to be *rational* in order to make it a
rebellion. Without a context, rational rebellion is impossible. Thus, crime,
murder, is itself an act of rebellion if the circumstances are deemed unjust, if the
environment—slavery—created the crime. Even if we only recognize the unjust
causes one hundred years after the murder is committed, it still makes the crime
a political act, a rebellion.

Jordan lists the sorts of "spontaneous outbursts" of slave violence that he, and
most others writing from our vantage point today, would define as acts of slave
rebellion:

. . . recurring instances of masters, mistresses, overseers, even whole
families murdered by their slaves—variously strangled, clubbed,

stabbed, burned, shot, or (most commonly the colonists felt) poisoned. Some of these instances might perhaps be properly regarded as ordinary crimes, *yet it is impossible to separate slave crime from resistance to slavery*; slashing an overseer with an axe might stem from blind rage or a disordered mind, but it scarcely represented acquiescence in the role of a slave." [Italics mine]

As Blassingame reports in *The Slave Community*, court records show that from 1640 to 1865, 533 slaves assaulted, robbed, poisoned, and murdered whites in the United States territory. Can anyone say that this is a large number or a small number? That it proves or disproves how miserable slaves were? Personally, I'm surprised at how small the number is. I would have expected much more, something like thousands or tens of thousands of such violent attacks. But that is because, as a child of the seventies, I have been conditioned to believe that Americans always rise up against oppression and that the good side always wins. The reality is that the oppressed rarely rise up, they always lose (in this country anyway), and they always collaborate with the State against those rare rebels to make sure they remain oppressed. Today's propaganda distorts the picture of slave times as a period of constant whipping, groaning, and simmering rebellion, of brave and defiant slaves progressing from injustice to freedom, as if history itself was a progression from slavery to freedom, a Spielbergian triumph-of-the-spirit, when in fact it was much more banal than that. In today's official portrayal of slavery, all of the depressing similarities to our modern life are censored with just as much vigor as they once censored all that was inhumane and unjust about slavery. The emphasis may change, but the purpose for censoring, then as now, remains the same: to reinforce our belief that how we live today is entirely normal and to purge any evidence which might contradict that faith.

6

A Roman Catholic Plot

THE GREATEST SLAVE INSURRECTION in the American colonies took place in New York City in 1712. Two dozen slave-domestics—the "privileged" class in the slave world, the ones who had it best, relatively speaking—plotted a violent insurrection they hoped would turn into a general uprising. The accounts we have today vary in some of the details but all tell essentially the same story. Late at night on April 6, the rebel group prepared an ambush by setting fire to a building in the center of the city—some accounts say it was an outhouse, some say a building on the edge of town, but the most convincing account I found suggested it was a building in the center—and lay in wait for the white authorities to come put it out. Armed with muskets, hatchets, and swords, the African-born slaves vowed to each other that it would be better to die fighting than to live as slaves. When the white neighbors and townsfolk arrived to put out the fire, the slaves attacked and slaughtered nine of them by variously shooting, stabbing, and beating their victims, leaving another nine whites injured. Those whites who escaped the ambush told the local authorities, spreading panic throughout New York City. Now, if everything went according to plan, all the slaves throughout the region would rise up with their brothers and face down the oppressors.

Militia units from New York and Westchester were brought up, as were soldiers from a nearby fort. Eventually the slaves were surrounded, waiting for help from their oppressed brothers to appear. It seemed so rational to believe that they would. But the expected help from other slaves never arrived—no rebellion was sparked. The city's other slaves remained passive. The oppressors stuck together, while the oppressed hung one another out to dry.

The rebellion was brutally suppressed. Six of the slave insurrection leaders committed suicide rather than surrender. In all, twenty-seven were arrested, some under dubious charges. As one modern commentator, Douglas Harper, bitterly noted, it was "a crude rebellion that could have been much more deadly, had it been better planned."

The colonials were shocked and horrified by the sheer number of victims, especially considering that New York City's population was just under five thousand at the time. As Harper observed, "In considering the psychological impact on the survivors, imagine some sort of attack on modern New York, with its eight million people, that would leave casualties of 10,000 dead."

The justice sentence was particularly brutal even by early-eighteenth-century standards, and the white colonials meant it to be savage. Thirteen slaves were hanged, one left to die in chains without food or water, three were burned to death, and one left racked and broken on the wheel. Here is a description of what it is like to break a man on the wheel: the victim, naked, was stretched out on the ground tied to stakes or iron rings. Wooden pieces were placed under the wrists, elbows, ankles, knees and hips. Then limb after limb and joint after joint was smashed. After that the shattered limbs were "braided" into the spokes of the large wheel. They would then raise the wheel to the top of the pole, where the birds would eat at the flesh of the victim.

No group of white men in the colonies ever received such a harsh, medieval penalty for any crime.

This rare example of a group slave insurrection was marked by its bad planning, gory slaughter of "innocent" whites, its total failure to spark a wider rebellion, and the State's savage and successful suppression.

More significant was how the colonials grossly misunderstood the rebellion. To them, it made no sense except as a random act of indescribable evil. This is evident in the mass hysteria thirty years later when an alleged slave plot to burn down New York City was "uncovered." At the time, blacks made up about a fifth of the city's population. The circumstances of the plot have been challenged ever since, but nevertheless the hysteria was real: 154 blacks and 24 whites were arrested, and 31 blacks were executed.

As Jordan explains in *White Over Black*:

> The reaction of New Yorkers to what seemed a major slave conspiracy may best be characterized as one of thoroughly confused horror. In retrospect it is not the horror but the confusion which is revealing, for that confusion plainly demonstrated that New Yorkers had no firm framework of belief into which a major Negro uprising could be securely fitted. An absurd variety of self-conflicting explanations for the conspiracy were advanced. One of the participating judges, Daniel Horsmanden, published a lengthy justification of the court proceedings which variously treated the conspiracy as a Roman Catholic plot, as a monstrous instance of ingratitude toward kindly white masters who had retrieved these Negroes from the heathen barbarism of Africa, as a conspiracy of normally loyal slaves duped by utterly depraved white people treasonous to their natural loyalties, as an example of the dangerous villainy of slaves in New York, and as a revelation of the inherent baseness of Negroes in general.

It is easy to imagine Judge Horsmanden also blaming violent video games, the NRA, and Marilyn Manson for causing slave rebellions, if only those excuses existed in his day. Anything, no matter how bizarre, was cited as the cause for slave rebellions expect for the most obvious source: slavery.

7

The Battle of Negro Fort

Po' niggers can't have no luck.
—Huckleberry Finn

AS BRUTAL AND TRAGIC as these slave rebellions were, a few, read in terms of contemporary poetics, also had a painfully black comical side to them—black comedy in the sense that it was as if God himself had decided to punish the downtrodden merely for being . . . downtrodden.

After the War of 1812, as the British were evacuating the Spanish territory of Florida in 1815, they handed over a well-constructed and fully-armed fort to their local allies, a combined militia consisting of about three hundred runaway African-American slaves and another thirty Choctaw and Seminole Indians. The fort, which lay along the Apalachicola River, had been named Fort Prospect Bluff under the Brits. Under its new slave fugitive commander—whom we only know as Garson—and his Choctaw chief lieutenant—whose name we have never learned—

the fort was renamed Negro Fort. If the name sounds like a taunt, that's because it likely was meant to be a taunt. Garson and his men were not only ex-slaves, they were also feeling strong in a British fort with weaponry at their disposal. And they were itching for some payback.

News about Negro Fort traveled throughout the South, and as many as eight hundred black fugitives, from as far away as Tennessee, settled in the surrounding area. The Americans didn't like it at all. Slaveholders complained. They viewed Negro Fort as the center of gravity for a budding Jacobin rebellion against slave-holding America.

Garson and the Choctaw chief decided not only to create a safe haven for fugitive slaves and give the fort a taunting name, but they also started to launch raids across the Georgia border, a brave and just decision, but not wise. Garson, the Choctaw, and the others must have felt safe in Spanish territory, armed to the teeth, protected inside the walls of Britain's finest fort technology.

Responding to angry demands by Georgia slaveholders, in March of 1816, war hero General Andrew Jackson petitioned the Spanish governor of Florida to destroy the settlement. At the same time he ordered Major General Edmund Gaines, commander of U.S. military forces in the so-called Creek nation, to destroy Negro Fort and "restore the stolen negroes and property to their rightful owners."

Garson wasn't frightened. In fact, he was so confident that he started boasting, declaring that he would "sink any American vessels that should attempt to pass." Garson's reckless bravado reached a fever pitch when the American forces, along with five hundred Lower Creek Indian allies and a naval convoy, approached Negro Fort on July 27, 1816. As one account noted, when an American delegation tried to negotiate Negro Fort's surrender, "The American delegation reported that the black fugitive leader had 'heaped much abuse on the Americans.'"

Garson ordered his cannon to fire on the Americans in the river below. But the black militiamen, though incredibly brave and determined, lacked real military training. Their shot missed the American warship in the river below, falling wide of its mark. The rebels cheered, believing that they had just put the fear of Africa into the white devils' hearts. Justice, God, and history were on their side. The battle had begun!

Now it was the Americans' turn. They fired one cannon from the warship. And won. As luck would have it, that first shot was a direct bull's-eye: they nailed Negro Fort's powder magazine, which Garson's inexperienced men had carelessly left open. What luck! It was as if divine intervention had interceded on the slaveholders' behalf, as if Jesus appeared as a spotter, guiding the cannonball straight into the slaves' weakest point, incinerating Garson's entire force in a hellish explosion.

> Those who have will get more. From those without, even what they do have will be taken.
> —**Jesus Christ,** Mark 4:25

The Battle of Negro Fort was over as soon as it had started. The resulting explosion in the powder magazine was so powerful that it was felt all the way in Pensacola, some sixty miles away. Fewer than forty of the fort's defenders survived the awesome detonation. Many of them were so badly burned and mutilated that there was little hope for their survival.

Remarkably, Garson and the Choctaw chief survived the carnage. The Americans handed Garson and the Choctaw chief over to their Creek allies, who summarily shot Garson and scalped the chief. Other survivors were returned to their owners or auctioned off, while an American fort, Fort Gadsden, was eventually built over the ruins of Negro Fort.

What followed in Florida was cruelty on such a large scale that it rendered the tragic story of Negro Fort a mere footnote. In the 1820s and 1830s, Jackson initiated a campaign to exterminate the native Seminoles by forcing them out in mass population transfers, slaughtering the rest, and then replacing them with thousands of shareholders and slaves. By 1845, when Florida was admitted as the twenty second state, half of the population was slaves. By the end of the 1850s, there were only three hundred Seminoles left alive in Florida.

8

A Talent for Concerted Action

A chief source of danger, the colonists sometimes felt, was the Negro who was not a slave.
—**Winthrop Jordan**, *White Over Black*

THE SLAVE REBELLION plotted by Denmark Vesey in 1822 is cited by many as an example of the indestructible spirit of slave resistance and courage. As Sterling Stuckey wrote, "Vesey's example must be regarded as one of the most courageous ever to threaten the racist foundation of America. In him the anguish of Negro people welled up in nearly perfect measure. He stands today, as he stood yesterday . . . as an awesome projection of the possibilities for militant action on the part of a people who have—for centuries—been made to bow down in fear." But the dismal truth is that even among the few celebrated slave rebellions that we know about, such as Vesey's, it seems increasingly likely to scholars today that at least a portion of these "insurrections" were little more than outbreaks of white paranoia. That is, of these dozen or so slave rebellions, at least a few probably never existed except in the minds of fearful white slaveholders.

What made Vesey unusual was that he was a freed slave who had prospered as a carpenter in Charleston, South Carolina. We often forget this, but there was a significant population of freed slaves even in the South, muddying and complicating the facile picture of cultural evil we have in our heads. In Charleston in 1822, there were 3,615 freed slaves living among 10,653 whites and 12,652 slaves. James Stirling, a British traveler during the late slave period, observed, "I was struck with the appearance of the slaves in the streets of Charleston on a Sunday afternoon. A large proportion of them were well dressed and of decent bearing, and had all the appearance of enjoying a holiday."

In 1820, the state assembly, worried by these demographics, barred any freed slaves from entering the state, and disallowed any free blacks who left the state from returning.

Denmark Vesey was born Telemanque in West Africa, where he was thrown into captivity, taken to South Carolina and sold to a Captain Vesey in 1781. Vesey was said to have been impressed with "the beauty, alertness and intelligence" of his slave, who served him "faithfully" for twenty years. In 1800, Denmark Vesey won $1,500 in a lottery and used the money to buy his freedom and open a carpentry shop. Locals, particularly blacks, were impressed by his wealth, luck, and intelligence. He was one of the very few who could read—and he used his knowledge to argue for equality of the races.

Tensions rose when whites in South Carolina forbade a new black-led church—that had broken off from the Methodists—from preaching to slaves. Local authorities were afraid of what black preachers might say to their congregation, so they outlawed and harassed the church's members and leaders. In 1820, when Charleston moved to restrict the African Church, there were some three thousand black members, and Denmark Vesey was one of its leaders.

Within two years of the new oppressive legislation restricting black movement and worship in South Carolina, the greatest slave plot in American history was "exposed." On May 30, 1822, George Wilson, "a favorite and confidential slave" to his Charleston master, told his master about a plot led by Vesey which was to involve thousands of free and enslaved blacks, and even a few whites. The guerrillas were supposedly planning to take over Charleston, seize the munitions, massacre the whites, and sail on ships to Haiti sometime in July, just a couple of months away.

Authorities rounded up hundreds of suspects, extracted confessions, and in the end, executed fifty-five blacks (including Vesey), transported another nineteen out of the United States, briefly jailed four poor whites, and exonerated dozens of others. Some slaves informed on others, while a few, including Vesey, denied that there was ever a plot and refused to confess right up to their deaths, despite gruesome interrogation techniques.

Yet many believe that a plot never existed. Both then-South Carolina Governor Thomas Bennett and his brother-in-law, Supreme Court Justice William Johnson, were fierce critics of the Vesey trial proceedings. Governer Bennett wrote, "I fear nothing so much as the Effects of the persecuting Spirit that is abroad in this Place [Charleston]." They doubted that there ever was such a wild, bizarre plot involving thousands of insurgents and the takeover of the state's largest city. The fact that the slave-informants were later freed on state orders and given handsome rewards is just one of the reasons that some historians today doubt the plot's existence. A recent study by Johns Hopkins history professor Michael Johnson argues that the combination of rumor, empty boasting by slaves, and general paranoia among the local whites created a critical mass of the Salem witch trials sort, producing an entirely fictitious slave rebellion plot of monumentally absurd proportions.

As another historian, Philip Morgan, professor of history at Johns Hopkins University, noted, "We want to believe in the revolt. It points to the heroism of the slaves, that they were willing to lay down their lives to fight injustice." The real heroes, he said, were those like Vesey who refused to cave in and admit that there was a plot despite the torture and threat of execution.

Johnson's revisionist findings were praised, for example, in the *Nation*, because he "exonerated" Vesey and the other alleged plotters and indicted the evil white slaveholding culture that carried out the mass executions through sheer paranoia. Yet if Johnson is right—and it seems likely he is—then it deflates one of the few recognizable African-American heroes of the pre–Civil War period and forces us to consider the dismal reality of a three-thousand-strong freed-slave population that actually didn't plot to rebel against the slaveholders ever. Now, Stuckey's romantic description, "That a conspiracy on so large a scale should have existed in embryo during four years, and in an active form for several months, and yet have been so well managed, that, after actual betrayal, the authorities were again thrown off their guard and the plot nearly brought to a head again—this certainly shows extraordinary ability in the leaders, and a talent for concerted action on the part of slaves generally with which they have hardly been credited," is almost agonizing to read. And yet Stuckey's framing of Denmark Vesey's Rebellion, designed for a contemporary audience, was bound to look foolish someday, as all heroic, romanticized accounts created to meet audience expectations eventually do.

The whites in Charleston certainly believed in the slave rebellion plot, just as fiercely as they believed in the normalcy and virtue of their slave-based civilization. The single-day hanging of thirty-four blacks may be the largest mass state execution in American history—proof that the fear was real and deep and proof of their undying dedication to maintaining slavery. As was the case in other real and imagined slave rebellions, South Carolinians didn't blame slavery for inspiring the slave plot, but rather outside influences and the mental derangement of Africans.

As Edwin Holland, then editor of the *Charleston Times* wrote, "Let it never be forgotten, that our negroes are truely the Jacobins of the country; that they are the anarchists and the domestic enemy; the common enemy of civilized society, and the barbarians who would, IF THEY COULD, become the DESTROYERS of our race." If they could, that is.

Of course the complete opposite was true, the whites were destroying, and had destroyed, the black race. Yet such sentiments among whites were normal, mainstream. It was extreme and unrealistic to be for total abolitionism; it was normal, indeed respectable, to mass-hang black slaves on the belief that they were genocidal racists. The actual causes of rebellion are always avoided by the most respectable people—rebellion is always the fault of outsiders and evil. Postal workers rampage post offices not because something is wrong in post offices, but because Hollywood puts bad thoughts in their heads or because some postal workers are just lunatics with a penchant for snapping.

Vesey's example reminds us that the slaveholders felt most threatened by the freed slaves who lived among them. It's obvious their very existence reminded both whites and slaves that slavery was a condition, not a necessity or a favor. It reminded everyone that there was nothing inevitable about slavery, and therefore, perhaps, nothing normal about it either. A free black gave slaves hope, a model to aim for.

Who are the freed slaves among us today, and who our are bonded slaves? How are they treated by our ruling class? How do they treat each other? While we know that freed slaves were a threat to slaveholders for a variety of obvious reasons, they also were as much a threat to slaves. The envy and spite that freed slaves living in the South must have inspired among captive slaves is almost unimaginable—and something we'd rather not face today, as it muddies our simple moral framing of that time. Yet this division and resentment between bonded and freed slaves not only helps explain how authorities in South Carolina were able to coax their slaves into turning on Vesey (some, it seems, needed little coaxing), but it also should remind us of our own craven, submissive behavior today, in far less obvious manifestations. Moreover, it is easy to imagine freed slaves taking on some of the prejudices of the whites, in order to curry their favor. Some freed slaves even kept slaves of their own. As this chosen example shows, we are all potential slaves, and all potential collaborators.

> She was led, handcuffed, by Wildshaw's assistant, a black man, accompanied by Mr. Hope and some of his friends, to a field near at hand. There she was stripped naked, then the handcuffs were taken off, her arms put round an oak tree, and her hands tied together; her feet were also fastened to the tree. The coloured overseer took the cow-hide and fiercely swinging it round his head brought it down upon her shoulders. It was of no use to scream; thick came the blows, and freely poured the blood, whilst her master, her father! calmly speculated on the preventive effects of this infernal torture.
>
> —**John Hawkins Simpson**, *Horrors of the Virginian Slave Trade and of the Slave-Rearing Plantations. The True Story of Dinah, an Escaped Virginian Slave, Now in London, on Whose Body Are Eleven Scars Left by Tortures Which Were Inflicted by Her Master, Her Own Father. Together with Extracts from the Laws of Virginia, Showing That Against These Barbarities the Law Gives Not the Smallest Protection to the Slave, But the Reverse,* 1863.

This point is relevant because while from afar historical injustices seem simple to navigate morally, the closer one studies them, the more difficult and muddled the divisions between victim and victimizer become, the less heroic everyone seems. One would expect the entire class of oppressed to act as one, because it seems rationally to be in their interest to do so (and our cultural propaganda tells us that they do), but in fact the oppressed group often turns on its members with as much ferocity as allowed. Although it may seem crude to compare the two, consider once again Wesbecker's case. His fellow embattled employees taunted, brutalized, and turned their backs on him, even though he was essentially a victim of the same corporate forces and greed as they were. What inspired one employee to call Wesbecker "nuts" was the fact that he persistently demanded justice at his job, something the others didn't do. Slave-on-slave violence persists today, in a more subtle form. The fact that slaves didn't bind together in rebellion but rather often turned on those few rebels within their ranks to please their masters wasn't proof that they were happy with their lot and against the rebels; rather, it was proof that they were slaves with a slave mentality. Similarly, the fact that Wesbecker's co-workers didn't rally behind him but instead turned on him, wasn't proof that they were being treated well; rather, it was evidence of how successfully their union and their camaraderie had been destroyed.

9

"Without any cause or provocation"

THE MOST FAMOUS AMERICAN SLAVE REBEL is Nat Turner, whose insurrection in 1831 has all the brutality, strangeness, and bitter irony that typifies a doomed uprising in America.

Turner was born in 1800 in Virginia and was said as a child to have spoken about events from an earlier life. He was considered remarkably intelligent and was also deeply religious, to the point of being paranoid-delusional.

In 1821, Turner ran away from his master, only to return thirty days later because a Spirit had told him to "return to the service of my earthly master." Four years later, after being sold to another master, he had another vision. Having seen lights in the sky, he prayed to find out what they meant. Then, "while laboring in the field, I discovered drops of blood on the corn, as though it were dew from heaven, and I communicated it to many, both white and black, in the neighborhood; and then I found on the leaves in the woods hieroglyphic characters and numbers, with the forms of men in different attitudes, portrayed in blood, and representing the figures I had seen before in the heavens."

The visions didn't stop, but rather seemed to be building up to something. On May 12, 1828, Turner had his third vision: "I heard a loud noise in the heavens, and the Spirit instantly appeared to me and said the Serpent was loosened, and Christ had laid down the yoke he had borne for the sins of men, and that I should take it on and fight against the Serpent, for the time was fast approaching when the first should be last and the last should be first. . . . And by signs in the heavens that it would make known to me when I should commence the great work, and until the first sign appeared I should conceal it from the knowledge of men; and on the appearance of the sign. . . . I should arise and prepare myself and slay my enemies with their own weapons."

That time came in February of 1831 when a partial eclipse of the sun was interpreted by Turner to signify God's personal signal. Turner, a charismatic and popular figure on his plantation, gathered six of his most trusted fellow slaves and plotted an insurrection that they believed would be joined by thousands of slaves, freeing blacks throughout the South and ending in glory and liberty for all.

On August 21, at two in the morning, Nat Turner and his co-conspirators sneaked into their master's household and slaughtered the entire family, women and children included. Turner had spoken well of his master, calling him kind, and confessed that he "never had any complaints." But just because he liked him, didn't mean he didn't want to murder him. He could be both polite and grateful, and secretly boil with rage.

Emboldened by the successful bloodletting in their master's house, Nat Turner's band of rebels continued their rampage spree, going from white household to white household, slaughtering the masters' families and freeing the plantation's blacks. However, only about forty to fifty liberated slaves joined Turner's army, including a few on horseback, a far lower number than he had counted on.

The next day, as Turner's army marched on the nearest town, Jerusalem, they were confronted and scattered by a group of local militia. In the brief skirmish, the white militia quickly defeated the rebel slaves and sent them into retreat. Most of Turner's army abandoned him after this first encounter, leaving only about twenty sticking by their anointed commander.

Nat Turner's remaining rebels managed to find quarters in some friendly slave cabins, where they slept overnight, resting up for another day of liberation. Despite the defeat and loss of manpower they weren't entirely crushed. The next day they targeted a nearby plantation owned by a man named Blunt, who suffered from severe gout. Turner hoped that by launching an attack and slaughtering a large plantation owner as powerful as Blunt, he could rally new recruits to his slave army. However, incredible as it seems, Blunt and his family were defended by their own slaves, whom he armed and led against Turner's army. Blunt's slave army successfully crushed Turner's slave army, capturing two, killing one, and wounding another. After this debacle, Turner's army was essentially through. The few who stuck with him soon encountered state and federal troops, lost another skirmish, and scattered for good. Turner was the only one to escape from this last battle. He fled into the forest, dug a hole, and lived there for nearly six weeks before being discovered and arrested. In all, Turner's men managed to shoot, stab, and club to death fifty-nine whites, mostly women and children, in the area around Southampton, Virginia. Fifteen of Nat Turner's co-conspirators were caught and hung. In reprisal, a white vigilante group terrorized the region's blacks, killing hundreds in revenge pogroms that foreshadowed the rise of the KKK forty years later.

Turner was executed on November 11, 1831, and his body skinned as an example.

Several things are interesting about Nat Turner's doomed, gory rebellion. First, Turner was clearly delusional and yet his response to the madness of slavery was, from our vantage point today, the most sane and heroic of all. Joseph Wesbecker suffered from depression and was belittled for having a persecution complex and for being generally crazy, yet some of the normal people who worked with him sympathized with his attack on the company. The fact that Nat Turner may have been schizophrenic or delusional does not disqualify the inherent political nature of his rebellion. Rather, it suggests that sometimes only someone not mentally healthy—not normal—is capable of rising up against objectively awful injustice. A normal, healthy person finds a way to accept his condition, no matter how wretched.

The second most significant feature of Turner's rebellion was the white response. As always, the blame was assigned to unspeakable evil, savage Negroes, outside influences—anything but what was considered normal or inevitable at the time, namely, slavery. An account of the insurrection, "The Banditti," published in the *Richmond Enquirer* on August 30, 1831, reads, "What strikes us as the most remarkable thing in this matter is the horrible ferocity of these monsters. They remind one of a parcel of blood-thirsty wolves rushing down from the Alps. . . . No black man ought to be permitted to turn a Preacher through the country. The law must be enforced or the tragedy of Southampton appeals to us in vain." According to the *Enquirer*, Turner "was artful, impudent and vindictive, without any cause or provocation, that could be assigned."

This reality-inversion, this contemporary blindness to the obvious institutional cause of Turner's rebellion is almost a verbatim description used by most commentators today to describe Eric Harris and Dylan Klebold's murder spree at Columbine High School, in which fifteen were killed and twenty-three injured, as well as nearly every rage massacre before and after, whether in workplaces or schoolyards. *Slate's* Dave Cullen thought he solved the why riddle in his article, "The Depressive and the Psychopath: At Last We Know Why the Columbine Killers Did It," published on April 20, 2004, the fifth anniversary of the massacre. Cullen wrote, "[Eric Harris] was a brilliant killer without a conscience, searching for the most diabolical scheme imaginable. If he had lived to adulthood and developed his murderous skills for many more years, there is no telling what he could have done. His death at Columbine may have stopped him from doing something even worse." Cullen's breakthrough, like the *Richmond Enquirer's*, is essentially this: Eric Harris murdered because Eric Harris was an evil murderer. Cullen rides this line of reasoning further down the light rail line of idiocy, implying that Harris was a Hitler in the making who was stopped in the nick of time, and we should all be grateful that he only managed to kill a dozen students or else he surely would have gassed us all. Yet what's missing from Cullen's explanation is a context for Harris's rage attack on Columbine High School. Even Hitler is given a context by serious historians—the humiliation of the Treaty of Versailles and the failure of Weimar Germany—whereas rampage murderers, like slaves once before them, are portrayed as having killed without reason. Their murder sprees were and are explained as symptoms of the perpetrators' innate evil, or of foreign forces, rather than as reactions to unbearable circumstances. Blaming evil or psychology is far more comforting. Cullen even admits this, calling his explanation for Columbine "more reassuring, in a way." Indeed he's proud of this convenient "reassuring" aspect of his theory—he thinks it makes his version of events more palatable, and hence, more persuasive. Another journalist, Joanne Jacobs, summed it up even more simply: "Evil, not rage" inspired the Columbine killers, she wrote. Well, that settles that!

More depressing than the way slave rebellions were cruelly misrepresented is the role other slaves played in crushing slave rebellions, another awful aspect of slave life and the slave heart. As the *Enquirer* cheerfully pointed out in its account of the Nat Turner uprising, "But it deserves to be said to the credit of many of the slaves whom gratitude had bound to their masters, that they had manifested the greatest alacrity in detecting and apprehending many of the brigands. They had brought in several and a fine spirit had been shown in many of the plantations of confidence on the part of the masters, and gratitude on that of the slaves." Racists at the time saw this as legitimizing the virtue of slavery; the grim fact is that human psychology, and circumstance, caused black slaves to collaborate, and not just collaborate coldly but "in gratitude" and "a fine spirit." These cheerful, reassuring adjectives might be just a white fiction, but it is entirely believable that those slaves really did turn on their fellow slaves in "a fine spirit." Here is one of the finest expressions of successful slave management in practice, where the slave identifies his master's interests with his own, and his master's enemies as his also. Slave psychology and effective American slave management (which encourages a "cheerful disposition" and "initiative") combined to produce slaves which not only turned on their own liberators to protect their masters, but turned on them in "a fine spirit." Which helps explain again why there were so few slave rebellions. Not only were they doomed, and not only were they without context, but so often fellow slaves either refused to participate or worse, exposed plots and defended their masters with arms. These actions further reinforce the notion that a rebellion was not only doomed, but even the idea of rebelling was somehow not normal and perhaps evil. You really would have to be as crazy and schizophrenic as Nat Turner to not be affected; you'd have to have voices in your head louder than those around you to convince you that a slave rebellion was the right, sane response.

10

His Soul Is Marching On!

THE OTHER FAMOUS ANTI-SLAVERY INSURRECTION, John Brown's Harper's Ferry Rebellion, shares many of the same characteristics of the other rebellions: a mad religious fanatic embarks on an immensely sane mission to fight slavery, and fails spectacularly, largely because his plan was based on one wrong assumption: that slaves were ready to take up arms and risk all for freedom. All they needed was a little spark—like John Brown's army—to set their rebellion off.

In 1859, John Brown led a small army of fifteen whites (including two of his sons) and five free blacks on an attack against the Virginia port town of Harper's Ferry. The idea was to seize weapons from the munitions store, arm local slaves, and incite a larger slave rebellion that would finally end the wicked institution. Few free blacks joined Brown's army.

By 1859, two years before the start of the Civil War, abolitionism had suddenly gone mainstream in the North. Total abolitionism was now seen by a substantial number of Northerners, particularly the opinion-makers, as the only morally viable stand. This was a sharp and abrupt turnaround from previous decades, when abolitionists were considered marginal, fanatical, and unrealistic.

Still, it was one thing to propagandize for the abolition of slavery, but another thing to follow some Jesus freak into certain death. Even Harriet Tubman told Brown that she really, really wanted to join . . . but at the last minute she "fell ill and could not make it." As an African-American celebrity, Tubman had a lot more to lose than Brown's other recruits. Dying in the service of a suicidal honky's messianic mission was not how Tubman wanted to end her career, and her weak excuse provides at least one bit of comic relief to this tragedy.

When John Brown's army launched their raid on Harper's Ferry in the middle of the night, liberating blacks from their businesses and "arresting" their owners, seizing an armory with the aim of distributing weapons, none of the slaves in the surrounding region joined the rebellion. Even those slaves that they managed to liberate in raids around the town declined to take up arms with Brown. It was an inauspicious opening for a war of liberation. It had happened yet again, just as it happened to Nat Turner, and just as it happened to the slave rebels in New York City in 1712. The heroic poetics did not correspond to the hard reality of a slave population thoroughly conditioned not to act, not to try anything dangerous, not to step out of line, or threaten its masters or the general order of things, but rather to serve their interests, whether out of fear or a "cheerful disposition," and to do so of their own initiative.

A military force soon arrived led by Robert E. Lee and Brown and his band of twenty insurgents retreated into the armory with their captives and slaves. In the ensuing skirmishes, John Brown's army accidentally killed a freed black railway attendant, but they also murdered three whites, including the mayor of Harper's Ferry. None of this mattered, though: the slaves from the surrounding territories still wouldn't join Brown's call to rise up.

Lee's men, who surrounded the armory, suggested that Brown enter into negotiations to try to reach a settlement. Brown considered his position—no general uprising took place, no slaves joined the rebellion, and he was vastly outgunned. He sent out one of his sons to negotiate terms with Lee's men, but the minute Brown's son stepped out of the armory and into the open, Lee's men shot and killed him. This naturally poisoned the atmosphere, making further negotiations difficult—probably Lee's purpose. The South was in a fit of hysteria over the raid, and they wanted to make a brutal example of John Brown. The world trend against slavery, as well as hardened abolitionist sentiment in the North, threatened the South's slave culture and economy. Southerners viewed Brown's insurgency, however doomed and feckless, as a confirmation of all that they feared. It had to be crushed not only in blood, but in spirit. Lee stormed the armory, slaughtering ten of the white insurgents and two of the blacks. John Brown was taken alive, wounded, and paraded around, treated like the incarnation of evil. Virginia Governor Henry H. Wise described Brown's band as "murderers, traitors, robbers, insurrectionists . . . wandering, malicious, unprovoked, felons."

At his trial, Brown's lawyer argued that his client was insane. The lawyer read out a telegram which said, "John Brown, leader of the insurrection at Harper's Ferry, and several of his family, have resided in this country for many years.

Insanity is hereditary in that family. His mother's sister died with it, and a daughter of that sister has been two years in a lunatic asylum. A son and daughter of his mother's brother have also been confined in the lunatic asylum, and another son of that brother is now insane and under close restraint."

Brown was furious with his lawyer for disclosing his family's (and his) congenital insanity. Yet Brown's insanity was also crucial; given the pattern of rebels, it was his insanity that allowed him to wage a hopeless rebellion against the insanity of slavery. He may have known he was going to die, but now that slavery had been widely contextualized in the North (and Europe) as an evil and injustice of the first order, it must have made it easier to face death. Put another way, it seems to be no accident that John Brown, a white anti-slavery rebel, only appeared after the idea of radical abolitionism went mainstream, rather than before, when a rebellion would have not only been doomed but would have likely been contextualized in less heroic terms in the North, as that of a madman leading a bunch of bloodthirsty cultists on a murderous rampage. John Brown was hanged. But he died a martyr, one of the few martyrs that America has ever officially recognized. Within four years of his hanging, slavery was abolished.

As seemingly foolish as Brown's tactical plan was, it actually succeeded in its goal: to provide martyrs and an example, a spark perhaps, on the eve of a war that would eventually end slavery. Unlike Nat Turner, Denmark Vesey, and other black rebels before him, Brown went to the gallows a celebrated figure. He knew, as he died, that his death would resonate. Today, Nat Turner may be as important an anti-slave rebel as John Brown, but the fact that he died broken, defeated, and vilified, even repentant to a degree, in an ideological vacuum raises a question: if Joseph Wesbecker or Dylan Klebold and Eric Harris murdered for just reasons, will the time come when their crimes are vindicated in a future moral context that emphasizes the forces that drove them to murder, rather than the murders?

11

Our Founding Fleecers

IF YOU LOOK AT ANY DOMESTIC REBELLION throughout American history, you see the same pattern of cruelty, false attribution, and cruel irony/black humor.

Shays's Rebellion, a mostly lower-middle-class yeoman uprising in rural New England against the Boston elite, fought against unfair property and poll taxes enacted by the new Revolutionary government powers, as well as against court proceedings that the rebels believed favored the rich. The rebellion's goals were quite similar to the Revolutionary Americans' goals against the British—and yet the newly independent American leaders branded Shays's rebels "a party of madmen" who were conducting "a formidable rebellion against reason." They were officially portrayed as "knaves," "thieves," and "madmen," which made repressing them an absolute necessity. Chief Justice William Cushing labeled the rebels "evil minded persons . . . [waging war] against the Commonwealth, to bring the whole government and all the good people of this state, if not continent, under absolute command and subjugation to one or two ignorant, unprincipled, bankrupt, desperate individuals."

In fact, many of the rebels, like their leader Daniel Shays, were distinguished Revolutionary War veterans who had been driven to desperation by a bad postwar economy as well as rapacious absentee landlords and discriminatory taxes—exactly the same conditions that sparked the Revolutionary War. But there was a new Man in control now, a much more effective Man than the British Royal Crown—the American power structure. As so often happens in colonial revolutions, the new power imitates the vices of the old colonial power that it has defeated, the only difference being that the new native power succeeds in suppressing its insurrection where its colonial predecessors failed.

A militia army was raised by the new American government and called out to quell Shays's army of small farmers in 1787. In the ensuing skirmishes, four rebels were killed and the rest were forced to surrender. They were sentenced to death for treason, but eventually, unlike African rebels, pardoned. Pardons were not too popular among the new elite. Samuel Adams, once a human rights revolutionary, was now lieutenant governor of Massachusetts. He demanded that the rebels all be executed forthwith, and was livid at their pardoning. "Rebellion against a king may be pardoned, or lightly punished," he said, "but the man who dares to rebel against the laws of a republic ought to suffer death."

A few years later, the novice American government under George Washington faced the Whiskey Rebellion in rural western Pennsylvania. Locals, who relied heavily on local whiskey production and barter trade for their livelihood, protested a new federal tax on illegal whiskey distilleries imposed from Philadelphia. But the federal government didn't care. The coastal elite loathed the rebellious frontiersmen, describing them as "the scum of nature" and "a parcel of abandoned wretches" who lived "like so many pigs in a sty." Indeed they were desperately poor, unkempt, and a number of them were one-eyed, victims of eye-gouging, one of the most popular sports among frontiersmen. Both President Washington and his rightist right-hand man Alexander Hamilton wanted to make a swift example—which they did by violently suppressing the Whiskey rebels with a large army raised by the federal government.

Another, less publicized reason that they chose to go after the rebels was that President George Washington had a personal financial interest in seeing the rebellion quashed . . .

Several years before independence, then–Virginia colony governor Robert Dinwiddie offered as many as two hundred thousand acres of land as bounty to encourage enlistments in the local militia to fight against Indians, the French, and anyone else who got in the way of the Anglo-Saxon land-grab. The French and their Indian allies were impeding the Ohio Company's trade business in the frontier area, and Dinwiddie was a top-ranking officer, or rather profiteer, in the Ohio Company. Therefore, war. Dinwiddie didn't actually own the land he promised to give his militia. Instead, he gave the militia volunteers vouchers, essentially land

IOUs, and told them that if the campaigns were successful, the vouchers would be redeemable for property rights. Washington joined Dinwiddie's militia and quickly rose up its ranks.

When the fighting was over, the Virginia colony's House of Burgesses dragged its feet in funding the purchase of the promised land, making the vouchers increasingly worthless pieces of paper, broken promises. Washington, however—much like the Russian oligarchs of the 1990s—saw the value in those vouchers, and how they could be manipulated to his advantage. Starting in 1754 all the way through 1769, Washington acquired as many of his soldiers' vouchers as he could, offering as little as ten pounds for every two thousand acres, preying on militiamen who were too ignorant or cynical to place their faith in the word of the Virginia governor. Others began to suspect that their commander was up to no good with his voucher-mongering scheme, thus making it harder and harder for him to get his militiamen to dump their vouchers at clearance prices.

Washington's scheme had been smoked out. So he enlisted his brother Charles Washington to help, advising him to find out "in a joking way rather than in earnest, at first," what value his militiamen put on their land claims. "Do not let it be known that I have any concern therein," he told his brother, instructing him to purchase vouchers worth up to fifteen thousand acres in his own name. Washington used his scouts and officers to locate the best plots of land, and by the time he had twenty thousand acres under his belt, he petitioned Governor Dinwiddie to make good on the vouchers' promise, which Dinwiddie did. Only after the vouchers had been scooped up for a song and Washington had all the land IOUs in his pocket did the Virginia House of Burgesses authorize the money to convert the land vouchers into real land. The vouchers were cashed, and Washington was suddenly a very wealthy real estate magnate. The wars were extremely profitable for George Washington. Eventually he managed to acquire some sixty-three thousand acres in the Trans-Appalachia region, using all sorts of schemes to circumvent laws—like subdividing lands that exceeded the maximum allowable acreage and then registering each land separately. As historian Thomas Slaughter wrote, "Washington's methods for acquiring frontier acreage were machine-like in their efficiency."

And while Washington may not have been able to tell a lie, he sure was capable of playing the role of heartless absentee slum lord. Even as the economy in his fiefdom worsened, Washington was notorious for kicking squatters off of his land.

In rural western Pennsylvania, life became increasingly difficult from the 1780s through the 1790s. For frontiersmen, the Revolution brought Hell. In 1780, just one-third of western Pennsylvania's settlers were landless; by 1795, that figure was up to 60 percent in many townships. Most scraped by at a subsistence level, barely surviving. The socioeconomic situation devolved over time into an almost exact replica of feudal Europe. In 1780, the top 10 percent owned 26 percent of the land; by the mid 1790s, they owned 35 percent of the land. Conversely, the bottom 10 percent owned 2 percent of the land in 1780, and just 1 percent of the land in the mid-1790s.

By the time of the Whiskey Rebellion in 1792, a quarter of the frontiersmen lived as "croppers," laborers who farmed the land of their overwhelmingly East

Coast absentee landlords like George Washington. The croppers—essentially serfs—paid their rent in crops and kept the remainder for themselves.

In the early 1790s, just thirty-six men dominated the western counties of Fayette and Washington. While a few, like John Neville, George Washington, and the county sheriffs prospered mightily, many settlers felt that they had been fleeced by land speculators who had promised wealth and prosperity, but delivered poverty and despair.

One of the first acts of the new United States Congress was to pass the Whiskey Excise Tax in 1791, going against a promise to impose such taxes only as a last resort. The frontiersmen in western Pennsylvania, already destitute and desperate, for whom whiskey and their last pennies were a matter of life and death, ignored the excise. They tarred and feathered or harassed the few federal representatives who tried to set up excise offices or register the local distilleries. And they were right to do so: why should the "scum of nature" be forced to pay up what little they had left in order to cover the states' debts, while the new oligarchy, which had benefited so greatly from the war, bore so little of the war's costs?

Alexander Hamilton enlisted the comical figure of George Clymer, who was in charge of collections in Pennsylvania, to be his eyes and ears in the rebellious western regions. Clymer accepted, but was intensely paranoid . . . and extremely silly. Like a three-pointed-hat Inspector Clouseau, Clymer adopted various aliases, each with slapstick effect. On his way west from Philadelphia in September 1792, Clymer first tried to pass himself off as Henry Knox, the secretary of war. However, Knox was widely known to be among the most obese Americans alive, so locals took the much thinner Clymer-Knox for just another bad imposter looking to get comped. Realizing his mistake, he then named himself "Smith" and traded horses with his servant, in a classic switcheroo that he must have picked up from some bad European opera. Clymer quickly abandoned this scheme when a local called him "an ill-looking fellow" who "did not know how to rub down a horse." Furious, Clymer next tried to pass himself off as just an ordinary person. The sad thing was that no one recognized Clymer even when he admitted his true Clymer self, despite the fact that he was one of the signatories to the Declaration of Independence.

When Clymer arrived in Pittsburgh, he roomed in the most luxurious hotel for a few nights, unable to resist the need for civilized comforts. After getting his humors back, he transferred to a more ordinary hotel, the Bear Inn, hoping no one noticed that he had just checked out of the five-star around the corner. Locals quickly put two and two together. They knew that he had come to Pittsburgh on behalf of the excise and asked him to leave the Bear Inn. Clymer agreed, but now he was too terrified to venture out of the city, as per Hamilton's instructions, and into the rural frontier areas to conduct the investigation, as was his assignment. And yet the worst he'd have had to put up with were a bunch of dirty looks and unfriendly words. They weren't going to harm him—they told him so explicitly. But Clymer couldn't be convinced. After a few days, he lost his nerve completely, gathered some militiamen to act as bodyguards, and fled Pittsburgh in a panic, heading at great speed back to Philadelphia with absolutely no one in pursuit.

When he returned to the capital, he was horrified to discover that word of his comical adventures had followed him. Clymer denied everything, but no one bought it. So he switched tactics, fiercely defending his disguises and flight, claiming that locals were in "an actual state of insurgency against the government," including "magistrates, other public officers and clergy" of the region, and that his own bold venture was "more hazardous perhaps than to have taken an honorable chance in an Indian War."

The effect of his buffoonery was tragic: government officials took his panicked word for it, and raised an army to crush the supposed mass rebellion. And this is where the story starts to mirror that of so many doomed slave rebellions: hysteria among the dominant classes over perceived lower-class-savage murder plots, violent crushing, and slave turning against slave to please the master class.

The battles that followed were sloppy and dismal. In one battle, an army of rebel frontiersmen attacked a local oligarch, John Neville, who had helped bring in federal excise authorities and personally hosted them. The rebels lay siege to Neville's house, where the federal excise taxman hid inside. Just when everything looked doomed, Neville was saved by his slaves, who attacked the poor white rebels in a surprise rearguard action. Slaves fighting the poor in order to protect the oligarchy.

The federal forces tried cracking down in their usual brutal way. Eventually their tactics pushed most of western Pennsylvania's population to the side of the rebels. As a critical mass formed, the majority switched hearts. If a rebellion is small and just starting, it looks crazy; but if it begins to succeed, lasts, and builds up momentum, it inevitably legitimizes itself. This legitimacy is all the persuasion most people need. From 1793 to 1794, what started as a rebellion against an unfair excise tax transformed into broader class warfare, pitting locals against absentee landlords. This transformation of the rebellion's context is instructive— it doesn't mean that the rebels were losing control, but rather, that their ability to frame injustice grew as the rebellion seemed to take hold. The context started to take on a meaningful shape. Just as the American colonials' consciousness expanded from rebelling against unfair taxation in the 1760s to wider noble revolutionary goals touching on the inherent rights of mankind, so the Whiskey Rebellion guerrillas took on broader themes as injustice increasingly framed their consciousness. Once you start seeing injustice in one place, it's like taking off blinders—you start to see injustice everywhere, and how it is all connected. One horseman reportedly rode through Pittsburgh yelling, "This is not all that I want, it is not the excise law only that must go down; your district and associate judges must go down; your high offices and salaries. A great deal more is to be done; I am but beginning yet."

In 1794, President Washington raised an army of 12,950 men and led their march on the rebel counties to restore order and to protect his landholdings. The resulting show of force was brutally effective. The rebels melted away, faced with certain defeat, while the fence-sitters and even most who professed sympathy with the rebellion returned to the federal government's side. In the end, only a couple dozen Whiskey Rebels were brought to Philadelphia to be tried for treason, only two were convicted, and even they, unlike African slave rebels, were pardoned. There were casualties, but only ridiculous casualties. One rebel, a drunk in a local tavern, kept trying to grab the bayonet of a federal officer's musket while muttering taunts and threats, and he was eventually run through; the other was a cripple who happened to be in the area of a passing federal detachment when he was ordered to stop. He couldn't manage to comply quickly enough due to his disability, so a trigger-happy militiaman shot him in the genitals. He died "an excruciating death."

Yet in spite of the feckless comedy and brutal suppression of this rebellion, in the end the Whiskey Rebellion was, in a way, successful. From that time until the Civil War, it became de facto government policy (as well as standard American belief) that no government could impose a national excise tax on liquor except during a time of war or national emergency. Although all domestic rebellions are doomed, for some, partial justice does result. The rebellions may be brutal, misunderstood, and defeated . . . but the martyrdom isn't always in vain.

PART III

Ragenomics

Boss: Pretend you're me. You find this. What would you do?

Jack rises slowly, walks to his door, shuts it.

Jack: Me? I'd be very careful who I talked to about this. It sounds like someone dangerous wrote it . . . someone who might snap at any moment, stalking from office to office with an Armalite AR-10 Carbine-gas semiautomatic, bitterly pumping round after round into colleagues and co-workers.

Jack moves very close to Boss, picks up the PAPER and starts tearing it into pieces.

Jack: Might be someone you've known for years . . . somebody very close to you. Or, maybe you shouldn't be bringing me every little piece of trash you pick up.

—Fight Club

DO PEOPLE JUST SNAP WHEN THEY GO POSTAL? Do they act "without any cause or provocation," as Nat Turner supposedly did? Or are they reacting to grievances both specific and institutional: grievances that we are barely able to see because we lack distance, grievances which seem as banal and part of the natural turn-of-the-millennium landscape as strip malls and stress-palpitations, yet grievances which will be perceived as obviously unbearable twenty, thirty, fifty years from now? What, in the case of *Fight Club*, are the grievances that lead Jack to wage a violent revolution against Middle America? Some are easy to put your finger on; other grievances are impossible to verbalize, they could sort of be summed up as "life." Yet the millions who saw that movie and sympathized with its message understood what it was that drew Jack to violent rebellion. There was another, more comforting explanation for his violence too: Jack, as we learn at the end of the book, was mentally ill. As all rebels-before-their-time are ill. (The movie version wisely left that cheap escape-hatch ending more vague than the book, which is why the movie was far more effective than the book.) The huge underground popularity of *Fight Club*'s message makes another point: it takes someone who is mentally ill to see, and fight against, the sense of oppression that healthy people otherwise accept to such a degree that they can't even see it.

Everyone today agrees that slavery caused slave violence, and that inner-city poverty and pressures breed violent crime. Why is it so awful to suggest that offices, such as they are today, breed office massacres?

The school and the workplace are the two most important physical spaces for modern Americans—they are life's settings. This has become increasingly true over the last thirty years, as the family has withered away and as community has transformed from a concrete feature of life to an abstract, pathos-heavy myth whose demise is invariably rued in popular mainstream culture, such as in books like *Bowling Alone*. At the same time workloads and competition have increased, keeping Americans' lives more intensely focused on those two physical settings, the office and the school. While home and family have served as traditional settings for violence throughout human history, schools and offices had always been considered safe—until now.

1

Rage Against the Gipper

What the hell's going on, man? I thought you were going to come in here and start shooting.
—*Office Space*

ON AUGUST 20, 1986, Patrick Sherrill fired fifty shots heard 'round the nation's post offices.

Sherrill had worked at the Edmond, Oklahoma, Post Office branch for eighteen months before he "went postal." He pulled into the parking lot in his blue automobile right next to fellow postal employee Michael Bigler. It was around 6:30 AM; the muggy Great Plains furnace was warming up for another wretched day. Bigler, an evangelical Christian, noticed a large bulge in Sherrill's postal satchel, which lay on the passenger's seat, even though it should have been empty. Inside were two .45 semiautomatic pistols, up to two hundred rounds of ammunition, protective sunglasses designed to keep gunpowder and shrapnel from getting into his eyes, and ear plugs. He had checked out this gear from the Oklahoma Air National Guard base a couple of weeks earlier in preparation for a national marksman contest.

Bigler went to work sorting mail, joining about fifty other employees in the sorting area. Shortly before 7 AM, Sherrill entered through the east side of the building, his mail delivery bag strapped over his left shoulder, pistol in his right hand. The first two people he shot were Rick Esser, his supervisor, and Mike Rockne—grandson of the famous Notre Dame coach Knute Rockne. That's right: the same Knute Rockne who was the subject of Ronald Reagan's most famous movie, *Knute Rockne—American Hero*, the one where Reagan played George "The Gipper" Gipp, a star Notre Dame football player dying of pneumonia (the same condition that Reagan really died of, and the most common killer of homeless people, Reaganomics' most visible legacy), who tells Rockne, "Just win one for the Gipper." Reagan used this same line to great effect forty years later to help get himself elected, and re-elected. The first rebellious uprisings against Reaganomics broke out in America's post offices in the mid-1980s. The real spark, Sherrill's massacre, was set off with a gunshot to Mike Rockne's head, meaning at least one Rockne lost on account of the Gipper.

After killing Esser and Rockne, Sherrill chased down Bigler through the exit and shot him in the back. Sherrill ran into the front lobby, firing in a circle, and as employees fled towards an exit through the back, he pursued them, shooting. He killed his third victim, postman Jerry Pyle, as he tried to duck behind his old Volkswagen in the parking lot. Next Sherrill returned to the post office. He bolted the doors, then methodically walked through the building, from post station bay to post station bay, shooting those cowering under cubicles or hiding in their stations, sparing some, slaughtering others.

Debbie Smith was sorting letters when the shooting started. "I froze. I couldn't run. He came to shoot the clerks in the box section next to mine. I just knew I was next." But as she hid, Sherrill passed her by and opened fire on the next section. As Smith ran for the front door, she said, "I could hear all the clerks screaming as they were shot."

"I heard two quick shots and then a single shot," one survivor later recalled. "I thought it was a bunch of the guys clowning around, that maybe one of them had dropped a mail tray or something. But then I saw a guy fall with blood all over him. Then I heard another shot. And someone yelled, 'No! No!' Then another shot. And someone screamed, 'Oh, my God!'"

One witness said that Sherrill "shot anything that moved," yet another survivor told of how Sherrill targeted some and deliberately ignored others.

Hubert Hammond, a postal employee working that morning, said, "I saw Patrick Sherrill walking towards C-9 (William Nimmo) and shoot him twice. Then he turned toward me and lifted his gun at me, but didn't shoot. By then I was running with my back to him, to the front of the office. As I got out, I heard a lot of shooting inside."

Another employee, Tracy Sanchez, was also spared: "I was at my case near the break room and I heard a series of bangs. I looked across the room and saw people yelling and falling on the floor. Then Sherrill walked by with a gun, shooting people. . . . He walked right past me and I ran to the back door, but it was locked. Another man tried to get out with me. We ran back and there was a storage closet nearby. We hid in there, but we couldn't lock it so we turned the light off and stayed quiet. Sherrill stood by our door and kept emptying his shells and reloading his gun—about three times. Each time we could hear him walk around the room shooting, over and over. People begged him and he would yell at them and shoot them several times. Then, finally, it got quiet. But we stayed hidden until we heard the police."

One survivor said he heard a supervisor, perhaps Patty Husband (who was just promoted not long before), yell at Sherrill, "Get out of here, you crazy son of a bitch!" The survivor explained what happened next: "Then there were three more shots. He got her." Husband apparently had seen too many movies; either that, or she thought, like the drill instructor in *Full Metal Jacket*, that her new senior status, applied with confident determination, would reduce her murder-crazed subordinate to submission.

Five women huddled in terror, trapped in their station, walled in on all three sides. Sherrill shot and killed four of them and wounded a fifth. One of those he killed, a platinum blond from Georgia named Judy Denny, had just arrived from Atlanta with her husband, who also worked in the USPS. They moved to Edmond to escape their Atlanta station where a post office shooting rampage took place a year earlier, leaving two employees dead.

Sherrill kept on killing. He murdered Billy Miller, a young employee who had brought his wife's chocolate chip cookies to work and handed them out before Sherrill showed up. One young employee rounded a corner carrying a bundle of papers. Sherrill shot him—his body was found still clutching the newspapers.

At last Sherrill headed to the same last spot Wesbecker ended his spree—the break room. He found his fourteenth murder victim there, Leroy Phillips, and shot him. Police soon arrived, including a SWAT team. After they arrived, they heard only one shot—believed to be the bullet Sherrill put into his own head. As one officer testified, "A couple of minutes [after we arrived], we saw a subject inside the post office walk up and bar the back doors, look out the windows for an instant, then disappear from view. The man was bald-headed and there was blood on his forehead. . . . Approximately thirty seconds after he walked away [from view], at approximately 0715 to 0720, I heard the distinct sound of a muffled gunshot."

In the end, fifteen postal employees lay dead and another six were injured. It was the third largest mass murder in American history, and, although it wasn't the first post office massacre (there were four smaller attacks from 1983–85), it was the first postal rampage to burn itself into America's conscience, and still the largest workplace massacre to date. As Dr. S. Anthony Baron noted in *Violence in the Workplace*, "Probably more than any other single individual, [Patrick] Sherrill was responsible for making the general population keenly, painfully aware of a kind of terrorism that had been increasing annually but had for the most part been overlooked or ignored. He was soon to bring the issue of violence in the workplace into the media spotlight."

What could have caused it?

Media accounts noted that Patrick Sherrill had been nicknamed "Crazy Pat" by neighborhood kids. They called him that because Sherrill always thought that they were laughing at him. He was six feet tall and two hundred pounds, he had started balding back in high school. He lived alone with his mother in her white frame house in a working class section of Oklahoma City. She developed Alzheimer's in 1977, and died in 1978, leaving him alone. Eventually he got himself a pit bull—his only companion.

Sherrill sometimes mowed his lawn at night; he also was caught staring into neighbors' windows. He was desperately lonely, lower-middle-class, stuck in the flat middle of Middle America. In his house, after the massacre, investigators found numerous copies of *Penthouse* and *Playboy*, along with *Soldier of Fortune* magazines, and copies of *Soviet Life* and *Russian Made Simple*. They also found a pamphlet titled *Dying: The Greatest Adventure of My Life—A Family Doctor Tells His Story*.

Sherrill was dismally lonely, a loneliness far more common in Middle America than we are allowed to believe. Loneliness led him to anger, to blaming himself and those around him, to desperate sexual acts like making obscene phone calls and peeping into windows, to war-nerding and death-courting, to a fixation with ham radio (the predecessor of the Internet chat room), and to an intense sensitivity. Loneliness can create a vicious circle of strange behavior, which only increases the loneliness and alienation, which then increases the weird behavior.

A female civilian employee of the 219th E-I Squadron in the National Guard unit where Sherrill had served said, "I just got the impression, you know, he's a weird guy," while an FAA manager who supervised Sherrill's brief stint there as a file clerk called him an "odd duck" who was "hard to talk to." He wore "pants that people wore back in the fifties."

Others saw him differently. Vincent Stubbs, who was assigned to the same Air Force Reserves barracks as Sherrill in the early 1980s, described him as an "overweight bachelor who always expressed concern that he was going nowhere" and "the loneliest man I have ever known." A neighbor, Charles Thigpen, told *Newsweek*, "He wasn't a Rambo . . . shy but gentle, [he] liked the words 'thank you' and 'please.' We live in a time when we want quick answers. And since Pat's not alive to defend himself, they don't have to be the right answers." When Sherrill's cremated remains were buried at the grave site of his parents in Watonga, Oklahoma, twenty-five people attended his private ceremony. A picture in a local paper showed one woman, a customer on his route, kneeling at his burial site. A bouquet had been sent to Sherrill's service from letter carriers in Irving, Texas, (headquarters of the Boy Scouts). A card with the bouquet read, "To those who understand what he went through as a carrier. No one will ever know how far he was pushed to do what he did."

A postal union official blamed management for Sherrill's attack. Even some of his fellow employees said that they thought Sherrill's rampage was an act of revenge. The villain in this case is a supervisor with the unlikely name of Bill Bland, whom Sherrill accused of singling him out for harassment. In a way it fits: the blandness of Sherrill's job, loneliness, house, even the bland state he lived in, all made it somehow necessary that he would be terrorized by a superior named Bill Bland.

About nine months before the massacre, Bland suspended Sherrill for seven days for "failure to discharge your assigned duties conscientiously and effectively." In his letter, Bland wrote, "On September 19, 1985, you did fail to protect mail entrusted to your care, as evidenced by the fact you left two trays of mail and three parcel post items unattended, overnight, at 601 Vista Lane. Your failure to discharge your assigned duties conscientiously and effectively resulted in a one day delay in delivery of approximately 500 pieces of mail which had been entrusted to your care." Sherrill was written up a few months later for macing a dog that barked at him, even though the dog was behind a locked fence. The dog's owner witnessed it and reported it to the post office. Sherrill admitted his infraction, commenting that he didn't think anyone had seen it.

Sherrill was sure that his supervisors were "making book" on him—that is, compiling every tiny infraction in order to set up a record that would allow them to fire him. They timed his routes on days when his load was heavy, but, he told a friend, they timed a female carrier on the same route on days when her load was light.

On August 19, the day before the rage murders, Sherrill sat through another chewing-out session led by Bland and another supervisor, Rick Esser. One carrier who witnessed the dressing-down through the office window said, "Although I could not hear, it was obvious that Pat Sherrill was being reprimanded. I could see the look on his face which struck me as being very strange, eerie." By some accounts, Sherrill left the meeting convinced that he was going to be fired the next day, that the book had already been made on him.

Ironically, Bill Bland slept in late on the morning of August 20. He missed the show that Sherrill had put on especially for him. In case after case, we see this: the local petty tyrant always manages to have luck on his or her side on the day of the massacre, leaving others, subordinates and secretaries usually, to take the bullet. It is as if their luck is a permanent condition—luck that helped them attain their overlord position, luck that helped them advance further, luck that saved them from the bullet with their name on it.

2

"This has put a damper on our day."

> Q: What does it mean when you see a flag flying at half-mast outside of a post office?
> A: They're hiring.
> **—Contemporary American joke**

THE "GOING POSTAL" PHENOMENON began with U.S. Post Office massacres. In the popular mind, these post office murder sprees still have no context. They were too bizarre, too ridiculous. Post offices are quiet, colorless places in the public eye. Nothing could be more dull, even comically bland, than a United States Post Office. And no one could be more harmless than the mailman in the blue-gray shorts, driving his white delivery truck or power-walking in his pith helmet. Think of a postal employee and you tend to think of a friendly neighborhood fixture, a kind of fifties throwback to the happy days of community-oriented neighbors waving hello to each other. A general assumption is that a postal employee is someone who wanted a simple job for reliable wage and benefits. Some are liberal arts intellectuals who want to live the kind of life you imagine a Western European bureaucrat lives—relaxed work, steady pay, plenty of spare time to work on the Great American Novel. Others come from run-of-the-mill stock attracted to the womb of a large, secure structure, including former military people. Unlike the DMV, a post office feels almost as quiet, relaxed, and clean as a community library. It is, in a sense, Middle America itself, the Middle America of the *Andy Griffith*

Show. This hasty misperception of the post office culture made the murders there seem completely out-of-the-blue, surreal, and without context. If that can happen in a post office, where next?

When massacres started breaking out in our post offices, most people reasoned that it was merely another symptom of our violent culture. The post office massacres just confirmed the fear that the country is full of nut cases and they could be anyone, not just your neighbor, but even your mailman. *Killerus americanus* was merely innovating and morphing, launching a new post office product to add to its line of murder styles. And that made some people proud in an ironic, contemporary way—hence, the water cooler jokes, the "going postal" expression, the absorption into black humor.

One reason the whole rage murder phenomenon may have started with post offices is that the eight-hundred-thousand-employee-strong service, the nation's second-largest employer, was one of the earliest and largest agencies in the post–New Deal era to be subjected to what was essentially a semi-deregulation and semi-privatization plan, in what the neoconservative American Enterprise Institute calls "the most extensive reorganization of a federal agency." The Postal Reorganization Act of 1970, signed by Republican president Richard Nixon, aimed to make the USPS self-sufficient, running on its own profits. Before then, the USPS operated at a loss for 131 of the 160 years that it was in operation. The reform was pushed through in the wake of a growing nationwide postal worker lockout in 1970 to protest falling wages, a strike so effective that Nixon called the National Guard to New York to end it. Under the act, the postal workers union could no longer call or threaten strikes, but rather were required to solve all disputes through collective bargaining, and failing an agreement, hand the dispute over to binding arbitration. Postal workers have never gone on strike since. And the postal market was opened up to greater competition. In 1973, Federal Express started delivering. In other words, the postal service was the first post–New Deal experiment in loosening a large number of workers' rights and opening up their company to the brutal world of competition. Today, even with competition, USPS employees earn better wages and higher benefits than FedEx employees, something that the postal service is criticized for by reformers.

The U.S. Postal Service was able to function more profitably through the ususal tactics of pushing its workers to work harder and of creating an increasingly stress-jammed atmosphere, thereby squeezing more work out of them, or "increasing worker productivity" in the value-neutral language of economics. Oddly enough, the first year that the federal government stopped subsidizing the USPS, 1983, was also the year of the first post office shooting, in Johnston, South Carolina.

Perry Smith worked for the USPS for twenty-five years. In late 1982, his son committed suicide, devastating Smith. The death of his son naturally affected his work. He lost weight, stopped grooming himself, and generally looked and behaved like a man in a downward spiral. His supervisors responded not by showing sympathy, but by reprimanding him for every minor violation they could find. One time, a supervisor discovered that Smith left his letter satchel unattended for a few minutes and warned him that he faced disciplinary action. When it happened again, he was suspended. They rode him hard if he exceeded his lunch break or if he delivered a letter to a wrong address. The stress pushed this already cracked man beyond the threshold, and the constant harassment by his supervisors fed his anger. He blamed his downward spiral on the station's new postmaster, Charles McGee. Everything got worse after McGee took over.

Perry resigned from the service, miserable and harassed, about six months after his son's suicide. In August, he heard that McGee was leaving the post office job. Smith had not gotten over the postal service's mistreatment at the worst time in his life. On the postmaster's last day at work, Smith appeared at the post office, carrying a 12-gauge shotgun.

He told the first former co-worker he saw, "Jo, don't move." Then he told the others, "Don't move or I'll kill all of you."

McGee was in an office down the hall. He caught sight of Smith brandishing the shotgun and bolted out through a side exit. One employee who had worked there for ten years saw McGee take off and decided to make a dash with him. That was a bad move. Smith fired at McGee, but wound up dropping the younger employee behind him, tearing his ear off and damaging his spine.

McGee ran across the street into The Pantry, a convenience store. He yelled at the two clerks inside, both women, to take cover and then locked himself in the storage room while the clerks hid in the women's locker room. Smith followed McGee into The Pantry, reloaded the shotgun, and headed straight to the storage room. He broke down the door and faced McGee. "I told you I'd get you," he shouted, blasting McGee in the stomach. He pumped and fired a second time, blasting McGee in the chest. "I told you I'd get even with you, you sonofabitch!"

Smith ran out of the convenience store then raced across to the rear of the post office. There he was confronted by a police officer. Smith fired and hit him with buckshot. The cop gave him one more chance to surrender, and Smith did, as if suddenly losing all of his anger. The object of his oppression had been taken down. There was no reason to continue. As the cop cuffed him, Smith looked into his eyes and finally realized who he was. He told the cop, "Oh, I didn't know it was you. I didn't mean to shoot you."

The judge at his first trial declared Perry Smith mentally incompetent to stand trial. Smith apparently thought that he was Moses. A court-appointed shrink testified, "It was [Smith's] mission, like it was the mission of Moses, to rise up against these forces of evil." One is reminded of Nat Turner and the voices he thought he heard.

A few months later, a fifty-three-year-old postal employee in Aniston, Alabama, shot and killed his postmaster after taking his grievances about forced overtime and undercompensation first to his union, and then, when the union failed him, to the National Labor Relations Board for mediation. In the final settlement, the postal employee, James Brooks, agreed to drop his complaint. Brooks was not satisfied with the arbitration, so he took his complaints directly to the postmaster, Oscar Johnson—shooting and killing him with a .38 caliber handgun. After killing Johnson, Brooks ran upstairs to the second-floor office of his immediate supervisor, Butch Taylor. Employees heard Taylor beg, "Please man, no! No!" before hearing two loud bangs, silence, and then another shot. Taylor survived with wounds to his stomach and arm, but Johnson died from gunshot wounds to the head.

Just over a year later, in Atlanta, Georgia, a postal employee named Steven Brownlee took the rage torch from Brooks. As is the pattern with these shootings, the initial reports painted Brownlee as a lunatic who had snapped for no apparent reason and who fired at random. It was only later that his workplace was considered as a possible reason his attack. Brownlee, a thirty-year-old African American, had been forced to work seventy to eighty hour workweeks to keep up with the supervisor's demands and the heavy volume of mail. He worked the night shift sorting letters on a wrenchingly loud machine. Brownlee was already mentally fragile, but as his lawyer contended, the stress and overwork, combined with the nature of the job, pushed him over the edge. On the day of his murder spree, the mail load was so exceptionally large that he and other sorters were asked to come to work two hours early. At midday, Brownlee produced a .22 pistol and shot and killed his supervisor and two co-workers on the sorter line. As one employee said, "I don't think it was random."

These shootings were the prelude to the Mother of All Rage Massacres, the shooting spree in Edmond, Oklahoma, that blasted a new expression, "going postal," into the national lexicon and into the collective conscious.

Rather than shock the USPS management and staff into making fundamental changes, the stressful atmosphere and institutionalized top-down harassment only increased as the new Reaganomics corporate culture strengthened—and so did the number of post office massacres. With a new language to express their anger and frustration at mistreatment, post office workers rose up everywhere. In December 1988, Warren Murphy shot and wounded his supervisor at a New Orleans post office. In all, three were wounded in the shooting rampage. When Murphy was arrested he said he was "happy to get the attention of management" at the post office, saying he was "disgusted and aggravated" by them. His supervisors had been making book on him ever since his girlfriend moved out a couple of months earlier, causing Murphy's work efficiency to slip.

In March 1989, Don Mace became so frustrated with the petty harassment and bullying by his supervisors at his San Diego–area post office that he wrote letters to the media detailing his grievances. When pleading and negotiation failed, he drove to his post office in his uniform, walked into work, pulled out a .38 caliber revolver, and shot himself in the head. The supervisors' harassment methods included telling him by written memo that he was to go to the bathroom on his own time and not on the post office's time, and having a supervisor stand outside of his house during his lunch break, watching him through his kitchen window, clocking him when he ate lunch at home with his wife. After the suicide, a spokesman claimed that Mace had a "disciplinary history."

In San Diego County alone that year, four postal employees committed suicide. A year later, in the same area, John Merlin Taylor, a respected middle-aged family man, shot and killed two co-workers before turning the gun on himself. His supervisor was out that day, luckily for him. Taylor, a model employee who started to bend under the stress, spoke increasingly about the Edmond, Oklahoma, massacre before the shooting. When the Orange Glen postal workers discussed

Sherrill's massacre with Taylor, "[S]omeone wondered what could have happened to make a guy go berserk like that. And then someone said, 'job stress.' And we all laughed at that. John laughed too." Was he a loon also? One supervisor said, after the massacre, "He was always unfailingly friendly and congenial, always had a smile on his face. If you were to make a composite model of a model employee, you'd come up with John Taylor." He received numerous awards and bonuses, and was loved by most everyone. One stunned co-worker commented, "John, he never voiced a complaint as far as I know, not to anyone about anything. The rest of us, we'd always have something to gripe about. But John—John was just too nice to gripe about anything. That's what makes it all even more horrible and frightening. My God, John Taylor? Who's next?" It was hard to blame this case on racism or a "sad, lonely" freak. Taylor, in fact, had become increasingly upset over the change in the post office's culture, what he saw as its increased stress and loss of camaraderie. He also complained about the effects of increased automation. The day before the massacre, as Taylor left the office, he quipped that he was going home because there wasn't enough mail to keep everyone busy. A co-worker later said, "I figured he was just being sarcastic because there was a ton of mail in there."

Two years after that, a fired postal employee in Ridgewood, NJ, hunted down his former supervisor in her apartment and killed her with a samurai sword while she was sleeping in bed. Afterwards he raced to his former post office and executed two workers before surrendering to police. Before starting his murder spree, armed with his samurai sword and gun, Joseph Harris wrote a two-page note in which he complained about the "unfair treatment" at the hands of his former USPS supervisors, referencing the Edmond, Oklahoma, massacre.

Just a few months later, in November 1991, a postal employee in Royal Oak, MI, walked into work with a sawed-off .22 caliber rifle and four twenty-five-round banana clips. Thomas McIlvane was the object of a grotesque harassment drive by his supervisors. For example, three days after Christmas 1989, his supervisor handed him a letter notifying him that he was being suspended from duties for fourteen days due to such violations as failing to clear ice from the right-side window of his vehicle, making it "unsafe to drive," for leaving his engine running while he used the restroom for two minutes, for going thirty-one to thirty-five miles per hour in a thirty-miles-per-hour speed zone, and for engaging in "unnecessary conversation" with a secretary, thereby squandering company time. Declaring "I'll make Edmond look like a tea party!" McIlvane gave up on his grievance claim and turned to the bullet, killing three and wounding six before putting the gun to his head. Around that same time, complaints about the work environment at the USPS as well as the rash of massacres triggered a Congressional investigation headed by Michigan senator Carl Levin. Levin's report on the USPS documented "patterns of harassment, intimidation, cruelty and allegations of favoritism in promotions and demotions."

In spite of the report and its recommendations to ease the stress and bullying, little changed. A year after the Royal Oak shooting, Roy Barnes, a sixty-year-old postal employee in Sacramento, California, who was sure he'd been "singled out" by his supervisors finally folded under the pressure. Barnes showed up to work one day, stood up in the workroom floor in front of all of his co-workers, pulled out a .22 caliber pistol, and shot himself in the heart. A spokesperson for the Sacramento division told reporters, "We don't know why it happened." As it turned out, the postmaster's harassment was so brutal that Barnes had managed to obtain a kind of informal "restraining order" on his supervisor with the help of the local union—but to no avail. After Barnes's suicide, the postmaster in his station was suspended and transferred.

And then in May 1993, just fifteen miles from Royal Oak, Michigan, another angry postal employee who had filed a grievance went postal. After scrawling a message in the men's bathroom that he was going to "make Royal Oak look like Christmas," the forty-five-year-old rage insurgent went on a suicide mission. He killed one employee, wounded three, including the supervisor with whom he fought, and ended it with a bullet to the bridge of his nose. As one co-worker later said about the murderer, "[He] felt a lot of intimidation by upper management. That's the way they motivate you at work. It's a prehistoric era there, really."

After the Royal Oak shooting, the postal service set up a hot line for employee-snitches. It was deluged with thousands of calls, resulting in three hundred serious investigations and seven arrests for threats against supervisors and co-workers.

But why the dangerous atmosphere of rage and threats?

A report issued in 1994 decried the postal service's "adversarial relationship" between management and employees. The report noted the sharp increase in grievances filed (and their backlog time, which by 1994 was so bad that a grievance could take a year to reach arbitration) and the doubling of required overtime work just in the period from 1989 to 1994. Moreover, half of all employees thought that they had been unfairly disciplined for taking off legitimate sick leave—one example cited a postal clerk who asked his supervisor for a day off to attend his father's birthday, but was only allowed two hours off. The clerk's father became ill and had to be taken to the emergency room for care, and even though the clerk provided a certificate from the emergency ward proving his father's treatment, his supervisor suspended him, charging "there were other relatives at the party who could have taken the employee's father to the hospital and that the clerk could have reported for work."

The USPS has tried to counter the "myth" that life in the post office is more stressful or dangerous than other jobs, noting, for example, that the homicide rate in other fields, like retail trade and taxi driving, is higher than at the post office.

However, as Gloria Moore, a shop steward for the National Association of Letter Carriers Branch 132 in Dallas, said, "Cab drivers aren't shooting each other. We are shooting each other. We are assaulting each other."

Consider this testimonial by a postal employee, which painfully mirrors the kind of schoolyard bullying school rage murders. The testimonial is taken from one of several Web sites set up by and for disgruntled postal employees.

> Jim, 24 years old, a 6 ft 4 inch tall thin letter carrier with the smile of an angel, and the looks of a bookworm was bullied by my five foot manager who publicly humiliated him on the workfloor before all of us. She was a "holy" terror as she screamed, ranted and raved.

She was such a nut that daily she would post our names up on large cardboards listing the type of letter carriers we were. Everyone could see the cardboards as they were placed directly in front of the entrance to the workfloor where it looked obvious that she probably hoped we would all be publicly humiliated. There was the A List (with no names of course), the B list, C letter carrier, D, and "F" list. One of the letter carriers remarked, "Maybe if we all do "F" work it will lower her numbers, and they'll get rid of her."

Miss Janet would just scream pitifully at everyone on the workfloor, but she targeted Jim because as tall as he was he couldn't harm a fly. His face said so. We weren't sure why she did this, but humiliation seemed to be her tactic for teaching the rest of us. Daily she stood by his work area for hours tapping her foot, staring him down with this wretched angry look on her face as she would glance at her watch. He never said a word and silently continued to work.

Suddenly, he died. He developed meningitis and died within a couple of days. And then her mistreatment backfired. Quickly the rumor spread through the workfloor that "she killed him." Top management and union arrived to see what the discord was about. I was asked if I thought she killed him. I said, "No, but she made his life hell. I wouldn't be surprised if he didn't want to live."

On the day of Jim's memorial the workfloor in tears and sobs gathered together to say a prayer. Miss Janet Manager remained in her glass office locked up with her head resting on her desk. We wondered if it was guilt or just her mean spirited ways that kept her away from saying a kind word.

We posted our tributes to Jim by the exit of the building, and Miss Janet came over to me with my tribute in her hand and removed from the others. "You are not to speak of God in this job." she ordered.

She threatened to write me up with discipline. I had written, "Don't worry, Jim . . . now you're with the REAL BOSS."

She was transferred out to a new station where those employees all joined together to submit transfer bid slips to vacate the entire station and escape from Miss Janet's management style.

Miss Janet was then relocated and promoted to Acting Area Manager in charge of districts of stations. One could conclude that cruelty to workers is rewarded.

3

Disgruntled Employees

Main Entry: dis·grun·tle
Pronunciation: dis-'grun-tel
Function: transitive verb
Inflected Form(s): dis·grun·tled; dis·grun·tling /-'grunt-li[ng], -'grun-tel-i[ng]/
Etymology: dis- + gruntle (to grumble), from Middle English gruntlen, frequentative of grunten to grunt
: to make ill-humored or discontented—usually used as a participial adjective
—Merriam Webster's Dictionary

PATRICK SHERRILL'S MURDER SPREE set off a series of post office shootings. Wesbecker cited Sherrill's example, applying his rebellion tactics to the private sector.

After the Standard Gravure rage attack in 1989, the office shooting spree phenomenon spread across America. It seemed no workplace was safe.

Here is an incomplete list of some of the more prominent attacks that followed:

June 18, 1990: James Edward Pough goes on a shooting spree in a General Motors Acceptance Corp. office in Florida, killing ten people and wounding four others before killing himself;

one dead, two wounded by a disgruntled employee at the Fairview Development Center, Costa Mesa, California, 1991;

a fired employee shoots three at Elgar Corporation, San Diego, 1991;

also in 1991, a female employee unhappy with how she was being treated kills the plant manager at the Eveready Battery Co. in Bennington, Vermont, wounds two, tries setting the plant on fire;

fired employee from Fireman's Fund Insurance kills three, wounds two in Tampa, Florida, 1992;

December 2, 1993: Alan Winterbourne, thirty-three, an unemployed computer engineer, opens fire in a state unemployment office in Oxnard, California, killing three state workers and injuring four others. Winterbourne flees, killing a police officer before police fatally shoot him;

March 14, 1994: Tuan Nguyen, twenty-nine, recently fired from a Santa Fe Springs, California, electronics factory, uses a still-valid security code to gain access and shoot three people to death before killing himself;

fired employee kills supervisor and co-worker at the Richmond Housing Authority, Richmond, California, 1995;

three killed, four wounded by fired employee in Asheville, North Carolina, 1995;

recently-fired refinery inspector kills five co-workers, self in Corpus Christi, Texas, 1995;

September 15, 1997: Arthur Hastings Wise, forty-three, opens fire at an Aiken, South Carolina, parts plant, killing four and wounding three others. Wise had been fired two months before from his job at the plant;

June 5, 1997: Daniel S. Marsden, a plastics factory employee in Santa Fe Springs, California, fatally shoots two co-workers and wounds four others after an argument at work, then kills himself less than two hours later;

December 18, 1997: Arturo Reyes Torres, forty-three, walks into a maintenance yard in Orange, California, with an AK-47 and kills his former boss and three others. Torres, who blamed the supervisor for getting him fired, is later shot by police;

nine white-collar workers massacred by a day-trader in Atlanta's financial district in 1999;

November 1999: Brian Uyesugi, a Xerox employee, kills seven co-workers in Hawaii;

again, seven murdered, this time by an employee at Edgewater Technology, a Massachusetts internet consulting company, December 2000.

A typical lead from these massacres looked like this:

WORKER KILLS 4 AT CONN. LOTTERY
Connecticut lottery accountant Matthew Beck shot to death four senior executives before killing himself.

By Blaine Harden
Washington Post Staff Writer
Saturday, March 7, 1998; Page A1

With lethal volleys of gunfire, a disgruntled accountant shot to death four senior executives at Connecticut lottery headquarters today and then killed himself, playing out a tragedy that has become dismayingly frequent in the American workplace.

The casual-day corpses have piled up right through the new millennium. An incomplete list of the more gruesome office massacres of the Bush era include four dead and four wounded at a Navistar plant in Melrose Park, Illinois, in February 2001; two killed and six injured at a shooting spree at a Goshen, Indiana plant in late 2001; nursing school massacre in Tucson, Arizona, resulting in four dead in October, 2002; fifty-four year-old employee walks into his aircraft parts plant in South Bend, Indiana, kills four co-workers, wounds two, then commits suicide following a high-speed chase, March 2002; three dead and one injured in a Providence, Rhode Island, newspaper massacre in late 2002; seven murdered at a Chicago warehouse company by an employee about to be laid off in August, 2003; shooting massacre at a Merian, Mississippi, Lockheed-Martin plant that ended in five dead and nine wounded; employee at a Jefferson City, Missouri, manufacturing plant, Modine Manufacturing, kills three employees, self, July 2003 . . .

The list reads like a briefing from the Coalition Military Press Center in Baghdad.

And it hasn't slowed down in 2004. In Pleasant Grove, Utah, a recently suspended employee at the Provo River Waters Association shot and killed his supervisor, then locked himself in the company restroom and shot himself, but missed and survived; two workplace shootings in the Central California city of Visalia, one in December 2003, the other in April 2004, resulted in a total of two dead and one injured (one of the shootings took place at PrintXcel, a printing press; the other was sparked when the shooter wanted to bring a union into their plant, and the victim, also a blue-collar worker, argued against the union); one dead at a Hendersonville, North Carolina employment office, February 2004; two shot dead in a Phoenix office in April 2004; and five were killed, two injured by a disgruntled employee at the ConArgra plant in Kansas City, Kansas in July 2004, an episode ending with the familiar gunman-turning-the-gun-on-himself.

This is the world Joseph "Rocky" Wesbecker bequeathed to all the "sad, lonely" workers of corporate America. The crime wasn't invented by him, but the rage murder phenomenon only became relevant once it spread from the narrow boundaries of U.S. Post Offices to the broad everyworld of America's workplaces. It was Wesbecker who blew the doors off of the office world's sanctity. Before him, office massacres initiated by employees weren't even imaginable. It just had never occurred to anyone that the office could—or even should—be a place of mass murder, that the workplace itself should be murdered, or that the workplace inspired suicide attacks.

Consider, even fifteen years later, how shocked and surprised Americans are each time a rage massacre takes place:

> Everybody's in shock. You don't expect it. It's just mind-boggling how this could even happen or why.
> —**Steve Stacy**, thirty-eight year-old employee at Watkins Motor Lines, West Chester, Ohio, where two were killed and three injured in a workplace shooting spree in November, 2003.

> You always hear about the post office having problems like this, but I guess you never think it will happen to you.
> —**Laura Green**, North Carolina Employment Security Commission spokeswoman, following an office shooting in February 2004.

My brother was almost a victim of one of the earliest and bloodiest of California's many post-Wesbecker office massacres. After graduating in the top 10 percent of his law school class, he was offered a job at Pettit & Martin, one of San

Francisco's top corporate law firms, in the early 1990s. He was considered lucky to have landed such a choice, high-paying job. California was in the depths of a long recession at the time. Pettit was suffering along with the economy as a whole when my brother worked there.

Real work as a law associate is wretched stuff that one day will be recognized as such. Consider this resignation memo that a friend of mine forwarded to me. The names and locations have been changed:

-----Original Message-----
From: XXXX, XXXX X.
Sent: Tuesday, May XX, 200X 12:36 PM
To: All Boston
Subject: FW: Goodbye...
As many of you are aware, today is my last day at the firm. It is time for me to move on and I want you to know that I have accepted a position as "Trophy Husband." This decision was quite easy and took little consideration. However, I am confident this new role represents a welcome change in my life and a step up from my current situation. While I have a high degree of personal respect for XX as a law firm, and I have made wonderful friendships during my time here, I am no longer comfortable working for a group largely populated by gossips, backstabbers, and Napoleonic personalities. In fact, I dare say that I would rather be dressed up like a piñata and beaten than remain with this group any longer.

I wish you continued success in your goals to turn vibrant, productive, dedicated associates into an aimless, shambling group of dry, lifeless husks.

May the smoke from any bridges I burn today be seen far and wide.
Respectfully submitted,
XXXX XXXX
ps. Achilles absent, was Achilles still. (Homer)

My brother didn't last long in the corporate law world of Pettit, eventually going into employment law defending employees against corporations. Nine months after my brother quit his job there, Gian Luigi Ferri, a pear-shaped fifty five-year-old nerd who'd fallen through corporate America's cracks, indeed who was crushed by corporate America—specifically, as he claimed, ruined by Pettit & Martin in a litigation suit where they represented him and lost—entered Pettit's offices at 101 California Street wearing a dark suit with suspenders. Security thought he looked just like every other office-deformed businessman, so they let him in. When the elevator door opened on the thirty-fourth floor, Ferri whipped out two semiautomatic TEC-9 pistols from a duffel bag he'd pushed up in a dolly and slaughtered seven people, ending with a bullet to the brain in the stairwell.

Pettit & Martin, one of San Francisco's elder statesmen of the white-shoe corporate law world, closed down within a year after Ferri's murder spree. Just as Standard Gravure closed shortly after Wesbecker's massacre.

At the time of Ferri's massacre, it didn't strike me as part of a process, as a symptom of profound and brutal socioeconomic changes in America. It seemed more like a bolt from Hell, like something from the fascinating/violent American underbelly and part of the same logic of Jeffrey Dahmer or the Zodiac Killer, the serial murderers who were the underground pop stars of my generation.

Ferri's massacre seemed to fit into the emerging pattern of office massacres. The new-brand murder was only defined by its unique setting, the office, or by the large number of dead capped by the inevitable suicide; and yet, in hindsight, Ferri's attack didn't really fit the definition. A rage massacre in the workplace, as defined for the purposes of this book, is when a current or former employee attacks and murders his co-workers in his workplace. Ferri's rage may have been framed by the post office and office massacres that were gaining popularity, but Ferri wasn't an employee. He was a disgruntled customer. At the time, the setting—an office—was bizarre enough to justify itself as the definition of a workplace massacre. But now, with time and distance, considering the upheaval within corporate culture, it would be more appropriate to categorize Ferri's massacre as a "related rage massacre:" in the broader picture of post-Reagan office stress and devastation, his motivation, to destroy the corporation that he felt destroyed him, is the same motivation that drives the workplace rage massacres covered in this book.

My brother missed Ferri's rampage only by months; while a friend of his was killed by Ferri. This massacre brought the rage murder phenomenon home to me in the most direct way possible.

4

It Permeates the Entire Culture

Sometimes they just want to kill the company.
—**James Alan Fox,** professor of criminal justice at Northeastern University

ONE MORE RECENT RAGE MURDER SPREE which stood out in my mind from the rest took place in Hawaii. It was a classic rage murder in one sense: an employee once considered a quiet type suddenly snaps, walks into his office, and calmly blasts his co-workers. Uniquely disturbing in another sense: the setting, Honolulu, where people are supposed to live in an idyll beyond the pain and stress of the mainland; and the rage attacker, a Pacific-Islander, not the generally accepted profile of the type who'd snap (portrayed by some heavily flawed studies to be a white, male aged twenty-five to forty). The fact that a rage massacre could take place in even the unlikeliest of settings suggested that something deeper and unexplored in the culture was causing these murders.

The rage killer was Bryan Uyesugi, a forty year-old Xerox employee. Uyesugi lived at home with his brother and father at 2835 Easy Street—the real name of the street, not the metaphorical easy street—in the suburb of Nuuanu, where he kept a collection of rare goldfish . . . and guns. Twenty-four rifles, shotguns and handguns. Uyesugi's father, oddly enough, was a retired letter carrier for the U.S. Postal Service. The fact that the rage attack took place at Xerox gave it a metaphor-rich literary context. Particularly since many of these rampage sprees are often conveniently bracketed as "copycat murders."

Uyesugi showed up to the office at 8 AM, Standard Rage Murder Time, took the elevator up to the second floor, and started firing from his Glock 9mm handgun. He emptied a total of twenty-eight bullets from the seventeen-clip gun, reloading once during the massacre, at times crouching in what was described as a "combat stance." Police later found one victim slumped in a computer cubicle, another sprawled on the floor, and five dead in the conference room. Some had been shot up to five times. Uyesugi was a marksman with guns. The dead included his supervisor, Melvin Lee—who had earlier "chewed Uyesugi out"—and six fellow-repairmen. The court denied Uyesugi's insanity plea because he deliberately spared others, including one quiet co-worker, Randall Shin, who once saw Uyesugi sitting alone in a restaurant, went up and talked to him for ten minutes, wished him well, and left. On the other hand, another co-worker, described by both his wife and the prosecution as a "prankster" who "loved to have fun," was specifically targeted and murdered. Uyesugi apparently didn't find him to be all that entertaining . . . so he gonged him. When he was done shooting, according to survivors, he "waved goodbye to those he left unharmed" and calmly headed out of the office, down to the parking lot.

After the massacre, employees at Xerox's Hawaii headquarters a couple miles away were evacuated in the belief that Uyesugi was heading there to take his murder spree to the executive level. He was eventually arrested at the Hawaii Nature Center in Makiki, where he parked his van and contemplated suicide during a five-hour standoff. In a scene reminiscent of Cleavon Little's escape from the frontiers-men mob in *Blazing Saddles*, Uyesugi held off police with a gun to his own head, threatening to shoot if they came any closer.

After the massacre, Uyesugi was portrayed as a violent, ill-tempered freak. It was noted that he had sought help for depression, was a loner type, and that he was once reprimanded for "kicking an elevator." Yet friends of Uyesugi spoke differently of him.

"He didn't seem weird," said Victor Cabaltera, who served with Uyesugi on the high school ROTC rifle team. "I know he wasn't a loner in high school. He was funny. Just the things that would come out of his mouth, you wouldn't expect it because he seemed so innocent."

Brian Isara, who had known Uyesugi since kindergarten, said, "He had plenty friends. Plenty people liked him." He noted that Uyesugi held season tickets to the University of Hawaii Rainbows football team, liked tailgate partying, and was at Aloha Stadium just three days before the massacre watching a game in which the Rainbows lost to Texas Christian.

Yet Honolulu mayor Jeremy Harris said it appeared "as though it was a dis-gruntled employee who snapped," and observed that, "to have someone snap like this and murder seven people is just absolutely appalling." And then he made, perhaps inadvertently, perhaps subconsciously, a startling admission: "A mass murder like this is a shock to everybody. It shows this *violence permeates the entire culture.*"

Mayor Harris should have phrased his admission the opposite way—that the entire culture permeates these office massacres. Not one narrow part of the culture, the violent-media part, or the NRA-mad part, but the *entire* culture. It permeates the cubicle partitions, the little Dilbert cartoons taped to the computer monitor, the memos about downsizing and the hours worked, the benefits slashed, the friendly co-workers who strive to undercut each other, and the empty slogans about teamwork and pride.

Take for example the comments by Glenn Sexton, vice president and general manager of Xerox Hawaii, who called the shootings "by far the worst tragedy in the history of Xerox Corp."

"Like all of us at Xerox, you undoubtedly have questions," he continued. "Why? How could this happen? Only time and the work of HPD will determine that. Perhaps we'll never know. Hopefully we will."

Every massacre is followed by one of these disingenuous whys, and each time, the larger cultural tendency is to move on. Yet Uyesugi's massacre suggested that rage murders had a context. Something in modern America that was hard to frame was causing them to break out only in America and only in our very recent history. These weren't just any old murders, they were part of something hard to define. Yet they were all related, Xerox, Columbine, post offices, offices . . . in fact, it seemes to me *obvious* that school and office massacres had to be linked—the story-lines were almost identical including duffel bags, quiet types, and shooting at random, and the community reaction that followed always repeated itself. Incapable of even conceiving an explanation, the public would ask why and then blame the most convenient villain it could drag out to the rigged lineup: violent culture, lax gun control laws, video games, people who just snap . . .

Michael Moore successfully debunked these fatuous, diversionary explanations in his documentary *Bowling For Columbine*—but like everyone else Moore failed to consider the possibility that schools themselves incited the kids, just as offices may have incited the workers.

One cause that reporters might have considered for Uyesugi rage massacre was the culture at Xerox, which had been undergoing one of the largest downsizings in corporate America in the 1990s. Just a year before Uyesugi's massacre, Xerox announced that it was laying off nine thousand employees, or 10 percent of the workforce—part of the post-Reagan corporate culture of mass-firings during boom times.

Harry Friel, an office manager at the Hawaii state capitol, where Uyesugi regularly repaired photocopy machines, told one reporter, "He was frustrated, but in a quiet way. You had to pull it out of him. It eventually came out that he was under stress, something was bothering him, and it wasn't right, but he would shrug it off. He didn't want to talk about it."

He was stressed, yet he didn't talk about it—a recurring theme in rage massacres. Even when the stress is too much the sufferer doesn't want to talk about it, since even admitting one's unhappiness or inability to deal with the stress is to be a loser.

Uyesugi's father's first reaction to the media was that his son believed that he was being laid off. Xerox officially denied that, although reports say that he was in for a reprimand. Uyesugi certainly thought that he was going to be fired. He had been warned by a co-worker that the company was "going to come down hard on him" due to customer complaints; he had just been "chewed out" by his supervisor; and he was stressed from the workload and from the supervisor's insistence that he learn to repair a new, state-of-art machine that had recently been introduced, a job Uyesugi complained he wasn't up to.

But besides these seemingly petty complaints, Uyesugi also expressed a broader reason for his massacre. As one of the policewomen who negotiated his surrender recounted: "He continued to stress that he did what he had to do because he had to make a point." Time and again, these rampage murderers give the same vague, broad, *Fight Club/Falling Down*-like reason. They murdered and destroyed because they had to make a point.

5

Let Them Eat Prozac

> Why don't they get new jobs if they're unhappy—or go on Prozac?
> —**Susan Sheybani,** Bush election campaign official, July 29, 2004

THERE IS A SOCIOECONOMIC CONTEXT FOR THESE SHOOTING SPREES.
The rage murder is new. It appeared under Reagan, during his cultural economic revolution, and it expanded in his aftermath. Reaganomics has ruled America ever since. For all of the Right's hysterical attacks on Clinton as a leftwinger, the fact is that it was Clinton who administered a lethal injection to the welfare system with his Orwellian-named Personal Responsibility and Work Opportunity Reconciliation Act. Under Clinton, Wall Street flourished with greater deregulation, globalization accelerated as never before, downsizings soared, and the anti-union, pro-shareholder corporate culture that Reagan launched went from being a radical experiment to a way of life. By the time George W. Bush took office, the cultural-economic transformation had become so deeply entrenched that what once would have been considered extreme and unacceptable was cheered and praised, even by those who suffered. The change was radical and traumatic, so much so that historians may look back at this time and wonder why there weren't more murders and rebellions, just as it is shocking today to consider how few slave rebellions there were.

Rather than looking outside of the office world for an explanation for these shooting sprees—rather than blaming violent films, gun proliferation, the breakup of the family, the lack of God, or a fear-mongering media—why not consider the changes within America's corporate culture itself? We avoid this topic in mainstream discourse, and there are powerful reasons for self-censorship: if the workplace is responsible, then that means every working American is potentially in peril, living in unbearable circumstances, yet too deluded, or too beaten-down, to recognize it.

Under Reagan, corporations transformed from providers of stability for employees and their families to fear-juiced stress engines. Reagan's legacy to America and modern man is not the victory in the Cold War, where he simply got lucky; it is instead one of the most shocking wealth transfers in the history of the world, all under the propaganda diversion of "making America competitive" and "unleashing the creative energies of the American worker." New corporate heroes like General Electric's Jack Welch spoke of "unlimited juice" to squeeze from his employees—and wring their rinds did he. While work became increasingly stressful and time consuming with fewer rewards for the majority, capital was sucked from the middle and lower classes of working America and deposited into the offshore accounts of the very highest layer of the executive and shareholder class. As the Economic Policy Institute reported, "What income growth there was over the 1979–1989 period was driven primarily by more work at lower wages."

People's memories are short and America's propaganda is so powerful that most, even the greatest losers of this appropriation, have forgotten that a profound change occurred, which we now take for granted. We have been conditioned to react skeptically, even hostilely, to criticism of our current corporate values, values which form the foundation of everyday life today. What's more appalling is that huge numbers of those left behind in the wealth transfer genuflected to the new plutocratic class, celebrating the most vicious of the uber-CEOs. This craven CEO-worshipping is still going on today—middle Americans drag themselves home after work in order to gather around the television and watch billionaire ass-hole Donald Trump deliver his "You're fired!" line to some desperate, stressed-out Smithers-abee. Entertainment is no longer about joy or escape. It's about reliving life at the office, even if you just left the office fifteen minutes ago. It is about fetishizing the stress. It's as though the conditioning worked too well. This worship of the new plutocrats is reminiscent of medieval peasant adulation of the royalty that stomped on them. Indeed, serfdom is a good analogy considering the kind of neo-feudal divisions that arose in the wake of Reaganomics.

An example of this feudal divide was revealed in a *USA Today* article published in 2001. "Mega-Mansion Upsets Tiny Town" described how it's not enough any-more to just be rich and living in a mansion. America's mere millionaires have been demoted to a kind of resentful artisan-class, shaking their fists in hopeless envy at the new mega-rich up on the hill: "Frustration with increasing numbers of huge mansions here [in Medina, Washington] boiled over last month. . . . The Medina City Council slapped a six-month moratorium on construction of homes over 13,500 square feet," *USA Today* reported.

Medina is where some of Microsoft's oligarchs live, including Bill Gates, whose house is a whopping 52,944 square feet.

The article continued, "Medina is not alone. Civic battles challenging the right of the super-rich to build estates that dwarf the homes of their neighbors are playing out in cities all across the nation.

". . . Efforts to reign in these homes are underway in Palm Beach, Fla., New Orleans, Aspen, Colo., the suburbs of Washington, D.C., and throughout the Los Angeles area, mostly by limiting square footage, building heights and lot coverage."

The grim facts about the transformation of corporate America, and this mas-sive wealth transfer's effect on the American landscape, are undeniable. Exposing this used to be confined to the left-wing press, allowing the gullible, team-playing Middle Americans to safely dismiss what went on right before their eyes. Yet in the last few years, more mainstream books like *White Collar Sweatshop*, *Nickel and Dimed*, and *Working Poor* have, to one degree or another, attempted to reposition the centrist discourse.

One problem is that most left-wingers still reflexively focus their energies, and sympathies, on the plight of the industrial proletariat, a long-declining species in America. We all know how they got screwed under Reagan. We remem-ber how the blue-collar unions were broken in the rust belt and beyond, and how the manufacturing industry was forced into a false choice between breaking its unions or shutting the plants down and shifting production overseas. In fact once given free reign under Reagan, corporations did both—they had their cake and ate it, first breaking their unions and then shutting down their plants and moving them overseas to cheaper climes. Since 1980, according to the Bureau of Labor Statistics, the number of manufacturing jobs in the United States has fallen by about 25 percent, to 14.4 million from 19.3 million, while the overall population has grown by 70 million in that same period. The government has also quite literally legislated greater poverty for its worst-off workers. According to the Census Bureau, in 1981, when Ronald Reagan took office, a worker's annual earnings at minimum wage put him at 98.2 percent of the official poverty line; by the time Reagan left office in 1989, minimum wage brought that same worker's annual salary to just 70.4 percent of the poverty line. The reason is simple: Reagan didn't raise the minimum wage once during his term. In 1981, the minimum wage was $3.35, and in 1989, after the great wealth boom we've all been led to believe benefited every living American, the minimum wage was—*drum roll, maestro*—$3.35! In the sixties, the minimum wage was raised seven times; in the seventies, it was raised six times. But over Reagan's dead body would the poor get another red cent, and he even took a chunk of that red cent away. To put this into modern terms, 1981's $3.35 would be worth $6.53 in 2001 dollars, while 1989's $3.35 would be worth only $4.78. In real dollar terms, Reagan actually slashed the poorest Americans' earnings by 27 percent, during the same period Wall Street and the plutocrats saw their earnings soar by triple-digit percentages! With tax cuts thrown in as sweeteners! As of the summer of 2005, the minimum wage has not been raised for nine years, and Bush has been resisting the call because, you see, it would be "bad for business."

All of this would not have been a big problem for a majority of the country. Middle-class Americans bought into the argument that what was bad for the working class was good for America (i.e., the middle class), under the false assumption that the same dark capitalist force that sucked the juice out of blue-collar Americans would never dare sink its fangs into the white-collar world.

But it did. And now a new and no-less-brutal dialectic has developed as the working class has declined, one that divides increasingly desperate middle-class Americans from the increasingly fatter executive/shareholder class, which has been admiringly named by the obsequious American press the "mega-rich." (Incidentally, the shareholder class here refers not a little old blue-haired lady who owns $42,194 in Fidelity funds, the focus of so much deceptively feel-good pro-capitalist propaganda in the eighties and nineties, but rather, to those shareholders who actually affect corporate policy and profit from its new priorities—the so-called "major shareholders.")

According to the Bureau of Labor Statistics, there are some eighty million white-collar workers in America. How are they doing today, in post-industrial America, as compared to a generation ago? In spite of our self-image of progress, in 1997 white-collar males earned just six cents more per hour in constant dollars—or $19.24 on average—than they earned in 1973. Since President George W. Bush came to office, hourly wages actually declined in 2003, so the majority of workers lucky enough to have found new jobs actually get paid less than what they made in their previous jobs. According to a study by Harvard Law Professor Elizabeth Warren, the proportion of middle-income families who would be considered "house poor"—who spend over 40 percent of their income on mortgage payments—has doubled since 1975.

By contrast, CEO compensation has skyrocketed. Between 1990 and 2000, CEO pay skyrocketed by 571 percent, while the average worker's paycheck in the same period grew only 34 percent. Not only did their pay soar, but their pay relative to their average workers also widened dramatically, even recklessly. In 1978, CEOs earned just under 30 times their average workers' pay; by 1995, that figure rose to 115 times, and by 2001, CEOs of large corporations earned 531 times their average workers' salaries. One leading economist, Robert Frank, found that the top one percent captured 70 percent of all the earnings growth since the mid-1970s. The beneficiaries aren't just the CEOs—they're the shareholders, the real new feudal aristocracy. In just the period since Bush took office until the middle of 2004, for example, corporate profits grew 40 percent while real wages barely registered a 0.3 percent blip. And the Congressional Budget Office estimated last year that more than half of all corporate profits go directly into the pockets of the wealthiest 1 percent of Americans.

"We're back to serfs and royalty in the Middle Ages," says Edward Lawler, professor of management at the University of Southern California's Marshall School of Business.

Bush's tax policies are exacerbating the feudal tendency. The moves to eliminate taxes on inheritance and on dividends mean that the country is moving towards a model in which Paris Hilton would pay a lower rate of taxes than her cleaning lady, according to Martin Press, a high-profile tax attorney and registered Republican.

This wealth transfer is evident in every statistic. From 1979 to 1998, those who earned in the top fifth of income grew 38 percent wealthier while the bottom fifth's lost five percent of real income. Today, the financial wealth of the top one percent exceeds the combined wealth of the bottom 95 percent—America has the worst wealth distribution of any first-world nation.

Even the corporate world couldn't ignore this disturbing trend, engaging in periodic hand-wringing. A *Businessweek* article published in early 2000, "Not Enough is Trickling Down," found that from 1988 to 1998, family incomes for the middle 20 percent rose $780, while incomes for the upper 5 percent rose $50,760 in the same period. The *New York Times* came to the same conclusion in an August 31, 2001, article, "Boom of the 1990s Missed Many in Middle Class, Data Suggests," which begins: "The booming late 1990s appear to have left the middle class in the New York region and California no better off than it was a decade before, an analysis of Census Bureau data suggests. The poor got a little poorer, the rich got a lot richer, and the large group in the middle emerged slightly worse off than when the decade began. . . . Andrew A. Beveridge, a professor of sociology at Queens College who conducted the analysis, said he also found that the gap between rich and poor throughout the country had inched wider during the 1990s. In Washington, D.C., for example, the average income of families in the wealthiest fifth of the population, once adjusted for inflation, grew to 24 times the average in the bottom fifth, up from 18 times."

So while most middle-class Americans' incomes fell and their workload turned into work-overload, executives hogged almost the entire windfall for themselves. All that was missing from this neo-feudal picture was the introduction of the tithe, and a lot of dung.

In 1999 alone, the average CEO's pay soared 37 percent, led by Michael Eisner's obscene $576 million compensation that year, while the average worker's salary increased only 2.7 percent, leading John Cavanagh, director for the Institute for Policy Studies, to declare on the *McNeil-Lehrer News Hour*, "This year we almost fell out of our chairs. . . . The economy is doing well, but one group is benefiting enormously, another group not at all—in a sense, the emergence of two Americas." The "we fell out of our chairs" line is a testament to the success and power of America's propaganda—this bifurcation had been going on for twenty years, yet it even shocked the very people whose lives were dedicated to studying it.

Another change was that compensation was no longer linked to performance and output. Instead, pay increase was decided upon according to what might be defined as a "class" basis—the rich robbing the middle-class to make the rich into the mega-rich. So while workers may have worked more for less pay under the constant threat of being downsized, even those CEOs with the most disastrous track records were still able to rake in obscene remuneration packages and set themselves up for life. In Silicon Valley, executive pay for the top 150 companies actually doubled to $5.9 million on average from 2000 to 2001, even though their businesses in that period had literally collapsed in one of the greatest financial catastrophes of our time. Cisco Systems CEO John Chambers pulled in $157.3 million during the downturn, even though he oversaw a massive oversupply of his company's products to the tune of $2.25 billion.

Silicon Valley proved to be the nation's source of innovation in a lot of areas, especially in wealth transfer. In a *San Jose Mercury News* study of insider transactions at forty Silicon Valley companies that went belly-up after the March 2000 bull market peak, the executives, board members, and venture capitalists earned $3.41 billion, while the value of the companies they profited from plunged 99.8 percent to just $229.5 million at the end of September, 2002. As the *Mercury News* observed, "It represented a remarkable transfer of wealth from the pockets of thousands of anonymous investors—from day traders to pension funds—into the wallets of executives and directors who turned out to be winners even when their companies became some of Silicon Valley's biggest losers." It is interesting that they don't even consider the wealth transfer out of the employees' pockets of these companies, as if it's a given by now that employees are merely a fungible expense. The lesson is simple: in the post-Reagan era, hard work isn't what pays; rather, paying yourself pays.

It isn't just start-up companies either. Lucent Technologies' former chairman and CEO Richard McGinn was ousted in 2001 after a ruinous tenure that nearly sank the company, sending its stock down 95 percent. In spite of that he was handed a $5.5 million severance package, the company assumed $4.3 million of his personal loans and offered him health benefits for life, and best of all, a one million dollar per year pension. His CFO, Deborah Hopkins, was ousted along with him . . . and rewarded with a $3.3 million severance, which, added to her $4 million signing bonus just a year earlier, made her one-year catastrophic tenure very uncatastrophic for this lucky gal.

Of course, someone had to pay for Lucent's huge executive payouts, as well as its financial collapse. Guess who that someone—or rather, *someones*—was? The same year those severance deals were inked, Lucent began massive layoffs—sixteen thousand just in the months following McGinn's ousting. And cuts continue: on top of further layoffs, today, even Lucent retirees are losing their health insurance benefits, in spite of their employment contracts, forcing them to pay for insurance that many cannot afford. As the *New York Times* reported in early 2004, Lucent and other like-minded companies are spearheading a new trend in corporate America to do away with health benefits for retirees, employment contracts be damned. Ten years ago, half of all companies with five hundred or more employees offered health insurance to retirees who didn't yet qualify for Medicare; today, less than 36 percent do.

"Twenty years from now, no company will offer retiree health care," Uwe Reinhardt, a health economist at Princeton University, told the *Times*.

Leaving aside the elimination of the once-sacred retiree health benefit—after all, those people don't add value to the company any more—corporations have also slashed medical benefits for employees still working in the company.

It wasn't always this way. At the end of the 1970s, on the eve of the Reagan Revolution, health insurance was practically universal for employees of large businesses. From the end of World War II until Reagan took power, the number of insured Americans steadily increased every year. By 1993, the number of private-sector workers on employer-sponsored health insurance programs had fallen to 63 percent. Ten years later, that number fell to 45 percent. At the same time, the number of uninsured Americans rose from 31 million in 1987 to 45 million in 2003. Over a two-year period from 2003 to 2004, over 85 million Americans had no health care coverage for at least some period of time. Put another way, from 1981, the year Reagan took office, to 2001, the number of families declaring bankruptcy due to a serious illness multiplied by 2,000 percent.

And the quality of insurance has also worsened. Even in 1991, two-thirds of all full-time employees at large companies were covered by fee-for-service plans, allowing them to choose their doctors. By 1997, only 27 percent of full-time employees for big companies had this type of coverage, the rest forced into some kind of managed care. The same kind of managed care that treated Bryan Uyesugi for his depression, six years before his Xerox massacre. His HMO doctors declared him cured in 1993 and sent him right back on the job. Meanwhile, the average employee contribution into these degraded health plans has rocketed to 75 percent in the last ten years.

That's if they're lucky enough to have health insurance. Along with the poor, unemployed, and retired, millions of working Americans—twenty million, or more than one in ten—have no health insurance whatsoever. In some states—Texas, Oklahoma, Louisiana and others—the number of uninsured workers is more than 20 percent of the workforce. Bush's experiment with creating a no-healthcare working population was such a success during his governorship that he's applying it to the whole country. No Ailment Left Behind!

Like everything else in this book, America's health care feudalism is either appalling or appallingly funny, in a "kill the poor" sort of way, depending on the time of day you read it, your state of health, and how deeply you want to allow these facts to penetrate. Studies have shown that health insurance is literally a matter of life and death. Leaving aside its obvious benefits, people without insurance are less likely to see doctors, more likely to be diagnosed with illnesses late, and report being in poor or fair health more often than those with insurance. Moreover, according to a 1999 World Health Organization report titled "Social Determinants of Health," inequality is itself a killer. As *Forbes* noted in an article titled "Why the Rich Live Longer," "[L]ow status translates into insecurity, stress and anxiety, all of which increases susceptibility to disease."

In other words, millions of Americans not only accept lower relative wages, but they are literally dying in order to help fatten up the plutocracy as socioeconomic inequalities continue to widen into canyon-like proportions. And that's just swell news for employers, because cutting health insurance for employees saves money, and if unhealthy workers start slacking off, just announce a restructuring and downsize the whole lot of 'em! You can always call Manpower if you need another cubicle serf.

Along with vanishing and increasingly expensive health insurance benefits, employees also find themselves forced to pay far more of the cost for pensions. Companies contributed sixty-three cents per hour for pension costs related to employees in 1979; by 1996, the employers' share was down to forty-five cents. The next logical step is for companies to phase out pensions altogether. The government is hoping to lead the way. The Bush administration openly pushed for the bankruptcy of the Social Security and Medicare systems in an attempt to privatize them while driving up massive deficits that will hasten their doom. The only people who will benefit from privatized Social Security and Medicare are those with private wealth.

Other traditional middle-class benefits disappeared too. The annual Christmas bonus, once almost taken for granted as an affirmation of corporate America's moral decency, is now looked upon as a relic of the past. In 1950, almost half of corporate employees received Christmas bonuses; today, that's down to 36 percent, with most of that decline occurring in the 1990s.

Vacation time has also shrunk. After thirty years of steadily increasing paid holiday time, during Reagan's presidency, American workers got an average of three and a half *fewer* days off per year. Today, half of all vacations are now weekend vacations. In fact, it takes the average American fifteen years with a company to earn as many paid vacation days as an Australian worker receives after one year, while our fourteen day average is just half of the European worker's vacation time. That's if an American even gets paid vacation time: today 13 percent of all companies don't even offer it, up from 5 percent in 1998. But even this exaggerates American workers' holiday time. Many Americans are reluctant to take even those few days off that they're allowed, fearful of falling behind or giving the wrong impression to their superiors—so companies may as well slash it.

A full quarter of Americans don't use their meager vacation holidays. Their fears have been confirmed by management surveys, wherein managers gave lower performance ratings to employees who took more holiday time. According to a 2003 study by Boston College, 26 percent of American workers took no vacation time at all in the previous year. Many employees will say this is because they genuinely prefer working at their job to relaxing—because relaxing requires a completely different set of social skills that many overworked, company-obsessed Americans increasingly lack.

Here is one typical example, from an article in the *Pittsburgh Post-Gazette* titled, "Who Needs a Vacation? Not These Happy Workers," dated August 24, 2003:

> E.J. Borghetti [is] a Pitt employee who's never taken off more than two consecutive days from work in seven years—by his own choice.
>
> "I can explain it in four words: I love my job,' declared Borghetti, 33, a bachelor.
>
> "The personnel office will send me notes saying, 'You're losing these vacation days,' like they feel sorry for me, but it's a choice to me. It doesn't bother me in the least."

> Those slaves who have kind masters are, perhaps, as happy as the generality of mankind. They are not aware that their condition can be better, and I don't know as it can.
> —**William Grimes**, *The Life of William Grimes the Runaway Slave, Brought Down to the Present Time.*

Everyone has worked with infuriating model-employees like Borghetti, who raise the stress bar and increase the pressure within companies to eschew vacation time for greater professed love of—and time at—the office. The fact is that most Americans are more comfortable at work—where they are defined, controlled, and conditioned--than they are on vacation, on their own, with their families. Away from work they suddenly find that they have to make conversation not directly linked to the office, invent plans that result in pleasure, and keep themselves entertained rather than merely busy carrying out other people's orders. Overworked Americans have been conditioned to elevate their office lives into their own personal epics, while their private lives and off-hour skills have atrophied. A vacation away from the office therefore can be joyless and daunting, and most Americans who travel find that their only wish is to get back into the office, back to a clearly defined world with an overseer and responsibilities, and back to a familiar script where they know their lines well.

Not only has vacation time been slashed, but so has free time within the office: the traditional one-hour lunch break has fallen now to an average of twenty nine minutes.

Part of the problem is the technology boom. Several decades ago, optimists predicted that technology would eventually free up the American worker to spend more time than ever with his or her family, at home or on vacation, reaping greater benefits for less and less work. The official optimism reached a crazed peak in the nineties with the rise of the so-called Internet Revolution, which supposedly subverted all of our paradigms. What we know today is that the complete opposite has taken place. Anyone who has worked in the 1980s and 1990s knows that technology—

through cell-phones, pagers, Blackberries, the Internet, and so on—has blurred the line between work hours and off hours. Or rather, there is no such thing as off hours anymore.

Of course, this isn't the first time that technological advances made workers' lives miserable. The invention of the cotton gin at the end of the eighteenth century made cotton growing exponentially more profitable for Southern farmers, and this meant more slaves to man the cotton fields and gins in order to crank out the profits. With Eli Whitney's invention, Southern plantation owners were producing one-fourth of the world's cotton supply: in 1801, 100,000 bales of cotton were produced, a figure that soared, thanks to the cotton gin, to 4.5 million bales in 1860. Not coincidentally, the number of slaves used to service the cotton also boomed, rising from fewer than 1 million in 1800 to nearly 4 million by the start of the Civil War.

6

Making an Empire State Building Out of an Anthill

When I see someone who is making anywhere from $300,000 to $750,000 a year, that's middle class.
—**Rep. Fred Heineman,** Republican of North Carolina

SO HERE WE HAVE THE LIFE of a post-Reagan era white collar American: his benefits have been slashed, his pay stagnated, and his vacation time dwindled. Life is objectively worse. Yet for the American employer, this has been a time to celebrate. Their American workers work more hours than ever before, to such an inhuman degree that one wonders why the knit-cap anti-globalizationers don't produce empathy-puppets in defense of America's white-collar servants.

Over the past three decades, the average American's work year grew by 184 hours, an additional four and a half weeks on the job for the same or less pay. By contrast, Americans work 350 hours more per year than their European counterparts. Overtime has almost no meaning. Today, nearly 40 percent of American employees work more than fifty hours per week.

This workload increase grew even more in the last decade: Eileen Appelbaum of the Economic Policy Institute reported that a typical husband-and-wife household worked five hundred more hours in 2000 than they did in 1990. As work time skyrocketed to the maximum level humanly possible, President Bush delivered corporations yet another gift in the summer of 2004: new legislation stripping millions of workers of the traditional right to overtime pay for overtime work.

While Americans are spending insanely longer hours at the office, the physical space where they spend this time has simultaneously shrunk. Just over a ten year period from the mid-1980s to the mid-1990s, the average workspace has reduced in size anywhere from 25 percent to 50 percent, according to a 1997 *Businessweek* article, "Help! I'm a Prisoner in a Shrinking Cubicle." Thirty-five million people work in cubicles, which, by design, are a "mechanism of constant surveillance," a demeaning, identical honeycomb structure created to remind its inhabitants in no uncertain terms how much less privileged they are than their office-enclosed executive supervisors. Cubicles also heighten the sense of alienation within the workplace. As Dr. Paul Rosch, president of the American Stress Institute, said, "People sit six feet apart in little cubicles and never speak with each other except by computer. You never hear a human voice and it's 'press one' or 'press three', it's very frustrating." It is a familiar alienation, almost identical to the special alienation of the suburban subdivision where these same cubicle workers spend their mornings and nights, with neighbors who never speak to each other and rarely even see each other.

> Human beings weren't meant to sit in little cubicles, starring at computer screens all day, filling out useless forms and listening to eight different bosses drone on about mission statements.
> —*Office Space*

And cubicles aren't the worst modern corporate inventions. By the end of the nineties "hotelling" or "open-space" workspaces became increasingly common, whereby the employee has no fixed workstation and often no privacy, increasing both the sense that he is being watched as well as the sense that he is replaceable and meaningless. It got to the point where *Fortune* magazine named Plante & Moran, a Michigan accounting firm, the tenth best place in America to work in 2001 because it offered such benefits as offices with a door, a desk, and a computer for each staff member.

And we're the only idiots in the world eagerly signing up for this slavish life.

Remember the Japanese, those robotic workaholics whose secret to success in the late 1980s was an inhuman, ant-like dedication to their corporation, something we individualistic, freedom-loving, fun-obsessed Americans could never emulate because we were just too damn human, too creative, and too frontier-spirited? Welp, nowadays Americans work total hours that add up to nearly a month per year longer than the Japanese, and nearly three more months per year more than Germans, according to an International Labor Organization study. How so? All our overtime. And all those vacation days we can't take, and those vacations days we can, but won't. And remember, Germans and Japanese get full health coverage and double our holiday time without having to wait thirty years—or any years—for that benefit to kick in! Compared to Americans, the Japanese are the corporate world's Jeff Spicoli-san—it's Fast Times at Matsushita High for Japan Inc.'s workers, while the famously obedient-to-authority Germans party hearty in a corporate culture that looks like Der Animal Haus next to our wretched arrangement.

Yet we Americans think we're just plain nuts, a barrel of laughs with a zany next-door neighbor to complete the picture. Life really is a series of trivial yet entertaining domestic dramas, just like on *Seinfeld* or *Friends*—if only we were able to spend a few minutes at home, then surely that laugh-o-matic wackiness that our culture tells us exists would appear.

Speaking of wackiness, it must be a hell of a lot of fun to be a corporate executive in the post-Reagan era. If you were the type of kid who liked pulling wings off flies or stuffing firecrackers up cats' asses, then you'd probably find the philosophy of a post-Reagan CEO much to your liking.

Corporate America's executives managed to do more than corner nearly all of the new wealth produced in the last twenty years at the expense of their employees. They also appropriated their workers' happiness. This wasn't an inevitable, organic process, as the business elite's mandarins tell us, but rather a conscious management philosophy policy peddled by its new executive barons. The essence of that corporate philosophy was to instill fear into their workers in order to increase productivity with the aim of extracting the maximum value from them in as brief a time as possible.

One of the office world's most celebrated plutocrats was General Electric CEO Jack Welch, who coined the famous Welchism that employees have unlimited juice to squeeze, and who loved to tell people to "face reality." He earned the nickname Neutron Jack for having fired one hundred twenty-eight thousand of his employees and later boasting that all that was left after his mass-firings were the buildings. That, and an enormous amount of cash for Jack and his happy shareholders. Yuk-yuk-yuk. Some people may not find his kind of humor to their liking, but it probably bowled 'em over in Kennebunkport, or the Hamptons, or the Berkshires, or any number of corporate billionaire hangouts.

> From the ski slopes of Aspen and Gstaad to the beaches of Mustique and the Hamptons, instead of staying at a resort many billionaires (and millionaires) prefer to own multiple homes around the world—partly because it's always nicer to sleep in your own bed and partly because, well, they can. Of course, when you're an ultra-high net-worth individual your home can be as big as a resort—and also as luxurious, complete with maid service, golf, tennis and a private chef.
> —**Christina Valhouli**, "Billionaires On Vacation," *Forbes,*
>   September 19, 2002

Of course, this doesn't mean that Jack Welch doesn't have a heart. In his autobiography *Straight From the Gut*, a New Age–infused ego-romp that sold like hotcakes to the credulous masses, Welch did manage to share his thoughts with us on the importance of friendship . . . buried in the section "A Short Reflection on Golf." Just in case you didn't think he was, uh, human, you see.

But Welch would rather have us remember him as a plutocrat, and he ain't ashamed to admit it. "Sure I'm one of the fat cats," he was quoted saying in the *Wall Street Journal*. "In fact, I'm the fattest cat because I'm lucky enough to have this job."

How fat 'n' lucky was he? Welch earned $150 million between 1996 and 1998, $83.6 million in 1998 alone.

United for a Fair Economy, an advocacy group, described Welch's feudal wealth this way: "If Mr. Welch's $83 million total compensation in 1998 were represented by the height of the Empire State Building, how tall would the buildings represented by other GE workers be? The typical factory worker, earning $40,000 a year, would be represented by a building just eight inches tall. A well-compensated General Electric manager, earning $100,000 a year, would be represented by a building less than two feet tall. Considered globally, a typical employee working in a GE factory in Mexico and making $4,500 a year would be represented by a building less than one inch tall—smaller than an anthill."

Welch retired just a few days before the terror attacks of 9/11 and was awarded a severance package worthy of a Saudi prince. GE gave Neutron Jack an annual pension of $9 million, health and life insurance, a $15 million Manhattan penthouse, unlimited use of the company's private Boeing 737 jet, a limo, country club memberships, VIP seats at New York Knicks and Yankees games, $7.5 million in furnishings and decorations for his four homes, and more. All this for a man who amassed a personal fortune thought to be close to a billion dollars during his years at GE, while firing one hundred twenty-eight thousand workers. The extent of Neutron Jack's pillage was only revealed after his wife busted him sleeping with another woman. She filed for divorce and sued when Welch offered her a typically Neutron Jack settlement of $15 million, a sum her lawyer termed "offensive." The ensuing Clash of the Gargoyles in the cracked Welch mansion exposed the grotesque size of his compensation, leading to an Securities and Exchange Commission investigation and eventually a pledge by Welch to pay back to GE a part of his retirement package.

In spite of his loathsome, King George personality, what is most appalling is how Jack Welch managed to become absolutely adored by corporate America's white-collar suckers. His minions, who stood absolutely nothing to gain and everything to lose by worshipping his philosophy of destroying tens of thousands in order to enrich a few, called themselves "Welch-heads" in another example of our Reagan-era peasant-like behavior.

Take for example this Welch-head reviewer on amazon.com from Texas, who in October 2001, gushed over Welch's autobiography for the whole world to see:

> I shouted 'yeah!' to myself over and over as I read a couple chapters of this book. For example: the chapter about rating and rewarding his employees was excellent. For example, giving Class A employees 3x the salary increases over Class B employees—Great!! Giving NO increases to Class C employees, and getting rid of them sooner rather than later what can I say, I LOVE IT!!
>
> He's so right about the fact that it's more cruel to let Class C workers attain and maintain an certain income level (that they are not really worthy of), and waiting til they're older, with a large mortgage and kids in college before finally telling them that they're not making the grade.

Eventually those people *do* get weeded out (I'm seeing it happen right now in this economy). Sooner is better than later, both for the employer and the employee. I also enjoy not having to work with those types.

Presumably, all of this obscene wealth concentration in the hands of a tiny oligarchy is for everyone's good. At least that's what we were told at the beginning of the Reagan Revolution, and what we've come to implicitly, almost genetically believe in the years since, as all challenges to the Reaganomics theory have been squeezed out of mainstream discourse. The Reaganomics theory, when they still needed to sell it to America, was that we were all supposed to be people in our own unique boats, with the sea representing wealth, and as the rich got richer, the sea would rise, and supposedly our humble boats would rise along with theirs, as though the polar ice caps themselves would melt for the benefit of all mankind. Moreover, somehow only the people with the huge yachts were capable of raising the level of water for all of us. The rising-boat metaphor always struck me as strange, because it implied that the land would become submerged, and those of us not in the QE2 cruise ship would be forced to row around the high seas for the rest of our lives, bailing out water as fast as we could. Which is exactly what happened.

7

What Human Flesh Tastes Like

WHO EVER DECIDED that Americans were so bad off in the seventies anyway? From the right-wing revisionist propaganda that has since become accepted as fact, you'd think that Americans under President Carter were suffering through something like the worst of the Weimar Republic combined with the Siege of Leningrad. The truth is that on a macroeconomic level, the difference between the Carter era and the Reagan era was minimal. For instance, economic growth during the Carter Administration averaged 2.8 percent annually, while under Reagan, from 1982 to 1989, growth averaged 3.2 percent. Was it really worth killing ourselves over that extra .4 percent of growth? For a lucky few, yes. On the other key economic gauge, unemployment, the Carter years were actually better than Reagan's, averaging 6.7 percent annually during his "malaise-stricken" term as compared to an average 7.3 percent unemployment rate during the glorious eight-year reign of Ronald Reagan. Under Carter, people worked less, got far more benefits, had greater job security, and the country grew almost the same average annual rate as under Reagan. On the other hand, according to the Statistical Abstract of the United States for 1996, under Reagan life got worse for those who had it worse: the number of people below the poverty line increased in almost every year from 1981 (31.8 million) to 1992 (39.3 million).

And yet, we are told America was in decline until Reagan came to power and that the country was gripped by this ethereal malaise. Where was this malaise? Whose America was in decline?

The problem with the 1970s wasn't that America was in decline, it was that the plutocracy felt itself declining. And in the plutocrats' eyes, their fortunes are synonymous with America's. The plutocrats felt they were in decline because they weren't living lavishly enough—they needed 531 times their average worker's salary, not 30 times. The people were getting far more than they deserved!

Americans are probably the last people on earth who stubbornly and irrationally accept Reaganomics as both inevitable and for the greater good. They have waited twenty-five years for the effects to positively benefit their lives, and even though life gets objectively more wretched, they still believe that in the end it will work because there is nothing worse than "big government." Critics of the Reaganomics model of relentless privatization and deregulation, and the constant lowering of taxes on corporations and the wealthy, are still marginalized as left-wing radicals or quacks—even by Reaganomics' victims, which is to say the overwhelming majority of Americans. It's a reflex by this point. Like Dana Carvey's Grumpy Old Man, we like it this way—we work harder, stress more and earn less while the rich get richer. That's the way it is and we like it! We love it! Hallelujah!

One cutting-edge corporate philosopher from this period whose sadism would have appealed to the Grumpy Old Man was Intel's CEO Andy Grove. He preached for ever-greater fear in the workplace with the fervor and compassion of Torquemada. In his book *Only the Paranoid Survive*, Grove wrote:

> The quality guru W. Edwards Deming advocated stamping out fear in corporations. I have trouble with the simple-mindedness of this dictum. The most important role of managers is to create an environment in which people are passionately dedicated to winning in the marketplace. Fear plays a major role in creating and maintaining such passion. Fear of competition, fear of bankruptcy, fear of being wrong, and fear of losing can all be powerful motivators. How do we cultivate fear of losing in our employees? We can only do that if we feel it ourselves.

Grove, who became famous for such personal management innovations as the "Scrooge Memo" reminding employees that they had to work a full day on Christmas Eve, wasn't shy about his fear-management philosophy. In a *Forbes* interview, he boasted, "It's fear that gets you out of comfortable equilibrium, that gets you to do the difficult tasks. [Fear is] healthy, like physical pain is healthy. It warns your body that something is wrong."

A typical example of this fear-and-stress governance from the top down is revealed in this memo from the CEO of Cerner Corporation, a healthcare information systems company, to his managers, dated March 13, 2001:

-----Original Message-----
From: Patterson,Neal

To: DL_ALL_MANAGERS;
Subject: MANAGEMENT DIRECTIVE: Week #10_01: Fix it or changes will be made
Importance: High

To the KC_based managers:
I have gone over the top. I have been making this point for over one year. We are getting less than 40 hours of work from a large number of our KC-based EMPLOYEES.

The parking lot is sparsely used at 8AM; likewise at 5PM. As managers—you either do not know what your EMPLOYEES are doing; or YOU do not CARE. You have created expectations on the work effort which allowed this to happen inside Cerner, creating a very unhealthy environment. In either case, you have a problem and you will fix it or I will replace you.

NEVER in my career have I allowed a team which worked for me to think they had a 40 hour job. I have allowed YOU to create a culture which is permitting this. NO LONGER.

At the end of next week, I plan to implement the following:
1. Closing of Associate Center to EMPLOYEES from 7:30AM to 6:30PM.
2. Implementing a hiring freeze for all KC based positions. It will require Cabinet approval to hire someone into a KC based team. I chair our Cabinet.
3. Implementing a time clock system, requiring EMPLOYEES to 'punch in' and 'punch out' to work. Any unapproved absences will be charged to the EMPLOYEES vacation.
4. We passed a Stock Purchase Program, allowing for the EMPLOYEE to purchase Cerner stock at a 15% discount, at Friday's BOD meeting. Hell will freeze over before this CEO implements ANOTHER EMPLOYEE benefit in this Culture.
5. Implement a 5% reduction of staff in KC.
6. I am tabling the promotions until I am convinced that the ones being promoted are the solution, not the problem. If you are the problem, pack your bags.

I think this parental type action SUCKS. However, what you are doing, as managers, with this company makes me SICK. It makes sick to have to write this directive. I know I am painting with a broad brush and the majority of the KC based associates are hard working, committed to Cerner success and committed to transforming health care. I know the parking lot is not a great measurement for 'effort'. I know that 'results' is what counts, not 'effort'. But I am through with the debate.

We have a big vision. It will require a big effort. Too many in KC are not making the effort.

I want to hear from you. If you think I am wrong with any of this, please state your case. If you have some ideas on how to fix this problem, let me hear those. I am very curious how you think we got here. If you know team members who are the problem, let me know. Please include (copy) Kynda in all of your replies.

I STRONGLY suggest that you call some 7AM, 6PM and Saturday AM team meetings with the EMPLOYEES who work directly for you. Discuss this serious issue with your team. I suggest that you call your first meeting—tonight. Something is going to change.

I am giving you two weeks to fix this. My measurement will be the parking lot: it should be substantially full at 7:30 AM and 6:30 PM. The pizza man should show up at 7:30 PM to feed the starving teams working late. The lot should be half full on Saturday mornings. We have a lot of work to do. If you do not have enough to keep your teams busy, let me know immediately.

Folks this is a management problem, not an EMPLOYEE problem. Congratulations, you are management. You have the responsibility for our EMPLOYEES. I will hold you accountable. You have allowed this to get to this state. You have two weeks. Tick, tock.

Neal Patterson
Chairman & Chief Executive Officer
Cerner Corporation www.cerner.com
2800 Rockcreek Parkway; Kansas City, Missouri 64117
"We Make Health Care Smarter"

One of the most enraging things about this memo is Patterson's sly use of hip, torn-denim colloquialisms like "sucks." Hey, it's hip to be a slave-driving vampire! It's cool to be a terrified manager! Pushing your already stressed-out subordinates beyond the breaking point tooootally fuckin' raaaawqs, dude!

Just a few months before this memo was issued, Cerner was named to *Fortune* magazine's list of the 100 best companies in America to work for—so Patterson is about as good as CEOs get today.

Incredibly enough, Patterson explained away his cruel memo as a product of his upbringing in the countryside: "You can take the boy off the farm, but you can't take the farm out of the boy," he told reporters. Yuk-yuk-yuk. In other words, shucks, he ain't no high-falutin' Wall Street elitist! That's jus' straight-talkin', folks. Right. And as of March 1, 2004, this country boy Patterson still owned 3,426,936 shares in Cerner, making his net worth a whopping $159,695,217.60 just in stock options—not including the shares he's already unloaded over the years, or his high-six-figure executive pay, or his bonus. As John Denver once sang, "Thank God I'm a country boy!"

Patterson's objective in that memo was to transmit hellfire and fear into the hearts of his wage-slave foremen, so that they in turn would whip the 5,100 wage-slaves into shape, so that Patterson's net worth, and the net worth of the shareholders that he answered to, would skyrocket into further obscene wealth stratospheres. For some reason the vicious attitude expressed in Patterson's memo came as a shock to the public, even though everyone in a corporation seems to work for a Patterson. As Jeffrey Pfeffer, a professor at the Stanford University Graduate

School of Business, commented, "It's the corporate equivalent of whips and ropes and chains." Indeed.

So why was it such a shock? Because according to the official propaganda, we had actually moved beyond this kind of malicious, authoritarian work environment. According to the cheerleaders of the post–Industrial Revolution, technology and progress were leading mankind into a kind of egalitarian paradise beyond traditional hierarchical structures. According to another Stanford professor, Stephen Barley, author of *The New World of Work*, "Management's traditional source of legitimacy will begin to wane . . . the likelihood is that managers, unable to make knowledgeable decisions autocratically, will find themselves relegated to the important but less heady role of coordination."

As we know, the opposite has been true. Fear, imposed from the top down—from shareholder to senior executive, senior executive to executive, and so on down the chain right to the maximally squeezed Manpower temp—is the dominant trope in post-Reagan corporate culture. One of the simplest ways to instill this fear is to make employees acutely aware that their jobs are never safe. Grove's successor at Intel, Craig Barrett, was later quoted as telling shareholders, "The half-life of an engineer, software, hardware engineer, is only a few years."

Constant restructuring, downsizing, and layoffs became the dominant *modus operandi* for corporate America in the 1980s and 1990s, in spite of the prosperity and profits. It doesn't make rational sense but it's a fact: *corporate layoffs increased substantially as corporate profits increased.* CEO heroes like Jack Welch led a layoff-craze that saw 6.5 million Americans downsized just in the 1995–97 period alone. And in 1998, 10 percent more Americans were laid off than at any point in the previous ten years. Mass firings were no longer a symptom of economic downturn; rather, they were considered a necessary ingredient to ratcheting up employee fear—and rolling up huge CEO bonuses. Indeed, from the time Reagan took office through the end of the 1990s, forty-five million Americans were fired. White collar workers now faced the same uncertain job prospects blue-collar workers did in the early 1980s; moreover, white collar jobs are now also being outsourced to Third World countries, following a trend once thought confined to manufacturing. In finance, insurance and real estate industries, the odds of getting downsized have tripled since the mid-1980s.

> "The workplace is never free of fear—and it shouldn't be. Indeed, fear can be a powerful management tool."
> —**Wall Street Journal**, "Manager's Journal: Fear Is Nothing to Be Afraid Of," January 27, 1997

This trend of downsizing and outsourcing only worsened during the Bush the Younger recession. Recently, a congressional report doubled previous estimates of the number of American jobs shipped off to cheap labor markets like India from 200,000 per year to 406,000 outsourced in 2004. So it doesn't matter anymore if America's economy is expanding or contracting. There is no way out for America's middle class, through good times and bad they will always get squeezed and dumped, like rock star groupies.

There is a reason for that. CEOs who implemented mass layoffs were show-ered with cash and stock by the shareholding class that benefited from the pink slip massacres. Al "Chainsaw" Dunlap became a celebrity in the 1990s famous for taking over companies, firing thousands, and walking away with hundreds of mil-lions in bonuses. He took over Scott Paper Co. in 1994, fired 11,200 workers or one-third of the workforce, and sent the stock up 225 percent, allowing him to cash out with $100 million in just nineteen months. And he was a helluva guy at home too. When his first wife divorced him, she charged that one time he pointed a knife at her and said, "I've always wondered what human flesh tasted like." He forced her to dye her hair blond because it reminded him of his previous girlfriend, threat-ened to divorce her when she got pregnant, and submitted her to frequent "dust inspections," when he would wear white gloves and inspect the house for dust, and if he found any he would unleash a torrent of abuse. Dunlap's sadism was pathological. "He said one of his favorite tricks was to wait until a two- or three-year-old child approached, then to stomp on its feet and laugh as the infant hob-bled away crying." And not surprisingly, Dunlap used fear as a leadership tool: "His people are living in fear of him—absolute fear."

Al Dunlap was only able to flourish and become an adored celebrity in the 1990s because the culture had altered so much by then. Years of Reaganism had finally made it possible for a vile ogre like Al Dunlap to come out of his lair with-out fear of being run through with a stake by his employee-victims. This wasn't always the case. When he took over as general manager at Sterling Pulp & Paper in 1967 and applied his "mean business" philosophy of bullying and firing, he soon began receiving death threats. In the 1990s, on the other hand, not only was Dunlap not threatened by the tens of thousands of employees whose lives he destroyed to enrich himself and his shareholders, but worse, he was worshiped for it by the same people who stood to lose if Dunlap's "mean business" philosophy was applied to them. This is a clear and noteworthy example of how deeply the cul-ture had been altered by years of Reaganomics' cultural propaganda. The accultur-ation of a slave-like attitude had taken hold.

Take this Amazon.com reader's review of Dunlap's 1996 memoir, *Mean Business*:

This book gets better the more I read it, October 22, 2001
Reviewer: Collin Kinning (see more about me) from Alpharetta, GA United States

Its amazing to me, that there are people who still disagree with his meth-ods. Pardon me, but what ever happened to putting the shareholder first in a company?, I mean, isn't it THEIR money on the line? And since when is a business supposed to be a leader of social change? Last time I knew, businesses were supposed to be lean, efficient and prof-itable, not some over blown behemouth that was supposed to play nice with its competitors. This book is lean, its mean and its supposed to be painful to those who disagree, because turn-around artists would not be needed if companies would think more of their shareholders first and foremost.

In 1998, Citigroup CEO Sandy Weill earned $167 million, at the same time that he cut 5 percent of his workforce and reduced 401(k)s, pensions, and other benefits.

Another example, drawn from *White Collar Sweatshop*, revealed that in February 1993 Bank of America announced that its massive downsizing of 28,930 employees had paid off to the tune of a $1.5 billion profit, the largest in banking history. CEO Richard Rosenberg followed the profit report with a fresh announcement: in order to save another $760 million, eight thousand of the bank's white collar employees were reduced to part-time status of nineteen-hour workweeks, one hour shy of eligibility for benefits, meaning now they were stuck with smaller paychecks, no healthcare, no vacation, and no retirement.

Neither 9/11 nor the Dubya recession has altered this cruel tendency. A 2002 report by the Institute for Policy Studies and United for a Fair Economy revealed that CEO compensation rose considerably when the CEO fired employees, cut their benefits, or moved operations offshore even in the new millennium, even after the corporate scandals and media attention and all the talk of patriotism and America pulling together. While median CEO pay increased a modest 6 percent in 2002, those CEOs who announced huge layoffs in 2001 saw their 2002 packages soar 44 percent—in the middle of the worst recession in decades! At the thirty companies in 2002 that had the greatest shortfalls in their employee pension funds, the CEOs of those same companies saw their pay rocket 59 percent over the median. In other words, the more callous/feudal you are, the more you get rewarded no matter what is going on in the economy at large.

8

Putting Their Heads on Pikes

> They tell you, "You're too old. There's no way we can help you." You just get to the point where you want to kill someone. It was very tough.
> —*White Collar Sweatshop*

NOT ONLY HAVE LAYOFFS BECOME A PART OF CORPORATE RELIGION, but they are executed in ways far more brutal and humiliating than before. Whereas in the past, a sacked employee was generally given two to four weeks' notice, today, white collar employees are routinely fired in the most degrading manner possible. As in everything else in today's corporate culture, all consideration is given to the interests of the executives and shareholders, while employees are considered little more than expenses and possible threats. Fired employees are told to vacate the premises immediately, ordered to hand over their security badges, and escorted to their workstations by security and management, in view of all their co-workers, to ensure that nothing is stolen while they clear out their belongings. All thought is given to protecting the company; no thought is extended to the sacked employee, who often is thrown out in order to transfer a few more bucks into the executive's bonus. Moreover, this brutal firing method serves as a warning to all the others. It adds to the sense of fear, the fear of humiliation, the fear of fucking up even once.

One typical story comes from the dot-com bust in the summer of 2001. Real Networks laid off 15 percent of its workforce, or 140 employees. According to one bitter account, "It was heartwarming the way they did it—people came back from lunch and their passcards didn't work. People who were still in the building were escorted out the door by security and were SEARCHED upon exit."

A day later, another firing story came from Citrix, which let sixty-five of its one thousand employees go. Witnesses said that the laid-off were led out of the building by security guards and told that their personal items would be boxed by a bonded firm and sent to the address on company file at a later date. Armed guards were hired to patrol their offices for the next several months on the look-out for ex-employees, according to those who worked there. If a former employee was spotted near Citrix, they were told that they would be reported to police. If Citrix's employees were seen talking with fired employees on company grounds, they would be fired on the spot.

I saved three typical reactions to the Real Networks firings from the message board of the once-popular Web site, Fuckedcompany.com, which covered the collapse of the dot-com ponzi scheme:

> It's crap like this may cause some disgruntled employee to go beserk. Why not just put a sign on the door the next morning with a list of employee names that can no longer enter? Why the he** do companies fire employees in the middle of the day???

> I just don't understand why companies use these gestapo procedures when they lay people off. I mean, the "lucky" people who still have jobs see this shit and start thinking "uh-oh, there but for the grace of God go I"—I'll bet a lot of hardware disappears between now and the _next_ set of layoffs at Real.

> It's the fine art of diverting attention. If you actually looked at how the money was pissed away, you will see that the higher ups (plus family and friends that came along for the ride) almost always made millions, with outrageus salaries, selling worthless stock and lavish expense accounts. so how are you gonna divert attention from all the money you've swindled? hey look! some guy is stealing a paperclip! Smithers, release the hounds...

All of this takes place in office settings that increasingly resemble something between Fort Knox and Camp X-Ray. Armed security is standard at offices, as are magnetic-coded tags with picture IDs and security cameras. Many companies also install keystroke software on their employees' computers in order to monitor them.

According to an American Management Survey, more than three-quarters of major companies spy on their employees, double the number just seven years ago. Nearly half of all companies pay someone to monitor their employees' e-mails and Web surfing habits, and about the same number audit their employees' e-mails on a regular basis. TruePitch markets software that records an employees' every keystroke, even deleted lines, and at the end of the day bundles and organizes all of the employees' e-mails, instant messaging chats, and documents and sends it to the supervisor in a daily report.

Companies routinely install audio and video equipment to monitor their employees' movements and conversations. Cards with computer chips are standard now for parking in company lots, entering offices, and changing workstations, allowing employers to monitor their employees, and reminding employees that they are under constant surveillance. Even America's slaves generally weren't fenced in and guarded by security.

To make sure that uppity employees aren't plotting anything or talking bad about the company, old-fashioned spying is becoming more common. Companies are increasingly hiring actors to pose as new employees whose job is to report to management what the other employees are saying or doing.

In Soviet times, workers often had to show an ID to enter their factories, which usually had a security entrance, but once a worker was inside they were never subject to the degree of full-spectrum dominance as today's American workforce. In 1991, I visited a television factory in Leningrad. I remember being shocked that at the gate to the half-idle factory, security checked IDs to restrict movement into and out of the factory. It seemed a clear example of evil Soviet authoritarianism. Yet once inside, workers casually lounged, talked, smoked in the hallways, and even drank. In 2001, I worked as a data entry clerk for National Processing Center in Louisville, Kentucky, where all employees were required to pass by a security post manned by three or four armed security guards behind bullet-proof glass, monitoring an array of video cameras trained on the workforce inside. To enter the office, you had to swipe a magnetic card at the front door. The offices themselves consisted of a massive honeycomb of cubicles with shoulder-height partitions, allowing anyone to see everyone at all times. The few offices allotted to senior supervisors had glass walls facing inside, but no windows out onto the street. Everyone could see each other inside—no one could see the free world outside, and no one from the free world could see us. Banners were stretched high along the walls, cheering the workforce on with slogans reminiscent of Soviet factories. In my section, merchant services, the banner read: "PRIDE of Merchant Services" with the word pride broken down: "Proactive Responsive Innovative Delivering Excellence." Across the street from NPC was a special branch of the Jefferson County Sheriff's Department, ready to provide overwhelming backup in case one of the company's fourteen hundred employees went postal.

The strangest thing about all of this is that if you were to tell an American that his workplace is more Soviet than what the Soviets ever created, he would think you're simply a nutcase or a troublemaker. And who knows, maybe he'd be right. Maybe the normal thing is to accept all of this. Only a nutcase would object.

9

Workers Complain, But They Don't Quit

WHY DO THEY TAKE IT? Why don't they do something about it? As this recent, anonymous Livejournal posting from the spouse of an employee for the gaming software company Electronic Arts shows, even when people are completely aware of their misery and sense of injustice, even when their health declines, when their spouses suffer and their marriages fall apart, they still accept even the most wretched arrangements, soothed only by their private, anonymous grumblings:

> My significant other works for Electronic Arts, and I'm what you might call a disgruntled spouse.
>
> I am retaining some anonymity here because I have no illusions about what the consequences would be for my family if I was explicit. Our adventures with Electronic Arts began less than a year ago. I remember that they asked [my husband] in one of the [job] interviews: "how do you feel about working long hours?"...
>
> Within weeks production had accelerated into a 'mild' crunch: eight hours six days a week. Not bad. When the next news came it was not about a reprieve; it was another acceleration: twelve hours six days a week, 9am to 10pm.
>
> The current mandatory hours are 9am to 10pm—seven days a week—with the occasional Saturday evening off for good behavior (at 6:30pm). This averages out to an eighty-five hour work week. Complaints were ignored.
>
> And the kicker: for the honor of this treatment EA salaried employees receive a) no overtime; b) no compensation time; c) no additional sick or vacation leave. The time just goes away. Additionally, EA recently announced that, although in the past they have offered essentially a type of comp time in the form of a few weeks off at the end of a project, they no longer wish to do this, and employees shouldn't expect it. . . .
>
> The love of my life comes home late at night complaining of a headache that will not go away and a chronically upset stomach, and my happy supportive smile is running out. . . .
>
> Amazingly, Electronic Arts was listed #91 on Fortune magazine's "100 Best Companies to Work For" in 2003.
>
> EA's attitude toward this has been (in an anonymous quotation that I've heard repeated by multiple managers), "If they don't like it, they can work someplace else." EA's annual revenue is approximately $2.5 billion. This company is not strapped for cash; their labor practices are inexcusable.

I look at our situation and I ask 'us': why do you stay? And the answer is that in all likelihood we won't.

But the sad truth is that in all certainty, they will stay. And even if they don't, someone else will take her husband's place, meaning no skin off EA's back. As one respondent to her note wrote, "Well, I know this doesn't help you any, but you're certainly not alone, and EA certainly isn't the only publisher pulling this sort of crap. I've been wanting to leave my job for quite some time, but it looks like all of the major publishers are following the same plans. . . ." Like the slaves of Frederick Douglass' time, today's American workers would rather "bear those ills we had/than fly to others, that we knew not of."

It is the feebleness and powerlessness that is most shocking. Josh Pastreich, a union organizer from the International Alliance of Theatrical Stage Employees Union (IATSE) Local 16, suggested in a posting that the white collar EA developers form a union, which got this lightbulb-flash response: "A union just for Game Developers or the entire IT industry? I have worked in the IT industry for 10 years now and while I know that it's not nearly as long as most, I have seen my wages stay virtually the same while my hours go up. We don't even get raises here, just bonuses. I am forced to work almost every day of the week most of the time."

In a private interview, Pastreich was not optimistic: "[M]any developers are interested in forming a union, but they work project to project. The biggest issue is that workers are afraid they are going to get blackballed if they are seen as supporting the union and they will never work again in the industry. That is a very high price because they have invested so much in terms of time, effort, and money to get up to where they are." If this sounds so very pre-1930s, it's because it is. Only in one way it's even worse. Thanks to years of effective Reagan-era anti-union propaganda, the new generation actually identifies their employers' anti-union interests with their own interests, so companies needn't fear them organizing and fighting for a better life: "Now you have much younger workers coming directly out of school, they have no experience with unions and often think they are too good for a union even though they are getting screwed." The way Pastreich sees it, a pronounced lack of bravery and courage keep white collar slaves like the EA employees from fighting for their interests: "They push on, hoping it will get better, or that the next studio won't be as bad. It is going to take a group of brave workers to stand-up and change things because as long as EA is making money they don't see a problem."

Nowhere is the slave mentality more evident than in the final paragraph of the disgruntled spouse's posting, appealing to the ogre's heart:

If I could get EA CEO Larry Probst on the phone. . . . The main thing I want to know is, Larry: you do realize what you're doing to your people, right? And you do realize that they ARE people, with physical limits, emotional lives, and families, right? Voices and talents and senses of humor and all that? That when you keep our husbands and wives and children in the office for ninety hours a week, sending them home exhausted and numb and frustrated with their lives, it's not just them you're hurting, but everyone around them, everyone who loves them? When you make your profit calculations and your cost analyses, you know that a great measure of that cost is being paid in raw human dignity, right?

If, in a fantasy confrontation with her tormentor, posted in the safety of an anonymous forum, the best shot that this "disgruntled spouse" can imagine delivering to Probst is to "look into your heart," then frankly, the Larry Probsts of corporate America have nothing to worry about. These people still believe, after all of these years, that the plutocrat class has a conscience they can appeal to? What movies have these people been watching? To consider how feeble the spouse's thinking is, imagine Probst's answer: either he could say, "Yes, I think about it," which means he has no heart because he exploits his workers anyway; or he could answer, "No, I don't think about it," which means he has no heart, period. As it is, if I were a Larry Probst reading this posting, I'd sleep pretty well at night. The main thing is that no one is considering real action. There is no serious threat of a company-wide or industry-wide white-collar collectivization, no threat of street action, no death threats of the sort that "Chainsaw" Dunlap once endured in the late 1960s. Slaves always grumble when they're safely away from the boss's eyes. So long as they put in all the work, they can let off a little steam at night.

For five years now, you've worked your ass off at Initech, hoping for a promotion or some kind of profit sharing or something. Five years of your mid-twenties now, gone. And you're gonna go in tomorrow and they're gonna throw you out into the street. You know why? So Bill Lumbergh's stock will go up a quarter of a point. Michael, let's make that stock go down. Let's take enough money from that place that we never ever have to sit in a cubicle ever again.
—*Office Space*

Most Americans today take it for granted that the workplace is unbearably stressful, fearful, and organized to transfer much of the wealth up to a tiny, privileged class of executives and shareholders at the expense of the many. But it wasn't always that way.

Long before Neutron Jack, General Electric's stated relationship to their employees was deliberately paternalistic, respectful, secure, and symbiotic. In 1962, right around the time that young Jack Welch joined GE, Earl S. Willis, the manager of employee benefits at General Electric, wrote, "Maximizing employment security is a prime company goal." Later, he wrote, "The employee who can plan his economic future with reasonable certainty is an employer's most productive asset."

Contrast this to Jack Welch, who bragged after one hundred twenty-eight thousand firings, one hundred twenty-eight thousand potentially ruined families, that "only the buildings remained standing." Oh, and his billion dollars in savings, his $15 million annual pension, and his company 737. "Loyalty to a company, it's nonsense," he told the *Wall Street Journal*.

In 1941, an AT&T employee handbook stated, "By means of this [pension plan] and other welfare practices, the Company endeavors to 'take care' of its employees throughout their working careers, and beyond. In return, it naturally expects employees to be genuinely concerned with the welfare of the business and to feel personally responsible for its reputation and continuing success."

In 1996, James Meadows, vice president of human resources for AT&T, said, "In AT&T, we have to promote the whole concept of the work force being contingent, though most of the contingent workers are inside of our walls."

Clearly, for most Americans, everything is getting worse and worse. The only beneficiaries are the Chainsaw Dunlaps and Neutron Jacks.

One phenomenon that allowed CEOs to implement this feudal solution was the rise of the temp worker, a rare species before Reagan came to power. Across America, temp employment quadrupled from 1986 to 1998. As the *New York Times* noted, "Until the 1970s, temps and contract workers hardly existed," and yet according to a recent survey, a typical company today uses temps to meet 12 percent—and oftentimes up to 20 percent—of its manpower needs. Temps are the perfect post-Reagan employee: they receive no benefits, earn less than full-timers, and keep the permanents properly scared, allowing employers to work everyone harder and keep them motivated through fear of getting fired. It is not uncommon these days for a temp to stay with a company for years in prolonged temp status— cheap, easy to get rid of, no benefit worries . . . Why give 'em health care when you don't have to? Why give 'em job security when you can just tell Kelly Services that their services are no longer needed?

This contingent-worker philosophy keeps fearful workers working harder to keep from getting replaced, and keeps worker costs down so that a greater share of the company wealth goes into the pockets of the executive/shareholding elite. That's the sum of it all. With low-cost, no-benefit temp slaves working in the same cubicle row as full-timers, employees are not only less likely to make uppity demands for raises and increased benefits, but more important, they'll be more likely to accept cuts in their compensation package just to keep from getting downsized. In other words, executives and shareholders get more for less, and keep the difference for themselves. Its effect is to create one of the world's most submissive workforces in the civilized world—Reagan-era Americans refuse to see their struggle in collective, class terms. Rather, each is conditioned to see their fate individually, as protagonists facing a personal test of character, which serves the oligarchy just fine.

Contrast this with France, where, in May 2004, part-time actors (!) were so incensed about planned cuts to their welfare benefits that they planned to storm the Cannes Film Festival, forcing officials to bring in six hundred riot police for protection. As economist Lester Thurow observed, "[E]xamples abound of profitable firms that simply marched in and dramatically lowered the wages of existing workforces by twenty to forty percent. Workers complain, but they don't quit."

So today's American white-collar worker is oddly passive, considering that even many American slaveholders rejected the high-stress, high-fear, juice-squeezing tactics of today's CEOs. One famous slave memoirist, Henry Clay Bruce, wrote in 1895, "The master who treated his slaves humanely had less trouble, got better service from them, and could depend upon their doing his work faithfully, even in his absence, having his interest in view always." But today's workers don't even need to be treated well in order for companies to squeeze the maximum amount of work out of them and gain the maximum level of self-initiative. In fact, like victims of domestic abuse, the more poorly American workers are treated, the more they work and the less they demand. It is as if they have no dignity left.

10

The Cost of Stress

TODAY'S MIDDLE-CLASS EMPLOYEES may force themselves to appear as cheerfully enthusiastic workers to the public eye—indeed they have to. In *White Collar Sweatshop* an executive VP at Lehman Brothers recounts how a managing director confronted her in the hall and told her to "smile more often so that people would know just how grateful she was to still have her job."

They may smile, but the effects of this new corporate culture are quantifiably disastrous. Stress is a word that seems too trivial to describe the state of so many middle-class workers pushed to the edge.

One study estimates that stress costs the American economy $300 billion in diminished productivity, employee turnover, and insurance. The European Agency for Safety and Health at Work reports that more than half of the 550 million working days lost annually in the United States from absenteeism are stress-related. In public, Americans smile and tough it out, unable to show the strains of stress for fear of being lumped in with those who can't deal. But a 2000 Gallup Poll found that 80 percent of workers feel stress on the job and nearly half say they need help coping with it. Twenty-five percent have felt like screaming or shouting because of job stress, 14 percent felt like striking a co-worker, and 10 percent are concerned about a colleague becoming violent.

How dangerous is stress? Stress can lead to hypertension, heart disease, heart attacks, and other problems. According to the National Institute for Occupational Safety and Health (NIOSH), early signs of job stress are headaches, short tempers, trouble sleeping, and low morale. This naturally affects the workers' psychological health. The American Psychological Association estimates that 60 percent of work absences are due to psychological problems, costing over $57 billion per year. Healthcare costs are 50 percent higher for workers suffering from stress, according to the *Journal for Occupational and Environment Medicine*. And there's plenty of stress to go around: the number of workers who report high job stress is still boiling over, climbing from 37 percent in 2001 to 45 percent in 2002, including 40 percent who describe their work as "extremely stressful" and 25 percent who label it "the number one stress" in their lives, according to the NIOSH.

Stress on this level is an entirely new health problem in the middle-class workplace. Like workplace massacres, stress only entered our lexicon as a widespread life-destroyer in the aftermath of the Reagan Revolution. According to a 1997 report by the Princeton Survey Research Associates, three-fourths of American workers believe there is more on-the-job stress than a generation ago. As a sign of how minor a role stress previously played in the workplace, the University of Chicago's National Opinion Research Center, funded by the National Science Foundation and described as the "gold standard for surveys in the social sciences," only began asking workers about workplace stress in 1989, even though the social survey started in 1972. In other words, workplace stress didn't even cross the minds of the country's top social scientists until Reagan's term ended.

Stress and fear are so rampant that another new buzzword has recently appeared, "presenteeism," which describes the increasingly common phenomenon of workers showing up to the office even though they are too sick, for fear of falling behind.

While the new corporate culture afforded America's plutocrats an obscenely decadent existence, for middle-class Americans life became an increasingly intolerable struggle—both at the office and at home, what little time was spent there. A study by Harvard Law School Professor Elizabeth Warren showed that even though the average two-income middle-class family earns more than the single-breadwinner from a generation ago, given mortgage costs, car payments, taxes, health insurance, day-care bills, tuition costs, the need to move into an area with a good school district (due to the increasingly unbearable competition among kids), and so on, the average two-earner family actually has less discretionary income today than single-income families a generation ago. Based on current trends, one of every seven families with children, or more than five million households, will have filed for bankruptcy by 2010. Home foreclosures in 2002 were triple the rate twenty-five years earlier; and mortgage payments have not only risen in real terms, but they've soared 69 percent as a portion of family income from 1973 to 2000. Here is a clear example of the downside to a home ownership–based econ-omy in an era where the middle-class is increasingly squeezed. If interest rates rise above their historical lows, the problems will only multiply. Car repossessions doubled between 1998 and 2002. In fact, more than 90 percent of bankruptcies are declared by people who would be described as middle-class.

For women, single mothers in particular, it is worse. Over the past twenty years, the number of single women who have filed bankruptcy has increased by 600 percent—nearly one in six will likely go bankrupt by the end of this decade.

And in the midst of all this Americans let their leaders blame them for their problems. Republican Senator Orrin Hatch said millions of Americans are going bankrupt because, "they run up huge bills and then expect society to pay for them," while his colleague, Republican Congressmen Henry Hyde sneered, "Bankruptcy is becoming a first stop for some rather than a last resort." Amazingly, the abused, half-bankrupt middle-class continues to reward the Hatches and Hydes—whose careers are underwritten by banks—ever-greater election victories in perfect synch with their own increasingly untenable debt load.

One of the main causes of this explosion in foreclosures and bankruptcies is the Reagan-era deregulation of the credit and mortgage lending industries. It was thought that through deregulation, and following America's great wealth boom, foreclosures should fall; but in fact today's homeowners are three times more likely to foreclose than before deregulation. The reason is "easy credit" sold to increasingly desperate, struggling middle-class families, and a consumer lending industry run wild with its schemes to rope in customers. Meanwhile, to keep up, credit card debt rocketed 570 percent between 1981 and 1999.

Corporate America's white-collar and blue-collar masses have not only seen their pay stagnate and their debt burdens increase, but their benefits have been slashed and are no longer considered safe. Today an American is 49 percent more likely to be without health insurance than before the Reagan Revolution began. At the same time, over the past twenty years, the number of families declaring bankruptcy due to a serious illness has soared more than twenty times, or 2,000 percent. Perhaps this is what the Reaganites mean when they talk about people taking "personal responsibility for their lives." That is to say, the middle and lower-middle classes need to take the blame for their own wretched impoverishment, not the plutocrats who tweaked the machine to work exclusively in their favor. If you point the finger at them you're not accepting personal responsibility—instead, you're playing class warfare.

The bottom line is that the middle class no longer exists as we once knew it, before Reaganism destroyed the postwar ideal of a comfortable, happy, home-by-six middle class. It's gone. A certain demographic may still be called that based on the statistical definition, but it ain't the same middle class it used to be. Today, the middle-classes struggle under increasingly unbearable conditions and are only able to maintain the trappings of a middle-class lifestyle thanks to cheap imports produced by near-slave laborers in the Third World and easy credit that is slowly picking them off one by one.

If Ward Cleaver were alive today, he'd rarely be home to see his wife and children; and when home, he'd be an impossible crank, always getting called on the cellphone or buzzed on the Blackberry. The stress from seeing his health insurance get slashed would only be overshadowed by the fear caused by another round of white-collar downsizing and vicious memos from the senior executives implying that more fat was yet to be cut from the company payrolls. Mr. Cleaver would work weekends and forego vacations, and likely vote Republican, forced to choose between the hypertension medicine and the blood-thinner pills since he can't afford both, not under the new corporate HMO plan. . . . His anger and stress would push him into cursing Canada for being a hotbed of anti-American liberalism while at the same time he'd agonize over whether or not to order his medicines from their cheap online pharmacies. He'd have no time for imparting little moral lessons. "Not now, leave me alone," he'd grumble, washing down the last of his Cumadins with a low-carb non-alcoholic beer while watching *The O'Reilly Factor* through clenched teeth. His wife June would be stuck at a three-day merchandising conference at a Holiday Inn in Tempe—if they weren't divorced by now—while the Beaver would be standing in front of his bedroom dresser mirror in his long ck trenchcoat, clutching his homemade pipebombs, plotting revenge on Eddie

Haskell and all the other kids who call him "gay" and "bitch" and make his life a living Hell.

PART IV

Wage Rage

Maybe it's time to start handing out bulletproof vests along with IDs. Homicides committed by disgruntled employees and former employees at the workplace are on the rise. That kind of killing was virtually nonexistent before 1980. But since 1988, the number of office slayings has increased disturbingly.

—"News Section," *Fortune*, August 9, 1993

1

Hire One Bourgeois to Alienate the Other

BY ANY HISTORICAL STANDARD, the ground was—and is—fertile for rebellion in America, thanks to the Reagan Revolution. Any time wealth inequities diverge as abruptly and hideously as they have over the past twenty-five years, particularly as expectations for our lives have grown, a society can be expected to explode. Rebellion is even more likely if there is an ideological or intellectual context to give form to the discontent, or "disgruntlement" to use the current term.

What's strange, from an historical point of view, is that there haven't been large-scale domestic rebellions against the Reagan Revolution. This doesn't mean that the Reagan Revolution was actually fair and equitable. Domestic rebellions inspired by gross social injustice are extremely rare in this country, as we have seen, and all rebellion is doomed to end in violent and brutal defeat.

What is really striking is not the paucity of open rebellions in American history—which the more credulous American mandarins inevitably point to as proof of this country's infinite virtue (just as Southern whites have pointed to the striking lack of slave rebellions as proof of the slaves' happiness)—but rather that there have been people willing to risk rebellion of any kind. Given the odds—that is, the null set over zero—it takes reckless bravery or mental illness or suicidal desperation to launch an insurrection.

That explains why so much rebellion in America is expressed in less obvious, less direct ways. For example, in slave times, while there were only a few rebellions, there were numerous instances of vandalism, mysterious fires, poisonings and crop-sabotage. As Harding writes in *There Is a River*, "One of the most universally popular [forms of struggle] was arson, which minimized the danger of direct confrontation and certain death. Fire could destroy property held so dear by a property-based system." Similarly, a recent problem facing companies is what the *New York Times* calls "Layoff Rage." One downsized IT manager, for example, sabotaged a company's computer systems, causing $20 million in damage on the eve of the company's public stock offering. The fifty-six year-old manager, who made $186,000 a year and had a wife and three kids, left an anonymous note explaining why: "I have been loyal to the company in good and bad times for over thirty years. I was expecting a member of top management to come down from his ivory tower to face us with the layoff announcement, rather than sending the kitchen supervisor with guards to escort us off the premises like criminals." He got busted, of course. Pinkerton, the security firm, estimates that only 1 percent of laid-off workers strike back against their former companies, so it is still rare—just as, again, slave arson and vandalism was relatively rare.

What makes rebellion more impossible is if it lacks context and resonance. The triumph of Reaganomics occurred right at the total collapse of the Left and at the "end of history" in mainstream American ideology, ceding debate just when a new social injustice desperately needed to be framed. Labor unions in America were destroyed in the 1980s. Indeed, the percentage of private-sector employees who belong to unions in 2003 was half of what it was in 1983, according to the U.S. Labor Bureau.

Unions became identified with something un-American, immoral, and corrupt. The repeated, grotesque corruption of America's banking elite, which required hundreds of billions of taxpayer bailout money in the wake of the S&L scandal, never led Americans to view banking as inherently immoral or un-American. The unprecedented corruption of America's CEO class in the 1990s, including its multi-hundred-billion dollar schemes to pad books and siphon cash to offshore companies, never led a sizable number of Americans to view our dismally regulated corporations as un-American and immoral. Yet corruption in the unions was, thanks to Reaganism, seen as proof of the institution's congenital malevolence, as well as its anti-Americanness. Labor unions were accused of holding back America's progress. In the popular conscience of anyone who came of age in the Reagan era, unions are seen as inherently working against American values. This sentiment is so powerful that today even workers who would benefit from unions are generally disinclined to support them. Such workers see themselves as patriotic and individualistic in the American spirit, putting their faith in the alleged level playing field of the free market, much to their employers' satisfaction. This sentiment reached its *reducto ad absurdum* point in the 1990s with Wal-Mart employees or Amazon.com workers accepting lower wages and meager benefits in exchange for being referred to as "associates" rather than as workers. Even white-collar high-tech employees mimicked the Wal-Mart employees' gullibility, by taking worthless and meager stock shares and the title "associate" or "partner" in exchange for low wages and inhuman work hours, reduced benefits, and the promise not to unionize. All because the white collar worker sees the company's interests (that is, the major shareholders' interests) as his own too. The goal of every slavekeeper.

And if they tried to unionize, they were crushed. Amazon.com, for example, quashed a union drive at its Seattle customer service center by simply downsizing the workforce and shutting the Seattle center down. They thereby destroyed a nest of unionization, all in the name of the New Economy where "old" rules like unions don't apply.

The very idea of collectivizing to protect their interests is anathema to white-collar, middle-class American professionals. They have always seen themselves as the class in adversarial relation to unions. Which is why white-collar workers could not even conceive of collectivizing to strengthen the precarious position they find themselves in today. Can you imagine law associates locked in collective bargaining to reduce their work week from ninety hours to eighty-five? Picketing accountants demanding two extra days of vacation a year? Data entry clerks across the country staging a walk-out to win a fifteen-minute paid coffee break?

The ghost of Western Union founder Jay Gould, who once boasted, "I can hire one half of the working class to kill the other," is back, only the middle-class is now in the same galley ship that the working class once was. "I can hire one bourgeois to alienate the other"—this was something Marx had never foreseen.

In this highly atomized corporate culture, it is no wonder that workplace rage rebellions should take place in the form of one-man suicide missions. If the idea of banding together to fight for something as obvious and vital as one's own self interest—unionizing for a dental plan or to keep wages and pensions from being slashed—is frowned upon, then who would consider raising arms with fellow employees to wage an insurrection against the company that oppresses them? No employee would be able to trust another to keep the plans secret; moreover, no employee is ever aware that anyone else is as miserable and desperate as he is. The culture demands that people smile and love their work—and most do, or at least most believe they do.

2

Profiling Anyone

NEITHER THE FBI NOR THE SECRET SERVICE has been able to create a profile for a rampage murderer—not in the office world, not in the schoolyard world.

The inability to profile these rage murderers is important because it strongly suggests that external factors, that is environmental factors, create the rampage murderer, rather than the internal psychological disorders of the rampage attacker. Serial killers, for example, can be profiled because they share distinct psychological characteristics. But nearly anyone is a potential rage murderer. They spring out from anywhere in that vast unrecognized middle. Some are single, some married. Some are anti-social loner types, some friendly and well-liked. Most have been men, but there have been women. Most have been white, but there have been a number of black, Latino, and Asian-Americans. Many served in the armed forces, but so have countless millions of Americans; many collect guns, but then again, few things are as American as collecting guns.

There have been attempts to draw a profile of these rage murderers. But the profilers end up either using a brush so broad as to be meaningless, or they contradict themselves within the set of characteristics of their profile in order to create a pattern that fits with the crimes. For instance, one study profiles potential office rage murderers as white males between twenty-five and fifty years old, with low self-esteem, loners fascinated with weapons. However, a caveat is that within that group, those under thirty and with a history of violence and substance abuse were more likely to commit non lethal violence, while those over thirty, with no history of violence and no substance abuse and "unable to release their frustrations" were more likely to commit lethal violence in the workplace. Therefore you look for those over thirty years-old who have no history of violence or substance abuse, because they're the most dangerous employees of all. That really narrows it down. The only male employees left under this profile would be student-interns, retirees, and minorities.

Another profile, in *Violence in the Workplace*, claims that "history of violence" is a sign of a potential rage murderer contracting the profile above.

Anyone could snap anywhere; anyone's a suspect. And that means that employees go out of their way to make sure they're not perceived as being potentially dangerous, no matter how cruelly they are treated. Employees are so terrified of uttering the wrong quip, one that could be misconstrued, as even the slightest hint of disgruntlement could be grounds for a visit from police, a forced psychological examination, and a destroyed career. No, the only hope is to smile all the time and pray that no one notices how miserable you are—pray, in fact, that you yourself never know how miserable you are. And if you snap, then don't let it show until the morning you appear with your duffel bag.

3

Secrets to Company Hunting

CONTRARY TO THE GENERAL PERCEPTION of office massacres as random shootings by crazed loners who snap, nearly every rampage murderer targets both specific oppressors—usually supervisors—as well as the company in general. Targeting a company through murder and destruction might strike us as totally irrational, not to mention tactically unsound. In the first place, the shareholders are generally people or organizations far removed from the company premises. Second, a company isn't really a tangible thing. It is a structure, a legal setup, a concept, a link in a distribution chain. This is what makes a company seem so invulnerable and daunting to a disgruntled employee—the enemy is some kind of bewitching abstract. Its center of gravity is dispersed and diffused, so perfectly hidden that it makes going after the *Predator* monster seem like shooting fish in a barrel. The company is also a set of implanted impressions and emotions: the company is the routine, the system, the partitions and industrial carpeting, the workstations and company parking lot, the memo board and the gossip, the buzzing overhead fluorescent lights, the stench of cheap coffee grinds and morning breath, the other people's moods, the petty intrigues, morale, the Friday Casual Day, and the box of Krispy Kreme donuts in the break room. Yet the abstract company is also made up of concrete assets, and those assets include not only its cash, buildings, and equipment, but also its personnel. And, as the rampage murderers demonstrated, the abstract company is concretely represented by its image or its sanctity or its karma. Whatever you call that intangible, this "image" or "sanctity" is the company's soft underbelly. The rampage murderer who attacks his workplace seeks to kill the abstract company by killing its literal assets and splattering the image in blood, thereby killing both employees and company. Indeed, it is hard for a company to recover from a rampage murder. Some, like Standard Gravure, close forever.

4

A Mom and Pop Operation

LARRY HANSEL WORKED as an electronics engineer for Elgar Corporation, a San Diego tech company.

Elgar's description of itself in the early 1990s is impossibly saccharine in a familiar sort of way: despite annual sales of over $40 million, "it liked to think of itself as a mom and pop operation" that, they claimed, "strove to foster a family feeling among its employees."

An upsurge in orders forced Elgar's supervisors to assign Hansel a heavier workload, pushing him into more and more overtime. He apparently wasn't happy with the increasing burden, but the ma and pa corporate culture wouldn't listen. One could argue that Elgar's callous attitude towards Hansel's complaints fostered a truly genuine "family feeling"—anger and frustration. As the stress increased, Hansel ominously started name-dropping the post office massacre that took place in nearby Escondido two years earlier, resulting in three deaths.

So in 1991, as Hansel was buckling under the stress, Elgar fired Hansel. The firing came in response to a new policy in which Elgar ranked their employees in terms of their performance, and slashed the bottom five, Hansel being one of those five. At the meeting where he was fired, he "seemed calm enough," according to a supervisor. And who would know better than family? Not that there was a Ma and Pa Elgar present for the firing, or for the months of stress or the harassment and pressure that preceded the firing. News of Hansel's downsizing was handled by Hansel's supervisors.

Three months after getting fired, Hansel returned to Elgar Corp's office. He drew up a hit list of six executives—the Moms and Pops, if you will. When he

Ames

. reception area, he asked the woman at the phones for three of the exec-
. the list and was told that each of them weren't in. Hansel couldn't back
.ow or the element of surprise would be lost. He walked out of the building,
rig... .1 up several radio-controlled homemade bombs, stashed a mountain bike
not far from the entrance, and returned to the lobby, this time with a bandolier of
ammo draped over his shoulders and a shotgun held upright in one arm.

Hansel fired into the receptionist switchboard, blowing out the phone lines
(just as Wesbecker had started his spree). He set off two diversionary bombs in the
rear of the building by radio control, then walked up to the second floor, the executive floor. There he found two men standing near a fax machine—one, a general
manager on his hit list, and the other, a sales manager, just an innocent bystander.
Hansel shot and killed both of them.

Then he walked down the hall and entered the office of one of the targeted
executives, who had heard the blasts and darted underneath his desk. To Hansel,
the room appeared empty—the executive watched Hansel's feet as he sniffed the
room like a rage-raptor. Finally Hansel left and as he passed by the two sprawled
victims by the fax machine, he shot each of their corpses again for good measure.
Satisfied, Hansel walked downstairs and out of the lobby, chewing his gum, shotgun slung over his shoulder.

Now came the getaway, phase two of his plan. He hopped onto the mountain
bike and peddled away from the office—middle-aged technician with blood on his
hands. He peddled up to his pickup truck, which he'd parked far enough away to
make sure it wouldn't be spotted by employees. He ditched the bike, leaped in the
truck, and sped away, getting as far as Palm Desert, 130 miles to the east, before
turning himself in to police when he couldn't think of a phase three.

Hansel pleaded insanity "due to stress from work." According to Dr. S.
Anthony Baron, who studied the Elgar massacre for his management guide,
Violence in the Workplace, "He had been pushed to the breaking point by the loss of
his job. The focus of his fury was the company that dismissed him, specifically
Hansel's superiors. He made a decision to sacrifice himself for a cause against all
management."

Elgar Corporation survived the massacre. But it needed to make some changes
and reform. It finally understood that merely telling its employees and each other
that they were one big happy family without actually treating its employees like
family—unless you accept Joan Crawford as your model parent—wasn't working.
They might actually have to treat their employees like . . . human beings.

Hansel's gruesome murder may have brought about some good for the others,
but he hardly cuts a heroic figure. He was not a model of mental health. To begin
with, Hansel served as a delegate for the extremist Democratic presidential candidate Lyndon LaRouche in 1984, earning 521 votes in his district. That's 521 Hansels
just in one district! He believed that UFOs were landing in his backyard. And he
became increasingly obsessed with the Bible. Of course, if obsession with the Bible
and UFO landings were admitted as signs of mental illness, then roughly nine-
tenths of the American population would be strapped into asylum beds tomorrow,
and force-fed an IV-cocktail of Thorazine and Lithium. But even within this 90-per-
cent demographic, Hansel proved that he had gone the extra mentally ill mile with

his murder spree. That's about the most basic definition of good mental health there is: you only kill people when your government tells you to. Murder under any other circumstance—particularly if because you feel aggrieved—is ipso facto a sign of severe illness.

Insane or not, Hansel's bloody insurgency against his company had a surprisingly rational effect:

> Management agreed with the need for improved communication and the need to improve conditions at the plant. They realized that a gap existed between supervisors and employees, whose perception was that management didn't care, that they were only concerned with profit . . . . A new security system was implemented. Employees and visitors now wear badges.

Hansel the rage guerrilla may not have slain the beast, but he did force the corporation to change and become more just . . . and more militarized.

While the uninformed, general perception of the Larry Hansels is that they are simply nutcases who snapped, those closer to the case treated it not simply as an act of random lunacy, but rather something as rooted in the environment. The workplace helped incite the workplace massacre. Faced with the possible collapse of the company after Hansel's attack, Elgar's management was forced to at least pay lip service to humanizing their company culture, although they coupled this with the more common military American response—increased security. At the same time, Dr. Baron acknowledged that even though Hansel clearly had mental health issues he was also pushed into snapping, rather than snapping "randomly." Yet while Dr. Baron recognizes the role Elgar's callous and stressed corporate culture played in Hansel's rampage, and while he also notes that the crime of office rampages is entirely new, he doesn't draw larger conclusions about the cultural changes and causes of this crime. Rather, he offers management advice on how to profile potential rage-murder employees—what warning signs to look for and how to prevent rampages. In other words, like Kelleher and others who have looked closely at rage murder attacks in the workplace, the focus is not on the larger socio-economic shifts that produced this unique crime, but rather on helping corporations adjust their cultures in order to prevent these crimes from happening. By ignoring the broader underlying causes of these rage massacres—grotesque pay inequality, unbearable stress, job insecurity, and more work for less pay—Dr. Baron strengthens the current setup by helping managers make their corporations safer while continuing these practices, rather than arguing for a better life for its employees.

It is interesting that nearly all of the books on this crime are manuals and handbooks designed for management, published by specialized professional publishers, rather than books for a wider audience published by trade publishers. It is as if the broader implications—of linking rage massacres to changes in the corporate culture—are being held back from a wider audience.

5

Termination! Termination!

ROBERT MACK BEGAN WORKING for General Dynamics in San Diego right after high school, starting at age nineteen. His first assignment was in the plastic fabrication line. He never worked for another company in his life. Through twenty-five years of dedication to General Dynamics, Mack reached a fairly senior position as a "floater" on the assembly line, which meant that he would work in a number of different areas in the plant or on different missile lines. He had fairly high security clearance and used it to run errands or to move in and out of the plant at will.

Twenty-five years after starting his job, at the age of forty-two, Mack was fired. Fired, it should be noted, during the Christmas season in 1991 in the depths of California's worst recession since Reagan took office. Before he was fired, he had a paid vacation day docked for showing up one minute late to work.

Management's reason for firing Mack was that he had been slacking off at work. His supervisors kept a record of each tardiness or truancy. After twenty-five years of dedication to General Dynamics, Mack had started to slip. Management wasn't interested in why his performance had suddenly worsened, they just knew that he was starting to show up late at times and so they suspended him and sent him home over the Christmas holidays. Mack was divorced with three children and had a live-in girlfriend whom he was engaged to marry.

In a rare interview with Mack in the Department of Corrections San Louis Obispo Men's Colony (where Larry Hansel is also housed)—rare because Mack is alive (most rage murderers kill themselves), willing to talk, and very normal—he gave some amazing insights into the mind of a rage murderer, and into the world that drives a once-healthy worker insane.

The general foreman invited Mack to the industrial relations room, where he was brought before his direct supervisor, James English, and a young management representative named Michael Konz. Mack had been cornered without a union representative to protect him. Konz told Mack that he was being investigated for taking trips in and out of sensitive areas, which Mack agreed was reasonable given his security clearance. Then they sent him home without pay for the holidays. He was told the suspension was for three days and that they would notify him when the next meeting to discuss their problems would be.

As Mack told the interviewer, Steve Albrecht, "They took my badge and everything and they sent me home. . . . I had to go two long weeks without any pay. So what little Christmas money I had left over, I had to use that. . . . I'm hurting by then. This is a Merry Christmas and Happy New Year's and all that other stuff."

It is frightening—like having a terminal disease, like facing extinction. Mack, an African-American devoted to his factory job, felt the holiday pressure as deeply as any other white-collar worker.

But there was another twist here which Albrecht finally caught:

Albrecht: Let me see if I understand this. They suspend you for three days and then they told you not to come back for three more weeks until this hearing date?

Mack: Right.

A: So you sat home all that time?

M: All that time without pay. No welfare, no unemployment. No nothing, no organization, no nothing.

A: No help from the union?

M: Nothing from the union either.

Finally the termination letter comes—and it's a bombshell. Mack's account of how his mind reacted to what was essentially a death notice is one of the most poetic accounts of credulity cracking I have ever read, as if lifted straight from a Philip K. Dick nightmare:

M: When the letter came in the mail to me, I said to myself, "I finally got a letter to go back to work."

A: What were your thoughts and feelings?

M: Like my whole career is gone. I got a letter, right? And the letter said "termination." And I was stunned by termination. I tried to ball this letter up and it wouldn't ball up. It was still in my hands. So I tried stomping it with my feet and the letter was still in my hands. Then the letter burst into flames, and I sat there and shook it and tried to get it to go out until it finally went out.

A: That's what you were thinking or that's what was happening?

M: That's what was happening. And it kept saying "termination, termination." But I plugged my ears up so I couldn't hear the word termination. So, after that incident there, then it finally cooled down. I went and got some cold water and put the letter on top of the TV. When I came back into the room, termination, termination was what went through my head, termination. I've lost everything, everything I've worked for is gone. I'm not going back to work. What will the people think? How will I tell the people?

By "the people" Mack meant, first of all his fiancée, and then his family, friends, and co-workers. It was total devastation.

M: Everything was racing through my head, you know. And I went and sat down on the side of the bed and the TV burst into flames. Termination, termination. So I turned the TV off and I got into bed. I was laying in the bed and my pillow burst into flames—termination. Every time I would stop to sleep this letter would appear. It would appear and sometimes, it would chase me around the house and say, "termination,

termination." And no, I couldn't turn this off because it was consistently chasing me, consistently appearing for maybe five days in a row. Every time I napped. I couldn't sleep at night. I had to leave my leg hanging over the side of the bed, swinging it. So in case the letter came, I'd be able to wake up.

Over five days Mack, cracked, terrified, and despondent, sat alone in his house, never leaving, trying and failing to come to terms with his brutal termination. Twenty-five years—his entire adult life—gone. "I figured it was time to terminate myself," he said. "I couldn't stand it anymore." Mack bought a gun through an acquaintance, a .38 caliber revolver. Unlike so many abused American workers, Mack wasn't going to let the people who essentially killed him get off lightly with a clean conscience: "If I would have killed myself at home it would have been a domestic problem. So, I had to go back to work where the problem all started from."

Mack's girlfriend drove him to the termination hearing at General Dynamics. "I told her a few little small things, you know, goodbye, I loved you. I did everything I could to take care of you all." But he didn't tell her why he was saying that.

Mack entered the hearing with the two men who had terminated him, James English and Michael Konz, as well as his union representative. It was here that they dropped another little bomb: now he was being fired not for going in and out of the plant gate, but for absenteeism, which wasn't the reason he was initially suspended. The union rep tried to stand up for Mack but was ineffective. Mack here beautifully expresses the debilitating power of authority:

M: I kept wanting to talk so I could tell my side, and they wouldn't let me talk. . . They kept telling me to shut up and so I did. And I kept trying to talk about my absenteeism. I sat there in anger, trying to get my words out, and then my mouth started getting dry, and I couldn't get any saliva in my mouth. My head started tingling, my hands started tingling, and then I knew I had to get up and get some water. These are the same symptoms that came when the big flash came.

A: Did you get some water or anything?

M: I wanted to get some water. And when I went to get some water, this big blur came over me. And that's when the shooting started . . . something like a blackout. I call it a stroke, because I lost a lot of my memory and stuff like that. . . . After the shooting took place, I went outside [the hearing room] or I was already outside when the shooting took place. I had already shot one man in the back of the head.

A: English or Konz?

M: And English had already been shot and now Konz has been shot now. After shooting Konz, there was this Mexican man who was in the room. He worked in that room there. He was jumping up and down saying, "Don't do it, don't do it!" and that caught my eye. And when that caught my eye, it made me look back around to where I could see there were two men laying down on the ground.

What is so fascinating about this part of the interview is ⬛ artlessly Mack describes the actual cracking of a post-Reagan ⬛

In fact Mack was one small tragedy in a larger transfor ⬛ Dynamics. The company's culture underwent a radical shift aw ⬛ role as pillar of the sunny community to becoming an object of plunder for a lucky few executives and shareholders.

According to a PBS documentary, *Surviving the Bottom Line*, trouble began when local hero and Apollo astronaut William Anders took over as the new CEO of General Dynamics in 1991 and proceeded to fire thousands of workers. The reason for the firings? "Anders had worked a deal so that he would reap a huge bonus as General Dynamics's stock rose. And, catering to Wall Street by selling off divisions and laying off workers, Anders kept pushing the stock higher and higher."

While thousands of families were destroyed, Anders proved he had the right stuff to make it as a Reaganomics-fueled CEO, pocketing more than thirty million dollars in cash in three years and scoring about the same amount in stock options, while essentially junking the company. He fired thousands, spun off divisions with the usual devastating results, and stripped the rest of the company for his and his shareholders' personal stash.

As the PBS documentary showed, many or most of the jobs could have been saved—the same General Dynamics products were still being produced and sold, only now by spin-off firms stripped down and on the cheap. But that kind of sentimental claptrap doesn't hold water in the new corporate culture. The whole point of the asset-stripping, division spin-offs, and labor layoffs wasn't to "increase competitiveness," as the PR machines tell us, but rather to melt down the company silver and cash out quick.

It was in this climate of callous employer-employee relations that Mack was summarily fired without the company giving any thought to how it would affect his life.

Mack told Albrecht that Anders' brutal corporate policies directly affected worker morale, and the sense of rage:

A: When you read in the newspaper and see that [GD CEO] William Anders makes millions of dollars in salary and bonuses, and then they have all these layoffs, I'm sure that adds fuel to the fire?

M: Yeah, that adds fuel to the fire.

A: Do people talk about that on the line?

M: Yeah, they talk about that on the line. We can't get a nickel raise out of them but they can make $25 million. If that million dollars would float down through the system, it would make everyone a little more comfortable. That's management. That's the way management operates. . . . It used to be one, two people got laid off and that would be all right. Now you're talking about thousands of people getting laid off. Thousands of people losing their jobs and their homes, and stuff like that. This is where the pressure comes in.

Michael Konz, the management rep in the termination meeting whom Mack killed, was both a symbol and a manifestation of this newer, even more vicious mutation of the post–Reagan era corporate culture:

> **M:** It was the fact that they put that young kid [Konz] in there in a position to terminate people. . . . [T]hey put that young kid in there, knowing he's going to try and do his best job to be a "company man." But there should have been something in his mind that day that said, "Hey wait a minute, I'm only twenty-five years old. This man has worked here for twenty-five years. How can I terminate a man that's spent twenty-five years working here on the job, and I'm only twenty-five years old?"

What made this murder so significant is that Mack's lawyer, Michael Roake, managed to shift the focus away from a seemingly senseless crime committed by a crazed individual who snapped to putting General Dynamics and corporate America on trial. In San Diego, where everyone knew what General Dynamics had done, Roake found a sympathetic ear.

"It was necessary," Roake said, "because we had to remind the world that something caused this and, if nothing else, to echo the fact that the company's behavior brought this to a crisis point."

Mack directly responded to this issue in his interview with Albrecht when he managed to pose exactly the question that this book asks:

> **A:** Do you think that General Dynamics has policies that lead to this kind of [workplace violence] behavior?
>
> **M:** They have a policy there that makes you lose your wife, your house, your kids, your cars. . . .
>
> **A:** Do you feel that their policies put people in fear for their financial well-being?
>
> **M:** They put them in fear. Yes, that's true.
>
> **A:** How do you think you're different than the guy who's also treated like you but doesn't go back and do what you did? What's the difference between a guy who works for a boss who's a jerk and doesn't do anything, and the guy that works for a boss who's a jerk and does take some kind of violent action against him?
>
> **M:** Some people are afraid. Some things [the company does] put a lot of fear inside of them.
>
> **A:** So they're afraid to react or afraid to do something?
>
> **M:** They're afraid to react, plus [the company] is trying to create that atmosphere where it equals fear.

The Ticking Timebombs authors note: "It's hard to make much sense of this last exchange. Is Mack saying the work rules at General Dynamics make people afraid?" This is 1993: in just a few years, instilling a climate of fear would be openly acknowledged as an effective, if not the most effective, form of human resource exploitation. And fear works. Fear is what keeps all downtrodden people, whether slaves or dissidents, from rebelling.

By standing up for himself and fighting back, Mack comes off as a kind of R. P. MacMurphy at his workplace, rather than a loony murderer. Referring to an August 11, 1992, article in the San Diego Union-Tribune ("Workplace Traumatized by Slaying at Convair") Albrecht notes, "When you look at this piece, they talk about the fact that there are a lot of people who are sort of on your side. There are people at General Dynamics who claim, 'I'm not going to say that he did the right thing, but I can understand where he came from, and maybe if I had been in his spot, I'd have done it too.' How can this be possible?"

M: That's right. There's that much tension there.

A: How do you think you're perceived now by the people on the assembly line? Are you sort of a hero to them, or do they distance themselves from you?

M: Some of them feel like that, "That's the man, that's the one that broke the camel's back. Now the pressure won't be on us as much." Because now [General Dynamics management] are starting to change their ways. . . . Union and management policies. I'm sure that I'm not making any remarks for anyone to go out and do the same thing I did, but I'm sure that it's going to continue happening.

Just as some of the survivors of the Standard Gravure massacre expressed sympathy with Joseph Wesbecker, Mack was, to many, a kind of hero. This is a crucial point, because in the case of real random murders like serial murders, survivors never express sympathy with the murderer. However, in rebellions, survivors of attacks often do sympathize, particularly if the rebel belongs to the same oppressed group as they do.

Roake argued successfully that Mack's sole intention was to kill himself in a manner and in a place that would call media attention to what he perceived to be the callousness of corporate America. The jury could not reach a verdict, and the judge declared a mistrial. In a retrial, Mack copped a plea bargain getting life imprisonment with possible parole after seventeen years.

A: This is kind of a hard question to answer. If you had to do it over again, everything being the same, would you have chosen the same route or . . . ?

M: No. But then again, I was at the point where there was nothing left in my life.

In other words, yes.

6

A Mellow Guy

WILLIE WOODS FELT LIKE his supervisors were singling him out for harassment. For six months now they were "picking on" him. He was sure he was on the way to losing his job as a radio repairman at the Piper Technical Center in downtown Los Angeles.

On July 19, 1995, Woods appeared at work on a day when he decided that enough was enough: he wasn't going to take their harassment. He wasn't going to allow the bastards to ruin his life and get away with it. Sure enough, the supervisors were on his case again. First thing in the morning, Woods was brought into a meeting with his bosses, given an official reprimand, and notified that he faced getting fired. Witnesses reported hearing shouting coming from the meeting. At 10 am, Woods left the supervisor's office, grabbed a nineteen-round Glock semiautomatic pistol from his belongings, and returned to launch his preemptive strike. He shot and killed two supervisors whom he believed had been terrorizing him while they were still seated in their cubicles, then headed out of the office and downstairs in search of his other tormentors. He found one, also a supervisor, in the hallway. Woods shot and killed him, then hunted down the fourth supervisor who was hiding in an office, crouched and cowering against his desk. Unlike Hansel at Elgar, Woods was a thorough rage murderer. He entered the fourth victim's office, peered around, found the crouching supervisor, and shot and killed him.

After the massacre of four supervisors, co-workers who knew Woods expressed surprise and confusion, saying Woods "seemed like a mellow guy."

Indeed, after getting his sense of justice, he returned to his mellow state. Two cops from a police gang unit happened to be in the building during the shootings and responded to the gunfire. Woods quickly surrendered to them without resistance. He was sentenced to life without parole.

7

Tuan & Song

ABOUT TWENTY MILES SOUTH of the Piper Technical Center, in an industrial South-Central L.A. suburb deceptively named Santa Fe Springs, Tuan Nguyen pulled up to the company that had fired him two weeks before.

It was cool that day, March 14, 1994, when Nguyen approached Extron Electronics' factory entrance. He punched in the five-digit security code, opened the door, and stormed onto the assembly floor, clutching a high-caliber pistol. His objective: the supervisor's office at the other end of the plant. As is often the case in these murder sprees, the killer wound up paving his path to the supervisor's throne with the bodies of seemingly innocent fellow workers, the inevitable collateral damage in these rampage rebellions. As he crossed the factory, Nguyen shot several co-workers, starting with Chris Newell, an electronics repairman who had just earned his B.A. in engineering, and had announced to the crew that he'd gotten engaged. Nguyen fired two bullets into Newell's back, killing him almost instantly.

To be fair, Nguyen shouted to the panicking, scrambling workers, "Get down or get out of the way!" One man who didn't heed him was Son Van Truong, one of the plant's most skilled repairmen, who had been saving up to open his own TV repair shop. Nguyen shot him in the back of the head.

A nearby worker heaved and vomited, then dove under a table head-first, his ass sticking out. It was too tempting a target to pass up: Nguyen nailed the exposed ass with a single shot.

Nguyen paused to reload his gun. Cocked and ready, he literally sprinted across the cement floor, underneath the powerful fluorescent lights, to his true target—the supervisor. On his way to the management offices, he bumped into Song Sabandith, a thirty-nine-year-old Laotian immigrant, who in a fit of panic raised his hands and pleaded in his native language, "Man, don't shoot! I surrender!" It could have been a replay of the centuries-old Vietnamese domination of the Laotion people, except that as is so often the case in these rage murders, potential targets perceived as particularly friendly, sympathetic, or harmless are often consciously spared. In this case, Nguyen elbowed the pleading Sabandith aside and shot another man standing nearby twice in the back.

Sabandith fell to his knees in tears, but Nguyen resumed the sprint to his ex-supervisor's office and kicked the door down. The supervisor's desk was empty—she had just left for lunch when Nguyen entered the building, just as Bill Bland happened to sleep in late on the morning of Patrick Sherrill's postal spree, or as Michael Shea happened to be out on the day of the Standard Gravure massacre. This common plot twist to rage attacks—that the targeted supervisor often happens to be out of the office while his or her minions take the bullets—is a fitting metaphor for the entire post-Reagan era. Nguyen apparently decided that he had to kill some kind of supervisor or all this would have been for naught. So he shot the most convenient person, Teresa Pham, in the heart. Pham had once trained Nguyen to assemble computer interfaces. She died instantly.

Satisfied that he had killed at least one member of the supervisor class, Nguyen completed the operation by pressing the gun to his temple and blowing the side of his head out.

8

"I'm not gay!"

THREE YEARS LATER, in that same industrial suburb, another office rampage murder took place. Two rampage murders in one suburb, Santa Fe Springs, population fifteen thousand. Daniel Marsden, a quality control inspector at the Omni Plastics Factory, complained that employees were mocking him behind his back, accusing him among other things of being a homosexual. On June 5, 1997, Marsden was heard getting into a shouting match with some fellow employees. He burst out of the factory, grabbed a 9mm semiautomatic handgun, and stormed in blasting everything and everyone, all the while screaming, "I'm not gay! I'm not gay!"

In the melee he managed to kill two workers, one Latino the other Arab. He wounded another four.

Employees at the plant did a good job of keeping mum on the circumstances of Marsden's snapping. One said he "appeared to be firing at random," even though the report showed that after hitting his first two victims Marsden ran into a meeting room and shot three company employees. One man tried to escape the room; Marsden chased him down and shot him dead. In all, he fired fifteen or sixteen shots.

He fled in his car and parked outside a Mexican grocery store. He told two passing women that today was the last day of his life . . . and after they rolled their eyes, he made good on his word, shooting himself in the mouth.

Afterward, an Omni Plastics vice president maintained that the murder made no sense and that Marsden had been shooting at people "with whom he had seemed to enjoy conversations."

At the very least we can say that Marsden was victimized by bullying and harassment of the sort that pushed Wesbecker and others, including many schoolyard rage rebels, over the edge. Indeed many schoolyard shooters, such as Columbine's Eric Harris and Dylan Klebold, or those in Paducah and Santee, were called "gay" and "fags" by their tormentors. Patrick Sherrill was also rumored to be a homosexual by co-workers at one job. The VP's complete misunderstanding of the circumstances that led to the shooting spree—insisting that Marsden somehow "enjoyed conversation" with the people he then shot, is sufficiently deluded and likely points to deeper corporate culture problems at the plant. But what we can say is this: Marsden felt abused, and he rebelled in the same way that increasing numbers of workers had rebelled before him and after.

Marsden's example is also useful because it is packed with all of the painful black comedy that seems to accompany so many American rebellions, whether officially recognized like the Whiskey Rebellion or Negro Fort, or the as yet unrecognized solo uprisings of our time. The idea of a middle-aged quality control manager screaming "I'm not gay! I'm not gay!" while shooting his co-workers brings to mind South Park's Mr. Garrison: "Gee Mr. Hat, I can't wait till this rampage murder is over so I can get myself some poontang." You can say that again, Mr. Marsden.

9

A Nondescript Warren of an Office

The first reports of the lottery rage massacre at the Connecticut state lottery gave the impression that the shooter, thirty-five-year-old accountant Matthew Beck, was a barking lunatic: he had been treated for mental illness and suicidal tendencies, and now he had finally gone over the edge, slaughtering his co-workers with all the deranged purpose of a Freddy Krueger. He played paintball, they noted. At his father's house, where Beck lived his last six months, a sign read, "Trespassers will be shot. Survivors will be shot again." But the most chilling image was that of Beck standing over his last victim in the office parking lot with the gun aimed at the man's head. The victim pleaded for his life and the frightened co-workers, who were hiding in the nearby woods, yelled for Beck to spare him. But Beck just smiled and shot the man in cold blood before turning the gun on himself.

Yet what emerged later from more comprehensive accounts was far more ambiguous than first allowed.

Matthew Beck worked at the Connecticut state lottery as an accountant for eight years. He was considered a hardworking and loyal employee, but near the end he grew angry and disgruntled because he was not getting the promotions he felt he deserved. In our post-Reagan culture, most Americans would instinctively side with Beck's supervisors, operating on the assumption that corporations generally operate like efficient meritocracies rather than crude popularity contests. Yet in each American's own private experience, we know how profound a role the supposed non-occupational factors—office politics, personal relations, connections, petty malice, attendance at the company barbeque, hygiene, fashion, one's ability to smile and make it look sincere, a sense of humor (or what passes for a sense of humor in the office world), as well as sheer luck and circumstance—play in an employee's ability to advance up the company ladder.

Beck was described by his co-workers as a "diligent and quiet" employee, a subtle way to describe an employee who doesn't play for the company softball team or peck his fellow workers with wacky jokes and anecdotes. Beck had hoped to get promoted at last to associate accountant, which would have made him a supervisor and increased his pay. But he was skipped over, despite his work and seniority. To make matters worse, less than six months before his murder rampage he was assigned to do data processing on top of his stagnating accounting duties. This was adding insult to injury—especially as they underpaid him for the new work by roughly two dollars per hour, according to a grievance that he filed and subsequently won.

Was he passed over for promotion because of poor performance? One supervisor whom he spared, Karen Kalandyk, admitted that when it came to computers, "He was so much beyond the rest of us that you tried to use his talents." His problem then? He couldn't communicate. "He couldn't tell us what he knew," Kalandyk said. In other words, he didn't join in the depressing Soup Nazi citation-tournaments with other employees over by the water cooler.

In August 1997, Beck filed a grievance against the state to complain about his unfair treatment. Fellow employees say that around this time Beck changed, both physically and emotionally. He went from being a quiet, diligent worker to a broken and bitter man.

"He was always angry about not being promoted," one supervisor said.

"He became visibly withdrawn into himself [around the time that he filed his grievance]," said John Krinjack, a lottery sales rep. "He took on a severe look, an angry look. He looked like he had lost weight and gotten pale. For a while there, I thought he was really pale."

There is no indication that this obvious physical deterioration elicited any sympathy or support from Beck's supervisors or co-workers. Rather, what they conveyed to reporters is something like revulsion. Clearly he didn't fit into the frat-house, and they did their best to push him out.

"He looked a little evil in a way," said another accountant, David Perlot. "He talked a little sinister, like. He struck me as odd, not the kind of person that I wanted to get close to."

Was he always this way? Was he born weird and evil, or did his experience at the Connecticut lottery somehow deform his personality? Here is how a shocked childhood friend, Herbert Vars, described Beck: "He was the all American guy. He was Mr. Clean-cut."

Another childhood friend said that going back to elementary school, he had never even seen Beck argue with someone. "I would never have expected it from him," he said, noting that they had continued to hang out and even hike together until Beck's downward spiral.

Yet after eight years as an accountant with the state lottery, he was "odd," not the type that "I wanted to get close to." His missed promotion had less to do with his work performance, and more to do with the conditioned behavior his superiors wanted of their underlings. Beck did not have the cheerful attitude that masters prefer.

Two months after filing the grievance, Beck took a medical leave, suffering from the effects of stress. He was falling apart. It must have been painful for Beck to not only work for and take orders from people who refused to promote him, but worse, for people who ordered him to work more for no extra pay, people who must have been quietly and subtly getting their revenge on him for filing the grievance. Beck's relationship with his girlfriend suffered. He moved back home with his parents, underwent treatment at a psychiatric hospital, and started to take psychiatric medicines. He even tried committing suicide.

For someone clearly intelligent, industrious, and quiet like Beck to get rejected and mistreated by his workplace after eight years of hard, quiet, diligent work, which even after his shooting spree was described as "so much beyond the rest of us that you tried to use his talents," must have struck him as an injustice of cosmic proportions. When he was finally denied his promotion, he essentially saw it as the end of his life.

I loved my job. That's all I lived for, was to go to work and come home.
—**Robert Mack,** fired General Dynamics rage killer

While on leave, Beck turned whistleblower. He went to the local newspapers exposing corruption in the Connecticut Lottery. In November 1997, lottery officials admitted that they had inflated their figures for years by rounding up numbers to the nearest half million.

"They need to increase (revenues) by thirty million dollars and they're under a lot of pressure to let other things take a back seat," Beck told the *New London Day* newspaper.

He also exposed to the *Hartford Courant* how some store clerks were cheating the system by "fishing" for instant winning tickets. The clerks would punch code numbers into lottery computers until they came up with the winning combination and then they'd take the cash. Lottery officials at the time of the shooting spree refused to comment on this allegation.

Beck also tried to interest reporters in his own employment grievance against the lottery. But they didn't bite. According to an Associated Press story, here is why: "The *Courant* described him as frothing at the mouth and said his eyes were 'wild,' while the *Day* described him as 'scruffy' in appearance." There's quite a difference between appearing scruffy and frothing at the mouth—perhaps what they simply meant was that Beck didn't smile much.

Try to understand Beck's profound sense of dislocation. Here he worked for the state lottery, which by definition is already a sleazy enterprise, a government-run scam that preys, like all gambling dens, on the desperate dreams of predominately lower-class fools. And even in this officially sanctioned scam, the state was scamming its own scam to make the scam look like it was working! Yet the same corrupt supervisors who were fixing the scam were, at the same time, passing judgment on Beck's life, condemning him to stagnation not for being a bad worker, but for not being one of the boys. And Beck was the crazy one? He was expected to shut up and take it?

> "I saw no prospect that my condition would ever be changed. Yet I used to plan in my mind from day to day, and from night to night, how I might be free."
> —*The Narration of Lunsford Lane,* a slave memoir published in 1842

Otho Brown, the lottery president, told the media that the lottery's practice of inflating figures had been stopped. Brown was the man Beck later shot in the parking lot.

In January 1998, Beck won the first part of his grievance against the lottery. So he wasn't imagining his injustice. But the damage had already been done—he was crushed. While still awaiting the grievance board's ruling on his back pay, Beck decided to return to work. His colleagues were openly hostile upon seeing him return. They had him marked as a loser.

As one employee, who asked to remain anonymous, told the *New York Times,* "He knew he wasn't going to go anywhere. Management distrusted him."

In February 1998, just a week after returning to work at the lottery, one of Beck's supervisors gave him the task of tracking lottery employees who were given state vehicles as a fringe benefit. It must have been like salt in the wounds: "Why don't you monitor other privileged employees who gets the perks we've denied you?"

The office massacre took place on March 6. Like the word "stress," "office" is far too simple a word to describe both the oppressive spirit of the place and also the typical degrading interior. It cannot describe how, by sheer dehumanizing design, it flattens you with that horrible fluorescent light, those white walls, beige cubicle partitions, the trim industrial carpeting, the disinfectant-scented restroom stalls, and the buzzing vending machines . . .

One local reporter described the state lottery office as a "nondescript warren of offices . . . a maze like collection of cubicles and small offices, connected by narrow hallways to still more offices in the one story concrete block building."

The *New York Times* reporter on the scene offered this picture:

> It is an ordinary building, beige, with a warehouse in the back, but to many people, the headquarters of the Connecticut Lottery is a place of fantasy where the big winners go to pose with the big cardboard check. They follow the bright yellow "Prize Claim Center" sign into a special reception area and collect jackpots from six hundred to hundreds of thousands of dollars.
>
> There is another entrance, one used by the secretaries, accountants, data processors and other employees who keep the Connecticut Lottery humming. They must punch in a security code to enter the rabbit's warren of cubicles and partitions.
>
> An outsider could easily get turned around in this maze, but Matthew Beck, an accountant, had worked at the lottery for more than eight years. He knew where he was going, and on Friday morning, he knew what he wanted to do.

In other words, an office just like any other. Did the journalists who wrote these descriptions understand that they were describing part of the murder spree's cause?

It was Casual Friday at this nondescript warren of offices, a day which most well-conditioned American workers greet cheerfully. But in its own subtle way the concept of Casual Day is just another demeaning reminder of how much power the company has over you, even commanding how you look and dress, when you need to stiffen up and when you can relax. Even slaves had their version of Casual Friday. As Robert Anderson noted in *From Slavery to Affluence*, "The slave on a plantation could get together almost anytime they felt like it, for little social affairs, so long as it didn't interfere with the work on the plantation."

Matthew Beck wore jeans and a brown leather jacket for Casual Day. At the start of the workday, Beck was seen speaking to his former data processing supervisor, Michael Logan. Logan was the first to deny Beck's grievance over his non-promotion, before the complaint was taken to a higher authority. And Logan was the IT manager who oversaw Beck's humiliating and illegal added workload for no extra pay the year before, when he was moved to data processing work. A co-worker said that Beck looked "real ticked off" while talking to Logan.

Linda Mlynarczyk, the chief financial officer and Beck's senior supervisor in the accounting wing (another key oppressor from his experience), walked past and told Beck to take off his coat. It was thirty minutes into the work day and keeping your leather coat on was not in the spirit of Casual Day. But Beck wasn't in a Casual Day mood. So he answered her curtly: "No."

Logan finished talking with Beck and walked back to his office. Beck sat at his cubicle for a few minutes, staring off into space. At 8:45 AM he stood up and walked into Logan's office. After a brief confrontation, Beck pulled out a military-style knife and plunged it into Logan's stomach and chest, killing him.

He then backtracked toward the front of the building and barged into a meeting room. Again, the privileged-class meeting room acts as focal point for the raging insurgent. The meeting was led by Mlynarczyk and attended by four other employees in the accounting department.

Beck keyed in on his objective: the CFO herself. He pulled out a Glock 9mm semiautomatic handgun from his coat, pointed it at Mlynarczyk, and said, "Bye-bye." He shot Mlynarczyk three times, killing her. Just a few days before she had met with Beck to explain to him his new duties, now that he had returned to work. It is not hard to imagine how uncomfortable that meeting must have been for the humiliated, aggrieved Beck; nor is it difficult to imagine the subtle way that a supervisor who dislikes her employee can transmit contempt.

Mlynarczyk had previously served as mayor of nearby New Britain, a city of seventy thousand with a large ethnic-Polish population. She was the first Republican to be elected mayor of New Britain in twenty years—and she was tossed out after just one term. Her single term was marked by controversy over the fact that she had privatized the city cemetery and named her fiancé the corporation counsel. She also forced the city union to make concessions to lower expenses and make New Britain more "business-friendly." While she may have been for the free market and fair competition, when it came to her own fortunes Mlynarczyk practiced familiar Old Europe rules of the back-scratching nepotism sort. She was the first mayor in Connecticut to endorse Republican John Rowland for governor, so when she lost re-election and he won, the victorious Rowland duly appointed her CFO of the state lottery. As CFO, she was responsible for the lottery's numbers which were later admitted to have been cooked—though she never took a fall for the lottery accounting scandal. Beck got destroyed by her and other supervisors for much less. Meanwhile, her patron, Governor Rowland, was forced to resign as governor in the summer of 2004 in the wake of a federal corruption probe and numerous ethics violations that were building toward an impeachment. He was the first Connecticut governor ever to have been fined for ethics violations prior to his resignation.

Beck shot Mlynarczyk dead. But rather than shooting the others in the meeting room, employees whom Beck knew well, "He just lowered the gun and walked away," said mid-level supervisor Kalandyk, the same one who had complimented Beck's intelligence in the *New York Times*. "I made eye contact, and his eyes were dead."

Another colleague in the room noted that Beck "gave him a grin or a smirk" before walking out.

In the hallway, there was pandemonium as workers screamed and fled through the maze of cubicles toward the warehouse.

Mlynarczyk's office was located in the executive suite, which worked out well for Beck. Her office was next Frederick Rubelmann III, vice president of operations, who opened his door and asked, "Is everyone okay?" Rubelmann was one of the executives who had rejected Beck's promotion to associate accountant. Rubelmann confronted Beck head-on—and was shot and killed.

By this time many of the hundred employees had escaped to the gravel parking lot. Beck sprinted after them, hunting down his last and biggest target, Lottery president Otho Brown. It was the fifty-four-year-old Brown who had final say on signing off on the rejection for Beck's promotion. Now, hunted and pursued by his disgruntled worker, Brown was leading the employees toward a nearby forest for safety. Beck staggered outside and sprinted after his co-workers, the left leg of his jeans soaked in his victims' blood. Some employees dove into ditches, others dispersed, sinking into the soft mud.

Brown apparently detoured back to the gravel parking lot. Some employees claimed that he was a hero, trying to save his employees by using himself as bait to draw Beck away from them and toward him.

Brown was caught alone in the gravel parking lot, trying to flee. Beck, an avid jogger and hiker, quickly overtook him. Brown backpedaled as Beck closed in. The Lottery president held up his hands and cried, "No, Matt!" then tripped and fell on his back.

Beck stood over his boss with the Glock aimed at his head. The employees who had safely hidden in the forest marsh yelled out at Beck not to shoot.

One fellow accountant yelled, "Matthew, don't! Matthew don't!" while others screamed. Brown pleaded for his life and held his hands up defensively. Beck stood over him for a moment, breathing hard. He raised his pistol—Brown put up his hand to shield himself—and fired twice. Brown went still as the employees in the woods screamed and cried. Beck stood for a moment, walked around Brown's limp body, then shot the corpse again, causing it to jerk.

Just then a white police car came tearing into the parking lot. Beck put the pistol up to his head and shot himself through the temple. Somehow the gun went off twice. His body collapsed to the ground.

Was Matthew Beck crazy? As one supervisor in the meeting room who survived described his choice of victims, "They were the people who had the power in the Lottery. They were the ones who had turned down his promotion."

His parents released a statement to the press, noting, "His murderous act was monstrous, but he was not a monster, as his friends and family can attest."

10

The Summer of Rage

THE TERRORIST SLAUGHTER on 9/11 seemed to put a temporary freeze on rage murders, both in schoolyards and in offices. A lot of stuff was put on hold then— including the Constitution and the Bill of Rights, and even this book, which was started and abruptly canceled after my first publisher's editor told me, in the aftermath of 9/11, "There's no way we can sell a book like this now."

As soon as the culture got acclimated to the terrorism-fear and constant war-footing, office massacres returned with a vengeance. In 1998, there were nine recorded workplace massacres; in 2003, there were forty-five, leaving sixty-nine dead and forty-six wounded.

The terrorist attack on 9/11 was a shock and distraction to the general population; however, the same underlying socioeconomic conditions existed as before. In fact, under President Bush, Reaganism only got Reaganier. Not only was there a recession that bordered on a crisis, but Bush's jaw-dropping economic policies further widened the socio-economic moat by transferring another couple trillion dollars of national wealth to the super-rich through unprecedented tax cuts for the top two percent and credits for large corporations, by record boosts in funding to the military-industrial complex, and by imposing further cuts in programs aimed at the middle and lower-middle classes. This final, gargantuan wealth transfer push will outlast Bush for decades. Indeed, when Bush first took power, his administration floated the idea of ending corporate taxes altogether, shifting more burden onto the "individual" (a euphemism for the middle class). The first part of Bush's second term was devoted to the "privatization" of Social Security, a thinly disguised trick to eventually kill the whole program and further enrich a few plutocrats. A study by University of Chicago economist Austan D. Goolsbee showed that Wall Street firms stood to earn up to a trillion dollars in trading fees if the plan goes through.

Bush's rush to make America feudal has become so obscene that it straddles the line between cheap comedy and gratuitous evil, as if his economic policy was the product of a plutocrat's gag, just to see how far they could take things, to see how much they could get away with. Here, for example, is a typical article that will come to define George W. Bush's presidency:

YACHT OWNERS ENJOYING HUGE PERKS, TAX BREAKS
Law allows wealthy to write off pricey purchases in several ways
By Eric Nalder
Seattle Post-Intelligencer
Wednesday, November 10, 2004

Some ultra-rich yacht buyers are expecting to deduct millions from their income tax next year by depreciating their pleasure craft under the provisions of the Bush administration's tax-relief program passed by Congress in 2003. About 500,000 boat owners nationwide can decrease

their income-tax bill every year by declaring their vessels a second home.
. . . Several yacht sellers gathered at the floating boat show on South Lake Union last month said most of the big pleasure boats on the water are supported by tax incentives.

This is the setting for the Summer of Rage. The months of July and August, 2003, which were among the bloodiest ever in the brief history of workplace rage murders, built on a trend since 1998 of increasing numbers of workplace homicides. The bloodbath began promptly on July 1, when an employee at Modine Manufacturing in Jefferson City, Missouri, shot and killed three co-workers, wounded four others, and later killed himself as police closed in. Some said he seemed to fire at random, but others on the scene said that he clearly picked out targets and deliberately spared others. Ironically, his .40 Glock handgun was a Missouri State Highway Patrol–issue gun that he bought at a local dealer—it even had the MSHP markings. One co-worker claimed that the suspect, twenty-five-year-old Jonathon Russell, was on probation at work for having clocked out early on some overnight shifts, but a company spokesman denied this. A local CBS affiliate reported that the plant, which had 140 employees, was planning layoffs. Russell had recently separated from his wife and moved into a trailer home with his mother. Neighbors and employees described him as "quiet" and "nice" and "not at all the type." Russell also reportedly had a crippling gambling habit. He would frequent the Isle of Capri casino in nearby Boonville, Missouri, with his mother. The casino's website cheerfully proclaims, "Grab your own slice of paradise at the only tropical oasis of fun and excitement in the heart of Missouri. Our 28,000 square foot casino will sizzle with 900 slots and 35 table games, three signature restaurants, a retail and entertainment center, and a historic display area in the pavilion." Russell and his mother went there often, gambling away his meager wages. He left the rigged game of the post-Reagan workforce for the even more obscenely rigged game of the legal gambling den. As Robert DeNiro says in Casino, "We're the only winners. The players don't stand a chance." The Isle of Capri's general manager told reporters that Russell was a good customer who "hit none of the triggers" of a problem-gambler. That is, he never got angry or asked for help after they cleaned him out. It's a depressing picture: these lonely, struggling middle Americans, mother and son, getting swindled in the air-conditioned, carpeted comfort of an officially sanctioned fleecing scheme. You can almost hear the cheesy country pop cover band playing, smell the mix of old stale tobacco smoke and Freon, as Russell and his mother glumly spend another losing night at the Isle of Capri.

The very next day, in San Angelo, Texas, a fifty-year-old Verizon Wireless employee, Rodney James Moncke, shot his supervisor four times in the torso, killing him, and then turned the gun on himself. A message board for disgruntled Verizon employees, Verizoneatpoop.com, posted this comment on the day of the massacre, showing yet again the common yet censored sympathy for these murder sprees:

Name:	Anonymous
Date/Time:	7/10/2003 2:09:14 PM
City:	n/a
State:	New York

Grievance: I heard an employee in Texas went postal—shot a manager then himself! Has anyone heard about this? What department was he in? Management should take a look at the situation, could become an epidemic due to working conditions! I'm surprised it took so long for something like this to happen. Then again, Verizon will eliminate all employees one way or another. Layoff, suicide . . . stock goes up as the head count & service levels go down. If the manager weren't dead VZ would prob. give em a big bonus for eliminating yet another worker. Then again, the dead manager's boss will likely get a promotion for eliminating 2 employees. If that doesn't make any sense to you, then you obviously have never worked for VZ!

Incidentally, just as I wrote this chapter, a twenty-two-year-old Verizon customer in Fargo, North Dakota, went berserk at a local mall to protest the awful service he was getting from the company. Here is what happened:

May 14, 2004
FARGO, North Dakota (AP)—A man who said he was fed up with his cellular phone service went to a Fargo mall and started hurling phones across a store, striking an employee and causing more than $2,000 in damage, authorities said.

Jason Perala, 22, of Fargo, told The Forum newspaper that he planned only to yell at employees at Verizon Wireless.

"Then I just lost it," he said. "I just started grabbing computers and phones and throwing them. I just destroyed the place. . . . I kind of regret that I did it, but I hope my message got across."

Police said Perala took off his shirt and put on safety glasses before throwing around computers, phones and other items.

One employee was struck in the shoulder by a phone before he and other workers dashed into an office, locked the door and called police, Sgt. Kevin Volrath said. Other businesses in the West Acres mall lowered their steel security gates during Thursday's incident.

This isn't a classic case of employee rage, of course, but clearly there's something wrong with Verizon's human relations strategy—and its corporate culture. In 2002, Verizon cut eighteen thousand jobs, and in that same year it earned $4 billion in profits on $67 billion in revenues. The downsizing worked so well that in 2003 they started laying off workers in union-friendly states and shifting the jobs into union-free states, as well as announcing new massive layoffs, sparking large-scale telecom union strikes. To no one's surprise, the union bent to Verizon's will, signing a deal in September 2003 on behalf of its worker-members allowing the company, in an unprecedented cave-in, to fire its workers at will in the future, as well as offering the usual concessions: wage freezes, healthcare and retirement benefit cuts, and so on and so on. All this while the company was making literally billions in profits. One wonders what the workers would have got had they not gone on strike. Sold as Soylent Green meat, perhaps? Meanwhile their executives were paid more than half a billion dollars in salaries and bonuses between 1997 and 2001. Verizon CEO Ivan Seidenberg earned more than $58.4 million in 2002 alone. In the months after the union caved, they downsized another 21,000 employees and earned $1.6 billion in profit. Wealth transfers just don't get much more clear-cut than that.

The Piccolo Petes and Roman candles had just been cleaned up when, on July 8, a worker at a Lockheed-Martin plant in Meridian, Mississippi, shot and killed five co-workers, wounded seven, then killed himself with a shotgun blast to the heart right in front of his live-in girlfriend. Initial reports painted the killer, Doug Williams, as a racist freak who targeted blacks. However, a deeper look at the murder spree, once again, provides a far less conveniently evil portrait of the murderer. For one thing, Williams shot an equal number of blacks and whites (though more blacks died as a result of their wounds than whites), and Williams clearly avoided shooting some blacks during the spree. Lauderdale County Sheriff Billy Sollie said that Williams "passed by several blacks during the shootings, first aiming his shotgun at them, then raising it away."

If anything distinguishes this spree from the others, it's the over-the-top irony of where it started: Williams opened fire during a mandatory sensitivity-training seminar for employees, seminars which taught ethics and respect in the workplace. None of the media's reports remarked on this obvious irony, nor the even darker triple-irony of a workplace massacre in a weapons plant (which produced parts for the C130-J transport planes and F-22 Raptor jets) that forced its workers to attend sensitivity courses. With distance, the irony is almost too obvious—it would get cut from even the lamest sitcom script. But for anyone who has had to endure these ineffective, ridiculous sensitivity seminars, the thought-police aspect is enough to set a person off. Companies hire these sensitivity seminar swindlers to bring their act to the company staff with only one goal in mind: to indemnify the executives and shareholders. Everyone knows that sensitivity training seminars don't work, especially when administered in a weapons plant in Mississippi. If anything, they engender more cynicism and anger. Like so many corporate policies over the past twenty-five years, sensitivity seminars are imposed on employees with little care for their effectiveness in creating a genuinely collegial atmosphere. If they wanted employees to love each other more, they should give them job security and a bigger cut of the profits. Employees aren't stupid either—they know they're being forced to attend for the shareholders' benefit, not for their moral betterment. It only adds insult to injury, rage to humiliation.

During the sensitivity seminar that morning, Williams angrily stormed out, returned with a 12-gauge shotgun, a .223-caliber semiautomatic rifle, and a bandoleer of ammunition . . . and opened fire. One of the first to die was a white co-worker, Mickey Fitzgerald, who turned to Williams and said, "Doug, you don't really want to do this." Williams replied, "Yes, I do," and shot him in the face. While Williams clearly wasn't enlightened on the race issue, an employee wounded in the shooting later testified that Williams was trying to shoot the plant manager and the production manager. He wounded one target but the other got away.

Williams, a father of two, got chewed out by his bosses in front of his girlfriend that very morning because he punched into work at a different spot than usual and was then forced by the same insensitive bosses to go to a sensitivity seminar that teaches respect for his fellow workers. It was also reported that he had been recently passed up for a promotion. Williams's relatives said the shooting was not racially motivated, but the result of a workplace climate that allowed the twenty-year employee to be "picked on" by other workers and singled out by management who ignored his concerns. One of those he injured was Steve Cobb, the plant manager. At the end of the ten minute shooting spree, he came upon his girlfriend, Shirley Price, who held up her hands and pleaded with him to stop. Williams put the shotgun to his chest and shot himself in the heart. A few days later at the memorial service held for the victims in the First Baptist Church, Price interrupted the mayor's eulogy and cried out, "Excuse me. Don't criticize this man. He was a human being, too." She waved the service's program, which included the names of those killed and wounded, and said, "His name was not on here . . . .He was a victim too . . . . He was a kind and loving man." Then, according to CBS, "Several people attending the service stood up and applauded."

Details like these repeat themselves often in rage murder cases. While the attacker is often labeled whatever the most evil strain of the day is (Nazi, racist, Jacobin), that motive doesn't hold up under further investigation, and instead it often turns out that the attacker was abused at work. Victims of a shooting don't usually stand up to applaud cries to recognize the murderer's humanity. But time and again, in these rage murders, we see victims and relatives of victims expressing this sympathy, proving that the real enemy isn't the criminal but the culture that made him snap.

The long, hot Summer of Rage was just picking up steam. On July 21, in the Detroit suburb of Livonia, Michigan, a twenty year-old man armed with a .25 caliber automatic pistol threatened to shoot a co-worker and himself at Iron Mountain Secure Shredding. He showed up for work and asked to see his supervisor before brandishing the gun. "His plan for today was take a gun to work, shoot the employee and then himself," said Lt. Benjamin McDermott. "But he couldn't bring himself to do it." The standoff ended four hours later with his peaceful surrender, making this rage-surrender a rare exception. Perhaps the twenty-year-old was still young enough to be lulled by hope. Perhaps he hadn't yet hit the existential dead-end that so many workers reach after too many years in the corporate rabbit warren.

Two days later, on July 23, a Century 21 real estate salesman, Ron Thomas, opened fired with a .357 magnum in his office in San Antonio, Texas, killing two female co-workers and wounding another with a bullet to her temple. Thomas, who was married with two children, was alleged by one policeman to have been angry over the fact that he had to answer to female supervisors. The forty-eight-year-old real estate salesman killed his sixty-one-year-old supervisor and his forty-year-old top competitor in the office as they were talking together in the copy machine room. "He didn't have to be a good shot," a policeman observed, sizing up the kill-zone. Interestingly, after the shootings some co-workers described Thomas, who was African American, as a "wonderful" office mentor and the office's top salesman. Moreover, on his way out after the massacre, he looked the receptionist in the eye but didn't shoot her, confounding reporters and police who wanted to paint him as a deranged misogynist. A few days after the shooting, an article in the *San Antonio Express-News* detailed long-simmering tensions between Thomas and the forty-year-old competitor he killed, a series of office politics stink bombs that look ridiculous from afar, but can feel like your own private Fallujah when experienced in the first person. One ex-employee described Thomas's bad relations with the woman, Anna Medcalf, as "office stuff" and the fallout they'd had as "a minor ongoing flap." At one point, police later said, Medcalf made a comment about the fact that Thomas's children were biracial, enraging him. As the police chief said, "In reality, I think in the end, we'll see that it wasn't quite the personality that was the real suspect."

After fleeing the scene in his Ford Explorer, Thomas was spotted by a trucker who reported him to police. "When police began following, they observed a gun flash from the cab of the vehicle, and the Explorer swerved and crashed," according to WOAI News. Thomas was found dead in the vehicle. One noteworthy detail about this massacre was how contrary it was to the standard rage murderer profile as a loner, angry white male. Thomas was married, successful, African American, well-liked. . . . and angry at his co-worker and those he perceived as part of her circle. As is often the case, the authorities will paint the killer as evil and deranged, saying he was motivated by misogyny (or racism or Nazism), rather than consider the possibility that culture in the office, and the larger socioeconomic squeeze that created the kinds of office politics we have today, really did make his life Hell. It's an easy way out of having to talk seriously about these crimes, and makes defending them impossible—if the killer is white, he is a crazed Nazi, and if he's black, he's a misogynist.

More than a few rage murderers have been African American: Thomas, Robert Mack of General Dynamics, Elijah Brown in the recent 2004 ConAgra plant massacre in Kansas City in which five were killed and three injured. And then the strange, unheralded case in 1987 of David Burke, an African American PSA airlines employee in California who was fired from his job after admitting to stealing sixty-nine dollars from an employee liquor fund. He pleaded to his supervisor, customer service manager Ray Thompson, not to fire him. He confessed, said he was "regrettably sorry," and noted "my children will have no one to feed them" if they fired him. Thompson would have none of this bleeding-heart mau-mauing. On Burke's way out of the office where he was fired, a secretary wished him, "Have a nice day!" Burke reportedly turned around and said, "I intend on having a very good day." (PSA called itself "The airline with a smile!" and painted a big corny smile on all of its airliner noses.)

The next day Burke boarded the L.A.-San Francisco commuter on PSA that Thompson regularly took. Using his company badge which he still had, Burke sneaked a loaded .44 magnum on board. When he boarded and saw Thompson, he scrawled a note on an air-sickness bag that read, "It's kind of ironical, isn't it? I asked for leniency for my family, remember? Well, I got none, and now you'll get none."

And he meant it: when the BAe-146 commuter reached its twenty-nine thousand feet cruising altitude, Burke calmly walked to the toilet dropping the air-sickness bag on his supervisor's lap. When he returned, he pulled out the .44 and shot Thompson. The sound of the shot was picked up on the cockpit voice recorder. Seconds later, the sound of the cockpit door bursting open is audible and a stewardess tells the crew, "We have a problem." The captain asks, "What kind of problem?" Burke bursts in and is heard on the recorder answering, in perfect timing, "I'm the problem," while firing two shots, one for the captain and one for the copilot. As the commuter plunged to the earth, another shot is heard—that of Burke committing suicide. The plane broke apart at thirteen-thousand feet feet and crashed into the Santa Ana hills, killing all forty-four passengers and crew on PSA flight 1771. In a sense this would make Burke's attack the largest mass-murder in U.S. history, and the largest rage murder. But for the purposes of my book, a rage murder takes place in the workplace, and Burke didn't work in the PSA planes; moreover, nearly everyone he killed was a customer, which defies the usual definition. On the other hand, Burke's attack was successful from a rage point of view: he killed the supervisor that fired him and the company he was fired from. PSA died shortly afterward, getting absorbed into US Air the following year -- a company that went on to become one of the poster villains for instilling a culture of mass-layoffs-with-management-bonuses.

Back to the Summer of Rage, 2003. After a three-week hiatus, another deadly shooting erupted at Andover Industries in Andover, Ohio. On August 19, a thirty-two-year-old factory worker named Ricky Shadle shot and killed one co-worker and wounded two others before he went into a metal room and shot himself in the head. A few weeks earlier, Shadle, who worked at the company for five years and had never missed a day of work, had incorrectly filled out a vacation form. Shadle suffered from a learning disability—he was injured during childbirth and had a low IQ. His mother, Rosalie Shadle, said that he always needed help filling out forms and that his company knew this. Nevertheless, when he started his two-week vacation, the payroll clerk, sixty-one-year-old Theodora Mosley, called and threatened to fire him if he didn't return to work immediately, citing the improperly filled-out form as reason for denying him his vacation. Shadle was deeply upset—his mother called Mosley to plead his case, but Mosley wouldn't budge, claiming that it was her son's fault for not filling out the form correctly. Mosley knew of Shadle's learning disability but wasn't moved. In fact, according to Shadle's mother, Mosley had earlier arranged to have Shadle suspended from work without pay after alleging that he made a "vulgar expression with his fingers" toward her, an accusation Shadle denied (but lost). Shadle, a six-foot-three-inch, three-hundred-pound "gentle giant" who lived with his mother, was often teased for his learning disability, both in school and in the workplace. He had recently been diagnosed with cancer in his leg and the doctor said the only way to save him would be to amputate. Shadle confessed to his mother that he would rather kill himself than have his leg amputated. The day he returned to work, he asked his supervisor to put him on a part of the assembly line where he wouldn't have to stand up, since his leg was hurting. The plant usually accommodated him, but on that day they told him he would have to stand. This led to another shouting match with Mosley and some other women in the office area. The heartless behavior of his supervisor may have made his death-wish a little stronger, and perhaps fueled an urge to take some bastards down into the dirt with him. After this last humiliation, Shadle angrily walked out of the plant, went home, grabbed four pistols, returned, went straight into Mosley's office, and shot and killed her. He then continued on into the offices of two others, shooting them, before putting the gun to his own head and killing himself.

People often express surprise that a "quiet, obedient" type like Shadle would be the one who snaps. As Ashtabula County Sheriff Bill Johnson said, "He didn't get along like normal people would in a job setting, in other words, talking to people or something like that." But in Shadle's case, he truly did have nothing to live for. There was no point in being obedient. For Shadle, terminal cancer was like a gift from Oz—it gave him the courage to rebel.

And then ten days later, in Chicago, a warehouse worker who had been fired six months earlier returned to his former workplace, murdered six co-workers, and then died in a shootout with police. Salvador Tapia, a thirty-six-year-old Mexican native, arrived at the Windy City Core Supply warehouse where he had worked armed with a Walther PP .380-caliber semiautomatic pistol and extra clips. He showed up to the warehouse bright and early, and shot and killed the owner's son before the first pot of coffee brewed. Then he found forty-eight year-old Eduardo Sanchez, who had just arrived and was putting his lunch away. He pointed the gun at him and gave him a choice: "Do you want me to tie you up, or do you want to die?" Sanchez wisely chose door number one, and was duly roped to a metal railing. Tapia told him, "You haven't done anything to me. I am going to kill all of them. I want to kill everybody." And that was exactly what he did—killing the two owners and three other employees as they arrived for work. During the shooting spree, Sanchez watched helplessly as Tapia shot himself a total of three times and survived each self-inflicted gun wound, spattered in blood. "He looked like the devil," Sanchez later said. The spared hostage managed to wriggle his way out of the ropes. He escaped while Tapia was shooting himself, and warned away two employees before calling the police, who shot and killed Tapia. Later, Acting Police Superintendent Phil Cline, displaying an enlightened Windy City attitude toward Latinos, told a newspaper, "We're not sure why [Tapia] didn't shoot [Sanchez]." Another report said that Tapia targeted his victims "at random," conveniently omitting the detail about how he spared Sanchez while targeting the owners and their sons.

All told, in two months, at least twenty-five were killed and seventeen wounded in eight workplace rage attacks. It was a long, hot summer indeed.

In fact, according to a study by the organization Handgun-Free America, the number of workplace shootings actually doubled from 2002 to 2003. Moreover, July was the bloodiest office-rampage month on record.

11

"Evil, not rage"

IF YOU LOOK AT A MAP of the shootings and how they spread chronologically as well as geographically, another pattern emerges. In the case of both postal massacres and workplace massacres, the first outbreaks appeared in rural America before spreading to the populated areas and the coast. With post offices, the first massacre took place in small-town South Carolina, spread to Alabama, then Atlanta, Edmond, and New Orleans before hitting coastal California with a vengeance and metastasizing everywhere and anywhere after that. In the case of office massacres, Wesbecker launched his rebellion in Kentucky and from there it spread quickly to the coasts of Southern California and Florida, and now appears literally anywhere in the country. Today these massacres can appear anywhere at any time, with all of the geographic randomness yet circumstantial similarity of a roving guerrilla war.

These patterns hold for the third type of rage murder: schoolyard massacres. Like postal and office shootings, schoolyard shootings got their start in small-town America in 1996, exactly a decade after Patrick Sherrill "went postal" in Edmond. The white, suburban middle-class massacres that Columbine popularized got their start in rural towns like Moses Lake, Washington; West Paducah, Kentucky; and Jonesboro, Arkansas.

In fact schoolyard shootings weren't entirely new. In Kentucky alone, there were two that occurred other than the Paducah massacre, one in Carter County in 1993 and another in Union in 1994. A new phenomenon was that the rebellions had spread and found sympathy with a broader audience. Never before had people considered that a schoolyard massacre could happen at any white middle-class suburban high school in America. But through the the Moses Lake-Paducah-Jonesboro rage, they entered the collective adolescent conscious. They provided a new context for something already felt, already brewing, but not yet expressed.

In his book *No Easy Answer*, Brooks Brown, a former Columbine student and childhood friend of one of the Columbine killers, explained how the rage rebellion context reached his school:

> The end of my junior year [1998], school shootings were making their way into the news. The first one I heard about was in 1997, when Luke Woodham killed two students and wounded seven others in Pearl, Mississippi. Two months later, in West Paducah, Kentucky, Michael Carneal killed three students at a high school prayer service. . . .
>
> Violence had plagued inner-city schools for some time, but these shootings marked its first real appearance in primarily white, middle- to upper-middle-class suburbs. . . .
>
> When we talked in class about the shootings, kids would make jokes about how "it was going to happen at Columbine next." They would say that Columbine was absolutely primed for it, because of the bullying and the hate that were so prevalent at our school.

There are good reasons why the rage craze started in small-town America and moved to the big cities. First of all, rural Americans are a little less conditioned and a little wilder than their highly socialized counterparts on the coasts. I grew up in coastal California and lived for nearly a year in Kentucky, so I've seen this difference myself. When it comes to the intense social pressures to conform, the suburbs of San Jose are like Bismarck's Prussia compared to Kentucky. It's easier to imagine that you can literally shoot your grievances away in rural America or that you have the "right" to fight fire with fire, rather than fighting a downsizing-mad CEO with a groveling smile as most coastal yuppies would. In coastal or big-town white America, if you are a failure, you are more inclined to imagine that it is your fault, that it is some kind of cosmic judgment on your innate base nature. You might accept it more passively, suck it up more, or just quietly end it in your garage with a garden hose and the idle running. But well before you'd snap in suburban California, you'd be giving it your 110 percent over and over and over, constantly convincing yourself and those around you of your optimism and determination, always being positive and trying to make sure that everyone thinks you're just swell. There is no room for eccentric behavior in coastal suburban America— unless it's the kind of eccentric behavior that's already considered cool in a recognizaby safe way.

In rural white America, expectations are different. A neurotic, metrosexual office slave slathered in Kiehl's cucumber-based facial lotion, always beaming about his wonderful career and how everything's "great!" would strike most there as repulsive. Sacrificing all of one's waking hours, as well as family, friends, and children, just to please an abusive boss and a disloyal corporation has not yet been fully absorbed as "normal." However, the "shootin' the bastards up who done you wrong" solution has a long tradition, and doesn't seem as bizarre a response to injustice as coastal America's cheerful slavishness.

What was significant about these rage murders wasn't that they started in rural America, but that they spread to mainstream America. Not that this hasn't ever happened. Other cultural trends, such as in arts and in language, often percolate "upward" from the rural lower-middle class to the larger middle class.

The shootings in Pearl, Paducah, and Jonesboro might have seemed little more than isolated incidents if they didn't already have a context in the office massacres that had been leaving behind blood-spattered workplace corpses for over a decade. The three schoolyard shootings happened one after another, creating a snowball effect that helped propel the schoolyard massacre coastward and into cities, to Pennsylvania, Oregon, and later, of course, to Columbine High in Littleton, Colorado. One way of wrongly interpreting this pattern was to attribute the crime's spread to "copycat" behavior, rehashing the ol' kindergarten question of "would you jump off a bridge if Johnny did?" This fatuous explanation allows observers to write off a profound crime with a simple catchphrase. After reading a newspaper article about a schoolyard shooting in Mississippi, some upper-middle-class suburban goth-brat decides, "Hey, I wanna be just like that hick! I'm going to murder and destroy my life so that maybe one day a hick I don't know will think I'm cool!" You have to willfully forget how you thought or felt as a kid— what your references consisted of, where you drew your borders—to accept an explanation as intellectually lazy and convenient as the copycat-made-him-do-it explanation.

In fact, many schoolyard shooters very consciously saw their massacres as rebellions, however poorly expressed or thought-through (just as many office and post office murderers did). Michael Carneal, who slaughtered three students in a high school prayer class in West Paducah, was found to have downloaded the Unabomber's manifesto as well as something called *The School Stopper's Textbook: A Guide to Disruptive Revolutionary Tactics; Revised Edition for Junior High/High School Dissidents*, which calls on students to resist schools' attempts to mold students and enforce conformity. The preface starts off, "Liberate your life—smash your school! The public schools are slowly killing every kid in them, stifling their creativity and individuality making them into non-persons. If you are a victim of this one of the things you can do is fight back." Many of Carneal's school essays resembled the Unabomber manifesto. He had been bullied and brutalized, called "gay" and a "faggot." He hated the cruelty and moral hypocrisy of so-called normal society and the popular crowd. Rather than just complain about it all the time like the Goths he befriended, he decided to act.

Luke Woodham, the high school killer in Pearl, Mississippi, whose murder spree preceded Carneal's by two months, was even more explicit in his rebellion. Minutes before starting his schoolyard rampage, Woodham handed his manifesto to a friend, along with a will. "I am not insane," he wrote. "I am angry. I killed because people like me are mistreated every day. I did this to show society push us and we will push back. . . . All throughout my life, I was ridiculed, always beaten, always hated. Can you, society, truly blame me for what I do? Yes, you will. . . . It was not a cry for attention, it was not a cry for help. It was a scream in sheer agony saying that if you can't pry your eyes open, if I can't do it through pacifism, if I can't show you through the displaying of intelligence, then I will do it with a bullet."

The Columbine killers openly declared that their planned massacre was intended to ignite a nationwide uprising. "We're going to kick-start a revolution, a revolution of the dispossessed!" Eric Harris said in a video diary he made before the killings. "I want to leave a lasting impression on the world," he added in another entry.

And that they did. If the immediate goal of an armed uprising is to spark wider sympathy and push the momentum further, then many of these rage uprisings succeed. One of the most troubling and censored aspects of schoolyard massacres is how popular they are with a huge number of kids. I felt that forbidden sympathy for Klebold and Harris as soon as I heard about Columbine, as did many people I know who range from white collar professionals to artists. Many of us experienced the same agony in suburban high schools, an agony that is dismissed and ridiculed because it doesn't conform to the officially recognized grievances that we allow. We are white and middle-class, therefore we are happy—and if we're not happy, we're whiners. We have freedom of speech; therefore, we have no censorship. The shootings are not really uprisings; the sympathy is not really widespread. Today's white middle class must be the only socioeconomic group in mankind's history that not only doesn't recognize its own miseries as valid, but reacts dismissively, sarcastically (dissidents are called "whiners"), even violently against anyone from their class who tries to validate their misery. But our ranking of what constitutes existential "pain" is purely irrational and arbitrary. In fact, if pain could be measured neurochemically, it is entirely possible that the pain felt by a white-collar office worker stressed from seventy-hour workweeks and Andy Grove–inspired office fear is equivalent to the agony felt by indentured servants. The point is that the middle class persistently denies its own unique pathos, irrationally clinging to an irrational way of measuring it, perhaps because if they did validate their own pain and injustice, it would be too unsettling—it would throw the entire world order into doubt. It is more comforting to believe that they aren't really suffering, to allocate all official pathos to the misery of other socioeconomic groups, and it's more comforting to accuse those who disagree of being psychologically weak whiners. Despite its several hundred million strong demographic, the white bourgeoisie's pain doesn't officially count—it is too ashamed of itself to sympathize with its own suffering. And yet all the symptoms and causes remain and grow worse even as the denial becomes more fierce.

The popularity of the Columbine massacre helped spawn several more schoolyard shootings and untold numbers of school-massacre plots, many of which were uncovered, and many of which were the inventions of paranoid adults. Just as post office rampagers cited Edmond, several schoolyard massacre plotters and gunmen referenced Columbine, often promising to top it, or to borrow from Royal Oak postal worker Thomas McIlvane, "Make [Columbine] look like [name of harmless, happy place for women/children]."

> "They said specifically it would be bigger than Columbine," New Bedford Police Chief Arthur Kelly said.
> —**Associated Press**, "New Bedford police say they foiled Columbine-like plot," November 24, 2001

Across America, Dylan Klebold and Eric Harris became anti-heroes. In a *Rocky Mountain News* article titled "Surfers Worship Heroes of Hate," dated February 6, 2000, the journalist details the mass popularity of the Columbine killers: "They made hate-filled videotapes about the day the deed they were planning would make them cult heroes. Now, they appear to have gotten what they wanted—at least online."

The article goes on to quote some of the message boards devoted to Klebold and Harris:

> In a Yahoo! club devoted to the killers, a 15-year-old Elizabeth, N.J., girl writes: "They are really my heroes. They are in a way gods . . . since i dont believe in 'GOD' or any of that other crap that goes along with it. They are the closest thing we can get to it and i think they are good at it. they stood up for what they believe in and they actually did something about it."

A fourteen-year-old Toronto girl is also cited as belonging to twenty (!) online fan-clubs devoted to Klebold and Harris. The point of the article is that the

Internet shows just how sick our kids are. It does not consider the possibility that maybe the kids aren't simply evil, but rather they have valid reasons for making Klebold and Harris heroes. Perhaps they are considered heroes for valid reasons and the Net allows us easier access into the unofficial truth.

Another article in the *Denver Post* a few months earlier noted with horror:

> They wanted cult-hero status. And they got it. At least by World Wide Web standards. . . . "Dylan Klebold and Eric Harris Rule," reads the subject line from the bulletin board. "Eric and Dylan should be praised for what they did, not be labeled as monsters. . . . They did what so many of us young people wanna do."

The reason Klebold and Harris's hero status is expressed online is obvious: it's the one place where you can exchange ideas with a reasonable hope of maintaining anonymity. Admitting your sympathy with the Columbine killers can, in today's paranoid, zero-tolerance school atmosphere, get you thrown out of school, forced into counseling, or sent to a boot camp in Central America. Literally. As this *New York Times* article, "Desert Boot Camp Shut Down After Suspicious Death of Boy," dated July 4, 2001, shows:

> The authorities here are investigating how a 14-year-old boy died this week while participating in a rigorous boot-camp program for troubled youth in the desert west of Phoenix. . . . It is by no means the first camp of its kind where children have suffered serious injuries and even death . . . . [Capt. Tim Dorn] said that investigators could not determine whether camp personnel had adequate amounts of food and water available to the children. When investigators visited the camp on Monday, he said, the temperature was 120 degrees. The *Arizona Republic* reported today that the boy had vomited dirt before he died . . . .Tony's mother, Melanie Hudson, who lives in Phoenix, said she enrolled her child in the camp to help him control his anger."

Even though rage rebellions hit schoolyards years after they started in the adult world, the juvenile perpetrators are generally more explicit about whom they are fighting and the significance of their operations. One reason they are often more direct about viewing their massacres as rebellions is that young people are more idealistic, even as schoolyard shooters. A man who has worked in the office world for twenty-five years no longer contemplates larger society or his ability to have any effect on anything outside of his rabbit warren of cubicles. Most adults stop talking about society and justice after a few years of getting squeezed in the work/debt vise. The best that most workplace killers hope for is to remove the immediate source of repression—the offending supervisor, and the company, if possible.

Like adult rampagers, schoolyard shooters are impossible to profile. Initially it was thought that Columbine's Dylan Klebold and Eric Harris were drug-addled dropouts, Nazi-enthused homosexuals, children of broken homes, Goth-geeks,

Trench Coat Mafioisi, or Marilyn Manson goons. But the truth was far more commonplace and that's what was so disturbing about their massacre. Both came from two-parent homes, both loved their parents and both were highly intelligent but erratic students. They weren't Nazis or drug addicts. They weren't Goths, Trench Coat Mafiosi, or Marilyn Manson fiends; they weren't even gay, as some had theorized.

An exhaustive attempt by the Secret Service to profile school rage murderers failed, as detailed in a government report released in May 2002. Some schoolyard shooters were honors students, some were bad students; some were geeks, some were fairly popular; and some were antisocial, others seemed to be easygoing and "not at all the type." Some have been girls, a fact strangely overlooked by most. Like their rage counterparts in the adult world, school shooters could be literally any kid except perhaps those who belonged to the popular crowd, the school's version of the executive/shareholding class. That is to say, about 90 percent of each suburban school's student body is a possible suspect. And once again, I believe this at the very least suggests that the source of these rampages must be the environment that creates them, not the killers themselves. And by environment I don't mean something as vague as society but rather the schools and the people they shoot and bomb.

It isn't the office or schoolyard shooters who need to be profiled—they can't be. It is the workplaces and schools that need to be profiled.

A list should be drawn up of the characteristics and warning signs of a school ripe for massacre:

complaints about bullying go unpunished by an administration that supports the cruel social structure;

antiseptic corridors and overhead fluorescent lights reminiscent of mid-sized city airport;

rampant moral hypocrisy that promotes the most two-faced, mean, and shallow students to the top of the pecking order; and

maximally-stressed parents push their kids to achieve higher and higher scores.

The profiling should be extended to the adult workplace as well. Then workers could know which companies to suspect and possibly shut down for posing a danger to society. Here is one possible profile:

employees expected to work in excess of a traditional forty-hour week without additional pay;

atmosphere of fear and stress intentionally imposed from above;

temp slaves hired alongside full-timers;

downsizing has occurred or will occur;

wages and benefits continually slashed;

union weakened or nonexistent;

promotions based on favoritism rather than merit;

management ruthlessly penalizes employees if personal tragedies affect productivity;

massive gap between upper echelon pay and other wages;

imposes Casual Friday; and

presence of co-workers who love their job too much to leave for vacation.

Unfortunately, this describes nearly every workplace. Which is why nearly any workplace can spawn a murder spree.

The collective resistance to considering the possibility that the workplace causes murders is effected by a kind of defiant amnesia. But schoolyard shootings are too shocking and subversive to forget. They remind us that we were just as miserable as kids as we are as adult workers. In fact, the similarities between the two, the continuity of misery and entrapment from school to office, become depressingly clear when you study the two settings in the context of these murders. Even physically, they look alike and act on the mind in a similar way: the overhead fluorescent lights, the economies-of-scale-purchased industrial carpeting and linoleum floors, the stench of cleaning chemicals in the restrooms, the same stalls with the same latches and the same metal toilet paper holders . . . Then, after work or school you go home to your suburb, where no one talks to each other, and no one looks at each other, and where everyone, even the whitest-bread cul-de-sac neighbor, is a suspected pedophile, making child-leashes a requirement and high-tech security systems a given.

If you consider it this way, it means our entire lives, except perhaps college and that one summer backpacking around Europe, are unbearably awful. As if our entire wretched script was designed for someone else's benefit (Jack Welch). This is too much to handle. So the inescapable suspicion that suburban schools cause murder rampages is rejected with unrestrained hysteria. Blame is hurriedly focused on the murderer, rather than on the environment. A typical example is an op-ed piece written by Joanne Jacobs for the *San Jose Mercury News* published exactly eight months after the Columbine massacre, in which she tried to reassure herself and her readers that, "Evil, not rage, drove these killers." I emphasize her quote because it's one of the most revealing yet widely held explanations among contemporary Americans. When you use a word as inherently meaningless as "evil" to describe something as complex and resonant as Columbine, you are desperately trying to recover the amnesia that once protected you, and told you how blissful and innocent your own school years were. The fact is that the schoolyard shooters were clear about their intentions: they wanted to "pry your eyes open." But sometimes we don't like what our eyes see, in fact, we refuse to believe what they see. You'd need to use *Clockwork Orange* eye-tweezers on someone like Joanne Jacobs to make her face this unpleasant fact.

If you accept that schools and offices, as compressed microcosms of the larger culture, create massacres, just as poverty and racism create their own crimes or as slavery created occasional revolts, then you have to accept that on some level the school and office shootings are logical outcomes and perhaps even justified responses to an intolerable condition that we can't yet put our fingers on. Justified, that is, if you look at these crimes from a historian's point of view. Imagine a historian one hundred years from now, with no emotional investment in our culture, looking back on how we live today, and thinking to himself, "My god, how could those poor wretches cope with such Hell?" In fact, unofficially, even today a lot of people look at these murders as justified, as vindication. Sympathy is all over the Web. It's revealed in black-humor, in "Wage Slave" T-shirts, and in movies like *Office Space* and *Fight Club*. It's revealed anywhere it can safely be expressed.

12

A Rebellion of One

ONE MAIN DIFFERENCE between adult rage massacres and schoolyard massacres is that many schoolyard shootings and shooting plots were the work of two or more students. The most obvious, tactical explanation for this is that there is a greater possibility for students to share plans for a rebellion than office workers. In schools, there is a greater distance in terms of communication between students and the adults who run the schools, and between cliques of students within the school. Adults are often laughably unaware of what kids do, what they talk about, and what bothers them. Kids are more adept at hiding things from adults. It's not as humiliating to lie and feign obedience to an adult as it is to submit to a fellow student. However, an adult who has to hide his feelings from adult office peers is far more likely to feel the pangs of humiliation and shame, which will increase over time as the evidence of his own cowardice builds into a case against himself. Then there's the question of snitching: children are also far less likely to rat on each other than office workers. Youth culture has always viewed narcs as the filth of humanity. The office world has no equivalent villain to the evil narc. Everyone in the workplace is a hall monitor. Any office employee would be happy to rat out a fellow worker who is, by definition in the post-Reagan corporate culture, a competitor rather than a comrade. With unions destroyed both in fact and in spirit, the idea of binding together for anything at all, whether to press for a company dental plan or to massacre the executives, is impossible. However, as Web postings and interviews have shown over and over, there is widespread sympathy in the office world with workplace massacres, a sympathy which is even more afraid of exposing itself than student sympathy with schoolyard shootings.

So circumstance has allowed one faction or demographic of this new rebellion to operate in groups, the student rage-murderer demographic. It is hard for us to consider a lone gunman engaging in open rebellion. By its very nature, rebellion should be a collective, with a manifesto and a clear context. Schoolkids can plot in groups more easily, but office slaves simply cannot. Yet even in the case of adult rampage murders, the gunmen don't act alone in spirit. They consciously build on previous office massacres, referencing them as inspirations in the way revolutionaries might reference other uprisings, to the point where the details of each incident practically blend into one, despite the fundamental differences of the perpetrators. Moreover, the fact that there is widespread sympathy shown in anonymous message boards gives the uprising a sense of collective uprising—at least, a collective cheers them on.

In some ways, today's American massacres resemble the numerous shooting rampages that take place almost every month in the Russian army. A regular feature in the Russian news is the army recruit who shoots a couple of fellow soldiers or officers on his base, then escapes into the woods where he is either gunned down or commits suicide. The figures are astounding: one leading liberal politician, Boris Nemtsov, claimed that some two thousand Russian soldiers died from rampage shootings or suicide in 2002 alone. The Russian government officially put the figure much lower, although a leading journalist reported that a confidential 2002 Defense Ministry report confirmed Nemtsov's claim, putting the figure at 2,070.

In America, the country scratches its head and asks why without wanting to hear the answer. In Russia, no one is fooled. Hazing, called *dyedovschina*, is notoriously brutal, as are living conditions. Soldiers literally starve to death and can often be found begging for change in Moscow metros just to survive or to hand over to their hazing elders to avoid getting beaten or raped. Organizations have been set up to try to change the army's culture, but the murder sprees continue to pile up. Everyone in Russia knows it is not that the recruits just snap, but rather that the brutal, medieval Russian Army causes the soldiers to snap. Their bloody rampages, while terrible, find sympathy in the mainstream heart.

In America, no one is calling for a fundamental change in the corporate culture or school culture (except perhaps the half-hearted attempts to regulate bullying). To consider a change in our corporate culture is far too threatening—it is tantamount to calling for the overthrow of everything we now believe, everything we take for granted as normal.

Detail by detail, the office and schoolyard rampages are so similar to other rebellions throughout our history that it is shocking to me that no one has considered these similarities until now. Like today's uprisings, the American slave rebellions were characterized by wanton brutality, a society that hysterically misrepresented the causes that seem so obvious today, perpetrators who were borderline schizophrenics, painful black comedy, and violent, tragic failure.

PART V

More Rage. More Rage.

"We, students at Westerburg High, will die. Today. Our burning bodies will be the ultimate protest to a society that degrades us. Fuck you all!"

—*Heathers*, 1989

1

I Don't Like Mondays

IN JANUARY 2004, I moved to Santee, California, a suburb of the greater San Diego region. People I knew, even journalists, couldn't understand why I would be researching rage murders in San Diego of all places—it was difficult to imagine that anyone could possibly have a reason to be angry there. If my move to San Diego sparked any reaction from my writer friends in New York City or Moscow, it was an ironic mix of envy and condescension. The day I arrived in San Diego, it was dry, sunny and seventy degrees. They had perfect weather all year around there, with perfect beaches, sunshine, surfers, and blonds in bikinis. Life was easy, right?

In fact, the warm coastal stretch from San Diego to Orange and Los Angeles counties has the largest concentration of rage murders—office, postal, and schoolyards—in the country, which only underlines the thesis of this book. If happiness cannot be found at the southwestern-most edge of America, the apogee of the American Dream, then rage has infected the very soul of the nation and nowhere is safe. If San Diego wasn't safe, then there was nowhere to hide, nowhere to run to, unless it was far away, across the border, or better yet, across the ocean.

Santee, a suburb at the eastern edge of greater San Diego, was the site of the last major school shooting that gripped America before the Red Lake school massacre in 2005. I happened to be visiting the U.S. from Russia when the Santee shooting took place on March 5, 2001. I watched it unfold live on CNN: fleeing students ducking for cover, SWAT teams manning the school perimeter, helicopters flying overhead, crying parents, emergency phone calls, and cries of "why?" It felt like a repeat of Columbine, except that the final death toll was much lower and the suspect, fifteen-year-old Charles "Andy" Williams, looked like the least threatening 15-year-old kid imaginable. The television footage of the scrawny, pale geek at his arraignment, wearing a jumpsuit and chains and smirking in barely-contained terror, was both sad and chilling. He looked so familiar and so harmless. It was impossible to make him larger than life and "evil" the way the media had managed to do with the Columbine killers.

Contrary to popular expectation, there is something about San Diego that brings out the rage in people. The most famous pre-Columbine school rampage murder took place in San Carlos, in San Diego County, in late January 1979. Brenda Spencer, a tiny, bespectacled sixteen year-old high school student, decided one Monday morning that she didn't feel like going to school. So instead, at 8:30 AM, she pulled out the .22 rifle that her father had given her for Christmas (along with five hundred rounds of ammunition in her stocking), opened her window, and started firing at students and teachers at Cleveland Elementary School, located across the street from the apartment where she lived with her father. Principal Burton Wragg, fifty-three, was killed, and Mike Suchar, fifty-six, the school's head custodian, was shot in the chest and killed when he ran to help Wragg. Eight young children were wounded as they ran for cover, and a police officer was shot in the neck. The shooting spree lasted for twenty minutes. Police arrived and took up positions. They commandeered a dump truck and moved it between the apartment and the school, cutting off Spencer's line of fire, allowing them to evacuate the wounded and those still hiding. After a six-and-a-half-hour standoff, Spencer finally surrendered. When asked why she did it, the nerdy little teenage girl told authorities, "I don't like Mondays," inspiring the Boomtown Rats' hit song. But Spencer gave other interesting reasons as well: she shot the school because "it was fun" and "this livens up the day." She also explained that she had targeted "no one in particular, I kind of like the red and blue jackets. . . . I just started shooting, that's it. I just did it for the fun of it. I just don't like Mondays. . . . I just did it because it's a way to cheer the day up. Nobody likes Mondays." Spencer was sentenced to two twenty-five-to-life terms. Her appeals for parole have been repeatedly denied, and her claims that she was drugged both during the shootings and during the court proceedings have been angrily denounced. Spencer at times has even denied that she was responsible for the shootings, charging that police fired on the school and later blamed her while she lay drugged up in the apartment on acid and angel dust. This miserable tale of Carter-era nihilism even has a love interest angle: Brenda's father wound up marrying her juvenile hall cellmate. The girl was only seventeen years old when Brenda's father first met her. While Brenda was transferred to rot out her days in prison, her father and former cellmate tied the knot and gave birth to a child, who they later put into a daycare center under the guidance of Christy Buell, one of the children whom Brenda had shot. Christy's father, Norman Buell, told a reporter in 1993 that he felt Brenda should be given parole. He believed that she had been abused by her father and that "she's served her sentence." The judge and parole board continued to see things differently. Taking into account her paranoid-delusional tales of being drugged up both while shooting and later during the trial, Brenda Spencer has consistently failed in her attempts at parole, the last denial coming in 2001, the same year as the Santee school shootings.

Spencer's school shooting was unlike those that sprang up in the mid-to-late nineties in that she didn't target her own school. In fact, she doesn't seem to have felt any rage whatsoever—her shooting spree was really an anti-rage murder. She killed because she was bored. It was the perfect crime for the Carter/New Wave era, the perfect material for the perfect pop song for a perfectly exploitative entrepreneur like Bob Geldof. Her shooting didn't spark any broader uprising, in part because she wasn't raging against anything that others might have raged against. However, she later expressed remorse over the possibility that she might have inspired the school shootings of today.

2

This Place Is the Pits!

SAN DIEGO COUNTY was also the site of several early "going postal" outbreaks. The first was on March 25, 1989, when ten-year postal employee Don Mace walked into the Poway Post Office where he worked, dressed in his postal uniform, intent on making a point to the callous management. He pulled out a .38-caliber revolver, pressed it to his temple and killed himself in front of his coworkers. Mace's suicide came after three other suicides by postal employees in the San Diego region. In just the previous five months there had been one in Encinitas, one in Pacific Beach, and one in El Cajon, the inland suburb adjacent to Santee.

Less than six months later, on August 10, 1989, postal employee John Taylor opened fire at the Orange Glen Post Office in Escondido, a northern suburb of San Diego, killing two coworkers before turning the gun on himself.

In Dana Point, a mostly white, overwhelmingly Republican coastal town of thirty-five thousand located about forty miles north of Escondido, another postal murder spree exploded in 1993. This story doesn't really fit the definition of rage murders covered in this book because the perpetrator wasn't filled with rage so much as genuine sickness, but its details do help readjust the reader's expectations about an idyllic San Diego and provide additional context to help understand how true rage murders happen.

USPS employee Mark Hilbun joined the Dana Point Post Office in 1988, and, although he was considered eccentric and even unpleasant, his performance was adequate enough to keep him employed. But in 1992 everything changed when he fell in love. Hilbun, whose curly sun-bleached mullet and mustache gave him a typical SoCal dude-look, developed an obsession with a new employee, Sue Martin. She rebuffed his advances, but like a tan, psychotic Pepe LePew, he was only more inspired by the chase. Hilbun was convinced that Sue was the one—she just needed to become enlightened about this fact. As he later told investigators, "Sue and I were chosen as, uh, husband and wife of, uh, the race, the human race." Hilbun tried to get Sue to date him, but she refused. He made obscene phone calls and sent her increasingly disturbing notes the more she continued to deny his advances. While she complained to the postmaster and other employees, his work suffered. Finally, in late 1992, the postmaster put Hilbun on leave. In December, after Hilbun called Sue and told her he couldn't live without her, Hilbun was fired. Now Hilbun was free to devote his every waking hour to harassing Sue Martin. Hilbun later told detectives that he had once managed to break into Sue Martin's apartment: "I thought for sure she'd be there. She wasn't. I looked at all her pictures and stuff. It seemed like she was just like me, not really fitting in . . . I wondered if she had a demon in her, and it's now in me." In April 1993, Hilbun sent her a note saying, "I love you. I'm going to take us both to hell." She panicked and left town with her boyfriend for two weeks.

On the day of her return, the thirty-eight-year-old Hilbun decided to act. Wearing a T-shirt with the word "Psycho" across the front, and a Pink Floyd baseball cap as a disguise, Hilbun began his operation with an early-morning visit to his mother's mansion in nearby Corona Del Mar. He slit the throat of his mother's cocker spaniel, tiptoed upstairs, woke his mother up, and stabbed her to death with a Buck filet knife. As he later told Sheriff Investigator Mike Wallace, "I said I was going to take off camping so I had a Mother's Day gift for her and then I just jumped up on top of her and showed the knife and she put her hands up and said, 'No, no.' And I said, 'I love you very much and here, you're gonna go see Grandma,' and I plunged the knife in her heart a couple of times and she died—no problem at all." Hilbun loaded his pickup with camping equipment and canned food, tied a blue kayak to the roof, and drove to his former post office in Dana Point. He marched inside through the rear loading dock with the aim of "rescuing" Sue Martin and spiriting her away to South America. Hilbun asked his one friend there, Charles Barbagallo, where he could find her. Barbagallo was cagey; seeing the blood-spattered "Psycho" shirt tipped him off that he should protect Sue. Hilbun had no time for dilly-dallying, so he shot his friend in the face, killing him instantly. After wounding another employee with a superficial gunshot wound to the scalp, Hilbun hunted down the postmaster, Don Lowe, who had fired him a few months earlier. Lowe, who had warned employees to be on the lookout for Hilbun because of his increasingly strange behavior, heard the gunshots and scrambled into his office in the nick of time, locking the door and praying. He was wise, as Hilbun later admitted: "I was angry at [Lowe] . . . for isolating me and not trying to help me in any way. . . . I think that he was the cause of all the problems." Hilbun fired into Lowe's locked door. Convinced that he had nailed Lowe, he abandoned the lucky postmaster. The lovelorn avenger raced out of the post office, figuring that Sue was out delivering mail (in fact she was hiding inside the station). He trawled Sue Martin's postal route, which he had staked out in advance. While driving around in search of his love, kayak rattling on the pickup roof, Hilbun spotted an old man, a retired probation officer, working in his garage. Hilbun hopped out of his car, told the man to freeze, cracked him in the back of the head with the butt of his revolver, shot him in the arm, and sped away without stealing anything. After failing to find his object of obsession, Hilbun decided it was time for plan B.

He headed north to Newport Beach, a famous upper-class surfer town. There, Hilbun pulled over and started swiping magnetic placards from the side of a parked car, placing them on his pickup windows. The owner of the car, a middle-aged businesswoman, busted Hilburn in the middle of his heist. Acting quickly, Hilbun jumped into his pickup and sped away, but the woman followed in hot pursuit. She wanted her magnetic placards back if it was the last thing she ever did. At one stoplight, Hilbun, in a rare moment of reason, warned the woman, "If you follow me, I will kill you!" She thought he was bluffing—either that or she was willing to lay down her life for those magnetic placards. So she kept after Hilbun, egged on by her dogs, a mini-schnauzer named George, and a Lhasa apso named Harri, who yapped their avenging master further into battle. Hilbun couldn't shake her, so he decided to get rid of her. He pulled over to the side of the road. She stopped her car behind his as if not taking no for an answer, that trait of success in the business world, would once again triumph. Hilbun got out of his pickup, trudged up to her window, saw the yapping sidekicks, pulled out a pistol, and fired six shots, hitting her in the face, neck, arm, and hand. Then he sped away in his pickup. The next night, Hilbun held up a man at an ATM machine, but when he pulled the trigger the gun wouldn't fire. Hilbun clicked a couple more times, laughed, and walked away. "I thought he was just some jerk," the man later explained. "I thought maybe it wasn't a real gun . . . just a joke." Shortly afterward, Hilbun attacked a couple at a different ATM, shooting the girlfriend in the head and seriously wounding the boyfriend.

Later that evening, Hilbun decided to take a load off. In roughly thirty-six hours of hard work, he'd murdered two people, injured five (three seriously), and executed a cocker spaniel sharia-style. Now it was Miller Time. He headed to a sports bar in Huntington Beach. He later explained that he hoped to meet a woman there, but his social skills were failing him: "I felt all wasted and I couldn't really . . . communicate at all." When news reports flashed his face on every TV screen in the bar, warning Orange County residents of a massive manhunt and asking people to be on the lookout, Hilbun, wearing a bright Hawaiian shirt and sitting alone, suddenly became the most famous patron the sports bar had ever hosted. Phone calls were made; police walked into the bar, tapped his shoulder, and walked him out. He was sentenced to eight consecutive life terms. And an extra eight months for cruelty to animals.

Hilbun was clearly insane. The jury in his trial reached a deadlock over his insanity plea, which was only broken when his attorney agreed to plead guilty in exchange for ruling out the death penalty. But when you relive his crime spree, following his blood-and-sand-paved trail along the famous Beach Boys coastline of Southern California, some of the innocent, easy charm of this region gets dragged down into depressingly familiar territory. The same Middle American illnesses—loneliness and violence—set in the same familiar, bland world of sports bars and ATM outlets, and people's fanatical attatchments to their magnetic window placards plague even paradise. (Dana Point, incidentally took its name from the nineteenth century novelist Richard Henry Dana, who named the point "the only romantic spot in California.")

Other notable San Diego area rage murders include Robert Mack's 1992 shooting at General Dynamics, as well as Larry Hansel's attack on Elgar Corporation, which resulted in the deaths of two supervisors. Hansel had cited the Escondido postal shooting as one of his sources of inspiration. But perhaps the most original rage attack in the San Diego area took place in 1995, when an unemployed ex-plumber, Shawn Timothy Nelson, stole an M-60 tank from a local National Guard armory, stripped himself naked, and drove it through central San Diego, into the tract home districts intersected by Interstates 5, 8, 15, and 805. Plowing over cars, signs, and sidewalk trees, churning up asphalt in the tank treads while being pursued by dozens of police cruisers. In all, his tank destroyed twenty cars, squashed a telephone booth, destroyed a bus stop bench, and toppled utility polls, leaving five thousand people without electricity. The tank was equipped with a 105 mm cannon, a 7.62 mm machine gun, and a 12.7 mm anti-aircraft gun—none of which were loaded. After leaving a six-mile trail of Godzilla-like destruction, the thirty-five-year-old ex-serviceman, who had served in the Gulf War, found his tank stuck on a freeway divider. While he tried to maneuver it out of the trap, police swarmed on top of the tank, cut the lock off the hatch, leaned in, and shot and killed Nelson . . . a finale caught on live television that many residents criticized as unnecessarily brutal.

San Diego's rage-fueled violence makes sense when you visit. The sprawling metropolitan area of 2.7 million, the seventh largest in America, is not only the southwesterly-most corner of the American Dream, it is also the most militarized region in the country and what the San Diego Chamber of Commerce boasts as "the largest military complex in the world." The county's twelve major military installations include the Marine Corps's Camp Pendleton in Oceanside, the San Diego Naval Station, the Marine Corps's Air Station Miramar, Naval Air Station North Island, San Diego Naval Submarine Base, and a number of training, command, and logistics facilities. One-fifth of the U.S. Marines and Navy are stationed there. The area has the largest number of active-duty military personnel in the country. Revenues from defense spending directly account for some 20 percent of San Diego County's GDP, according to the San Diego Chamber of Commerce's 2003 report. Not only is it a region saturated with men in uniform, but a large number of ex-military people from all over the country settle there, making it a solid bastion of the white right spite bloc. San Diego County has more than two hundred-sixty thousand military retirees, the largest concentration in the United States. When I lived there, I saw these retirees everywhere, generations of them. You can see them lingering around gas stations or in the driveways of their decaying Eisenhower-era tract homes, squinting through tinted steel-rimmed glasses. A lot of them have squat bodies with guts that hang over their belts and bumper stickers on the backs of their used SUVs bewailing big government. This is the real, representative face of San Diego—not bimbos in bikinis and loveable airhead surfers with glazed eyes and six-pack abs.

I've had my own run-ins with these people. Most recently, in June 2004, I published an article in the *New York Press* about the role of spite in the white male Republican base, and got this response, published in the following issue:

> Apparently Mark Ames is under the illusion that conservatives are gutless ("Spite the Vote," 6/9). Please pass along an invitation to that piece of crap: This former Marine will beat him to a pulp—just present himself in San Diego and we can lace up the gloves and let the games begin. Gutless is the pathetic crap he is, passing off for a journalist, or the staff allowing this crap. And stuff the 1st Amendment—he's gutless and the paper is not much better.

I'm praying for my prayer to be answered. You have my email. Let's rock and roll.
—**Jack Truman**, San Diego

Tom Metzger, former Grand Wizard of the California Ku Klux Klan, runs the *White Aryan Resistance* web zine from his base outside of San Diego. Indeed, San Diego has long been known as a haven for white supremacists, the Idaho of the southwest.

Pete Wilson, who as governor of California in the 1990s led bitter, racially-divided attacks on Latino immigrants, started his political career as mayor of San Diego during the Reagan Era. At the time he gained popularity by bashing Latino immigrants, to the approval of local white voters. The toxic culture of white tract-home malice is as strong in San Diego, if not stronger, as anywhere in the country.

3

"It's only me"

SANTEE IS A KIND OF HALF-SUBURB, half-rural junkyard sprawl of sixty thousand, located on the edge of the desert valley in eastern San Diego. The city is also known as "Klantee" because of the white supremacists and gun enthusiasts who supposedly live there, and because the city is nearly all white, over 85 percent at last count. In 1998, a black Marine at a party in Santee was attacked by five whites and left paralyzed in what authorities described as a hate crime. Santee's layout is familiar to anyone in Middle America, with its Wal-Mart/Target superstores on one edge, Barnes & Nobles/Old Navy-anchored malls on another, and, on the south end transmission repair shops and furniture rental stores, struggling Old America businesses with names like American Fence Company and Magnolia Mini Storage. There's a wealthier section of town nestled against the hills, with well-irrigated landscaping and fresh two-story homes in neat subdivisions. And then there are the mobile home parks and the decaying two-story apartment complexes deeper in the valley. East County is where coastal suburbia meets rural Middle America, a break point only twenty minutes by car from the Pacific Ocean and such fabled plutocrat enclaves as La Jolla and Costa Mesa. Along the coast, the sidewalks are lined with lush green stretches of perfectly groomed lawns, healthy palm trees, and rows of bird-of-paradise plants. Twenty minutes inland, this coastal beauty quickly gives way to Middle American flatness: Santee's older two-lane roads on the south end near the small airport are lined with tall dry weeds and shrubs, and red-white-and-blue pennant-lined trailer parks and old tract homes with campers and RVs parked in the driveways. Here, you might think you're in rural Kentucky or Arkansas, not California. As Santee Mayor Randy Voepel declared in 2001, "We are America." And not just because of the way it looks. Santee is red state country, a disregarded notch on the Bible Belt. It is the home of the Institute for Creation Research, a "Christ-focused creation ministry" devoted to promoting creationism in schools. Coastal San Diegans call East County residents goat ropers, trailer trash, and haze suckers—all of the haze and smog produced in greater San Diego settles down over the eastern edge of the desert-mountain-ringed bowl. The billion-dollar San Diego light-rail line, pushed through by former mayor Pete Wilson, runs from San Diego's beaches to Santee's largest shopping mall, anchored by an Old Navy. But the rail cars are almost entirely empty no matter what time of the day you see them pass. Few want to go into Santee, and few venture out from Santee to the coast, as one Army recruiter in Santee told me.

Andy Williams moved to Santee with his father less than a year before his shooting spree. Before approaching the California coast, he was a happy lower-middle-class white kid in lower-middle-class rural America. After he was thrown into the gladiator pit of suburban San Diego, the downward spiral was fast.

His parents had married in Lawton, Oklahoma, in 1981, and later moved to Knoxville, Maryland, a rundown town of eight thousand, where Andy was raised. Knoxville is in Fredericksburg County, a rural, white region that has far more in common with Lynndie England's West Virginia than with more familiar Maryland locales like Baltimore or Annapolis. Fredericksburg County was one of the last places in the country where you could still pop into a gas station and buy a jar of ephedrine capsules. Andy's parents divorced in 1991, when he was only five. The county court ordered his older half-brother to live with his mother while Andy stayed with his father.

In 1999, Andy and his father moved to Twentynine Palms in the California desert, forty miles north of Palm Springs. Unlike lush, hilly Fredericksburg County, Twentynine Palms is parched, beige, hot, and dusty. Andy was said to have been popular in the middle school there, a class clown known as "underwear man" because he came to school once wearing his underwear on the outside of his pants. In Twentynine Palms, Andy had a circle of friends and relatives, including aunts, uncles, and grandparents, that eased the transition from Maryland. He missed his friends, but he was able to adjust, making good grades, playing center-field on the baseball team, and acting the role of Linus, complete with blanket, in the school play.

In 2000, Andy's father found work as a lab technician in the San Diego Naval Medical Center, so the two of them moved to an apartment in Santee. And it was there, as a freshman at Santana High, that life became Hell. Santana High is a flat-roofed, dark brown, long, windowless, foreboding structure that looks more like a storage facility than one for youthful creativity and learning. Directly across the street from Santana High is a Mormon Church and an Army recruitment center. A white banner over the Army recruitment center reads, "Students! Need Money for College?" On the corner across from the school entrance was a popular strip mall with a Subway, Starbucks, Del Taco, and 7-11.

On the first day I visited, two men stood on the sidewalk in front of the school handing out orange-covered Bibles to students who mostly ignored them. One of the Bible peddlers was older, wearing a round straw hat and a corduroy jacket; the other was younger, with a dark goatee, wearing a gray windbreaker and khakis. According to one account, the year that Andy Williams started school, one of the trustees on the Santee school board, Pastor Gary Cass, used to stand outside of Santana High holding up pictures of aborted fetuses and anti-abortion placards.

From my own experience growing up in coastal California, it is far worse to be barely middle-class in the shadow of the wealthy than to be lower-middle-class among like kind. Santana High is located against the hills in the wealthy part of Santee. Andy Williams lived in one of the depressing apartment complexes amidst the dry scrub in the valley. The contrast was rammed home every day he arrived at school. In Knoxville and Twentynine Palms, Andy Williams would not have had to face the particularly nasty, devastating socioeconomic hierarchy and hazing that he was exposed to in more middle-class Santee. Here, a local bourgeois elite overlooked the lower-middle-class trailer trash below, while twenty minutes away, just over Interstate 8, the modern, wealthy coastal population sneered at all of East County, including the best Santee had to offer, intensifying the local micro-caste feuding and isolation.

The move to the apartment complex in Santee devastated Andy. He was never able to fit in. As a hick arriving from the sticks to a city that pretty much represented the top of the redneck food chain, Andy was marked. He was short, skinny, pale, and vulnerable. On Monday, March 5, 2001, he rebelled. He hid a German-made Arminius 8-shot .22-caliber pistol in his backpack, along with a Beanie Baby doll he called "Spunky" that his half-brother had once given him (it reminded him of happier times, he later explained).

Andy had been planning to shoot up the school for at least a few days already. In fact he could not decide if he wanted to kill, to die, or both. Just two days earlier, at a Saturday night sleepover party, he told friends that he was going to shoot up the school. Williams claimed afterward that his friends were at least as gung-ho as he was and that they egged him on because they hated Santana High as much as he did. He wanted to show them that he could do it. The friends' version is that Williams bragged to them about his plans to shoot up the school, but they thought he was joking and couldn't be serious. Williams's version was that they were all in it together.

Joshua Stevens, who held the sleepover, told reporters: "The whole weekend I was with him he was joking he was going to shoot people. . . . He invited us to come out and take part in the shooting."

That same weekend, his father took him to nearby Lakeside—a somewhat classier suburb which Santee residents call East La Jolla but which La Jolla residents still refer to as "hazesucker country"—to view a condo that he was planning to buy. Andy gave his father elaborate instructions on how he wanted his room to be decorated. His father later explained that he could never have imagined his son was planning a murder, not after he had shown such interest in the condo and his room.

On Monday, Andy arrived at school with the gun in his backpack. Before class he got stoned with his friends by the side of the school. Some of these friends claimed to reporters that they had patted him down because they were so worried about his weekend threats (yet they also claimed that they didn't take his threats seriously because he always joked about things). They also said they missed checking his backpack, a claim that the media bought wholeheartedly for its tragic detail.

Indeed the media, and most adults, take teenagers for their word all too often in these cases, forgetting how much kids hide from adults and how much dissembling they do.

Freshman student Analisha Welbaum told the *San Diego Union-Tribune* that she saw Andy at 9 AM. "He seemed carefree. I asked him if he was going to school and he shook his head and said, 'Yeah.'"

Andy later told investigators that he bragged about his plan to so many students—at least twenty knew in advance, probably more—in the hope that one of them would stop him. But no one came to his rescue. In fact, Andy felt they were "egging me on and egging me on." The fact that they didn't stop him only increased his sense of humiliation and desperation. It meant that they didn't take his threat seriously. It meant that if he didn't go through with it the taunting and humiliation would be unbearable for the next three years—which is a lifetime to a kid his age. He would essentially be dead if he didn't kill.

> "You can't go back, everybody would think you're nothing. Everybody would just have one more reason to mess with you."
> —**A friend's advice to Evan Ramsey** shortly before Ramsey's school-
> yard rage massacre in Bethel, Alaska, 1996

In the break between first and second period Andy went into the boy's bathroom, took a stall, and loaded the gun. The bathroom was full. At 9:20 AM, he opened the stall and shot the first person he saw, fourteen-year-old Bryan Zuckor, in the back of the head. He emptied the chamber on everyone in the bathroom, dropping one more student, seventeen-year old Trevor Edwards, with a bullet in the neck. When Edwards, lying on the floor, asked Andy why he shot him, Andy told him to shut up.

Richard Geske, a fifteen-year-old who was in the other stall when the shootings started, panicked as he saw blood pool around their bodies. At first he thought that the gun was fake, that the gunshots were bursting caps. But after seeing the blood, he sprang out of the stall and fled for safety.

Andy reloaded the gun and stepped out into the corridor. Using the bathroom as a base, he'd emerge into the hallway and fire at the scattering students, then retreat and reload. He hit Randy Gordon, seventeen, in the back, killing him. Gordon's best friend, Raymond Serrato, was standing next to him and was also hit. Serrato recalled catching Andy's expression just before he was shot: "There's a face smiling. Grinning. Just staring right at me."

Analisha Welbaum told a reporter that he saw her but spared her: "He's over by the bathroom and he's like freaking out. He's standing there shooting. He looks at me and then he just turned again and kept shooting."

One student, Matthew Harmon, claimed he action-heroed his way to safety: "All I know is he turned around and looked at me and shot at me. I hit the ground like stop, drop and roll, and I wasn't on fire." Bullets hit a locker behind him, he said.

After firing some thirty rounds over a period of about six to ten minutes, Andy Williams stopped shooting and sat on the floor of the restroom next to the bloodied bodies of Zuckor and Gordon. As he reloaded the gun, three policemen approached the restroom door. Andy told them, "It's only me." And put the gun down and surrendered.

A total of thirteen were wounded, eleven students and two adults, including, kids alleged, the school narc. Two students were killed. One of those, Zuckor, was still showing a faint pulse when paramedics reached him. At the hospital, the cell phone in his pocket rang. It was his mother calling to check on him; doctors told her that Zuckor was in emergency surgery. By the time Zuckor's mother arrived at the hospital, her son was pronounced dead.

Andy was interrogated just three and a half hours after the shootings by two sheriff's detectives. He was defiantly terse and cold. "I didn't want anybody to die, but if they did, then oh well," he said. "It was just a stupid thing."

"OK, you wanna tell us what all this was about?" Detective James Walker said.

"Mmm," Williams answered, according to a transcript of the interview in the the *Union-Tribune*. "I was just mad, I guess."

Over the next 51 minutes Walker and his partner, Detective Sharon Lunsford, probed and prodded the teen seated across from them. The transcript is littered with the phrase "NO VERBAL RESPONSE" to many of their questions.

Other times, they seem flabbergasted.

"Why—why shoot them?" Walker asked.

"They were just there," Williams said.

"Wrong place at the wrong time, huh?"

"Yeah," Williams responded.

But unlike Brenda Spenser, the original San Diego school shooter, who really did shoot them because they were just there, Andy Williams shot them for entirely different reasons. And many kids across the country who sympathized with him understood exactly why.

4

Sympathy Rage

IN THE DAYS AND WEEKS FOLLOWING Andy Williams's attack on March 5, an outbreak of school shootings and shooting plots swept the country, revealing a latent sympathy that we are afraid to acknowledge. Mass adult paranoia was also widespread, rooted in the fact that Americans are incapable of understanding why the sympathy exists or how deep it runs.

In the first seventy-two hours after the Santana High shootings, sixteen students in California alone were detained for making threats to students or teachers, or for carrying weapons to school. In one incident, on March 6, two seventeen-year-old students at the high school in Twentynine Palms, California, where Andy would have enrolled after middle-school had he stayed there, were arrested on charges of conspiracy to commit murder after authorities found a "hit list" in one of their homes and a rifle in another. The two were detained after a girl overheard them discussing the list and she told her father. In Perris, California, eighty miles north of Santee, a fifteen-year-old student was detained the next day after boasting that he could outdo the Columbine school massacre. Authorities found a four-inch knife in his backpack, and later recovered two rifles from his house. In Ontario, north of Santee, three Woodcrest Junior High students were arrested for threatening to put a bomb under the teacher's desk. No bomb materials were ever found. And in San Diego's Hoover High, a student committed suicide on campus the day after Williams's shootings.

But it wasn't only California that was affected. As reported on March 8 by CNN and ABC News, kids all across America rose up in rebellion:

in Washington state, a sixteen-year-old student allegedly pulled out a gun in class Wednesday, [March 7] at Kentwood High School in the Seattle suburb of Covington and ordered students to leave, authorities said. The boy surrendered without incident after about fifteen minutes. No one was injured;

in Savannah, Georgia, authorities said a sixth-grader was arrested on Wednesday for allegedly trying to bring a BB gun onto campus. No shots were fired and no one was injured. A parent and a school crossing guard spotted the fourteen year-old allegedly carrying the gun and reported it. Coastal Middle School Principal Alfred Howard confronted the boy, who dropped the weapon and ran;

in southwest Philadelphia, police arrested a twelve year-old student at Thomas Morton Elementary school, charging him with possession of a .22-caliber pistol;

another Philadelphia student, this one an eight year-old at Henry C. Lea School, allegedly threatened a "bloodbath" with a loaded shotgun on Monday before he was taken into custody;

a fifteen-year-old Camden, New Jersey, honor student was arrested for allegedly threatening to shoot members of a clique on March 6;

in Bradenton, Florida, Bayshore High School sophomore Philip M. Bryant, seventeen, was suspended from school after being charged March 7 with carrying a loaded semiautomatic handgun to school;

twenty miles away in St. Petersburg, John Wayne Morrison, seventeen, was charged with carrying a revolver with a sawed-off barrel at Meadowlawn Middle School, his former school;

in Davenport, Iowa, a fifteen-year-old Assumption High School student was arrested March 7 and ordered to undergo psychiatric evaluation after he threatened to get a gun and shoot everyone in school;
a Harlingen, Texas, high school freshman was expelled after he was caught with a hit list of his own;

in Arizona, three students were arrested March 7: an eighth-grader was accused of threatening to bring a gun to school to shoot sixth-graders; a thirteen-year-old was arrested after allegedly threatening to shoot class-mates who teased him; a thirteen-year-old-girl was arrested after a bomb threat was left on an answering machine on the night of March 6;

in Fort Wayne, Indiana, the day of the shooting at Santana High School, police arrested an Elmhurst High School student after finding a semi-automatic handgun in his locker;

in Las Vegas, Nevada, a seventeen-year-old junior at Western High School was arrested for possession of an unregistered weapon on school property after he was seen carrying an assault pistol. The gun was never brought into the school.

The day after the Santee shootings, an eighteen-year-old high school student in Maryland was arrested for sending death threats to Santana High students via instant messaging, telling one student, "I am going to finish what Andy started." He was tracked down, caught, and pled guilty to one felony charge of making a terrorist threat and a misdemeanor charge of making an annoying or harassing communication.

Two days after the Santana shootings, at a private Roman Catholic school in Williamsport, Pennsylvania, fourteen-year-old Elizabeth Bush walked up to fel-low eighth-grader Kim Marchese, thirteen, and shot her in the shoulder. Elizabeth, a bespectacled nerd who was constantly taunted and accused of being a lesbian by Marchese and her popular crowd, took her father's four-inch, nine-shot, blue-barreled .22-caliber revolver into the girls' bathroom, loaded it, and tracked her victim down in the cafeteria during the lunch hour. After wounding Marchese—the bullet passed just inches from her spine—Elizabeth put the gun barrel to her head.

"I don't want to live. I should just commit suicide right here," she said.

Brad Paucke, a freshman who had ducked under the table when the shot was fired, stood up when he recognized Elizabeth from the school bus. He begged her not to kill herself, moving to within five feet of her. Elizabeth turned and pointed the gun at Paucke. The principal screamed from a safe location at the far end of the cafeteria, telling Paucke to duck and run, but the student stood his ground.

Amazingly, the boy's tactic worked. "You could tell she was really mad, and she looked like she was about to go off on everybody," Paucke told reporters. Elizabeth Bush placed the gun down on the floor, and Paucke kicked it safely away.

It was all so cinematic, one almost wants to thank Hollywood for providing a peaceful, happy, heroic-ending script which both actors faithfully carried out, particularly since Hollywood gets so much blame for providing the script for the shootings.

Suddenly, in the wake of Andy Williams's rage massacre, it was harder to pass off these schoolyard shootings as evil, unrelated acts brought on by something outside of the school culture.

Elizabeth told the judge at her sentencing a month later that she shot Marchese because, "They just treated me as if I was lower than dirt."

Even the county district attorney, Tom Marino, agreed. "This was, in her mind, the only way to deal with the situation and the torment she had been going through."

Police described the shooting as the "culmination of a grievance between the two students." That grievance stemmed from relentless taunting and teasing by Marchese, the cheerleading captain, which came to a head a few weeks earlier when Elizabeth contacted her by e-mail pleading for her to stop and for them to make peace. Somehow Marchese convinced Elizabeth that they had made peace, because Elizabeth then sent her emails confiding her troubles and secrets . . . which, naturally, the cheerleader mass e-mailed to her friends, giving everyone ammo to mock Elizabeth Bush.

According to Elizabeth's mother, Catherine Bush, her daughter was called a lesbian and "vicious, vicious names" at the public school she was attending before switching to the Catholic school the year before the shooting. "She was being told to get out of town or school or something would happen to her or her family," Catherine Bush said. "Stones would be thrown at her after school on occasion." She was picked on so much at the public school that she started skipping class until the administration threatened legal action if she did not show up more regularly. "She is always someone who is for the underdog," her mother said, noting that Elizabeth hoped to become a human rights activist. "At one school she was friend of a girl who was in a wheelchair. She used to help her. If anybody is being picked on or there is a problem, she is usually right there to try to defend that person."

> "To me, high school is like Hell. You get up and go to Hell every day."
> —**Alex Frost**, the actor who plays Alex, the school rage killer, in *Elephant*

In an interview with ABC News shortly after the shooting, aired on March 9, Kim Marchese denied that she had bullied Elizabeth. In fact, she and others, even school administrators, denied that Elizabeth had been bullied by anyone at all. "I haven't talked to Elizabeth Bush for about a week or two," Marchese claimed.

Marchese used the shooting to both promote herself as the normal, saintly one, while portraying Elizabeth as a kook—a common tactic used in adult-world social battles. Her repetitve use of the word 'but' suggests a casual, detached, character--the character of the cool clique.

"I knew Elizabeth Bush I think a little bit more than other people did," Marchese said. "When she came to the school last year, I didn't really know her that much, but then as the year went on I got to know her. She was the kind of girl that was quiet, but I know she had a lot of problems with herself and her family.

"She wasn't in the best health mentally, but I know she used to cut her wrists last year, but she got help with that," Marchese added in what reads like a typical double-serrated-edged adolescent put-down. "She used to tell me she used to be able to talk to God, but she told me she doesn't hear him anymore."

It sounds convincing until you realize that Marchese denied ever having bullied Elizabeth, a denial police and reporters later found to be false. Remember, even school officials and fellow students had backed up Marchese, yielding to the fear of lawsuits, to the pressure to cover one's ass, and to the instinct to rally behind the popular girl and against the "weirdo." This deception and denial is repeated in the aftermath of school shootings everywhere, including Santana High, and is reinforced by a society that wants to believe that mental disorders trigger shootings, rather than school culture, a culture that pretends to root for the underdog, but in fact worships the popular people and protects the privileged.

About a month later, Elizabeth apologized in open court to Kim, while she, wearing a sling for her wounded arm, "cheerfully forgave her," according to a Reuters reporter on the scene: "'I could tell just by looking at her that she was really sorry,' a smiling Marchese said outside the courthouse before adding: 'Not to offend, but if she hadn't been in her right mind, it might have been harder.'"

Even though Elizabeth Bush got off with a relatively light sentence—juvenile hall until age twenty-one—the resulting Lifetime movie–like courtroom apology/apology-accepted ending reinforced the social feudalism which helped inspire the shooting in the first place: Elizabeth resumed her role as the weirdo, was forced to apologize to her tormentor, and paid for fighting back by losing her freedom; meanwhile the indestructible, popular Kim Marchese got to play victim, heroine, and merciful saint, forgiving her weirdo assailant, while letting the world know how difficult it was for her to offer this absolution, "not to offend" of course.

Of all the post-Santee shootings, the most shocking took place at Granite Hills High in El Cajon—just five miles from Santana High. In the days and weeks following Andy Williams's attack, rumors had been circulating on the campus that a shooting might take place there. Six students had been suspended over a two week period for making vague remarks about plots. On March 22, just three weeks after Andy Williams's rampage, Jason Hoffman, a student who hadn't been suspected or suspended in the rebel round-up, pulled into the high school parking lot at 12:55 PM, just as fifth period was starting. No two student-rebels could be more dissimilar than the diminutive, desperate-to-fit-in Williams and the two-hundred-pound, antisocial Hoffman who lived practically next door. Hoffman stepped out of his gold Dodge pickup, slung a 12-gauge pump shotgun around his shoulder and packed a .22 caliber handgun, then walked calmly toward the administration building. On his way, he was confronted by the school dean. Hoffman, a brawny, shaven-headed eighteen-year-old, eluded the dean and started firing into the administration office windows and into an open doorway. An El Cajon policeman who worked as a resource officer at the school chased down Hoffman in a running shooting battle. Hoffman lost. He went down with bullet wounds to the face and the buttocks, making a hero of the cop.

As Hoffman was being wheeled away to an ambulance, parent Renee Ditzler, who was at the school to deliver a wallet to her son Billy, approached the bleeding teenager's gurney. Police tried to keep her away, but she pushed into Hoffman's face. "I told him one day he was going to stand before God, and I hope He has no mercy," Ditzler later told reporters. Newly-appointed Attorney General John Ashcroft, a longtime gun advocate, reacted to the Granite Hills shooting by accusing Hollywood of "almost literally teaching shooting."

In all of the fear and paranoia that Hoffman's shooting caused, one important detail was left out: the school had already rounded up potential suspects before he attacked. Hoffman wasn't on that list. This is another reminder that the school rampage murderer can not be profiled. So rather than profile the kid, who could be almost anyone, the public should try profiling the schools that cause kids to murder.

Throughout that day, panic set in at schools all across San Diego. Rumors, alleged plots, and threats caused closures and lockdowns at schools in the entire region. Just a few blocks away at the local middle school, graffiti warned of a shooting plot that afternoon.

Hoffman pled guilty to attempted murder. Shortly afterward he hanged himself in his jail cell.

The student insurgency took weeks to die down. On March 27, all six public schools and one Catholic school in the Westchester County town of Harrison were forced to shut down due to threats of violence. "All the guy said was post office and school and click, that was it," Larry Marshall, a Harrison police lieutenant told CNN. Note how the threat links a post office and school massacres—they're seen as one crime, expressing one sensibility.

What was so shocking about these numerous sympathy-shooting outbreaks was that they destroyed the one possible theory for Andy Williams's rage attack—that it was the work of a lone psycho. The theory is that there are always going to be a few psychos out there, and sometimes they snap, and there's nothing we can really do about it. The mounting evidence, however, showed that Andy Williams was speaking for a great number of American kids from coast to coast. And this wasn't the first time that America had to face this disturbing fact.

Looking back two years earlier, the same pattern of sympathy shootings and shooting plots had broken out across the country in the aftermath of the Columbine massacre. In the days and weeks following the massacre of April 20, 1999, schoolyard incidents included:

four fourteen-year-olds arrested in Wimberly, Texas, for conspiracy to commit murder, arson, and the manufacture of explosives;

a seventeen-year-old arrested in Jackson, New York, when a "metal device with a fuse" is found in his backpack;

a high school senior arrested when he threatened to "blow up" his school in Princess Anne, Maryland;

a thirteen-year-old in Bakersfield, California, caught loading a .40 caliber handgun at school;

five teens at William McKinley Jr. High in Brooklyn arrested after boasting of their plans to blow up the school on graduation day;
on May 20, 1999—the one-month anniversary of Columbine—a student at Heritage High in Conyers, Georgia opened fire on students with a .22 caliber rifle, injuring several.

The actual number of sympathy rage attack/plot incidents is far greater than I have listed here. Many of the plots either don't get reported, or, when they do, they only make the local papers.

5

Frog-Marching Across the Quad

IN 2004 ALONE, SEVERAL SUCH PLOTS, some along the order of Denmark Vesey and Gabriel Uprising plots, have been "discovered" and "unmasked." Hysteria and paranoia are so common now that we barely even notice the plots unless they happen in our own hometown. Here is a sample.

On February 10, 2004, Sacramento police charged two boys, a fourteen-year-old freshman and a fifteen-year-old sophomore, with planning to use guns and bombs to pull off a massacre in the cafeteria at Laguna High. Headlines announced, "Columbine-Style Plot Averted"—news helicopters showed police descending on the school and parents evacuating their children. The cops claimed to have found swastikas and "Nazi drawings" in the boys' homes, as well as a .22 rifle. But the scariest allegation the cops announced was that the boys, both white, planned to massacre African American students, leading Cynthia Isais, a sixteen-year-old junior on the basketball team, to describe the plot as "scary." Later, Sacramento County police spokesman Sgt. Lou Fatur used slightly more careful language regarding the evil KKK angle. He said that the boys were targeting one specific black female student, and then added, in one of the worst examples of deductive logic, "There was an African American girl who is a student and was a target. And when one is a target, many can be a target. These kids are pretty disturbing." There was talk of the plot involving up to six kids, of bombs and guns stashed away. "This is the closest this area has ever had to a Columbine-style shooting," one cop said.

However, after the initial heavy television coverage of police and parents descending on the school, the story quietly faded away, as if authorities were hoping no one would remember.

The following day, hidden in Section B of the *San Francisco Chronicle*, it kinda sorta turned out that, well, the Sacramento County sheriffs mighta gone a little overboard. The headlines said it all: "Columbine-style attack averted" (February 11); "Plot to attack school a 'fantasy'" (February 12). There was no *Mississippi Burning for Columbine*. In fact, there was probably no plot at all. Whereas initially the cops fed the race-war angle, two days later, they still could not produce any evidence, leaving one cop to quietly suggest, "at least some of the intended targets were black." Since the school was one-quarter black, it would logically follow that some intended targets might be African American. Maybe they should teach basic syllogistic reasoning to the Sacramento Police Department:

A: The boys planned to kill Laguna High students.
B: Some students at Laguna High are black.
C: Therefore, all Klansmen are Socrates.

When the hysteria died down, students said that a gang of African Americans at the mixed-race school had bullied the white suspects, who had just moved to Elks Grove from Arizona. As with Andy Williams, kids who move from one shit-kicker region to another, higher-up Hell on the socio-economic-geographic ladder tend to get mauled. Several students denied that the boys' plot was racially-motivated. Close friends described the scheme as "bully-revenge," a "sick fantasy" and not a genuine threat.

The cops' claim of a weapon also turned out to be an exaggeration. The .22 rifle (really just a popgun) that the cops paraded before the media belonged to one of the accused boy's parents. The rifle was safely locked in the master bedroom when the police discovered and confiscated it. In other words, the kids had not taken it out and there was no evidence that they even had access to it—yet the cops declared that they had the weapon. Think about it: the police would have had to get the suspect's parents to open the cabinet and hand them the gun, unless they broke into the cabinet and took it. The cops knew where the gun was stored, and how they got it; yet they went public declaring the gun proof-positive of the plot. That is to say, they simply lied.

No other guns were found, nor were any explosives.

But it gets more absurd. The plot hinged on a caper that the two poor hicks planned to pull off at a local Big 5 Sporting Goods store. The dastardly duo hoped to break in, steal guns, escape scot-free, make it to the school for lunch break, and unleash a massacre signaled by a string of devastating pipe bombs. The only thing that got in the way of their brilliant Big 5 heist was a little something called a door. The suspects had failed to so much as pry open the back door of the targeted Big Five during their one feckless break-in attempt. Like common house pets, the suspects had no idea how to open the Big 5's back door—so they gave up and left. That was that, the culmination of their plot. If I know kids, then their lack of determination that means they didn't really want to break in. But we can't take any chances these days, not even on kids who have no weapons and don't know how to open doors. As for the pipe bombs, well, if cops believed that, then they probably believe that both boys left behind smoking-hot-model-level girlfriends in Arizona.

Now they face charges that could put them behind bars for up to ten years. These two boys, the real victims of their own wounded boasting, are ruined forever by a community that will gladly make an example of them. As in all periods of domestic unrest, the important thing is to make swift and brutal examples of suspected rebels.

Three days later, at a middle school in Sunnyvale, California (where I grew up), nine students at Cupertino Middle School, aged twelve to fourteen, were arrested by Sheriff's deputies for plotting to burn their school down. If you lived outside the Bay Area, you wouldn't have even heard about this middle school plot; but in the South Bay, after similar plot "discoveries" at Saratoga High (my high school), Bellarmine Prep, and farther away, at Laguna High, it was beginning to feel like Iraq. Every kid was a potential terrorist. No one stopped to ask whether the deadly cocktail of stress, brutal competition, and suburban California emptiness might be the source of all this violence. Nor did they ask themselves if they were being hysterical, or rather why they were being so hysterical. The next day, Saturday, the middle school arson plot accusation began to unravel. No dangerous materials were found on any students, just a pen-drawn plan. Many insiders and administrators said it was all probably just empty boast. Once again, the headlines tell a story of paranoia: "Plot foiled to burn school, cops say," (February 14); "Arson charge draws own fire," (February 15).

There had been numerous other plots in 2004, such as the case of two Dutchtown, Louisiana, students—Christopher Levins, seventeen, of Prairieville and Adam Sinclair, nineteen, of Geismar—who, local police say, planned to imitate the Columbine shootings on the massacre's fifth year anniversary—April 20, 2004. Police were tipped off by a caller, and in their search for evidence they found poems about being bullied, writings praising Eric Harris and Dylan Klebold, and drawings depicting the suspects massacring students and teachers and celebrating. Even though no weapons were found, detectives said that the boys had "obtained information on buying shotguns and rifles"—a rather strange accusation in a country, and state, where obtaining such information is a patriotic duty. In any case, they faced up to fifteen years prison for "terrorism," an example of the extreme punitive measures favored by this country and the very type of repression that reinforces kids' sense that they are growing up in a nasty, hateful society.

A few months later, on May 14, 2004, two middle school students in Winder, Georgia, one fourteen and the other fifteen years old, were arrested after police had been tipped off about their plan to launch a school massacre the following week. "They were planning on a Columbine-style killing," said Winder Police Lt. Kristi Schmitt. Police claimed to have found explosives and bomb-making instructions, as well as shotguns and rifles in one of the kids' closets. However, the "bomb" was a mix of drain opener and bleach, tree-fort-level weaponry which can maybe cause a little pop; the bomb-making instructions were downloaded legally from the Internet; and in Georgia, minors are allowed to possess firearms. In other words, they did absolutely nothing wrong except talk shit, which all insecure teenage boys do. Some, including the school principal, dismissed the alleged plot as hysteria, but authorities coerced the fifteen-year-old to plead guilty in return for not trying him as an adult, in which he could have faced up to sixty years in prison. The fifteen-year-old also agreed to testify against the fourteen-year-old. The excessive cruelty on the part of the authorities is reminiscent of the way hysterical slaveholders posted rebel slave heads on pikes, or coerced slave witnesses and turned them against each other to confirm the existence of non-existent plots. It is as if the authorities need to show that they can find and destroy student insurgents before they act, not in the interests of serving justice, but in the interests of serving society's fears. Just six months before that, in Lovejoy, Georgia, a fourteen-year-old student was arrested for planning to "make history by turning Lovejoy into another Columbine," according to Clayton County police Capt. Jeff Turner. You start to get the sense that Columbine is the *American Idol* of the new millennium. This plotter was caught after one student whom he'd tried to recruit turned him in. Police found "a diagram" after they arrested him—a drawing that for them was enough evidence to declare the existence of a plot, arrest the boy, and crush him.

One of the most widely-reported of these school plots took place in New Bedford, Massachusetts, in November 2001. A group of seven students planned to unleash a massacre at their high school that they hoped would be, once again, "bigger than Columbine," using bombs and firearms that they were amassing. They planned to videotape the massacre, then gather on the school rooftop and commit mass suicide. The plot was revealed when the lone girl of the group had a pang of conscience and warned her favorite teacher.

> An initial rising in 1649 "was abortive, for as usual one tender-hearted negro could not bear to think of his white master (a judge) being murdered, so revealed the plot in time for measures of repression to be taken."
> **—The Myth of the Negro Past**

The culture's reaction to the New Bedford plot reveals not only the country's mass hysteria, but also its mass delusions. A *USA Today* editorial, "Columbine's Lessons Learned," explained that kids have finally learned how to snitch. The editorial didn't mention how the culture should be shocked and trying to figure out why Columbine found so much sympathy, or why the plots are still happening; rather, "New Bedford showed that with careful plans in place, murderous acts by students can be thwarted." Indeed.

The hysteria has reached ad absurdum proportions. A third-grader in Pontiac, Michigan brought a one and a half inch by one and a half inch medallion in the shape of a gun to school—he had found it in the snow that morning—and was suspended. Parents pulled their children out of the elementary school en masse when they heard about the deadly medallion. Two days after the Santee shootings, a fifteen-year-old student at a high school in Belmont, California, was arrested and incarcerated in juvenile hall for two days after he wrote a "threatening poem." Charges were later dropped. In May 2004, a fourteen-year-old boy at a middle-class intermediate school in Walnut Creek, an upper-middle-class suburb east of San Francisco, was detained by police who stormed his classroom, cuffed him in front of the students and teachers, and frog-marched through the quad . . . for posting a flash cartoon on his web home page. The teacher had called him a "good-looking peacock" in class one day, so that night, the boy made a naughty flash cartoon that read, "He called me a good looking peacock, Maybe I should kill him and urinate on his remains." The boy's mother, who called the arrest absurd, noted that her boy was a graphic artist who often posted satirical art in the fashionable black-humor style of South Park, his favorite program. A few years earlier the kid would have been given a serious sit-down, but today, America has no patience for touchy-feely liberal crap. If you step out of line, Team America will be called in to destroy you. The boy's mother complained that she hadn't been notified before the arrest, and wondered why her son had to be cuffed in the class-room and led out of the school by police rather than, at the very least, arrested at home. Walnut Creek Police Lt. Damien Sandoval said the school has a no tolerance policy and the police also "take threats like this quite seriously." It is hard to imag-ine that the kid became a better person after this. More scared, more cautious, and more alienated from his peers, sure. Which perhaps is all we want.

The panic, and the over-the-top ruthless crackdown, is clearly reminiscent of the slave rebellion plot hysteria and reflects a deep-seated fear, a suppressed understanding, that the rage is everywhere in our middle- and upper-middle-class white schools. Any student is a potential rebel. Obviously there is a real reason to be afraid. How do you deal with a problem like this, where every student is a potential rebel? Our solution so far has been a militaristic, authoritarian crack-down, which, like all badly-executed counter-insurgencies, not only ignores the underlying causes but even exacerbates them. Zero tolerance policies, heavy police responses to what once would have been considered empty boy boasting, and the increased fear and suspicion that they inspire only fuel more rage. The toxic school culture is only reinforced by repressive measures.

6

Copycats on Copycats

As EXPECTED, Andy Williams's Santana High shooting and the wild aftermath brought out the same chorus of meaningless copycat explanations that followed the string of postal and workplace shootings before. This cheap framing is yet another way to keep from blaming the school.

> Kids see this and believe a copycat could be a quick way to be brought to the forefront.
> —**Andrew Vachss**

Maybe these are copycat cases, maybe there has always been violence in schools and [some] never got national coverage. The fact is, we shouldn't be surprised when after all the coverage a school shooting receives, there are going to be second or third incidents
—**Al Tompkins**, who teaches Broadcasting and Online Ethics at the Poynter Institute.

The copycat phenomenon is out there, and it is particularly damaging for certain kinds of individuals who are predisposed to this behavior in the first place.
—**Frank Ochberg**, a Michigan psychiatrist and a member of an FBI group that has assessed shooting threats.

There is clearly a copy-cat contagion effect at work.
—**James Alan Fox**, the Lipman Family Professor of Criminal Justice at Northeastern University and an expert on mass killings. In the 1970s, 1980s and early 1990s, Professor Fox said, there were a handful of rampage killings in schools by students, but they were isolated incidents and were not picked up by students elsewhere in the nation.

So who is the real copycat here, the experts or the kids? And what does Fox mean to suggest when he acknowledges that the few school shootings in the pre-Columbine area "were not picked up on"? That copycats hadn't yet existed? Is that the explanation for this crime's sudden explosion? Is he suggesting that copycating was introduced in the mid-nineties, out of thin air, rather than that some unbearable change in the school culture might cause them to "copy" each other?

The copycat explanation is no explanation at all for school rage attacks, just as it doesn't explain workplace or postal attacks. In fact it seems like another playground taunt. It is no more or less insightful than slaveholders assigning blame for slave rebellions on copycatting the Hispaniola revolution. Like blaming evil, the copycat rationale is so empty that it doesn't even qualify as a convenient explanation. At least Ashcroft argued that the kids were brainwashed by Hollywood; at least he's looking for a genuine cause and effect. But dismissing this rash of murder and sympathy—across the country, across a wide variety of students—as simply copycat shootings assumes that kids operate at about the same intelligence level as sardines. Stupider in fact, because the copycat theory assumes that man's survival instinct is inexplicably superceded by the infamous copycat instinct that kicks in anytime a school shooting is shown on television (or, in the case of working adults, a workplace shooting).

What these experts could be saying is that the deep-rooted desire to lash out merely needed a trigger event. Though what is relevant here is not the trigger-event, but the culture and environment that pushes a kid to such a point that all he or she needs is a trigger event to set it all off.

During the successful slave revolution in Hispaniola in 1797, newspapers in America attacked other papers that reported on the rebellion and on the black revolutionary leader's program, accusing them of inciting potential copycat rebellions in America. The *Richmond Recorder* announced in 1802 that "American editors had been fomenting restlessness among Virginia's slaves by reprinting the St. Domingo constitution." In the same way, in America many commentators blame the media for spreading copycat Columbine attacks merely by reporting them. In both cases, they're absolutely right: it puts ideas into people's heads, people who feel oppressed and desperate. It offers them an answer, a solution, to some awful condition. Today we know that the slave would have been right to take the Hispaniola revolution to heart and rise up, but at the time it was not seen that way. In fact the Hispaniola revolution was seen then as roughly the moral (and geostrategic) equivalent of the Khomeini revolution.

Surprisingly enough, in the wake of Columbine and especially Santee, society did start to take a look at something deeper than *Doom II* or the liberal/fear-mongering media to explain why the shootings were so widespread.

Had Andy Williams' face not brought a familiar, unsettling pathos to the school rampage murder picture, the debate following the Santee shootings might have once again centered on tired denunciations of violent culture, lax gun laws, the media, or moral decay, as was the case after Columbine. Something about the diminutive, scared-looking Williams struck a deep chord with young people and adults alike. He was a twerp of a more common, yet unrepresented sort: rather than a bespectacled, fat, pimple-faced computer geek, Williams, with his bedhead blond hair, scared, wolfish eyes, and wounded smirk, looked like the kind of kid who should have fit in a respectable mid-level clique. That is, if you forgot how high schools actually work. It was his vulnerability that was his doom in the corridors of his suburban high school. And this same pathos made him a kind of hero once he was in a jumpsuit and chains. This little dork was the cause of so much panic. He drew the nation's networks to film his shooting; he managed to attract an entire army of San Diego police, SWAT, and helicopter teams. Later, at his arraignment, TV viewers got to see this little wisp of twerp-dom, this Linus, dressed in a menacing oversized jumpsuit (his public defender didn't think of getting him proper clothes). The tormented boy next door had fought back. It was an inspiration to some, a real wake-up call to others.

7

An Entirely New Phenomenon

THERE HAVE BEEN SHOOTINGS and violence at America's schools for years now. But this book is focusing on what we all know to be a unique and deeply disturbing type of school violence—the rage attack, or "classroom avenger," as some mockingly call it. Throughout the eighties and into the early nineties, gang attacks in inner-city schools caused a number of shooting deaths and woundings. Middle America was horrified by the shootings, and by the news reports of metal detectors becoming common in these inner-city (read: minority-dominated) schools—but they weren't necessarily shocked. The ethnic riots of the sixties and seventies already provided a context for these school crimes. And with the rise of Reagan, as the country became increasingly polarized along class and ethnic lines, it became acceptable for Middle America to react callously to the inner-city school violence, just as they turned their backs on the crushing of America's blue-collar unions and the cuts in government assistance to the poor. For the most part, violence at inner-city schools was considered "their" problem. Just as the poor were essentially blamed for being poor under Reagan, so the schoolyard gang violence was blamed on the African Americans and Latinos who lived where the violence was greatest.

Underlying all of this was the sense that inner-city school violence was something foreign and contrained, something to be contrasted against middle-class school culture. Inner-city riots and violence of the sixties and seventies never spread to Middle America—white middle-class youths didn't set fire to their subdivision tract homes and 7-11s; they didn't turn their parents' station wagons into barricades to keep the Man from controlling the inner-suburban section from Pleasant Street through Chestnut Way. Hippies abandoned suburbia, taking their anger out on major urban military and government installations, or they dropped out altogether, moving to rural communes. But they never turned suburbia into a war zone. No one even considered the possibility of rage murders in white middle American schools. Such a thing was just not imaginable until the late 1990s, long after the phenomenon had broken out. We all knew that the blacks and the poor were left behind, but that was part of the deal struck with Reagan. Violence in inner-city schools was regrettable, but hey, life's tough.

What Middle America didn't expect was that eventually the Reagan Revolution would turn against them too. And yet it has always turned against them: downsizing started with blue-collar workers and eventually devoured the white-collars; outsourcing devastated first the manufacturing sector and now it's plundering the white-collar service sector; and violence thought only to wreak havoc on inner-city schools now infiltrates middle-class public schools. Of course, Middle America's parents were idiots for not seeing this: in 1980, Ronald Reagan pledged, as candidate for president, to abolish the Federal Department of Education. You don't hear too much about that now that Reagan has been officially canonized, but he was the first president in my lifetime, and perhaps in American history, who went out of his way to attack and demean education. It was the same inverted work-is-freedom rationale that he used to destroy unions (they hurt America's workers), the environment ("trees cause pollution"), the poor ("welfare queens"), and human rights ("the Contras are the moral equivalent of our Founding Fathers"). Reagan said that by abolishing the Department of Education it would somehow improve education. He didn't abolish the Department of Education, but he did make it respectable to heap contempt on public schools and to blame schools for their own problems, thereby making it easier to cut funding and deprioritize the nation's historical dedication to educating its citizens equally and for free. Reagan's contempt for public schools and the poor was most clearly manifested when he slashed federal funding for school lunch programs—and when he tried to have ketchup declared a "vegetable" on federally-subsidized school lunches in order to offset tax cuts for the wealthy.

I have already defined what constitutes a post-Reagan rage murder in the workplace. Here is a working definition of today's schoolyard rage attacks:

> attacker(s) attacks their own school with guns and/or explosives in order to fight something that takes place within that school (such as bullying, difficult-to-define evil, pressure);

> attacks are aimed at destroying the school as a symbol, with victims chosen either because they signified whatever enraged the attacker about the school or chosen "at random." Just as victims of terrorists tend not to have been specifically targeted but rather happen to be in the symbol that terrorists attack, many victims of schoolyard rage attacks are not specifically chosen but are part of the institution that is attacked, and therefore they are misidentified as having been shot "at random"; and

> attack takes place in middle-American school—that is, the school community should be predominately middle-class and/or predominately white.

There have been murders in schools for some time, but until lately, none fit this modern definition. One of the earliest known school massacres took place in 1927, in Bath, Michigan, when a "demented farmer" killed his wife, then planted dynamite in the Bath Consolidated School basement and detonated it, killing thirty-eight school children. He wasn't able to detonate all of the dynamite—otherwise many more would have died. Interestingly, this is how the hero of *Heathers* planned to blow up his school.

In the 1980s, there were five school attacks reminiscent of today's rage murders. In three of those cases, the student shot teachers or administrators rather than students, something rarely seen in modern rage attacks in American schools. In the early 1990s, there were four more shootings, again mostly targeting teachers and administrators. The most interesting—modern—of these was carried out by Wayne Lo, an eighteen-year-old student at Simon's Rock College of Bard, an experimental school for gifted students in Great Barrington, Massachusetts. Lo shot the female security guard in her security hut, then gunned down a professor as he was driving out of the parking lot. A student who heard the car crash ran out to see what happened. Lo shot and killed him. He then moved to the library, where he opened fire on students studying there. He followed that up with a shooting spree in the school dorm hallways. In all he killed one teacher, one security guard, and one student and wounded four others.

But the school rage murders didn't start in earnest until 1996, with fourteen-year-old Barry Loukaitis's attack on his Moses Lake, Washington, school. In just of a couple years, Loukaitis went from being an outgoing honor student to a withdrawn outcast in this desolate, small-town community (which boasts a grim sign reading "Welcome to Moses Lake, the Desert Oasis"). The tall, thin-framed boy's home life had cracked—his mother was suicidal—while students, particularly the popular Manuel Vela, called him "gaylord" and "faggot" and "dork." Loukaitis never wore shorts because he was ashamed of the bruises on his legs that resulted from the bullies' beatings. On February 2, he entered his ninth grade algebra class with his father's hunting rifle and two holster-held pistols beneath his trench coat. He shot and killed Vela and the algebra teacher and another male student, then delivered his coup-de-grace punchline: "This sure beats algebra class." The punchline was stolen from Loukaitis' favorite book, Steven King's *Rage*, making it, in retrospect, a pathetically unoriginal attempt at empowerment-through-evil. While he was in the process of "calmly" lining the students against the wall to make them hostages, he was overpowered by the gym teacher, symbolic of the triumph of the jock over the twerp. Loukatis was sentenced to two life terms plus 205 years in jail.

A year later, in Bethel, Alaska, another high school shooting occurred. Bethel, a remote town of five thousand, is sort of the Moses Lake of the Alaskan tundra. Evan Ramsey, a sixteen-year-old nerd, shot and killed a popular jock and the school principal, put the gun under his chin, but lost his nerve and surrendered. He had been egged on by two friends—a group of fifteen students who had been forewarned, and who watched the shootings from the school's second floor gallery. There was precedent in his family. Evan's father had been jailed eleven years earlier for storming the *Anchorage Times* office fully loaded and prepared to die because they refused to publish his political letter to the editor. "I had a [sic] AR 180-223 semi-auto, something like 180 rounds of ammo for it. A snub barrel .44 magnum and about 30 rounds for it," Evan's father said. Two weeks after dad's release from prison, his son done made him proud. Evan Ramsey was sentenced to two hundred years in prison. "I'm dead to the world," he said ruefully. "In a few months, nobody will really remember me. There will be other people that will commit other offenses and I'll be considered yesterday's news."

Ramsey was remarkably prescient. On October 1, 1997, Luke Woodham walked into the crowded courtyard area of his Pearl, Mississippi, high school and pulled out a 30/30 hunting rifle from under his trench coat. The star art pupil killed two fellow students, including his former girlfriend, and wounded seven others. His plot had initially involved several other students as co-conspirators, but they all backed out at the last minute, as many rebellions are deserted at the final hour. Woodham was sentenced to three life terms, and one of the plotters was sentenced to six months in a boot camp and five years probation.

Exactly two months after Pearl, fourteen-year-old freshman Michael Carneal opened fire on a prayer circle at Heath High in West Paducah, Kentucky, killing three students and injuring five more. Carneal came from a well-to-do two-parent home in an upscale section of the otherwise dreary, dying riverport town. A depressed, sarcastic nerd with a popular cheerleader for a sister, Carneal was accused of being gay in a rumor column published in his eighth grade school newspaper—he never recovered from the humiliation or the teasing that relentlessly followed. Immediately after the shooting spree, Carneal dropped the pistol, turned to the leader of the prayer group and said, "Please, just shoot me." The following morning, a small group of students gathered at the front of the school and unfurled a homemade banner across the entrance that read: "We forgive you Mike." Vicky Whitman, Michael Carneal's former girlfriend, told a civil attorney why she didn't take his earlier threats seriously: "Every school I've been to, someone would mention we should burn down the school. It's not strange for someone to not like school." It's not strange—but few seemed bothered by it, because that was just "the way things were." Carneal was sentenced to life imprisonment.

Five days after Carneal's massacre, Joseph "Colt" Todd, a fourteen-year-old, took up a position in the woods outside of his high school in Stamps, Arkansas, and opened fire on students, injuring two. Lafayette County Sheriff John Kilgore told reporters, "He said he had been living in pain for some time and that he was going to cause pain on someone else."

On March 24, 1998, Mitchell Johnson, thirteen, and Andrew Golden, eleven, pulled the fire alarm at their middle school in Jonesboro, Arkansas, took positions in a wooded hillside to create an enfilade, and opened fire on students as they filed out, catching them in the cross-fire. The two boys managed to kill four students and one teacher, and injured another ten. Eventually they were cornered into surrendering by police, who were stunned by the boys' age and their arsenal: Remington .20 caliber rifles, Smith & Wesson pistols, two-shot derringers, semi-automatics, and hundreds of rounds of ammunition. The day before the shooting, Mitchell Johnson told friends, "Tomorrow you will all find out if you live or die." But since Mitchell had bragged so much about belonging to gangs he wasn't taken seriously. Mitchell was one of those "invisible middle" kids who was part-bully, part-bullied in a school culture that tolerated and even encouraged bullying. John Marks, an administrator at Westside, boasted of his pro-bully sympathies to Harvard researchers working on a federally-funded study of the shootings: "Knowing Mitchell [Johnson], I'm not sure what he did to get picked on. [laughs] . . . . [Mitchell was] known as a whine-bag. I mean in football he was always whining because the other kids were bullying him. . . I talked to a lot of kids that get bullied, they brought it on themselves. . . ."

Exactly one month later, Andrew Wurst, a fourteen-year-old eighth grader, brought a gun to his middle school dance in Edinboro, Pennsylvania. Described as a loner, Andrew had planned to kill all the people he "hated" and then himself. He shot and killed a teacher, wounded three students, and surrendered. "I died four years ago," Wurst told police. "I've already been dead and I've come back. It doesn't matter anymore. None of this is real."

A few weeks later, on May 21, 1998, Kip Kinkel walked into his high school cafeteria in Springfield, Oregon, and opened fire on the four hundred students gathered there before classes. He killed two boys and wounded twenty-two other students, four critically, six seriously. As a student he had tried to play the class clown, much like Andy did, but his act crashed hard: he was voted "Most Likely to Start WW III" by his peers. Unlike many shooters, Kinkel was getting deeper into trouble with school officials and the law before the shooting—most rampage murderers do not have a history of trouble with authorities or the school, just as most office rage murderers don't have violent records before their massacres, one of the factors that makes profiling school shooters so impossible. The day before Kinkel's shooting he was caught at school with a stolen gun, arrested, suspended, and sent home. His father desperately tried to place him that day in a "boot camp" for troubled youth, a popular parental remedy in the 1990s. But the next morning, Kinkel took fate into his own hands. He killed both of his parents, brought a .22 rifle to school under his trench coat, and opened fire.

Thus ended the bloody 1997–1998 academic school year. Middle-American students across the country memorized a brand new subject—the school rage massacre—a subject that today is impossible to unlearn.

Some analysts argue that in terms of actual numbers of victims, the school rage murder phenomenon is still rather insignificant. The number of large-scale massacres is relatively small, less than a couple dozen in the last ten years by most counts. The Justice Policy Institute noted in a report issued in 2000 that even in the bloody 1998–1999 academic year, the chances of dying at school from homicide or suicide were less than one in two million, compared to an out-of-school rate that was forty times higher. Yet the fear is real: the same institute report noted that seven in ten Americans believed a shooting was likely in their school. Indeed the homicide rate is totally misleading—the number of plots, threats, and near-misses is many, many times greater than the actual shootings. The shootings are a shock. They are not supposed to happen in middle-class schools, and they didn't until now. The shootings are a direct assault on the American Dream—which is why they are so disturbing. The fear reflects how unsettling and piercing this crime is. And the fear reflects a still-censored recognition that the shootings have widespread sympathy among students, and that any student, at any school, could be next. This is a well-founded fear. The fact that there were only a dozen slave rebellions didn't make whites feel any safer, nor should they have felt safer, simply based on the low number of outbreaks. They knew that something was terribly wrong with slavery, but they couldn't consciously admit it.

Most Americans know that the low homicide rate doesn't mean that schools are really safe so much as it reflects effective policing, snitching, and zero-tolerance repression, keeping many more would-be rage murderers, by a factor of tens or hundreds, from crossing the line from plotting to killing.

8

Culturally Normative Behavior

AS MUCH AS THE 1997–1998 ACADEMIC YEAR SHOCKED MIDDLE AMERICA, it would pale in comparison to what came next. On April 20, 1999, the bloodiest of all school rage massacres took place at Columbine. Eric Harris and Dylan Klebold murdered twelve students and a teacher, wounded twenty others, and then killed themselves. Americans wanted to blame everything but Columbine High for the massacre—they blamed a violent media, Marilyn Manson, Goth culture, the Internet, the Trench Coat Mafia, video games, lax gun control laws, and liberal values. And still skipping over the school, they peered into the opposite direction, blaming the moral and/or mental sickness, or alleged homosexuality, of these two boys, as if they were exceptional freaks in a school of otherwise happy kids.

They searched all over the world for a motive, except for one place: the scene of the crime.

In fact, a typical Columbine school day for Harris and Klebold was Hell. Former student Devon Adams told the Governor's Columbine Review Commission that the boys were regularly called "faggots, weirdoes, and freaks."

As one member of the Columbine High School football team bragged after the massacre, "Columbine is a good, clean place except for those rejects. Most kids didn't want them there . . . Sure we teased them. But what do you expect with kids who come to school with weird hairdos and horns on their hats?. . . If you want to get rid of someone, usually you tease 'em. So the whole school would call them homos."

Harris got it worse than most, not just because he dressed weird or was one of the computer nerds, but also because he was short, he was a transplant from out-of-state (like Andy Williams), and, due to an embarrassing indent in his chest, he never took his shirt off during P.E., giving the jocks more ammo to attack him.

Former Columbine student Brooks Brown recounted one incident: "I was smoking cigarettes with [Klebold and Harris] when a bunch of football players drove by, yelled something, and threw a glass bottle that shattered near Dylan's feet. I was pissed, but Eric and Dylan didn't even flinch. 'Don't worry about it, man,' Dylan said. 'It happens all the time.'"

Once, a student reported them to the administration for allegedly having brought drugs to school, just to humiliate them for a laugh. Harris and Klebold were dramatically removed from class and searched—as were their lockers and cars. No drugs were found, but the damage was done. Another time, according to a report, students surrounded them in the cafeteria and threw ketchup at them.

They were so marked for abuse that even talking to them was dangerous. One female student recounted how, when she was a Columbine freshman, some jocks spotted her talking to Dylan Klebold in the school hallway between classes. After she walked away from him, one of the bullies slammed her against the lockers and called her a "fag lover." None of the students came to help her—and when asked later why she didn't report the incident to the administration, she replied, "It wouldn't do any good because they wouldn't do anything about it."

Klebold and Harris weren't the only victims of bullying. Debra Spears, whose stepsons attended Columbine in 1994–1995, said, "It was relentless. The constant threats walking through the halls. You had a whole legion of people that would tell you that just going to school was unbearable." Her stepsons both dropped out and never earned their diplomas—Columbine essentially destroyed their lives.

One favorite bullying game for the seniors was to "go bowling," in which they'd spread baby oil on the floor and throw a freshman on it, causing him to slide into the other kids. This was the original "bowling for Columbine." Another jock was notorious for forcing kids to push pennies across the ground with their noses in front of the whole school; teachers "would see it and just look the other way."

Regina Huerter, Director of Juvenile Diversion for the Denver District Attorney's office, compiled a report on Columbine's "toxic culture," as Dylan

Klebold's parents later described it. One Jewish student she interviewed told how jocks threatened to "build an oven and set him on fire," and how, during P.E. basketball, each time someone scored a basket, the bullies would cheer, "that's another Jew in the oven!" The student complained over and over, but, he said, the school administration not only didn't punish the jocks, they "did everything but call me a liar." Another student was physically and verbally abused by a group of jocks so badly that he refused to go back to the school. The father tried contacting the administration, but they didn't return his calls for six weeks, and when they did, they were curt and rude. The father pulled his son from the high school and told Huerter that "he still refuses to enter Columbine property to this day."

"All the students with whom I spoke, independent of their status at school, acknowledged there was bullying," Huerter wrote.

Students and parents all complained of Columbine High's exceptionally brutal culture, but the administration did nothing about it. Some who worked in the school district told Huerter that they kept mum about the bullying because they were afraid for their jobs. As Brown noted, "The bullies were popular with the administration."

Bullying was so deeply ingrained that, as the American Psychology Association Monitor wrote, "Columbine students said teachers and staff did not seem to notice the bullying and aggression; apparently such behaviors were culturally normative." Here again is a perfect, modern example of how what is considered normal is not only tolerated, but is simply not seen, no matter how brutal it is. From this example, it's a little easier to understand how whites accepted—did not even notice—slavery, in spite of its cruelty.

Many parents and students said that the reason for Columbine's bully-coddling culture went straight to the top, to principal Frank DeAngelis, himself a jock.

DeAngelis, along with district officials, disagreed. "We had problems just like any other high school," he said. The real problem, he implied in a statement to the governor's commission, was the lack of optimism expressed by his whiny detractors: "I'm a very positive person. That upsets people at times because they say, 'How can people be so positive? How can things be so rosy?'"

Most Americans, even today, essentially side with DeAngelis, the positive-thinking jock-principal. They still don't blame the school for causing the massacre. Even though all of the other alleged causes (liberal moral relativism/violent media/availability of guns) have left us unsatisfied, a poll taken five years after the Columbine massacre showed that 83 percent of Americans now blame the boys' parents above everything else. Just three years before that, 81 percent of Americans blamed the Internet.

Yet both Eric Harris and Dylan Klebold came from two-parent homes, and both openly confessed their love for their parents in their otherwise rage-filled video diaries. Their only regret was how their planned massacre would hurt their parents. In fact love for their parents was the only love that they are known to have professed. Eric Harris, considered by many to be the more "evil" of the two, said, "My parents are the best fucking parents I have ever known. My dad is great. I wish

I was a fucking sociopath so I don't have any remorse, but I do. This is going to tear them apart. They will never forget it."

Eric Harris was not the only one who wished he was a sociopath—so do a lot of people today who are still trying to frame the Columbine massacre as a product of something unrelated to the school environment.

Slate's Dave Cullen, commenting on Harris's Web diary rants (which are often comical in the list of things he hates, such as "Cuuuuuuuuhntryyyyyyyyyy music," "Star Wars fans," "all you fitness fuckheads," and "morons" who mispronounce words like "eXpresso"), concluded, "These are not the rantings of an angry young man, picked on by jocks until he's not going to take it anymore. These are the rantings of someone with a messianic-grade superiority complex, out to punish the entire human race for its appalling inferiority." Indeed.

Other, more serious psychology experts disagreed. In the *APA Journal*, the two development psychology academics observed, "Research indicates that chronic targets of peer harassment become increasingly withdrawn and depressed. The other, much less common reaction to bullying is hostility and aggression. Why did Eric Harris and Dylan Klebold have this more extreme reaction? It seems that bullying and victimization were not just individual phenomena, they were part of the school culture at Columbine High."

It was the school, and the larger middle-American culture that nurtured a school like Columbine.

Susan Klebold, Dylan's mother, told *New York Times* columnist David Brooks five years after the murder, "I think he suffered horribly before he died. For not seeing that, I will never forgive myself."

9

Anorexic Andy

There's a lot of hate around here.
—**Gentry Robler**, Santana High sophomore

THE SANTEE RAGE MASSACRE took place less than two years after Columbine, and this time, thanks in part to the pathetic figure of Andy Williams, people started to seriously consider the role bullying might have played. But there was resistance. In the immediate aftermath, Santana High School officials and local law enforcement officials either denied growing reports that he was a victim of bullying, or else they argued that even if he had been bullied it had nothing to do with the shooting.

Andy's appointed lawyer, Deputy Public Defender Randy Mize (his father could not afford to hire a private attorney), listed eighteen incidents of bullying just in the weeks leading up to the shooting, including "burned with cigarette lighter on his neck every couple of weeks," "sprayed with hair spray and then lit with a lighter," "beat with a towel that caused welts by bullies at the pool," and "slammed against a tree twice because of rumors." These "rumors" of course were rumors of the sexual orientation sort, the most devastating of all bombs you can drop on a newcomer kid who is incapable of defending himself. Jeff Williams, Andy's father, later said, "Some of the stuff basically borders on torture."

As Andy quickly learned, Santana High's culture combined the lethal cruelty of coastal California suburbia with familiar, rural trailer park hazing. He wanted out. He visited his mother in South Carolina a few months before his attack, and hoped to move back with her. When he visited old school friends in rural Maryland on that same trip, he told them that kids at his high school regularly egged his father's apartment or stole his homework and threw it into garbage bins. They called him "faggot" and "bitch" and "gay" and taunted him for not fighting back when he was bullied. Worst of all, much of the abuse came from the neighborhood "friends" he hung out with, got stoned with (he turned stoner to try to earn acceptance), and from whom he tried and failed to learn to become a skate rat. Some were students at the high school, some weren't. Andy's decision to hang out with students from another school, which suburban kids don't often do, in spite of the fact that these "friends" abused him at least as much as the Santana High "friends," says a lot about the choices he faced. If Andy could have learned to skate, he might have been accepted by a second-tier clique in the coastal California public school hierarchy. As it was, not only did he never live up to the skate rat standards on the ramp, but to punish him for being a dork, his skateboard was stolen on at least two occasions by his friends, who then taunted him for being too much of a fag to protect his board. In spite of their relentless taunting, Andy joined them at the local skate park, where they got buzzed on liquor and weed, skated on the ramps (he just watched), and tormented Andy Williams.

"His ears stuck out, he was small, skinny, had a high voice, so people always picked on him 'cause he was the little kid," said Scott Bryan, a friend of Williams.

He earned the nickname "Anorexic Andy."

"He was picked on all the time," student Jessica Moore said. "He was picked on because he was one of the scrawniest guys. People called him freak, dork, nerd, stuff like that."

Laura Kennamer, a friend, said, "They'd walk up to him and sock him in the face for no reason. He wouldn't do anything about it."

Even Andy's fifty-nine-year-old, neighbor Jim Crider, observed, "Williams looked like someone working hard to fit in with his peers—and not quite succeeding. His clothes did not match what the other kids were wearing. When he talked, others didn't always pay attention."

Anthony Schneider, who was fifteen when the Santee shootings happened, both confirmed Crider's observation and gave a small glimpse into the dumb, cool poison of this schoolyard culture there: "He didn't have that many friends. A lot of people picked on him. He was kind of a weirdo . . . He didn't talk that much. He just kept to himself. . . . One of my friends stole his skateboard [about a month ago]." Schneider's flat braggadocio about his friend who stole Andy's skateboard is a familiar cool tag for anyone who has experienced life in the suburban California school culture. I would have thought that his type had evolved by now—but no, like jellyfish, it turns out they're the same as they always were.

While visiting friends in Maryland a few months earlier, Andy was videotaped softly telling the camera, "My school is horrible. I hate it there." That was the same trip where he asked his mother to let him move in with her in South Carolina, anything to escape Santee.

On February 8, a few weeks before his shooting spree, one of Andy's best friends from Twentynine Palms, a boy described as a shy outsider suffering from muscular dystrophy whom Andy had essentially rescued from the lower rungs of twerpdom, was hit by a bus and killed. Andy was devastated by the news, though he never expressed his grief until after he was jailed. He couldn't show pain in the coastal suburbs, especially not over some dweeb who was a gimp.

So this was how the best years of Andy Williams's life began—in the words of his father, "border[ing] on torture." He was beaten up, taunted, set on fire, regularly burned with a cigarette lighter, had his skateboard repeatedly stolen, and his shoes pulled from his feet. He was taunted for being a fag, taunted for being taunted, and taunted for not fighting back, which only weakened his will and confidence more . . . and yet he was the weirdo in the eyes of the normal students. And he was only halfway through his freshman year.

His own explanation for why he shot at his fellow students was simple yet honest: "I was trying to prove a point." Word for word, this is the same reason Brian Uyesugi gave to Hawaiian police after his shooting spree in the Xerox office which left seven dead.

Prosecutor Kristin Anton told the *San Diego Union-Tribune* that authorities had failed to uncover any evidence that Andy Williams was the victim of a bullying campaign. "We've talked to hundreds of people . . . and frankly there isn't evidence to support this bullying theory," she said. Evidence that Andy's neighborhood "friends" had brutalized him was dismissed by Anton: "[T]hey did it in a way that they'd laugh about it and continue to associate with each other."

District Superintendent Granger Ward also denied that Williams's shooting was sparked by bullying, in remarks reported in the *Union-Tribune*: "Based on the district's own review last year and information from the District Attorney's Office, there is no evidence that Williams was bullied at school." Ward characterized Andy Williams's shooting as a criminal act by someone who brought a gun to campus and shot students and staffers. By shifting all of the blame away from the vicious school culture and onto the evil psychology of Andy Williams, Ward was essentially indemnifying himself. "It is unfortunate that the perpetrator of this crime is not the focus, and that's where the focus should be," he told reporters.

What was really unfortunate for Ward were subsequent media exposés which revealed that his school knew a lot more about the bullying problem than they had let on, and they had bungled and wasted a perfect opportunity to change the school's culture. In 1999, almost two years before the shooting, the U.S. Justice Department gave Santana High's school district a $137,000 grant to study the causes and effects of school bullying in partnership with the local Sheriff's office. The district could have chosen to give that grant money to any of its schools, but it chose Santana High. Why? The school later denied that the grant was given specifically to Santana High because it was a particularly cruel school beset by rampant bullying—they said that Santana was chosen essentially at random.

Almost all the grant money intended to study Santana High's bullying problem went instead to dubiously-related projects, like purchasing computer equipment and software for the police, including $3,400 for a computer image projector and $4,600 for mapping software. Money was also spent hiring "consultants" who were ineffective and generally ignored. As the *Union-Tribune* noted, "[P]articipants said a computer system to track juveniles wasn't used as planned, people received training they never used and little study was done of frequent bullies and victims." One "consultant," Nancy McGee, was paid twenty-five dollars an hour for organizing such bullying-reduction activities as the annual Peace Week, which included a school peace march and sensitivity training seminars, as well as a field trip for 75 students to the Museum of Tolerance in Los Angeles.

There were accusations that the money was wasted. As one parent, who was trained with six hundred dollars of grant money to act as a mediator, said, "I left there thinking, 'OK, we're going to do something with this.'" The parent was never called again.

After Andy Williams's shooting spree, the school had used some non-earmarked grant funds to bring in a bullying expert from Clemson University, Sue Limber. She interviewed students, parents, and teachers, and drafted her recommendations on how to change the school culture. The school board rejected her recommendations, charging that they did not apply to Santana's circumstances.

Remarkably, after three years and $137,000 in grant money, almost no actual interviews were conducted with bullies or bullied students in order to understand them better, no analysis was ever produced, and no recommendations ever forwarded. However, a more general survey of Santana High students and parents was conducted, and it yielded interesting results about the extent to which bullying was an integral part of the school's culture.

Roughly one-third of the school's 1,200 students surveyed said that they had been bullied, and nearly half said that they retaliated in some way. About one in five students were repeat victims of bullying, more often girls than boys. About 11 percent said they had brought a weapon to campus, and of those, a third said they brought the weapon for protection, while a tenth said they brought the weapon in order to intimidate. Most students—and even most parents—said that they did not tell school officials about bullying because they didn't think it would help. Remarkably, in spite of this perceived violence and threat of violence, and the lack of protection, only 7 percent of these same students said they felt unsafe at the school, and roughly the same percentage of parents felt that the school was unsafe for their kids. In other words, this prison yard culture in a white middle-American school was seen as normal by most people. And the principal and superintendent had this information two years before Andy Williams's shooting.

Their reading of the situation was right: it was normal. A national survey on bullying conducted by the Kaiser Family Foundation and *Nickelodeon* in mid-2001 showed that nearly one-third of all sixth through tenth-graders nationwide were either bullies or targets of bullying. Seventy-four percent of eight to eleven-year-olds say teasing and bullying occur at their school, while for the twelve to fifteen-year-olds, the number rises to 86 percent. And both age groups called the teasing and bullying "big problems" that rank higher than racism, AIDS, and the pressure to have sex or to try alcohol or drugs.

Time and again, students and parents complain of the devastating effects of bullying and their inability to stop it, no matter where they live. As one man in upper-middle-class suburban Iowa, whose son was savaged by local kids for being a "fag," said, "My son does not say if he's gay or not, but he is afraid to ride his bike, or even be out in the neighborhood alone. Our neighborhood has homes valued at $200,000 to $300,000 and he does not feel safe."

One reason why our society has failed to curb bullying is that we like bullies. Hell, we are bullies. Research has shown that bullies are not the anti-social misfits that adults, in their forced amnesia, want them to be. Rather, bullies are usually the most popular boys, second only on the clique-ranking to those described as friendly, outgoing, and self-confident. The Santana High kids and parents both felt that there was no point in complaining to the administration because they wouldn't have done anything anyway, a reflection of the fact that popular winners are treated better than losers. At Columbine, parents and students both felt that bullies were favored by teachers and administrators, and that complainers were often ignored or blamed. Indeed, losers pay for being losers twice over in our schools, taking both the punishment and the blame. Many kids (and adults) believe that victims of bullying bring it upon themselves; studies show how kids will often egg bullies on against their victims, in part to curry the bully's favor, in part to distinguish themselves from the victim class.

As we scratch the surface of this phenomenon, we start to see how miserable the school experience is for a great number of kids—white, middle-class, middle-American kids. It's a misery built into the modern school culture. In fact, it is so obvious, and so common, that only a kind of adult amnesia, combined with powerful cultural propaganda, could edit away such a widely-held bad memory.

10

I Would Have Done It Too

IT TOOK THE SHOCK AND PATHOS of Andy Williams's murder rampage to shake Middle America out of its previous smug attitude toward bullying.

As recently as 1999, just a few months after Columbine, *Time* published an article essentially designed to debunk a growing post-Columbine sensibility that perhaps these school massacres were trying to tell us something. The article, "A Week in the Life of a High School"—whose burlesque title, parodying Solzhenitsyn's gulag novel, belittled the notion that middle-American schools are Hell—essentially reduced the pain of countless traumatized adolescents to little more than pampered PC whining:

> So if you aren't allowed to wear a hat, toot your horn, form a clique, or pick on a freshman, all because everyone is worried that someone might snap, it's fair to ask: Are high schools preparing kids for the big ugly world outside those doors—or handicapping them once they get there? High school was once useful as a controlled environment, where it was safe to learn to handle rejection, competition, cruelty, charisma. Now that we've discovered how unsafe a school can be, it may have become so controlled that some lessons will just have to be learned elsewhere.

Note how the author casually equates bullying with fashion statements in the catalogue of zany, trivial adolescent worries. Nancy Gibbs, who wrote the article, is more than simply dismissive of victims' complaints—she thinks that bullying in schools is actually a good thing because it prepares kids for the real world, i.e., the office world. Rather than arguing that bullying is a serious problem that needs to be stopped, she accepts it and sneers at anti-bullying critics, implying that they are flaky and "unrealistic." Indeed she seems to rue the possibility that bullying might be curtailed in schools, and thus the valuable lessons of bullying will have to be taught elsewhere. This is emblematic of how deeply embedded cruelty is in our culture—it is considered respectable and mainstream to actually want our own children to be bullied. Bullying is just "reality."

Of course, one could make the same argument about sexual harassment that Gibbs makes about bullying—indeed, people often did—that it's not such a big deal, and that women who suffered from it needed to suck it up, get over it, and learn to deal with it or risk being handicapped in the real world. As we know, abolitionists in their day were not considered realistic either.

Nancy Gibbs clearly did not know schoolyard pain. Or if she did, she deleted it from her memory sometime during her climb to the top of the mainstream American journalism food chain. I don't know a single useful lesson that I or anyone else ever learned from being bullied—it only brought shame and debilitating memories. Getting bullied always leads you to wrong decisions and wrong conclusions. You compensate in all the wrong ways. You wind up looking for someone weaker to bully yourself, you lose confidence and hate your weakness, and you fear and distrust the wrong people, all of which are reasons why bullied kids overwhelmingly wind up as failures in the real world, according to recent studies. You have to have never been bullied to think that it teaches something valuable and necessary and makes you a stronger person. Dr. Tonja Nansel, who worked on a 1998 World Health Organization survey on Health Behavior in School-Aged Children, showed that both bullies and the bullied develop far greater problems later on in life—bullied kids particularly have difficulties making friends, and suffer from lifelong loneliness.

I know that I learned far more valuable lessons when I was the bully than when I was bullied. The lesson was simple: it felt better to be the one dishing it out. The pangs of remorse after pummeling a scrawny dork wore off pretty quickly; the humiliations of being on the receiving end, however, were replayed over and over and over, for years and years. I cannot imagine what kind of callous moron could possibly see anything valuable in being a victim of bullying. Maybe the idea comes from our cultural propaganda, where the bullied nerd, like *Back to the Future*'s McFly, always fights back in the triumphant climax, becomes a stronger person for it, and goes on to be a successful patron of a nuclear family, while the bully winds up washing his car. Bullying, in our cultural propaganda, is simply a dramatic plot device which the hero overcomes. Rarely, if ever, is it represented as it really works—as something privately eating away at kids, flat and uninteresting, and never overcome. But the school shootings, culminating with Andy Williams's attack, created a kind of cognitive dissonance—no one could explain why an everykid like him was shooting up his school.

As Dr. Nansel said, "In the past, bullying has simply been dismissed as kids will be kids," but that now we were waking up to its effects, "it should not be accepted as a normal part of growing up."

In the wake of Santee, a groundswell of opposition to schoolyard bullying finally broke through the resistance and censorship. Confessions about the life-destroying effects of bullying poured out from all parts of the country. It was as if Andy Williams had declared it was time to let a thousand flowers bloom. As if, like a rebel insurgent, he had sacrificed his life and other, likely innocent lives (as so often innocents die in rebellions) to force the issue, and perhaps save millions in the future.

This may sound melodramatic, but in fact, Williams's shooting had exactly this effect, inspiring some of the most pathos-heavy confessionals I've read.

One of the best post-Santee confessions was a brave op-ed, "Young Voices: Stop the Teasing, or More Kids May Die," by nineteen-year-old Michigan State freshman Emily Stivers, published in the March 20, 2001, edition of the *Detroit Free Press*:

> From as far back as I can remember, I was teased incessantly by my peers. I was "that short, fat girl with glasses," the one no one ever paid any attention to except to tease or spit on. But it would hardly have made any difference had I been tall and beautiful—kids will always find some way to make you miserable.
>
> . . . And often, you don't blame them. You blame yourself. You think "they must be right, I must be short and fat and ugly," and long after high school is done, you think that.
>
> I was tortured so badly that I seriously tried to commit suicide on three separate occasions in high school, and I filled up notebooks with violent pictures of all the mean, spiteful people I wished would just die. After those horrible 14 years of public education, I can certainly understand what drives a 15-year-old boy branded as "anorexic Andy" to bring a gun to school. Maybe a few more insults, a little more spit, and I would have done it, too.
>
> . . . That child was not concerned with consequences, he was only concerned with making his own pain go away. And no matter what he comes to regret later, I am certain that at the time, Charles "Andy" Williams knew that spending his life in prison was preferable to spending the next four years of it in the prison of his school.

This remarkably candid and courageous public confession gets closer to the heart of the conflict—that school, for most kids, is not at all the carefree, innocent, idyllic time we're told to believe it is, even against our own private experiences. As Carol Miller Lieber of Educators for Social Responsibility said, "The winners are a smaller group than we'd like to think, and high school life is very different for those who experience it as the losers. They become part of the invisible middle and suffer in silence, alienated and without any real connection."

The "invisible middle"—that is, in many ways, the very worst place to be. It is from this invisible middle that so many school shooters come. They aren't social outcasts and violent loners from broken homes. Andy Williams was a popular honor roll student in Maryland and, at least a normal kid in Twentynine Palms; after just six months in Santee, he was in armed revolt.

A few weeks after Stivers's op-ed, the *Detroit Free Press* published the article, "Mom's Group Tries to End Taunting," detailing the growing battle against bullying. Note how the dramatic rhetoric takes on the increasingly confident tone of a moral crusade, like civil rights or abolitionism:

> Chandra Sansom looks at her 13-month-old daughter and with tears choking her voice, explains why she started Parents Against Teasing and Taunting.
>
> "I don't want her to have to go through what I went through," said Sansom, 29, a bullying victim whose oldest child, Thaddeus Evans-Walker, 7, already has had regular run-ins with a school bully at Taft Elementary School in Ferndale.
>
> Her son's experience—which included being punched in the stomach by another first-grader—spurred her to start the group a few months ago with the goal of putting more anti-bullying material, such as a series of children's books about teasing and lying, in the hands of educators.
>
> . . . Bullying by fellow eighth-graders left Sansom with few coping mechanisms. She'd routinely fake an ankle injury so she could arrive at school 5 minutes late and leave 5 minutes early.
>
> But that didn't stop the constant teasing, taunting—including paint being poured on her hair—and fights, she said. It became bad enough during her senior year of high school, in 1989, that Sansom quit school just two months shy of graduation.
>
> "I let bullies rob me of my graduation," said Sansom, who a year later received a general equivalency diploma.
>
> Now she looks back on those experiences and vows she won't let her other children suffer.
>
> "I'm putting my arms around not just my kid but every kid."

The sensibility spread from coast to coast. At around the same time as the above article was published, another heartbreaking account, this by an Asian American parent named Chi-Dooh Li, appeared in the *Seattle Post-Intelligencer*:

A year after our family moved from the peace and homogeneity of Mercer Island to the noise and hodgepodge of the University District, one of my sons, then 14, told my wife and me, "You saved my life by moving here."

Little did we know then how literally he meant it.

My son, now 21 and making a life for himself in New York City as a professional musician, has since shared with us the agony that he went through, beginning in third grade, from being harassed and tormented by bullies. This included having a plastic bag tied over his head and being stuffed in his gym locker, and persisted until the middle of his eighth grade year, when we moved.

The Santee shootings and the ensuing spotlight on bullying have prompted long conversations and e-mail dialogues with my son and a number of others about their childhood experiences.

As suddenly as that, the once-accepted notion that bullying is just a part of reality is now considered atavistic and heartless. After Santee, society was ready to listen, confess, and act.

11

A Problem Overlooked

WITH THE CULTURAL ATTITUDE CHANGING, legal and political change soon followed. In recent years, lawsuits by parents of bullied students have been filed against school districts across the country. In January 2004, a Eugene, Oregon, school paid $10,000 for allowing the bullying of a student—one incident was caught on camera. The same year, the Anchorage School District settled out of court regarding a lawsuit brought by the parents of a bullied fourteen-year-old boy who attempted suicide and was left with brain damage. The school administrators knew of the bullying but did nothing about it, the parents alleged. And in rural Kansas, the parents of a boy who was taunted and called "gay," causing him to eventually quit school altogether to take his GED when he was sixteen, sued the district and settled for an undisclosed sum. "I called everyone I thought could help me, and I just couldn't get it stopped," the bullied drop-out's father told the Associated Press, explaining why he initiated the lawsuit. "It's like my son didn't matter."

His son is starting to matter, though. Today, pundits and experts debated bullying's effects and how to curb it, and state and federal legislators are introducing anti-bullying bills. By 2004, seventeen states had enacted anti-bullying legislation, nearly all passed in the aftermath of Columbine and Santee, while 16 more states have legislation pending. A federal anti-bullying bill is in the works in the

United States Congress as well, sponsored by California Congresswoman Lisa Sanchez and New York Congressman Jack Quinn.

"For too long, bullying has been a problem that has been overlooked," Congresswoman Sanchez said. "The consequences of ignoring this problem are very serious."

The cultural awakening against bullying is spreading. In a reverse of the office-to-schoolyard progression of rage massacres, recognition about bullying is moving up from the schoolyard to the office.

As a *New York Times* article, "Fear in the Workplace," noted, "Researchers have long been interested in the bullies of the playground, exploring what drives them and what effects they have on their victims. Only recently have researchers turned their attention to the bullies of the workplace."

By bullying in the workplace, the *Times* is referring to classic schoolyard bullying, the asshole boss or supervisor who abuses his or her power over subordinates. As the article leads, "Every working adult has known one—a boss who loves making subordinates squirm, whose moods radiate through the office, sending workers scurrying for cover, whose very voice causes stomach muscles to clench and pulses to quicken."

Carrie Clark, a fifty-two-year-old former teacher and school administrator in Sacramento, described what it felt like to be bullied by a boss, insulted repeatedly for ten months before she quit to save her health: "It got to where I was twitching, literally, on the way to work."

Long before this, the 1994 U.S. Postal Service commission report criticized the institution's "autocratic management style . . . tense and confrontational relations on the workroom floor."

On a fundamental level, the level of human relations, we are finally recognizing that the office world and the school world share a horrible trait: rampant bullying, in which the bullies are the winners. And, they share another awful trait: life in each setting is only wonderful for a very small elite—for executives and shareholders in the adult world, and for popular kids with happy home lives and bright futures in the school world. Meanwhile, life is a wretched time for many, if not most.

It hurts to consider that the flat cruelty of the adult world is merely a continuation of the school world. We need contrast. We can't believe that our own children endure the same awful treatment as we go through in the office . . . that they suffer for eighteen years only to graduate to a world that merely repeats all that is cruel, spiteful, and dehumanizing. Perhaps this is why, in spite of so much evidence of the similarities in the settings and the crimes, no one has seriously considered that school massacres and workplace massacres are products of the same socioeconomic squeeze.

While bullying (a playground word that seems to cheapen its truly devastating effects) is finally being recognized as wrong in specific settings where rage massacres have taken place, what is still being avoided is bullying on the broader, cultural level. We ignore the bullying of the Al Dunlaps, who abuses his wife, fires tens of thousands of workers and walks away with tens of millions for himself . . . and not only gets away with it, but becomes adored for his "mean business." Just as bullies are popular in schools. Or the bullying of Reaganomics, where the vulnerable were sacrificed in order to fatten up the rich, an uninterrupted policy that is only getting worse. Or the bullying of a popular new management style that pushes for increased fear and stress to squeeze "unlimited juice," and that creates a workforce that "never leaves" in spite of it. Not to mention, of course, the bullying of President Bush's brutish foreign policy, which has turned most of the world against America to a degree not seen in our lifetime, yet which has made Bush even more popular at home...that is until the bullied started fighting back.

That said, Andy Williams did manage to spark a significant shift in the culture, a mini-cultural revolution. If someone were to stand up in 2005 and argue, on television, that bullying is "not a big deal" today, they would be the weirdo, the one who would cause people to roll their eyes.

It is exactly this kind of transformation, of what is considered "normal," that is at the heart of this book. In a matter of a few years, the concept of bullying had gone from being considered "culturally normative" and part of reality, to being recognized as intolerable and lethal.

Was Andy Williams's uprising a success or a failure? His shooting did help change discourse, and legislation. He found enormous sympathy and sparked uprisings around the country. In that sense, it was a success. But is bullying really the fundamental problem? Laws were enacted in early America to mitigate cruelty towards slaves—but slavery still continued in a refined form.

For Andy Williams personally, the rebellion was a cruel failure. In the months after he was arrested, Andy hit puberty. Within a year, he went from being "Anorexic Andy" to a six-foot-three hulk, as stocky as a defensive lineman. Such a build would have changed his life at Santana High if he had held out another year. The only place where being a six-foot-three sixteen-year-old didn't help was where he was stuck. As Andy told an ABC *Primetime Thursday* interviewer, in his prison there are "five thousand bullies in one place."

"I don't really have a criminal background. I'm not really like a mean, like, hard-hearted guy. So I don't think I'm going to make it in prison. It's a tough place."

He was sentenced to fifty years to life. He will be eligible for parole when he turns sixty five.

12

No Profile Possible

KIDS ARE DEMONSTRABLY MORE MISERABLE TODAY than they used to ʰ According to the book *Kids Killing Kids*, as many as one in every four childrᵉ some form of psychological disorder, and one in every five has a moʳ severe disorder. Just twenty years ago, these disorders weren't viewed ʾ

more than normal growing pains. Today, the slightest aberration brings an avalanche of drugs and therapy—the pressure comes from parents, administrators, and rapacious drug companies which have bought off the politicians. America's kids are pumped full of legal drugs—particularly Ritalin and Adderall, which are essentially prescription speed, and Prozac, Zoloft, or other anti-depressants. At the same time school administrations constantly teach kids to "just say no to drugs." You start to get a sense of the madness of school life today.

The number of children and adolescents who take a wide variety of psychiatric drugs more than doubled from 1987 to 1996, according to a study reported in the *New York Times*. Today, 20 percent of high school students are on antidepressants or medicines for other psychiatric disorders. Another study done by University of Texas physicians estimates that Ritalin use among school-age children jumped from about 400,000 in 1980 to 900,000 in 1990—and then exploded to five million kids aged six to eighteen-years-old on Ritalin by the year 2000. Add to that another estimated three million kids who are on some other powerful psychiatric medicine—making the total of about eight million or 15 percent of the school-aged population.

Some might argue that these numbers simply show that kids are being diagnosed more closely and fed drugs more eagerly than before—that nothing has really changed except for the adults' hysterical doting, or the kids' whining. However, according to a government study conducted in 1999, one in five adolescents seriously considered suicide, and one in ten actually attempted suicide. This represents a 400 percent increase in the adolescent suicide rate since 1950!

It is difficult to argue, as some want to, that kids today are simply too pampered and whiny. They are demonstrably miserable, so much so that they're killing themselves and leading armed rebellions against their schools. And it's not just a particular type of kid who's doing this. Experts have been unable to profile the type of kid who would likely execute a school massacre. It's potentially any kid.

The Secret Service conducted the most exhaustive and authoritative attempt to understand and profile school massacres. In 2002, the Secret Service's National Threat Assessment Center issued a report called the "Safe School Initiative," and in it they concluded that no profile of a school shooter was possible, except perhaps that the attacker would most likely be a male. Which doesn't narrow it down much. This suggests that the kind of kid who would shoot up his school is not exceptional, but rather ordinary—from the "invisible middle." Given the data about how common it is to be suicidally miserable, this shouldn't be surprising.

Others have tried to offer up a profile. The FBI in 2000 issued a study which they cautioned, for good reason, was not meant to be a profile but rather provide warning signs of potential schoolyard rage murderers. Yet these warning signs would make suspects of about half the male school-age population:

signs of depression;

a pathological need for attention;

racial intolerance; and

an unusual interest in acts of sensational violence and a fascination with violence-filled entertainment.

The third warning sign, racial intolerance, is almost totally absent from all of the school rampage shootings that I and others have studied. In the initial days following a rage attack, allegations are often made of racism or Nazism as motivators—as was the case with the Columbine killers, who notably shot and killed the black football team star, and supposedly taunted him. But as others pointed out, the Columbine killers taunted most of their victims before shooting them, either for being preppy, God-fearing, jocks, or in the African American's case, a "nigger." In Eric Harris's diary, he writes, "You know what I hate? Racism. Anyone who hates Asians, Mexicans, or people of any race because they're different." It is as if the adult world needs to find racist motives in the school shooters and plotters in order to bracket them as exceptionally "evil," rather than, as is usually the case, typical.

James P. McGee, chief psychologist for the Baltimore Police Department, authored of a profiling study on schoolyard shooters. McGee's student rage murderer profile:

1. A white male between eleven and eighteen years old, of average intelligence from a middle-class background;
2. From a broken home;
3. Shows no symptoms of severe mental disorders such as schizophrenia or manic depression;
4. Small in stature and picked on by public-school classmates;
5. No history of serious conduct problems;
6. Access to firearms, and a penchant for wearing military garb;
7. Threats of violence before the shooting

Based on this, McGee boasted to the press after the Santee massacre that Andy Williams "came back with a high rating when compared to other cases." After he plugged the variables into MOSAIC, a computer-assisted risk assessment program used by the CIA, FBI, and other police agencies. "Here is your boy. He fits the pattern."

The only problem with this model is that the net is cast so wide as to implicate a significant minority, if not a majority, of eleven to eighteen-year old boys. We're talking millions of suspects here. What's the use of such a model, unless we're willing to treat all pubescent males as suspects, isolating all eleven to eighteen-year-old white males in barbed-wired education camps?

The first criteria implicates eleven to eighteen-year old boys from middle-class backgrounds of average intelligence. However, Andy Williams was from the rural lower-middle-class. Indeed many of the earliest shootings were carried out in rural white lower-middle-class America: Moses Lake, Washington; Bethel, Alaska; Jonesboro, Arkansas; and Pearl, Mississippi. The kinds of places they send Paris Hilton to to give the middle class a good laugh. Some take place in upper-middle-class schools, such as Columbine. And some involve girls, such as

Elizabeth Bush in Williamsport; a freshman girl in Hopkinton, Massachusetts, caught scrawling a hit list in a restroom stall in October 2003; or the girl involved in a large-scale Columbine-style plot in New Bedford, Massachusetts, in December 2001. As for "average intelligence," Andy Williams was an honor roll student until moving to California. Dylan Klebold and Eric Harris were remarkably intelligent and widely read for kids their age. In a video diary, Eric Harris quoted Shakespeare's *Tempest* to apologize in advance to his parents: "Good wombs hath born bad sons," he said. The thirteen-year-old boy who shot and wounded five fellow students at a middle school in Fort Gibson, Oklahoma, in December 1999, was a relatively popular straight-A student—and from a blue-collar town.

Next, the broken home theory. Many people assume that the Columbine killers came from broken homes—after all, most homes in America are broken and 60 percent of marriages end in divorce. Yet both Eric Harris and Dylan Klebold came from two-parent homes, and as we have already seen, both loved their parents and apologized to them in advance for the pain they would cause them. Michael Carneal, the Paducah, Kentucky, shooter who helped launch the whole trend in 1997, came from a two-parent home and had a popular older sister. Of the two Jonesboro, Arkansas, boys who followed up Carneal's shooting by pulling the fire alarm at their school, taking up position at the edge of a field, and picking off students and teachers, one came from a two-parent house, the other lived with his mother and stepfather. The Secret Service study found that two-thirds of the kids who launched rage murders at their schools came from two-parent homes. Even Andy Williams, who came from a profoundly broken home (after his jailing, both parents set up rival Web sites on behalf of their son), left a note before his shooting apologizing to his father; signing it, "Sorry Dad, I love you."

It is difficult to seriously argue with point three, that the murderers had no serious mental disorders. How do you profile and carefully monitor that demographic which is not mentally ill? The fact that these murderers are not mentally ill is, in itself, a disturbing statistic. It suggests that the kids who shoot up their schools are sane—meaning that their actions are guided by sane hands and sane thoughts. But even here the profile is flawed. Some shooters, like Paducah's Michael Carneal and Fort Gibson's Seth Trickney, exhibited signs of schizophrenia.

Small in stature. Sometimes true, sometimes not. Dylan Klebold was one of the taller kids in his class. One of the two Jonesboro shooters played on the basketball team. Jason Hoffman of Granite Hills High was over six feet tall and two hundred pounds. Luke Woodham of Pearl, Mississippi, was overweight. There are too many exceptions to this rule. Given different rates of puberty at this age, to suggest that "small in stature" is a warning sign or a profile is as useful as listing "young" as a warning sign.

Next, no history of serious conduct problems. Again, sometimes true, sometimes not. Klebold and Harris had been busted by police for burglarizing a van a year before their massacre. Eric Harris was also investigated for reportedly making a pipe bomb as well as for making death threats on his Web site. Mitchell Johnson, one of the two Jonesboro shooters, was taken to juvenile court and charged with molesting a two-year-old baby the year before his rage attack. Kip

Kinkel was arrested and suspended at his Oregon high school the day before the massacre.

Sixth, access to firearms. That really narrows it down. This is America, not Japan. You might as well include "access to a Starbuck's." There are some 200 million guns in American homes, twice the amount as just thirty years ago. According to one survey, 63 percent of rural or suburban teenagers either own a gun or live in a household with easy access to a gun. Gun ownership is a duty in this country. When I grew up, we had seventeen guns in our house. It is simply our cultural normative behavior, as they say.

Lastly, threats of violence before the shooting. This seems rather common— yet it is hard to distinguish a fake threat from a real threat. Massive murder plots have been unmasked with a lot of media noise accompanying them, only to evaporate under further investigation, leaving little more than destroyed young lives and embarrassed adults sweeping their mistakes under the courthouse carpet. In other words, hysteria has transformed what was once considered typical teenage boast into genuine threat—and lives are being ruined because of it. Today, given the paranoia and profiling that includes nearly every student, all threats of violence, no matter what the context, are assumed to be spoken with intent, and therefore prosecuted. Yet the school shootings and shooting plots continues. The zero-tolerance policy isn't stopping it—it's only increasing the culture of fear and suspicion, which in turn only increases the chances of another school shooting.

The one common denominator the Secret Service did find was that a majority of school shooters is that they were traumatized by bullying. This means that if a kid is unfortunate enough to be bullied, he becomes a shooting suspect. For obvious reasons, targeting bullied kids for surveillance or preventative detention is no solution, and cruel.

The fact is, adults, including law enforcement, are clueless because kids, if they're at all smart, know how easy it is to tell adults what they want to hear. This explains why, just months before the Columbine shooting, Eric Harris was praised by his court supervisor following his arrest for burglarizing a van. "Eric is a very bright young man who is likely to succeed in life," the court supervisor wrote. "He is intelligent enough to achieve lofty goals as long as he stays on task and remains motivated." The piling on of clichés with sunny optimism is almost comical, as is the court supervisor's assessment of Dylan Klebold: "He is intelligent enough to make any dream a reality but he needs to understand hard work is part of it."

13

Kids 4 Snitching

ON JANUARY 28, 2001, Al DeGuzman, a nineteen-year-old student at De Anza Community College, dropped off some rolls of film to be developed at a local Long's drugstore. De Anza, in Cupertino, California, is where many of my high school friends went for junior college. The rolls DeGuzman brought to be developed weren't filled with your stereotypical nineteen-year-old's photos of raucous beer bong parties and girls gone wild. Instead, they were snapshots of himself brandishing a variety of homemade bombs while wearing a t-shirt that read "Natural Selection." The girl working the film department that night, Kelly Bennett, a chubby eighteen-year-old San Jose State freshman, saw the photos and called her father, a policeman.

"I knew that theory from school about survival of the fittest and only the strongest will survive," Bennett said. "I knew if this guy was going around advertising that, that he was not all there. . . . I was 100 percent positive that this guy was weird."

The photographs would be ready in a day. Police staked out the drugstore and waited for DeGuzman to show—which he did, almost exactly twenty-four hours after he dropped the film off.

When he handed Kelly his receipt to pick up the photos, she was terrified and even surprised. He seemed much smaller and less frightening that she'd expected. She almost didn't believe it was him. But he held the receipt; there was no doubt. She signaled the stakeout cops, who moved into the drugstore, up separate aisles. DeGuzman spotted them, turned around, and tried walking out the door as inconspicuously as he could—but he didn't get far. Police detained him and brought him in for questioning. When they searched his bedroom—he lived with his Filipino parents in a middle-class section of San Jose—they found the rage murderer's loyal companion, the duffel bag. Inside were eighteen propane gas cylinders taped together. They found a backpack holding about twenty-five Molotov cocktails, and a plastic bag with several homemade pipe bombs, each with nails and screws taped to the outside. They also found guns, lots of them: an SKS semiautomatic, a sawed-off 12-gauge pump-action shotgun, a sawed-off Ruger 10/22 semiautomatic rifle, and an MDL 98 8 mm rifle. A black binder on DeGuzman's desk contained detailed plans for an attack at De Anza College: including drawings, maps, a minute-by-minute schedule, timelines—everything for a massacre. This wasn't one geek talking shit to another in order to impress a third—this was the real thing.

DeGuzman was thrown in jail and eventually hanged himself in Folsom State Prison in the summer of 2004, while Kathy Bennett briefly became the nation's most popular snitch. She was flown to the East Coast to appear on *Today* and *Good Morning America* to be hailed as the heroine-snitch who saved possibly hundreds of lives. The implication was obvious—if you're a chubby, lonely American all you have to do is snitch on someone more desperate than you, and you might become the apple of America's eye! It's your lottery ticket out of the Long's wage trap!

DeGuzman, on the other hand, became something of a laughing stock: ABC News declared "Vanity Helps Nab a Prospective Killer," while CNN shocked its viewers by revealing that DeGuzman wasn't like us: "Photo clerk says California bombing suspect was 'weird.'" The word "weird" has a particularly strong meaning in contemporary American discourse—in school it ranks, in its ability to destroy and expel, just a step down from the "gay" epithet, while in the office world, "weird" is the white-collar death sentence.

The current media blitz encouraging kids to snitch is perhaps understandable given our fear and given the failure to stop Santana High's shooting even though many kids knew about it in advance. But persuading kids to become informants is disturbing nonetheless. After DeGuzman, the pro-snitch propaganda has exploded recently, with students enlisted in a new push to help encourage a culture of snitching. In Oregon, a group of students called "By Kids 4 Kids" made a video arguing that snitching can save lives.

The video's language was eerily similar to Soviet snitch-encouraging propaganda and sloganeering. Everyone was encouraged to inform on everyone else— children who snitched on their parents were made into national heroes. Pavlik Morozov, the legendary Soviet boy who snitched on his father to Stalin's NKVD, resulting in his father's arrest and "disappearance," had finally found a new and welcome home: The United States of America.

ABC NEWS – SNITCHING IS GOOD
Breaking the Code of Silence
Students Are Now Willing to Snitch to Prevent Violence
By Michele Norris

ANNANDALE, Va., April 19, 2001—As threats of violence at schools across the country have increased, particularly since the Columbine High School tragedy in 1999, students have become more willing to break the code of silence and tattle on their peers.

It has been difficult to break the teenage mindset that snitching on one's friends is unacceptable.

Yes, it's difficult to break that anti-snitching mindset, but they're working hard on it.

Some would argue that since Americans are so different, we couldn't possibly be heading down the Soviet path. We're a freedom-loving, privacy-respecting people. We know the limits of intrusion. We're responsible enough to know where to draw the line, right?

This article in the April 9, 2001, edition of the *Des Moines Register* reveals not only how far down the Soviet road Middle America is willing to go, but also how crazy we can be when we go Soviet:

Cedar Rapids police are believed to be the first in Iowa to create a student hot line to take tips on illegal activity. Teens who call about classmates they believe to have alcohol, drugs or weapons on school property get $50 if the police recover anything.

You have to wonder who the cob-headed fool was who came up with this scheme. Anyone who remembers what kids are really like knows how dangerously flawed this snitch-for-cash scheme is. No teenaged boy could possibly avoid taking advantage of an offer like that. It's basically saying: "Narc on a weirdo, and earn fifty bucks!" That's called free money.

Cedar Rapids may have been the first in Iowa to create a student hot line—but they were hardly the first in the country.

Of all the examples of America's knee-jerk reliance on informants, none was as chilling as the WAVE America program, launched in North Carolina in 2000, with the backing of Governor Jim Hunt. WAVE stands for "Working Against Violence Everywhere." It was designed by the Pinkerton Service Group—the same Pinkerton notorious for violently destroying unions and halting strikes in the late nineteenth and early twentieth century. Pinkerton destroyed unions not only through direct violence, such as the slaughter of striking steel workers in the Homestead Strike of 1892, but also by infiltration and encouraging snitching, which led to blacklistings and a culture of mutual suspicion within the union movement. Some claim that Pinkerton was the forerunner of the CIA.

WAVE America relies on an anonymous tip phone line. Students are educated about WAVE through brochures and savvy info packets that encourage them to anonymously call in and report all "dangerous behavior" or students whom they suspect might be capable of committing violence. Pinkerton operators then interview the tip caller to see if its worth acting on, then forward the complaint to the relevant school. Among the "warning signs" students and teachers are encouraged to report are "social withdrawal," "excessive feelings of rejection," "feelings of being picked on and persecuted," "expressions of violence in writing and drawings," and even "being a victim of violence." In other words, if you bully a kid, afterward you can narc on him and make him a murder suspect, just in case you don't feel like looking at him anymore.

In the first year, according to Joanne McDaniel, acting director of the Center for the Prevention of School Violence, more than four hundred calls were received. "No guns or plans were revealed, but concerns about bullying, verbal abuse, and fighting were reported."

The frightening thing is that no one knows what happens to the files Pinkerton collects on the suspected students. McDaniel claimed they destroy their files after ninety days, but a Pinkerton spokesperson wouldn't confirm this.

The trend is alarming—but it isn't entirely surprising. The office world has been imposing snitch programs for some time now, and Pinkerton is one of the leaders. In order to guard against potentially disgruntled employees, Pinkerton designed the AlertLine 800 number, which encourages employees to snitch on each other. According to their Web site, the AlertLine 800 number services over a thousand companies—"including many Fortune 500 companies"—and seven million employees. Information about a potential problem employee is vetted by Pinkerton's operators and passed on to management and filed away in their Information Services database, which holds files on employees suspected of theft and other infractions, irrespective of whether or not they were charged or convicted of the crimes.

The WAVE America Web site (www.waveamerica.com) boasts, "Pinkerton Compliance Services has more than twenty years of experience in providing simi-

lar proactive programs for business and industry through its AlertLine®
Communications Services."

The workplace and the school are not only producing the same type of crime,
they are producing the same authoritarian response, encouraging mutual suspicion, turning not just one worker against the other, but one student against the
other. Video camera surveillance, metal detectors, campus cops, and narcs are the
norm in Middle American schools. Indeed, according to some Santana High students, one person that Andy Williams shot was the school narc.

Kids will usually rat out kids who are marked for abuse—the kids who the
adults instinctively distrust as much as the kids disrespect. As socialized
mammals, we give off and process all kinds of signals that we're not actively in
control of—studies have shown that bullied kids, for example, seem to attract
bullies just by their body language. As for encouraging snitching, the incident in
which Dylan Klebold and Eric Harris were falsely ratted out by popular bullies for
carrying drugs—the two were pulled from class in front of everyone, searched
thoroughly, and later released when it was found to have been a false accusation—
is a good example of how kids really (ab)use snitching, given the opportunity, and
how easily adults can be manipulated. That wasn't the only time Klebold and
Harris were narked on as a prank and subjected to humiliating searches. No one at
Columbine got in trouble for snitching on them—unless of course you count the
shooting victims as having been "punished." The point is that there will always be
a type of student you can safely snitch on without social repercussions, and a type
you can't and won't ever snitch on. Encouraging snitching just dumps more tox-
ins into the cultural mix. It encourages bullying, cynicism, and rage. Yet something tells me the Snitch Nation culture is only going to get stronger and bolder
the more destruction it brings. Petty malice is now the major premise of American
life. This meanness has become so common that it even dominates our leisure
time, with Americans worshipping mega-millionaire assholes like Bill O'Reilly
and Donald Trump. It's an utterly masochistic addiction--and no wonder, since
Middle America has taken so much shit over the past 30 years, we've grown not
only used to the meanness, but we can even get a rush off it. America is now Zed
Nation: addicted to the pain that our masters so lovingly deliver us, rewarding
them not only with greater incomes, but with our admiration, our leisure time,
and our souls.

14

St. Eric and St. Dylan

AL DEGUZMAN, THE SO-CALLED "DE ANZA BOMBER," is a perfect example of how a potential school murderer can be anyone, and of how widespread the sensibility is, and why profiling fails.

DeGuzman was a good student at Independence High School, but just missed getting accepted into the colleges of his choice. He was described by everyone who knew him as nice, artistic, intelligent, and not at all capable of carrying out the crime. As an elementary school student he turned down an opportunity to be placed in a school for gifted children.

"He's a choir boy, like a straight-up school boy," Bobby Playa, an eighteen-year-old Independence High student, told *Asia Week* shortly after the plot was uncovered.

Al suffered from depression; the rejections from colleges, as he said, knocked that depression into a bad place. Going to De Anza only made it worse. A large number of De Anza's students come from the west Silicon Valley suburbs. Many were popular, dumb jerks—not the types to be humbled by a junior college. It is hard to explain how invisible a small Filipino kid from the San Jose tracts could feel among the west valley's wealthy detritus. On his personal homepage, DeGuzman wrote of the De Anza students, "The people there are just as cliquey as they were in high school . . . maybe even more." According to the *San Francisco Chronicle*, he then launched into a profanity-packed description of the campus's students as either hypocritical wealthy liberals or people from poorer parts of the city who are "angry, on welfare, and hate the white man."

DeGuzman was an editor at the Independence High yearbook, which won several national awards. Everyone who worked with him had nice things to say about him. What's more, he had a strong group of friends, and even girlfriends. He got along with his parents, though in a cold, old-world sort of way. In a line that sums up how most kids and adults relate to each other, DeGuzman said, "It's just that as long as I gave the air of normalcy, they left me alone."

He wasn't a loner, he wasn't bullied, he wasn't a trouble-maker or abused. He just had this hidden side to him. DeGuzman was obsessed with Eric Harris and Dylan Klebold. On his homepage, he wrote, "The only thing that's real is the word of Eric Harris and Dylan Klebold—they knew what they had to do to change the world and they did it."

"There's so much stress nowadays—more than people can deal with," De Anza sophomore Matt Utterback, twenty-four, told *Asia Week* in their DeGuzman article. "People have breaking points."

Kids are more miserable, suicidal, and closer to mass murder today than ever. Bullying is clearly part of the problem. Yet efforts to stop bullying have not stopped the shootings. The urge to rebel and massacre is still there, even at the sites of the massacres, where anti-bullying measures and heightened security are most intense. On November 7, 2001, just seven months after Andy Williams's shooting spree, graffiti was discovered in a Santana High bathroom stall warning of an upcoming school shooting, forcing an evacuation. A few days earlier, similar graffiti, in different handwriting, also warned of an upcoming massacre. Some students at the school say that the culture hasn't changed much at all.

At Westside Middle School in Jonesboro, Arkansas, three days after the eleven and thirteen-year-old boys murdered five and wounded ten, the school gym had to be evacuated following a bomb threat. More threats have hit the school since. And so have strange characters—a clown was denied his request to perform for the students shortly after the shooting, but he was discovered later in the cafeteria performing magic tricks for the students before he was escorted out.

At Columbine, where new anti-bullying rules were introduced, student Aaron Brown, a freshman at the time of the shootings, said, "Things were better at Columbine, as far as how people treated one another. At least, that's how it was for the first month or so. But by two or three months after we got back, things were back to the way they had been before. The name-calling started up all over again. Some people had changed a lot, but others hadn't changed at all."

Six months after the massacre, Carla Hochhalter, the mother of one of the wounded girls at Columbine, went to a Littleton pawn shop, picked out a gun, agreed to buy it, and while the salesperson was turned around, she loaded the gun, shot, and killed herself. Her daughter, who today is confined to a wheelchair, cheerfully described life in an interview five years after the massacre as "amazing." In February, 2000, two Columbine students were shot and killed at a Subway sandwich restaurant a few blocks away from school. This double-murder at the popular high school hangout was never solved. A few weeks after the one year anniversary of the massacre, a star player on the Columbine basketball team hanged himself. More recently, in early 2002, two Columbine High students were suspended after a hit list they drew up of eleven students and two faculty members was found in a park across from the school and handed over to authorities. The boys were suspended from school and faced expulsion as well as felony charges of inciting the destruction of life.

The fact is that if schools remain wretched places, the shootings, and sympathy for the shooters, will continue. Sympathy for them is a common sensibility. The desire to destroy one's own school is expressed not only in pathos-drenched messageboards, but also in popular black humor.

Which reminds me of something I downloaded off the Web right around the time of the Subway sandwich shootings at Columbine:

CONGRATULATIONS! After year after year of jocks mercilessly beating on you, cliques looking down their noses at you, and teachers looking the other way because they only care about themselves, you've finally decided that you're Mad As Hell And You're Not Gonna Take It Anymore. You've decided to pick up the battle flag of St. Eric & St. Dylan and chosen the short but glorious path of the warrior over of the slow & degading death of the sheep.

But, there's more to getting ready for your "Day of the Last Laugh" than stockpiling on firearms and explosives, you know.

Several things you need to remember when you're getting ready:

Rule #1: TELL NO ONE! Not your friends, not your parents or relatives. Not even in your personal writings must you give away the slightest hint of the Doomsday you are about to unleash on these deserving saps. These assholes will crack down on you and have you hauled away at the first and tiniest sign that you may be harboring ANY thoughts of striking back. Wear a proverbial mask of "normality" that disguises the true face of the demon. When assaulted, keep your thoughts hidden from them and don't yell something like "I'm gonna come back here with a gun and shoot you all dead! You hear me? Dead!!" The less your tormentors know what's in store for them, the better the chances you have to prepare for your vengence.

Rule #2: LEARN PROPER MARKSMANSHIP! Hunting is not only permissable, but is even encouraged in society. Sharpen your skills with rifles and pistols when you're out with daddy out in the woods. Don't waste your ammo on small critters like cats, dogs or squirrels (that will only get the attention of the "Powers That Be" and use that as a hint of a potential serial killer, and you'll be condemned to spend afternoons with your school's local "Mister Mackey", thus giving the jocks and cliques even more excuse to pummel on your skull). Target bigger game that is around the same mass as your future victims. After a while, with each well-aimed shot, you'll start to notice how much a deer starts to look more and more like that jock who enjoys thumping you in the nuts as he passes you between classes.

Rule #3: LEARN WHAT *DOES* BLOW UP AND WHAT DOESN'T! One of Eric and Dylan's biggest mistakes is that they thought that a propane canister would explode if it was shot at. Even if it did, a big loud bang only does damage to the immediate vicinity. Exposives are good, but incendiaries are better. A burning agent not only damages everything in it's area, but can also spread out looking for other things to burn. This fact has been well proven in places like Dresden, Tokyo, and Waco. A cannister with gasoline & filled with 1/4 liquid detergent (for that sticky napalm effect) does the trick nicely.

Rule #4: KNOW YOUR VICTIMS' HABITS! You already know that they're assholes and they need to be destroyed before they are let out into the private sector and cause some REAL misery, but do you know what they like to do (besides tormenting you, that is)? Where do they hang out during lunch hour? Do they sit in a certain area each time (most cliques usually do)? Chances are you won't be able to get all of your intended victims to be all in the same place at the same time, so you'll need to use this data to determine what places and times the majority of your enemies will be, decide which ones are the most DESERVING to die, and plan your strategy (NOTE: DON'T write your data down [see rule #1]! If these notes are found, the teachers will call the cops to swoop down on your ass, and both you and your hopes of justice are forever fucked!).

Rule #5: REMOVE ALL TRACES OF YOUR LIFE! What this means is that after you've done your apeshit, no doubt Officer Barbrady and the media whores will tear through your house to look for signs of why you did what you did (always ignoring the obvious signs, like the cruelty inflicted by jocks & cliques, and sticking to the usual scapegoats like video games and EMINEM .mp3s on your computer). Before you embark on your mission, secretly prepare to erase all traces of what makes you as you are. Shred and burn all your letters and notes. Dump all your books & CDs off at the nearest Salvation Army drop-off center in the middle of the night (don't let your parents or friends find out, or they'll think you're about to commit suicide or join a cult and they'll interfere, thus monkey-wrenching your Grand Plan). Remove AND *destroy* your hard disc and any other data media from your computer on the morning of your mission (erasing data isn't good enough, because the porkers have ways to restore it later). When the cops and the retards from FOX NEWS start picking through your belongings, they won't find jack shit for them to use to further stereotype and persecute the next future apeshitter and his own mission. Think of the police and the media as where jocks and cliques go after they've graduated from high school. Do you REALLY want to make their jobs any easier?

Rule #6: And this one's the hardest rule to follow, but believe me, it's a very important one; SAVE THE LAST BULLET FOR YOURSELF! You've done your duty, and you've made sure that you've mowed down as many jocks and snottos as you could within your 15 minutes (or less) of Payback (their souls are already being prepared to work as your slaves in Hell). No doubt you've gotten the attention of the cops and they already have the SWAT teams surrounding the joint. Just a matter of time before they either mow you down (the ultimate daydream of every jock, young or old, is to legally blow away a "geek"), or to be dragged out alive in handcuffs to be paraded around in a humiliating baggy white jumpsuit in front of the media cameras and be degraded and abused for the rest of your life in prison (and you thought being picked on in high school was Hell). Better to deny these assholes the pleasure of hurting you some more than to just check out while you're still King of the World. Look at the examples of St. Eric and St. Dylan, who are now held in eternal reverence for their sacrifice, compared to the quickly-forgotten idiots who decided to remain alive and are stuck in the deepest hole society can cast them down into, where the abuse is greater than ever before, used as lab rats by psychiatrists to "find a root cause for why children kill", and there is NO way to defend yourself against it. Would you WANT to spend the rest of forever in a straightjacket & dog muzzle and wheeled around on a moving dolly? Remember, no one can put a dead person on trial.

Well, that's about it. Just remember, if you do decide to go through with your mission, I've never seen you before in my life, ng'kay?

15

Target: America

More rage. More rage. Keep building it on.
—Eric Harris

WHAT MAKES TODAY'S SCHOOL RAMPAGE MURDERS SO DIFFERENT from other school violence is that it is perpetrated by white middle-class kids—the same demographic that also sympathizes with the shooters. It's not supposed to be that way in America. The middle-class is supposed to be content, the bedrock of stability, especially the kids.

Today's schoolyard shootings are disturbing because they are attacks on the very core of our culture. Many rage massacres are directed not only at specific bullies, but at the entire school, "to make a point" or to "kick-start a revolution" in the words of Eric Harris. This is why, again like company massacres, there are no "random shootings." As Katherine Newman notes, "[J]ust about everyone at school—often a shooter's entire social world—is fair game." In this way, too, they resemble so many workplace massacres.

While several Columbine-style plots have been uncovered, even those which were clearly real threats didn't come close to matching the incredible arsenal that Klebold and Harris put together. Along with their guns—a TEC-9, a Hi-Point 9-millimeter carbine, and two shotguns—they rigged up ninety-five explosive devices, enough firepower to wipe out their school and slaughter hundreds of students, had they gone off. Among the bombs were forty-eight carbon dioxide bombs, or "crickets," twenty-seven pipe bombs, eleven one-and-a-half gallon propane containers, seven incendiary devices with forty-plus gallons of flammable liquid, and two duffel bag bombs with twenty-pound liquefied-petroleum gas tanks. One of the propane tanks was rigged to explode inside the cafeteria, which, if it had exploded, could have raised the death toll several times over. The timing fuse didn't work as planned, and the boys' attempts to shoot the tank to spark an explosion failed.

As Eric Harris explained in a diary entry dated April 26, 1998, "We use bombs, fire bombs and anything we fucking can to kill and damage as much as we fucking can."

> The slaves destroyed tirelessly. Like the peasants in the Jacquerie or the Luddite wreckers, they were seeking their salvation in the most obvious way; the destruction of what they knew was the cause of their sufferings.
> —**C. L. R. James**, *The Black Jacobins*

Clearly, they weren't just targeting some of the students—they were trying to wipe the school off the face of the earth. And not just Columbine, but Littleton, Colorado, along with it. As they perceived it, the school and the suburb were one symbiotic evil . "I live in Denver, and dammit, I would love to kill almost all of its residents," Eric Harris wrote in his diary. An article in the *Rocky Mountain News* about the video diaries of Eric Harris and Dylan Klebold revealed their widened net of rage: "They explain over and over why they want to kill as many people as they can. Kids taunted them in elementary school, in middle school, in high school. Adults wouldn't let them strike back and fight their tormentors, the way such disputes were once settled in schoolyards. So they gritted their teeth. And their rage grew." For Eric and Dylan, Columbine was Littleton was America—their rage was so great that according to CNN, had they survived the massacre, the two planned to hijack a plane and crash it into New York City. In his diaries, Eric Harris wrote, "If by some wierd as shit luck me and V [Klebold] survive and escape we will move to some island somewhere or maybe mexico, new zelend or some exotic place where americans cant get us. if there isnt such a place, then we will hijack a hell of a lot of bombs and crash a plane into NYC with us inside firing away as we go down."

No one can say that they hated America because we are free—they hated America because America loved Columbine High, and because they saw the same cultural evils at work nationally as they did locally. They hated America because there's a lot to hate, period.

In the aftermath of the Subway sandwich shop murders of two Columbine High students in early 2000, the media descended upon Littleton once again, warming the horrified public's hearts with ready-made tales of a grief-stricken community tightly drawn together in an outpouring of emotion and mutual support. This is what the country wanted to hear; and this is what the country got, regurgitated back as objective news. "Once more, a stricken community mourns its children," the *Denver Post* sobbed on February 15, 2000. Reuters got evangelical in their account: "One group came to the parking lot of the sandwich shop and wrote on the asphalt in blue chalk, 'For God so loved the world he gave his only son so that we shall not perish but have eternal life.' (John 3:16). Using pink chalk, they wrote, 'God is love.' The students also drew a circle around the word 'hate' and put a slash through it."

What that last line says to me is that *hate is a serious problem in Littleton*— otherwise the Christians wouldn't have to slay it. But, as always, no one explored why hate was such a problem. Instead, the focus was on the love which supposedly replaced it, a love officially on display for the whole media.

So why hate? What was so hateful about upper-middle-class white suburbia? And how exactly did the community really pull together?

Tom Galland, a pastor in Jonesboro where the eleven and thirteen-year-old boys shot up their middle school in 1997, had warned a Littleton minister who called him for advice after Columbine to expect lots of official grieving, but underneath it a nasty, callous reality. Six months after the Columbine massacre, the Littleton minister called Galland back and told him, "It's just like you said. We had a false sense of cohesion and togetherness, and now everyone is suing each other." That little detail never made it into the official grieving–community stories.

PART VI

WELCOME TO THE DOLLHOUSE

If little Susie doesn't get into the right nursery school, she'll never make it into the right medical school!

—Contemporary American joke

1

Bad Intentions

LESS THAN A WEEK AFTER I MOVED to Santee to research Andy Williams's shooting I got a phone call from my mother: the FBI and local sheriff's deputies had just arrested a student at my former high school for plotting to blow it up. The sixteen-year-old boy was busted while stealing explosive chemicals from the school's science lab and arrested at gunpoint. The news came in the wake of a massive cheating scandal at my old school, a story that made Bay Area headlines. Saratoga High School is one of the top-ranked public schools in the country—first in California by some academic rankings. If cheating scandals and Columbine-style plots could reach Saratoga High, the very top of the school hierarchy, then people figured that nowhere was safe. Others in the San Jose area savored the scandal like a delicious, hot serving of good old-fashioned *schadenfreude*.

In December 2003, two students swiped a multiple choice test from an AP history classroom, made copies, and passed it around to other students. Then administrators learned that the previous spring, students had hacked into the English 10 teacher's computer, stole her tests, and distributed them to others. In a third case, a student managed to install a keystroke-reading device, KEYKatcher, in his math teacher's computer—a small piece of hardware that you attach between the keyboard cable and the computer box. The device records the keystrokes over a certain period; when the device is removed and hooked into another computer, you can download everything that had been typed. The accused student managed to "read" the teacher's tests, which he then distributed to other students. In January, administrators discovered that he had hacked into the math teacher's files and changed one of his grades from a D to a B.

All told, eight students faced expulsion. Nearly all of them besides the KEYKatcher cheater were straight-A students or close. Parents of the accused students hired attorneys and appealed. The atmosphere was nasty, like a boardroom battle. By the middle of the month, news of the cheating rings leaked out to the *San Jose Mercury News*. The scandal made headlines and brought in local and national TV coverage, with large broadcast vans ferrying in aggressive reporters and cameras that chased the students across the quad. The reputation of the state's top public school, in Silicon Valley's wealthiest suburb, had suffered a major blow, and the rest of the Santa Clara Valley was enjoying the spectacle, seeing the smug Saratogans taken down.

Then it took a dark, familiar turn. Late at night on January 14 and 15, the high school's silent alarm went off. Police didn't find anyone and there were no signs of tampering except that the pins in the door to the science lab were missing. On the night of the sixteenth, police staked out the school. There, Sheriff's deputies and, by some reports, FBI agents caught a sixteen-year-old boy as he fled the science lab and arrested him at gunpoint. It turned out to be the same boy who was caught and suspended for installing the keystroke device. He was found with bottles of glycine and potassium nitrate, both potential explosive agents that he'd stolen from the classroom. He was taken down to the police station. Under questioning, which lasted five hours, the boy admitted that he wanted to "do bad things" to the school. Later, police changed their story about how explicit the boy was about his "bad" intentions.

> When our school blows up tomorrow, it's gonna be the kind of thing to affect a whole generation! It'll be the Woodstock of the eighties!
> —*Heathers*, 1989

The sophomore student was charged with burglary, possession of stolen property, possession of materials with intent to construct an explosive device, and obstructing an officer. And then he was released to his parents—a move that outraged residents in less affluent parts of the Santa Clara Valley, who rightly noted that if a Mexican from East San Jose was arrested and charged with those crimes, he would be frog-marched straight down to juvie hall, charged as an adult, and crushed for good.

Police managed to obtain a search warrant ten hours later. In the boy's bedroom they found a gym bag—the rage murderer's favorite accessory—and inside the gym bag cupric chloride, potassium permanganate, and ammonium nitrate. Most of those chemicals may not ring a bell, but the last one, ammonium nitrate, should: it's what Timothy McVeigh used to level the federal building in Oklahoma City.

Within days, Saratoga High School administrators managed to secure a restraining order on the boy barring him from coming within three hundred yards of the school, saying in their request to the court that the boy had "a clear motive for blowing up the school." He was placed under house arrest pending his hearing and slapped with an electronic monitoring device—a kind of human KEYKatcher—to be monitored by a probation officer until the suspect's first hearing at the end of February. Conveniently, both the student-suspect and the principal live in a new subdivision on the other side of Saratoga-Sunnyvale Road, across from the high school. The suspect's house was barely outside of the three hundred yard restraining order boundary.

On Monday, February 2, the accused bomb plotter's fifteen-year-old girl-friend, also a Saratoga High student, was pulled out of her morning class by

Sheriff's detectives for posting threats on her Instant Messaging profile to kill and mutilate the school principal's family—her IMs expressed her rage over the way her boyfriend was "unjustifiably portrayed as a psycho." The girl was arrested at school and released to her family.

2

The Maze

WHEN I HEARD THE NEWS about the bomb plot, I contacted Dan Pulcrano, the publisher of the *Metro*, Silicon Valley's alternative weekly, and he offered to fly me up from Santee to cover the story about my former high school.

I'd never really returned to Saratoga since graduating in 1983—I only rarely passed through on my way to or from another San Jose suburb. I had no desire to go back. I loathed the school and the town when I lived there, and once I got accepted into college I never wanted to see, hear, or smell the place again. It was goodbye and good riddance, and all of my close friends felt the same way.

In the seventies up through the early eighties, Saratoga was essentially a rich hick town. The local socialites took their relative provincial wealth very seriously, as did many of their children whom I went to school with. Saratogans lorded over all the other San Jose suburbs—Cupertino, Sunnyvale, Willow Glen, Almaden, Mountain View, Campbell, and Santa Clara. Ever-expanding San Jose was a depressing sprawl of sun-faded sixties apartment houses and tract homes, filled with struggling Mexicans and Filipinos and Hmongs serving their cagey white over-lords, a city criss-crossed by freeways, highways, and eight-lane, stoplight-filled prospects and boulevards jammed with delivery trucks and old station wagons—Saratogans were the barons of the South Bay shitkickers. Beyond our valley, no one really knew what Saratoga was, and no one cared, which is why most Saratogans never ventured outside of their tiny sphere of influence. Those who did know us—like Santa Cruzers or East San Josers—loathed us, and fights were common.

When I was a student, we became one of the first high schools in the country to have a computer lab and our school newspaper was said to be the first equipped with Apple's Lisa computers. The new tech culture was just starting to displace the post-war, post-Okie culture in the valley. And with the new tech culture came tech wealth, unbelievable wealth. Had I stuck around Saratoga rather than escaping to Berkeley and beyond or, had I returned to become a West Valley real estate agent like so many of my fellow classmates, I would be a petty marquis today. After the extraordinary wealth boom in the Silicon Valley region in the nineties, Saratoga became the top choice for the new IPO-rich executive elite. In the first quarter of 2004, the average house in Saratoga sold for around $1.3 million, ranking it at the very top in the nation. The hicks' dream of becoming genuine American royalty had finally arrived—which made returning there to cover the story of the school bomb plot and cheating scandal as humiliating as it was nauseating.

The town was always divided into two parts: the foothills, where the super-wealthy lived in their mansions and almost-mansions; and the flatlands, called the Golden Triangle by proud residents, although we called it the Maze when I lived there. Saratoga High is located at the western edge of the Maze, near the village center and at the base of the foothill aristocracy. When I visited they were building a new performance arts center at one end of the high school parking lot. Otherwise, the school looked exactly as I had remembered it—an ugly, gray cinderblock Hell with uglier red-coated trimming, flat-roofed, windowless, and degrading. The addition of several more portable classrooms, which look like the tornado magnets you'd see in Kentucky, was shocking in the midst of all the wealth. I thought it would change, that some of the new wealth would trickle into the school and make it less physically soul-sucking, but it hadn't. The school looked like a late Eisenhower-era army barracks, just as when I was there. It stands as a proud monument to the culture's priorities—cutting taxes.

The school parking lot reflected the Saratoga beyond the campus: students drove huge SUVs, including Lincoln Navigators, Mercedes Benzes, Jaguars, and, most popular of all, BMWs. I pulled into the lot in my rented Corolla, past cheerleaders whose SUVs were so high that all I could see were their huge wheels and the lower halves of their doors.

In the summer of 1976, with massive financial support from relatives, my mother, brother, and I moved into a small three-bedroom house on Junipero Way, at the very eastern edge of the Maze, in order to qualify for the Saratoga School District. Our address was quite literally the very last house on the edge of the school district—twenty feet from our backyard fence were the railroad tracks, and on the other side of the tracks the kids were zoned into a less-reputable district, I believe it was called Lynbrook. We lived in a genuine border region, where the pretensions of the provincial bourgeoisie gave way to an undisguised Okie culture filled with mag-wheeled vans and pickups. Ambition petered out right at our backyard. In this sense, the Maze was similar to what I saw in Santee. Saratoga High had a nasty mixture of California coastal cool, local wealth, and a dull, mean shitkicker sensibility. Steven Spielberg was a student at Saratoga for one year in the 1960s—he later said that his traumatic experience at Saratoga High School, where he was taunted and marginalized, inspired *Schindler's List*, openly accusing Saratoga's students of "anti-Semitism" when the movie was released. The accusation caused a great scandal in San Jose upon the movie's release. The sad truth is that Saratoga's students were probably too ignorant to know what a Jew was or why Jews should be hated. As most of his peers noted, Spielberg was bullied because he was considered a geek, not because he was a Jew.

In 1982, the year before I graduated, a sophomore student at neighboring Los Gatos High (the other high school in the Los Gatos-Saratoga Joint Union School District) was killed by a senior next to the Los Gatos creek, not far from the school. The killer was one of those small, boisterous, cool jerks common to that period. He killed the sophomore boy because he was "was a loser," as one student explained. After strangling him, stabbing him, and crushing his head in with a rock during third period, he left the boy's body in the creek-side foliage and later showeᵗ corpse to some of his friends. No one else at the school or in the suburb noticed that the boy was missing—police assumed he'd run away, and students and administrators gave a collective shrug. His scientist parents were sure something awful had happened, but the father was considered an eccentric, the type that the local rich hicks didn't trust. His sense that his son may have been murdered was dismissed by police and school authorities with a famous "rolling of the eyes." Rumors went around that he'd been killed by pot farmers in the hills above Los Gatos—the rumors even made it to my school, five miles up Highway 9. Students heard legends about the boy's corpse for years—my stepbrother heard them when he was a Los Gatos High student in the early nineties—and many probably saw it but kept their mouths shut. A homeless man stumbled across the boy's skeletal remains almost fifteen years after his murder. The bones dressed in denims, work-boots, and a thick belt with a large branded belt buckle, were like a punchline in a comic skit about waiting and waiting. The student who killed him, who had fought in Gulf War I and subsequently moved to Oregon, was tracked down, arrested, and sentenced to just six years in prison, with parole in two. None of the students who saw the body but didn't report it were charged. Los Gatos officials just wanted to "move on." The boy's boxed-up skeletal remains were misplaced somewhere inside a massive police warehouse. He has never been buried. His name was Russ Jordan, and he's in a lost box somewhere in a Santa Clara County warehouse.

Also in the early 1980s, in another San Jose suburb called Milpitas, a pothead high school student strangled his friend then showed her body to other friends over a period of a month. The story of how indifferent these Milpitas kids were to seeing their own friend's dead body, and how long they went without telling authorities, was made into the eighties youth-in-crisis movie *River's Edge*.

That was Santa Clara Valley's culture when I was there, before it became Silicon Valley.

Now that the valley is the center of the world—and in the middle of the post-Reaganomics vise—school violence has become thoroughly modernized. On April 30, 1999, three fourteen and fifteen-year-old boys at Willow Glen High in west San Jose were expelled for threatening to bring bombs to school. My stepmother was a librarian in the Willow Glen district at the time. The bomb threat was revealed just ten days after Columbine, so everyone was a bit jumpy and plot rumors were circulating all over. The boys showed some empty shells to another freshman. It seems they were just trying to scare him, but police took it seriously enough to cite the boys for terrorism threats and to take them down for questioning. The school's vice principal, Adrian Kirk, spoke as one of the few sane human beings in the entire school-security apparatus: "There is no substance to any of the rumors that are spreading," he said. "The Willow Glen Ed Park community was in a state of panic. They heard things they didn't know how to react to and the gossip mill is running wild and crazy with this." My stepmother backed up the vice principal's position that it was a dumb hoax. According to her, most of the Willow Glen students are bused in from the rougher parts of east San Jose, while the local whites send their kids to better schools outside the area. The minorities at Willow

Glen High are generally so relieved to be in a place as safe and quiet as Willow Glen compared to their violent neighborhoods that the last thing they feel is middle-American rage.

On March 16, 2001, a couple of weeks after Andy Williams's shooting in Santee, a fifteen-year-old boy at Westmont High in Campbell—the high school I would have gone to if we hadn't moved to nearby Saratoga—scrawled "Everyone will die on March 21" on two school desks. The messages were discovered, cops were called, kids were questioned, and finally the suspect confessed, saying he wrote it as a joke. He was arrested, booked, and faced expulsion. Despite the fact that they caught the boy and the potential danger had passed, 643 of Westmont's 1600 students stayed home from school on March 21. At Prospect High, which is the high school I would have gone to had we lived on the other side of the railroad tracks from our house in the Maze, a young male called in a bomb threat on the very day that the Westmont High hoaxer claimed everyone would die, causing a panic, with parents rushing to take their children out of the school.

Even my own high school uncovered an alleged massacre plot a few years before the 2004 bomb plot. A student at Saratoga High, an Asian American, was expelled from the school after he was caught with a hit list of students he planned to murder. I only found out about it while interviewing students about the bomb plot. Like a lot of school massacre plots and even some of the minor shootings, that one never made the papers.

3

A 4.0 Failure

WHEN I INTERVIEWED SARATOGA HIGH STUDENTS AND STAFF, one thing that surprised me was that everyone was much more disturbed by the cheating scandal than by the bomb plot and subsequent murder threat. The reasoning was simple: the bomb plot and murder threat were problems confined to just two suspected students. But the cheating scandal potentially affected everyone at Saratoga High. The school's academic reputation was compromised—students, administrators, and parents all worried that it would affect the students' chances of getting into a top university.

The competition and struggle to excel at Saratoga is brutal, a somewhat more exaggerated pressure-cooker than other middle and upper-middle-class schools. Almost one-third of Saratoga High's students today have 4.0 grade averages. Saratoga High School holds a top rank in the state of California for Academic Performance Index scores, at nine hundred points out of a possible thousand for the 2002-2003 school year, and an SAT average score of 1272. When I was a student at Saratoga we had maybe five or six 4.0 students in my class, and an 1150 score was considered good enough to get you into Berkeley.

But the culture changed in the early 1980s, starting around my sophomore year in high school. In the aftermath of the Reagan Revolution, fear and stress began to drive kids as much as it did their parents. An increasing number of people in America today believe that if you blow it once—even if you blow it in nursery school—then you're fucked for life. Part of the reason is scarcity. There are still just twenty "Top 20" universities, yet the population is constantly growing and the bar—the grades and scores required to get accepted into those elite schools—is constantly being raised. To get ahead, you have to start getting a leg-up on the competition earlier and earlier and in rarer and rarer ways. And if you don't get in, if you don't keep up, you'll be pushing shopping carts for the rest of your life. The kids are stressed out not only by their own pressure at school, but by the stress their parents endure in order to earn enough money to live in Saratoga High school district. This stress doesn't so much trickle down from parent to child as rain down, like acid rain, every day at home. The rules of the office world—if you screw up once, you're screwed for life—are applied to the school culture. Everyone is terrified of not "making it" in a country where the safety net has been torn to shreds, where failing to get rich is not just a material but a moral failure.

Applying to universities with a 4.0 isn't enough to ensure acceptance anymore. You have to have a 4.3 (meaning straight A's in AP honors classes) at a top high school—and Saratoga is tops in the brutal score–driven competition among schools. And within Saratoga, the competition is even fiercer. If one-third of the students have 4.0 grade averages, then you have to have a 4.3 just to stand out. The fear breeds more fear; the competition increases competition. It seems the bar cannot possibly be raised higher, and yet with every new class, it is climbs impossibly higher. As one parent told Saratoga High School's newspaper, the *Falcon*, "If you're just a 4.0, you're perceived by your family as a failure."

This insane culture has crushed many but has also produced a few exceptions. A graduate from the class of 1999, Ankur Luthra, became Saratoga High's first-ever Rhodes Scholar. Another recent graduate, Allan Chu, was named one of the nation's top twenty graduating high school seniors. Chu was entered into the national inventor's hall of fame while still at Saratoga High.

Over the past couple of years, parents have started pushing their children into SAT prep courses at an earlier and earlier age, some as young as fourteen. A teacher of the Princeton Review SAT course said, "I've had parents and children not satisfied with a 1,300 or even a 1,350, which is an incredible score. They feel like if it's not good enough to get you into the Ivies or Berkeley, they're not good people, and that's very sad."

The latest trend to give Junior an edge in the brutal struggle-to-achieve world is hiring high-end tutors for as much as $250 per hour to improve their grades. Once a few students hooked up, every parent in the West Valley had to have a tutor for their kid, or else he was doomed.

The squeeze on kids is so intense that even summer vacation is no longer a time for summer lovin' and havin' a blast, not if you want your kid to get ahead. Recently, college admissions prep camps have become the latest rage. As a *New York Times* article about these prep camps described it: "No campfires. No hiking. Just hours a day of essay writing, SAT preparation, counseling, mock admission interviews and a potpourri of workshops and college visits, all intended to give high school students an edge on the admission process." You have to almost wonder why a middle or lower-middle-class kid would even bother trying. Or why a kid wouldn't cheat.

Indeed cheating is a way of life these days—cheaters win, as we have seen from all of the "corporate malfeasance" scandals. Even some of Saratoga's prominent adults were caught up in their own high-profile cheating scandals. In March 2002, the Securities and Exchange Commission filed a civil fraud action against two Saratogans who headed Signal Technology Corp, CEO Dale Peterson and CFO Russell Kinsch, alleging that they inflated its earnings by over $9 million. Peterson once famously remarked that he was "sick of people thinking GAAP [generally accepted accounting principles] was important."

Roughly a year later, another wealthy Saratoga resident, Reza Mikailli, was convicted on ten counts of securities fraud and conspiracy charges for crimes committed while he was president and CEO of Unify Corp., a software company. And as everyone saw, the entire Silicon Valley "New Economy" boom was little more than an old-fashioned ponzi scheme whose proceeds allowed the best of the cheaters to buy a piece of Saratoga real estate, and a spot for their kids in the school district.

As in business and politics, cheating in schools is universal. And not small-time cheating, but cheating on the grandest scale imaginable. A Rutgers study of 4,500 high school students in 2001 revealed that 76 percent admitted to getting questions or answers to tests by someone who already took it, while 84 percent admitted to copying homework. And these are just the kids brave enough to admit it.

In a sense Saratoga's culture is built on a giant fraud scheme, or on an aggregate of ponzi schemes: parents cheat to get enough money to get into the Saratoga district; the school cheats to keep its test scores high enough to keep attracting the best cheating parents their school district; the kids cheat to get into the top universities so they will be in a position to cheat big-time in the corporate world instead of being a wage slave at the mercy of cheating executives; and once they successfully cheat in a big way, they can buy a house in a prestigious school district, putting their kids through the same corrupt cycle. Cheat to cheat to cheat to cheat.

It was within this desperate struggle that the kids at Saratoga High were compelled to cheat in the first place. And when one of them got busted, the devastation he faced—expulsion, which is the upper-middle-class's version of having your nose hacked off—incited him to avenge his murderers by blowing up the school, the source of his destruction. It was an attempt at vengeance, but also a futile effort to wipe his slate clean by destroying the records that implicated him, like the strategy of *Fight Club*'s guerrillas, who at the end blow up the nation's credit industries in order to liberate the population from this wretched modern squeeze. And really, in such a world, only a sucker-only a loser would play by the rules.

4

A Kind and Caring Stranger

> Several of the students who committed violent acts in school were thought to be depressed and oversensitive to others. Some of these symptoms are directly related to stress and the inability to cope with stress.
> —*Kids Killing Kids*

SLEEP DEPRIVATION IS A SERIOUS PROBLEM for Saratoga High's students. All-nighters are common for any kid in the competition. One of the students caught in the cheating scandal admitted that he routinely studied past midnight, sometimes until 4 am.

"Sleep schedules just get insane," Saratoga High senior Gene Wang told the *San Jose Mercury News*. "There are just days when people here melt from depression or exhaustion."

The problem is so bad that the school newspaper, the *Falcon*, published a story on sleep deprivation at the end of the turbulent 2003-2004 academic school year. One senior student, Ada Yee, told of how she got "three or four hours of sleep as a junior, and now I get five or six." The article notes that Yee was "a 2004 salutat-orian, corresponding secretary of the Interact Club, and a section leader in the band."

"Not enough sleep causes more stress," she said.

One of the most poignant examples of the intensity of Saratoga High's competitive culture was expressed in the personal homepage of a former Saratoga student, nineteen-year-old Daniel Walter Yang:

> By the time I started as a freshman at Saratoga High School, I had read all of Michael Crichton's books up until then and a lot more. But high school brought a halt to my reading as the homework increased significantly and there were other things to do. I haven't read much for pleasure since the start of high school.
>
> Junior year was tough, and I lost sight of many of my passions. My photography, my design, my running. I stopped a lot of them. I did win a [sic] illustration award for one of my designs at a national high school journalism convention in Boston though. But that was for work I had done the previous year. The homework load was just very heavy and that led to stress on some of my personal relationships.
>
> At the end of Junior year, I knew I needed to rediscover my passions and patch up rifts with other people if I was to lead a productive and full life.

Yang turned to Jesus after suffering the trauma of Saratoga High stress: "My struggles with following Christ's path and glorifying God is a key influence in everything I do," he wrote. It's a touching self-portrait; the stress he suffered at Saratoga, and the subsequent turn to Jesus, is reminiscent of the path taken by recovering addicts or trauma victims. Which is a good analogy for anyone sucked into our Reagan–era struggle—except that at least addicts were hooked on something pleasurable.

In fact the school pressure is so bad for these kids that many former students insist that the workload at the top-ranked universities in the country is a cakewalk compared to Saratoga High. Philip Sung's life became much easier after entering MIT: "I don't feel anywhere near as much competition here." Joyce Li, another former student, agreed that UC Berkeley was far less stressful and competitive than Saratoga High.

In May, 2000, Lancy Chui, a seventeen-year-old Saratoga student, committed suicide after writing a play for her English class about a girl who is saved from committing suicide by a kind and caring stranger. It was a fantasy—there were no kind strangers in Saratoga, not even kind friends or teachers. No one bothered reading into that play, even though the cry for help was staged as loudly as the play format allowed. Chui was an attractive Asian American girl—in a yearbook photo, her pale, softly-sculpted face stands out from the black top, black background, her jet-black hair cut into bangs over her forehead. Her high round cheekbones and distant smile add to a kind of eerie, tragic beauty. It looks as if she knew she was fated to die, and had come to terms with it.

Not long after presenting her play to the class and receiving a deafeningly blank response, Chui took a picnic blanket and a bottle of sleeping pills out onto a lawn on West Valley's campus, a local community college about a mile away from the high school. She swallowed the pills, laid down, and died in her sleep while giving the impression to passers-by that she was merely picnicking and resting. One educator I spoke to said that Chui's suicide note included an apology to her parents that she did not get accepted into Harvard.

5

The Post-Diaper Rat Race & Testing for Caldwell Brokers

Pressure is pushing kids to the limit.
—**Father of one of the students** suspended in the Saratoga High
    cheating scandal

THE STRESS STARTS AS SOON AS THE CHILD IS BORN. Parents leverage themselves to get into the right school districts, which, like every facet of our post-Reagan society, are becoming increasingly segregated along socioeconomic lines. Theoretically school is free and open to all—but the cost of living in the right school district already acts as a kind of tuition surcharge—a massive tuition surcharge. A property's attached school district can mean the difference in hundreds of thousands of dollars on each house. Parents have to work even harder and succeed even more in order to get their kids a decent education—to make sure they are poised to get the kind of job that will allow them to get their kids into the right school, thus maintaining this vicious lifestyle cycle. So in order to help their children get a leg up in this struggle, most parents today enroll their children in preschools.

In the 1960s, only four percent of children were enrolled in preschools. Today, over two-thirds of three and four-year-olds are placed in preschools. But you can't just be placed in any preschool anymore. Your child has to get placed—or rather accepted—into a top preschool in order to ensure that he or she gets into the right elementary school, which feeds into the right high school, which feeds into the right university. That means that the fight to get a child placed into the right pre-school is savage. As soon as the diapers come off, the child is tossed into the cage match. Preschools now have admissions requirements. Many children have to write essays or take an IQ test, called the ERB, to qualify for these elite preschools and kindergartens. To prepare their children for the test, parents pay tutors or psychologists to acquaint their children with the types of questions expected in the entrance exams. Many kids are tutored in "pre-reading" classes to help them stand out against the others. Tuitions for preschools run in the thousands of dollars. Top New York City preschool tuitions range up to $15,000 or more, while even at a Chicago public school district preschool tuition was $6,500 per year, more than the tuition at the University of Illinois, according to *Two Income Trap*. The best nursery schools have long waiting lists and stringent requirements, including interviews with the child and parents. The pressure to get one's child into the "right" preschool is seen as a prerequisite to putting the child on the path toward a top university, the only way to ensure that one's child might avoid the middle-class vise. And it's also about social prestige. Striving parents want to brag about which preschool their baby got accepted into just as badly as they want to brag about which university they get into later in life.

Perhaps the most famous scandal surrounding a preschool involves the recent securities fraud case of Citigroup chairman Sandy Weill and star telecoms analyst Jack Grubman of Citigroup's subsidiary, Solomon Smith Barney.

First, a little background on Weill, one of the grand dukes of the post-Reagan feudal elite. In 1998, he earned $167 million as Citigroup's chairman, just about the same time that his company was planning to downsize its workforce by 5 percent, and cut its remaining employees' 401K plans, pensions, and other benefits. Weill's success in transferring wealth from employees to his pocket clearly went to his head. In 1999, Weill pressured Grubman in 1999 to raise his rating of AT&T's stock in order to curry favor with AT&T's CEO, who also sat on the board of Citigroup. (Weill was in a vicious boardroom battle at the time, and he needed all the allies he could get.) Weill's offer was this: if Grubman would lie to investors about what a bargain AT&T stock was, Weill promised to help Grubman's children get accept-ed into a prestigious Manhattan nursery school. Grubman, who earned a $20 mil-lion bonus in his best year at Solomon, complained that the nursery school was "harder than Harvard to get into." Since Citigroup had donated $1 million to the school, Weill was able to successfully wield his influence, getting both of Grubman's children in.

"I tried to help Mr. Grubman because he was an important employee who had asked for my help," Weill admitted. In other words, countless numbers of Americans, perhaps tens of thousands or more, were tricked into buying lousy stock resulting in untold millions lost—so that an analyst could get his children into the right preschool. This was one of the biggest Wall Street scandals of the last few years—and the silliest. Yet it was also a grotesque reminder of how far the culture's pressure-cooked insanity had reached: even babies are no longer safe!

It may seem ridiculously funny, but the competition can be devastating—for the children, and for the parents who pass their disappointment and stress onto their children, as revealed in a *New York* magazine article about an ambitious couple and their four-year-old boy named Andrew:

"I doubted myself; maybe I overestimated my kid," Cynthia admits, referring to her disappointment when Andrew's scores arrived in the mail. "Maybe I'm looking at him with loving eyes, and maybe I'm wrong. He's very cute and animated and bright. But maybe that doesn't mean he's smart in an academic sense. I stopped trying with him. Before, we'd talk about the days of the week, or I would try to get into more detailed discussions. Now I felt it wasn't going to make any difference. I was so disappointed."

Although this post-diaper rat race has proved a boon to entrepreneurs—standardized test prep course programs, baby psychologists, and the shareholders in these expensive preschools all reap massive windfalls—it has demoralized traditional educators.

As the head of one preschool program explained in the same article: "I used to think it would get worse and worse and then get better. But now I know it gets worse and worse and worse and worse."

An educator who works with the Saratoga school district told me that the high school is under constant and intense pressure to achieve top scores on the standardized tests in order to maintain its top ranking in the state. The reason is obvious. If the school is ranked at the top then the students' chances of getting into top universities increase, which is why parents struggle to get property inside the Saratoga High district. The administrators pressure the teachers, who form their curriculum to "teach the tests," that is, to prepare them for the standardized tests, rather than to educate the kids. The educator I spoke to, who asked to remain anonymous, also alleges—as have some students—that the less-academically-successful students at Saratoga are often encouraged, or even pressured, into not taking the standardized tests, since their scores could lower the school's collective score. The educator told me that he was so incensed by this that he made sure some of the struggling students he worked with took the standardized tests just to upset the school administration—and bring the overall score down a hair. I talked to a few students who did not get good grades at Saratoga, and they agreed that they were essentially ignored and marginalized by the structure.

"They just don't even know I'm there, and they don't even really want me there," one Saratoga student, whose grades were merely average, told me.

"The school doesn't have time for these kids," the educator told me. "The administration there doesn't give a damn about the bottom half or about their lives or how this will affect them later on. All they care about is keeping the test scores high."

Kevin Skelley, who was the principal at Saratoga High at the time of the bomb threat in early 2004, has an education degree from Harvard and earned in the low six figures at the school. Dr. Skelley, as he was called, lived in Saratoga with his family, which is unusual considering how poorly educators are generally paid in America. He was said to be a member of the "Saratoga Society," hooked into the leading social clubs. The pressure to maintain the school's top ranking position starts with the parents and city elders—with whom Dr. Skelley hobnobbed—and is extremely intense. He could not afford to allow the school to slip from number one.

Dr. Skelley resigned a few months after the cheating scandal, bomb plot, and threats to murder his family, and moved to Southern California. As Dan Pulcrano, the *Metro* publisher, pointed out to me, part of the pressure to maintain those high scores is rooted in property values. The Saratoga school district's top ranking translates into the town's average $1.3 million housing price—many families, particularly Asian immigrants, reach into the extended family network and leverage everything to get an address in the school district (as my family did), driving the prices ever higher in a fixed-supply market. If someone were to buy Saratoga property when the school was ranked number one in the state, and try to sell it after the school's reputation had fallen, hundreds of thousands of dollars could be lost. Anywhere from 20 to 30 percent of that $1.3 million average home price comes from those standardized test score results—it's up to the kids to keep those property values rising. All eyes are upon them: parents, administrators, and real estate agents.

6

Globalization High

SARATOGA'S TEACHERS WERE FURIOUS and even hurt over the school's cheating scandal. They said that their trust had been abused. Some teachers blamed the students. Kim Mohnike, an English teacher at Saratoga High who once caught twenty-seven students in a class of thirty-one cheating on an assignment on *The Great Gatsby*—about a hero who cheated in order to make it in America— complained, "There's a lack of interest in the learning process. The most important thing for many of our students is the grade."

Some educators blame the school administration. Some school administrators blame the parents. And outside observers blame local financial interests, specifically, property values.

All of this is symptomatic of the high-tension link tying together the entire post-Reagan socio-economic system, a squeeze applied from the macroeconomic level to the micro-individual, all the way down to the stressed-employee's nerve-wracked three-year-old child who is forced to prepare for nursery school entrance exams. As Todd Dwyer, a popular economics teacher at Saratoga High, wrote in an op-ed published in the *San Jose Mercury News*, "Saratoga High School teachers and administrators did not create the hyper-creative academic environment our adolescents must deal with today: The deregulated free market did that. The competition is global and fierce. So the perception among kids is 'either I get into Cal or MIT or Harvard and develop the narrowest band of the most highly specialized skills, or I'm gonna wind up cookin' squirrels under a bridge.'"

The globalization of Saratoga High is not only an invisible economic force, but also a very real demographic force. While I was a student the school was almost all white; today's student body is half Asian American. Though few wanted to talk about it publicly, the town's worst kept secret is how the recently–arrived Asian Americans have raised the competition bar, thanks to pressure from the largely first-generation families. The journalism class I visited was overwhelmingly Asian American (East Asian with some South Asian) and yearbook photos revealed a Speech and Debate club that was also almost entirely Asian American. The whites, on the other hand, dominated the Christian Club, a far less significant achievement in the eyes of Ivy League schools. Saratoga's Christian Club might out-pray the South Bay Area competition, but elitist university admissions officers haven't heard the call.

It is a kind of celestial justice or blowback from globalization. The American elite export slave-wage jobs to Asia in order to boost shareholder profits, all the while touting the benefits of competition. What the rich beneficiaries of globalization meant was "competition for the rest of you, not for us." That came back to bite them on the ass, just as middle-class support for Reaganomics against the unions eventually came back to ruin their lives as well. Today, not only are Asian peasants out-competing American workers for factory jobs, but now, in the game of fair competition, Asian intellectuals and students are laying waste to middle- and upper-middle-class America's children. With borders falling, more and more Asians are making their way into the kinds of wealthy districts where the people who have profited from globalization put their kids—and if the assimilated, predominately-white upper-class insists on having an hour or two of fun per week, their kids are rendered testing-score-flotsam, as doomed in the Great Competition as all the steel mills and automobile factories whose demise we all so callously rationalized away. Now even the most privileged kids can barely keep up with the struggle, victims of the same globalization that enriched their parents. If they compete, they're miserable. If they drop out of the rat race, the rich kids will wind up slipping down to the middle class, where they will drain their parents' wealth . . . where they will actually need those cheap Asian-slave-labor-produced goods sold at Wal-Mart and Old Navy just to survive.

7

The Groaning Horde

ASIAN STUDENTS AND WHITE STUDENTS park their cars in segregated areas at the Saratoga High parking lot—no one could explain exactly why. There is little open ethnic hostility, only a grumbling mix of half-concealed resentment and resignation. It seems that both groups want it that way. One educator told me that when the Asian mothers pick their children up from school, the kids sit in the back seat even when the front passenger seat is empty. "They have a completely different ethic as we do," he said. "The pressure they apply to their kids is not something we're used to."

The only candid account I read about this touchy ethnic competition in Saratoga came from an Indian journalist, S. Muthiah, writing for an Indian newspaper, the *Hindu*, evidence that even Third World countries have less self-censorship than America: "A Chinese co-president of Saratoga High's Parent-Teacher-Student Association wondered after the [cheating] incidents in the school whether she was doing the right thing by her children by pushing them so hard . . . Not pushing a child or asking about his grades are concessions that I don't think Asian parents in the Valley would readily go along with; both parents and children sacrifice too much every day in search of the golden fleece—that sheepskin from a leading university."

Interestingly, according to this article, the cycle of ethnic competition and displacement is being repeated with new players in the ethnic struggle: "In this determined quest, Asian Indians are even more focussed [sic] than the Chinese if you draw conclusions from how little Indians participate in the wider school scene. . . . The results of inter-school matches in the Valley show several East Asians and Hispanics doing well for their schools in soccer (football), basketball, women's basketball and soccer (perhaps America's fastest growing sport) and swimming. The only Indian names to be found are, and rarely at that, in tennis. Their focus is the classroom—and exams."

Indeed there is a kind of pride on the part of the author because Indian children are clearly more miserable than even the Chinese, who come off as downright decadent for playing the "fastest-growing sport in America." The implication is that, because the Indians are more miserable, the Chinese are already as decayed as second-generation Americans and the Indians are poised to take their place. The more miserable you are, the more success you'll find.

The East Asians and South Asians aren't just competing at the high school level. They're already as deep in the diaper-less rat race as Jack Grubman and the rest of Middle America, as described in the same *Hindu* article. The author visits a top Silicon Valley preschool whose student body is 80 percent Chinese. The kids are pressured to learn early in order to get into one of the area's elite "lottery" elementary schools. "To gain admission to a lottery school, parents send in applications of intent for their wards and then wait in hope for their children to be short-listed for a test. Based on the results, a few high-scoring children are selected for each lottery school. And here they get a better, and more rigorously pursued, foundation that will give them an advantage in middle and high school where the pressures are even greater to perform."

The terrible Asian horde is upon us, and yet even the Asians are wretched and seething, groaning all the way to the No-Doz box. All of the students caught in the Saratoga High cheating scandal were Asian Americans, including the boy who then threatened to blow up the school. The local press would not discuss this ethnic angle to the cheating scandal and bomb plot, even though this was perhaps the most interesting part of the story.

Yet a closer look at the kids shows how, within his ethnic group, the factors at work were similar to other rage massacre suspects—thus reinforcing S. Muthiah's thesis that the Asian Americans really have become decadent and Americanized. The Saratoga bomber-suspect looked like a harmless and underdeveloped Asian kid, with a scrawny neck, a small head, and a skittish, cagey, expression. His eyes didn't meet the camera in his yearbook photo. The head is tilted back, as if distracted, or perhaps trying to add some menace. His fifteen-year-old girlfriend, who was later arrested for threatening to chop up Dr. Skelley's family, is also Asian American with a broad, fleshy face, flashing a mischievous, almost caustic grin in her yearbook photo.

"She was weird and depressed," one student told me. Some students said that the two of them had been dating since the seventh grade, which they saw as further proof of their "strangeness."

The boy's bomb plot wasn't taken quite so seriously by the kids or others because of the small quantities of explosives that he stole. Moreover, he took a solid chemical, glycerine, when he probably meant to take an explosive, glycerin, as science teacher Bob Kucer noted in a *Falcon* article.

"No one's scared that someone's going to blow up our school," a female *Falcon* staffer told me. "I heard from a science teacher that he didn't even have enough bomb material to like blow up a chair."

Indeed a lot of students thought it was kind of funny. The poor kid was not only a failure at school as a B student, he was a failure at Columbining as well. He flunked the biggest chem test of his life, one that would read something like: Dong wants to blow up his school. If the school contains 20,000 cubic feet of space with 20 reinforced concrete structures, and 1,300 students, how much ammonium nitrate, potassium chlorate, and glycine (or glycerin or glycerine) would Dong need to steal from the science lab? Explain your answer (30 minutes).

The most remarkable thing about the bomb suspect was how unremarkable he struck the students I spoke to. No one knew who he was, nor did they know people who knew him. He was lost in that "invisible middle," and now he was getting expelled from the herd altogether.

8

Every Child Left Behind

It wasn't just Grandma Millie who had money stolen, it was our children.
—US Representative Jay Inslee, Democrat of Washington

IN SNOHOMISH COUNTY, Washington, educators complained in July 2004, that in order to cover their energy bills to Enron—which were still locked in at artificially inflated rates—the district had to cut back on hiring teachers, purchasing textbooks, buses, and other children's needs. According to the *Herald* in Everett, Washington, school districts just in this modestly-sized county had to pay an additional $9 million for higher-priced energy thanks to Enron's power-market scam from 2000-2001. One local school district, Mukilteo, reduced spending for text books and library books and cut bus drivers, office staff, and after-school activities for children. Nearby Snohomish School District was paying an additional $420,000 a year in power costs. According to the *Herald*: "To balance the budget, the district has not hired teachers to match the growth in the number of students, and has left vacant positions unfilled, he said. That's driven up the average class size."

The same funding shortages occurred in the Mukilteo school district. Although the Mukilteo school district received extra state support in 2003, two-thirds of that assistance went straight to Enron's accounts (that is, somewhere in Antigua), according to Carolyn Webb, the district's executive director for business services. "Those were dollars intended to buy text books [and] computers and software," she ruefully told the *Herald*.

Incredibly enough, Enron sued the Snohomish County PUD (Public Utility District) for breaking an even more insane contract dating back to the peak of their 2001 scam. If Enron wins, they'll be able to squeeze another $122 million just from Snohomish County, meaning that the school districts will be forced to hand over another $2.5 million to the thieves at Enron. Rep. Inslee likened it to "Bonnie and Clyde suing the banks." The county's last hope lies in appealing to the Federal Energy Regulatory Commission—whose membership composition was heavily influenced by former Enron head Ken Lay! So it's really like Bonnie and Clyde suing the banks . . . in a court where the sitting judge was appointed by Bonnie and Clyde.

When this election [in 2000] comes Bush will fucking whack this shit, man. He won't play this price-cap bullshit.
—Enron trader, before 2000 elections

We will not take any action that makes California's problems worse and that's why I oppose price caps.
—President George W. Bush, May 29, 2001

Why do Americans take it? Why do they let it happen not only to themselves, but to their own children? Is there no one left in America with enough dignity to protect their own blood? Are we too deeply in awe of our masters, the CEO executives and heirs to the Reagan legacy? Are we so beaten down that we've actually come to like getting squeezed by them? The 2004 election victory of Bush, in spite of the record job losses and the worsening economic squeeze, suggests that worshipping the aristocracy has taken on a life all its own, totally separate from one's personal, financial, or health needs. I've been arguing the persistence of the slave tendency in this book and how it is highly adaptive, but at some point it becomes too much. Stories like this, of Enron stripping children of their education with the blessing of the President, who remains loved while it happens, are so enraging that you reach a point where you just have to stop and take a deep breath. It's shameful, disgustingly shameful . . . I don't think there is another country on earth where its citizens have so much potential power and are so fearful to use even one ounce of it.

All of this is a product of the larger cultural cruelty and bullying that has been going on since 1981, when Reagan slashed school lunch programs for poor children in order to offset tax cuts for the rich. It was a whopping success: in only a few years some three thousand schools and four million children were dropped from the school lunch program, including one and a half million children living below poverty and still qualifying even by the new meaner standards.

What was controversial then is just reality today. In 1999, one in every six children lived in poverty, in spite of America's unprecedented wealth boom during the nineties. And when they say "lived in poverty" they mean "Poverty"—the definition used by the Census Bureau is a family of three living on less that $13,290 per year. I don't know how it is even possible for a one person to live on that in America, but for one in every six American children, twelve million of them, it's not only possible, it just is. One way it's possible is to make sure Junior doesn't see a doctor. Some eleven million American children had no health insurance in 1999, something unheard of in every other civilized country in the world. Our child poverty rate, according to the Children's Defense Fund, is twice that of Canada and Germany, and six times the rate of France, Belgium, and Austria. We can't even treat our children one-sixth as well as Belgium. *Belgium!* In other words, when it comes to judging how a culture treats its children America can't even be compared to allegedly-stagnating, old Europe; America belongs in the Division-III conference competing with countries like India or Sudan—except that they at least have an economic excuse. We're the only wealthy nation on earth who treats its children this callously, and flaunts it like a virtue. We're the only country who considers it normal and "just the way things are" to choose, every time it grows wealthier, to divert that new wealth to the very richest while at the same time further cutting aid to the neediest. . . .We're crazy. Sick and crazy, and proud as peasants. We're convinced that it's everyone else, the thirty-five-hour-workweek French and the universal-health care Canadians are the crazy ones. For the simple reason that they aren't suffering enough. You start to see, consciously or unconsciously, why Eric Harris, Dylan Klebold, Patrick Sherrill, Joe "Rocky" Wesbecker, and all the others make sense. Rational debate is impossible in an irrational, cruel, and credulous culture.

9

Peggy Sue Got Buried

THE WRETCHEDNESS OF A HUGE PROPORTION of middle-American students, and their widespread sympathy with an almost jihadist response, is so familiar that it has seeped into the popular culture. When I was in school teen movies were fun, light comedies balanced with just enough pain to appeal to teens' manic sensibilities—*Sixteen Candles, Weird Science, Fast Times at Ridgemont High, The Last American Virgin,* and *Better Off Dead* all made high school out to be a romp punctuated by life's painful lessons. These films seemed plausible enough at the time— even if high school was a cruel place, students weren't squeezed then the same way they are today. Also, we didn't have murders yet to awaken our sense that what seemed to be normal was in fact unbearable and wrong.

That feel-good John Hughes script became less and less plausible as Reagan's presidency wore on until finally *Heathers* appeared and killed the feel-good teen comedy genre. *Heathers* was the first teen comedy that appealed to an emerging sensibility at the end of President Reagan's second term. It's about the sadism and lethal hypocrisy among striving students at an upper-middle-class high school, the losers who educated them, and a hero who murdered them because murder was the only rational, heroic response imaginable. The hero, played by Christian Slater, offers a solution to the school's noxious culture: kill the meanest, shallowest, most popular students. And kill the ones who take their place. And finally, when it becomes clear that each student is just waiting for the chance to bully someone beneath them, the hero resolves to blow the whole school up. That argument—of school as Hell and the cause of arguably-justified mass murder—caused a lot of controversy when Heathers was released. Today, this theme is the norm in teen movies: *Elephant* (2003), a verité-style film about a Columbine-like high school massacre; *Thirteen* (2003), about a middle-school girl's destructive climb up the school's vicious social ladder; *O* (2001), a modern adaptation of Othello that takes place in a high school and ends with a school shooting; and *Donnie Darko* (2000), an even more rage-filled attack on middle-class school culture and adult hypocrisy, in which the hero sets fire to the house of an "inspirational" teacher, and shoots and kills a student (also delayed due to Columbine). Even teen movies without school shootings, such as 1999's *Election* or 1996's *Welcome to the Dollhouse,* are such merciless attacks on middle-American school culture that you walk away hating not just the main characters, but their lives, their setting, and the broader culture that allows it all. The only likeable character in *Election* is the lovelorn lesbian rebel who nearly wrecks the "school spirit"—and gets herself thrown out of the school. The lesson being that you can only find happiness by opting out of the source of pain, which is exactly the opposite of what every fear-stricken, stress-squeezed American is made to believe.

The one exception to this school-as-Hell motif is *American Pie*, a callow retro rip-off of the eighties' teen comedies. The only reason that its characters can be so happy and shallow is that they were the popular crowd, and everyone knows that the real popular kids, that top 10 percent layer, never feel the sort of anger and alienation that leads to rage. The other popular feel-good teen comedy of the nineties, *Clueless*, is about the popular crowd at Beverly Hills High—in other words, the very elite of the schoolyard elite (just like the popular teen TV show, *Beverly Hills 90210*). A light teen comedy is only plausible when focusing on the elite. Interestingly, *American Pie* failed to spawn a new trend of feel-good teen comedies, largely because they're just not believable. The best teens can get are compromise movies like 2004's *Mean Girls*, a comedy about the nasty popular girls in a high school, whose happy resolution only comes after a violent accident; *Saved!*, a wretched movie about a Christian school's mean-spirited popular girls and the hypocritical teachers and adults; and *Perfect Score*, a teen comedy about a group of kids who conspire to cheat on the SATs by stealing the test because of the unbearable pressure they're under. None of these movies makes school out to be much fun at all. It's widely accepted today that high schools are miserable, nerve-pinching stress machines. They are governed by dim hypocrites; the climate favors the cruelest and shallowest students, and many, if not most students, are constantly suppressing a burning sense of injustice, shame, and powerlessness.

10

From Columbine to Bin Laden

WITH THE SARATOGA HIGH BOMB PLOT AND CHEATING SCANDAL, San Jose suddenly became hypersensitive to news stories about school rage across the country. Watching reports of schoolyard murders and murder plots became almost like watching war news—every day, something new went down.

On February 9, 2004, just as the Saratoga school district was debating what to do about their crisis, Jon Romano, a sixteen-year-old high school student, brought a shotgun to his school in Albany, New York. His school's name, Columbia High, eerily recalled you-know-where. Romano went in the boy's restroom, sent an SMS to a friend warning him that he had brought a gun to school and to leave, then pulled out a shotgun, and loaded it. Romano stepped out in the corridor during period break and fired at a student's head, somehow managing to miss. Students scrambled—Romano fired again, spraying birdshot, hitting the corridor walls, and tearing a small hole in a classroom wall. As he made to fire a third time, he was brought down from behind by an assistant principal, a diving tackle that prevented Romano from scoring a direct hit. As Romano fell, his gun went off, wounding Romano's football coach. Romano was arrested and charged with attempted murder. The nasty finger-pointing started immediately. A superintendent tried convincing reporters of his diligence and foresight by insisting that the school had instituted tight security measures well before Romano's shooting, creating only one entrance which secured the school. He said that no student could bring anything dangerous in or out without being noticed. Students listening to him speak to the reporters groaned out loud and openly contradicted him. "You can bring anything into this school you want," a freshman student told one local reporter. There were rumors, circulated by students, that Romano was either lashing out for having gotten into trouble for drinking at a dance the previous weekend or that he was a "loner" type. Another said he didn't seem the type to massacre—he'd played hackeysack with friends. Romano's lawyer, Attorney E. Stewart Jones Jr., disputed these theories and charged instead that his fellow classmates were "a large part of the problem."

The following day, Tuesday, February 10, police were called into nearby Corinth High School, in another suburb of Albany, after graffiti was found in the boy's restroom warning "Hell is coming 3-13-04." Police swept the school but found nothing. Students, parents, and teachers were all nerve-wracked after the Columbia shooting. Then someone looked on a calendar and found out that March 13 fell on a Saturday. It would be hard to bring Hell on an empty school. When a reporter suggested to Corinth's principal that the graffiti may have been written as a "copycat," his answer was surprisingly candid (and accurate): "I think that is a possibility," he said. "Although, from time to time, it happens without anything in the news."

"It happens without anything in the news." This is one of the more startling aspects of the school rage phenomenon. School massacres and plots are not only still happening, but the 2003-2004 academic year turned out to be the bloodiest since the Columbine academic year. As of early February 2004, there were twenty-one shootings with thirty-six school-related deaths, according to Kenneth Trump, a Cleveland-based school safety consultant. And almost none of it makes it into the news, perhaps because after 9/11 middle-American kids plotting and shooting their schools up just didn't fit into our new way of seeing things. Only Islamic extremists do that now. How could a middle-class white kid possibly hate one of the most sacred and beloved institutions in America, our schools, and so want to kill everyone inside?

Maybe they're raging against something larger in culture. Dylan Klebold and Eric Harris talked about hijacking a jetliner and crashing it into New York City in 1999. And just four months after 9/11, a fifteen-year-old honors student, Charles Bishop, piloted a small plane into an office high-rise in Tampa, crashing through the twenty-eighth floor of the Bank of America building, killing himself and terrifying the country. During his flight, Bishop violated the airspace of the MacDill Air Force Base, home to the U.S. military's Central Command . . . which was coordinating the war in Afghanistan and the hunt for Osama bin Laden. Later reports revealed that Bishop, who spent the last week of his life downloading maps of the base, had buzzed the MacDill control tower and had flown within one hundred feet of two parked and fully-fuelled KC-135 tanker fuel aircraft. Two F-15s were scrambled from a south Florida base, but they arrived too late, revealing a homeland security that had learned its hard lessons from four months earlier.

Bishop was a straight-A student, middle-class, white, and Christian. He left a suicide note expressing his support for Osama bin Laden and for the 9/11 attacks. That was impossible to accept, so his mother declared Charles a supporter of the War on Terror, and his teacher declared that Bishop was "very patriotic," even though he very clearly wasn't. The suicide note's disturbing message was dis- missed as "just trying to get attention," a common and meaningless epithet.

Since dead kids can't really benefit from attention the same way that living kids can, you have to ask, once again, Why was Charles Bishop trying to get atten- tion by crashing a plane into a downtown skyscraper? He answered that question himself in his suicide note, but no one wanted to listen. Instead, students and teachers started reciting the famous Collected Patriotic Sayings of Charles Bishop. Bishop's family released a statement claiming, "Charles and his family have always fully supported our United States war on terrorism and Osama bin Laden."

"He said he wanted to join the Air Force and do something for his country," said his journalism teacher, Gabriella Terry. His journalism teacher said she couldn't believe Charles would do what he did, saying she knew him well. "And I didn't miss a thing," she said, ignoring the overwhelming evidence that she had indeed missed every single thing about him. "He was a good boy."

The Charles Bishop suicide mission was a potentially fascinating, devastating story that could have inspired some serious self-examination in America, but did not. The fact that a good boy, nice and sociable, an honors student, could commit a terrorist act similar to Osama bin Laden didn't cause people to wonder what it was about his Florida school or America that drove him to imitate the most awful anti-American massacre in our history—instead, it led us to lying to ourselves. Mohammed Atta flew a plane into a building because he hates our freedom; Charles Bishop flew a plane into a building even though he loves our freedom. What's so hard to understand about that?

The Charles Bishop story ended even more grotesquely. Authorities, worried that the patriotic-suicide-pilot theory might not wash for long, came up with an explanation they thought would put all the doubts and fears to rest. They blamed the boy's acne medication, Accutane. That's right, acne medicine made little Charlie fly the plane in to the building. Super-Clearasil made him support Bin Laden. As Monty Python-silly as that last explanation sounds, it became the offi- cial version accepted by the *New York Times* and the broader media.

The Clearasil-made-him-do-it explanation not only reassured the country, it also stood to make Charles Bishop's mother a rich woman. She filed a $70 million lawsuit against Roche, the maker of Accutane. Later, Charles Bishop's mother was forced to admit that she and her husband had twice attempted suicide together. She blamed those episodes, conveniently enough, on drugs.

Ever wonder why a bright, likeable, handsome boy would hate his world?

Here, by the way, is Charles Bishop's suicide note, which was finally released to the public:

I have prepared this statement in regards to the acts I am about to com- mit. First of all, Osama bin Laden is absolutely justified in the terror he has caused on 9-11. He has brought a mighty nation to its knees! God blesses him and the others who helped make September 11th happen. The U.S. will have to face the consequences for its horrific actions against the Palestinian people and Iraqis by its allegiance with the mon- strous Israelis—who want nothing short of world domination! You will pay—God help you—and I will make you pay! There will be more coming! Al Qaeda and other organizations have met with me several times to discuss the option of me joining. I didn't. This is an operation done by me only. I had no other help, although, I am acting on their behalf. Osama bin Laden is planning on blowing up the Super Bowl with an antiquated nuclear bomb left over from the 1967 Israeli-Syrian war.

You can't read this note and say to yourself that he was a great patriot who was just trying to get attention. The kind of attention he was hoping to get was the same kind Osama was after—the attention that would wound America so deeply that it would have to adjust in some profound way. America is a hateful place for a great number of Americans, kids and adults alike. Charles Bishop didn't "hate us because we are free." He hated America because there's a lot to hate. Without much of a vocabulary to frame this hatred, he is left with the borrowed islamoscript of Osama bin Laden—Bishop's hatred perhaps hasn't yet been put into words, it hasn't been contextualized yet. He lacked the ability to express the sense of hatred and injustice in his own words, drawing from his own experience. Instead the enemy (Osama) of Bishop's enemy (America) became Bishop's friend.

11

Move On or Get Over It!

I ARRIVED ON THE SARATOGA STORY about a week after the bomb plot story broke. And everyone I spoke to, including Dr. Skelley, teachers, students, even the mayor, all said one thing: "We just want to move on."

"The students just want to move on and put this all behind them," Dr. Skelley told me. In fact, by the time I arrived, everyone in Saratoga had "already moved on." Even kids I spoke to said that.

There was something insidious about this rush to move on. I knew that this was one of one of the most popular phrases of the Bush Administration, and not surprisingly, the desire to move on always erupted whenever something awful happened and they wanted people to forget about it. They first employed the expression during the 2000 Florida voting scandal in order to give Americans the sense that Gore and his supporters were weak-willed whackos and sore losers. Winners always move on—losers can't. Since America is so winner-obsessed, the move on argument is essentially its own argument—it quashes debate far more effectively than any elaborate strategy Cicero could have come up with:

"It's Time To Move On, Mr. Gore"—*Hartford Courant*, November 28, 2000

"Time to Move On"—*Wall Street Journal*, December 13, 2000

"We have a winner, and it's time to move on"—Florida Agricultural Commissioner Robert Crawford, December 17, 2000.

"It's time to move on. This went on for too long."—George Bush, attending a ceremony in the Florida Senate officially certifying Florida's electoral votes in his favor, December 18, 2000

Telling people to move on is essentially the same as ordering them to go into denial, with the implication that if they don't put on their amnesia caps, there's something wrong with them.

David Miclean, an attorney representing one of the expelled Saratoga High students, cleverly turned this "time to move on" attitude on its head against the administration: "We'd like to think [Superintendent Cynthia Hall Ranii is] sincere in helping the family move on," he told the *Mercury*. In his framing, to move on is to let the kid off and put it all behind us; to not move on is to continue seeking a harsh punishment. His client received the lightest of the expulsion sentences, given to those kids caught in the cheating scandal allowed to attend neighboring Los Gatos High for a semester before returning to Saratoga in the fall.

In the aftermath of the school shootings at Westside Middle School in Jonesboro, Arkansas, and Heath High in West Paducah, Kentucky, these same urges and pressures to move on were employed, with devastating results, as revealed in the book *Rampage*, a Harvard study of the school shooting phenomenon.

At Westside the trauma was greatest because the two boys pinned down eighty-nine students and nine teachers, all of whom were caught in the line of fire of their enfilade. The shooting lasted five minutes, and the boys were apprehended ten minutes after that. Thirty shots were fired and fifteen targets hit. Teachers dragged children out of the line of fire and tried to stop their bleeding or comfort the wounded and dying. The experience was so traumatic that nearly all are still suffering severe psychological disorders.

Jonesboro's response? According to the Harvard team of sociology PhDs who studied the town for *Rampage*, Jonesboro's residents wanted the teachers, parents, and kids affected by the shootings to move on.

"You start hearing talk about 'moving beyond' this. When are we not going to hear about it anymore?'" Ron Deal, the Jonesboro Family Life minister, said. Beverly Ashford, a Westside teacher, told the interviewers, "You're dealing with parents that want to shove things under the rug."

They weren't even shy about their callousness and impatience. Mary Curtis, a teacher caught in the crossfire, told the Harvard team, "I heard secretaries [say], 'What's wrong with her? She needs to get her shit together.'. . . Some people didn't have to deal with the little bleeding, the little breathing. . . . By the time I ran back down that same hall, there was so much blood on it that I was trying to hold on to the lockers. There are people that judge me that don't know."

The call to move on is effective because it makes those who resist it look like losers and failures and weirdos. It works like bullying—the targets generally blame themselves. The mother of one Jonesboro victim said, "The people I work with avoid me because they don't want to talk about it. It's almost like I have a contagious disease." Betsy Woods, a Jonesboro counselor, told the Harvard interviewers, "The social norm is you don't [talk about the shooting]. Or if you [do, you] get an attitude from people like, 'What's the matter with you? Why are you still talking about it?'"

This attitude worked its way down to the kids' level in a particularly nasty form. The eighty-nine kids caught in the crossfire were offered the chance to attend Ferncliff, a camp for children traumatized by war or violence. Sixty-eight attended the first summer. The following spring, only twenty kids attended. The reason: pressure to move on, as described in *Rampage*: "The kids who continued to attend were sometimes mocked by classmates. Who was and who was not 'over' the shooting became a public label."

No one wanted to hear about the trauma anymore. And the longer the victims took to heal, the nastier the rest of the town behaved toward them. Many victims in Jonesboro found that they couldn't even talk about their pain or trauma with anyone. Some had to forge relationships with survivors of Columbine just to find a sympathetic ear. Even parents didn't want to hear about it from their children: "Some students complained to their teachers that their parents would not listen to them, saying instead, 'It's time to get over it.'"

If people who are suffering or upset don't move on, then the culture applies a more venomous voodoo incantation, "Get over it." Whereas the call to move on still implies a kind of patronizing "move on back to our state of denial, and we'll forget the whole thing" attitude, telling someone to get over it is the ultimate insult, the grown-up equivalent of sewing an "A" on someone's chest.

On the messageboard of Techrepublic.com linking to an article titled "Lost Your Job? Don't Look Overseas," message 104 of 107 reads, rather illiterately:

Yep, personal responsibility Some people take comfort in the fact that they can live off the government if something happens to their job, get over it. Everyone is dispensible. You can lose your job overseas, or you can lose it to your neighbor who is more qualified. From: ND_IT Date: 06/14/04

In the safety of messageboard anonymity, ND_IT managed to get an angry reply:

Get Over it?? That's easy for you to say. With twenty-four years professional and very successful IT experience, and 2 IT degrees, I have been trying to get back in for 2 YEARS with no success! Yes, there are some people competing who are more qualified than I. . . . that is always true for everyone... what's new is that now there are hundreds and sometimes even thousands competing for the same position! And THAT is thanks to outsourcing. From: Karl Jr Date: 06/14/04

The impulse to get over it is an example, caught in a phrase, of how profoundly normal it is for contemporary Americans to be callous and bullying. In a sexual discrimination and harassment suit filed by police recruit Kathy Durkin against the City of Chicago in 2003, she related how her instructor, Officer James Peck, abused her even over her father's recent death: "[G]et over it, my fucking father died too . . . you don't need your fucking father." When relatives of soldiers fighting in Iraq complained about a speech Bush gave that made light over the fact that no WMDs were found, Britt Hume of Fox News attacked the soldiers' families, saying, "[Y]ou have to feel like saying to people, 'Just get over it.'" Anyone who doesn't accept the way things are, no matter how cruel or destructive, needs to get over it.

In fact, grieving seems to be what draws out the very meanest in Americans. In a 1997 column in the *Waxahachie Daily Light*, columnist Paul O'Rear wrote, "Several months after Dad's death, Mom found herself dealing with the perceived attitude from some well-meaning people, that she needed to get over it and get on with her life."

Well-meaning indeed. Nancy Ruhe, executive director of Parents of Murdered Children in Cincinnati, told CNN, "People say to me all the time, 'When are these [victims] going to get over it?'"

This same heartless logic was applied, to the traumatized survivors of the Jonesboro, Arkansas, school shooting. A group of survivors wanting to erect some kind of meaningful memorial to the victims planted a garden. But the school wouldn't recognize it, and six months after they had designed, tilled, planted, and finished the memorial garden the school still refused to dedicate it. As a local minister observed, withholding his name, "That is a telling illustration of where we are as a community. We have tried to forget. . . . And they don't even know it's there." An artist painted a portrait of the five victims who were killed and offered it to the school, but they didn't want it. Three years later, the *Rampage* researchers found the portrait hanging in the Jonesboro District Attorney's office.

"Just when is it going to end?" Susan Miller, a Westside administrator, complained to the researchers. "The first-year, the third-year, and it will be the fifth-year anniversary. . . . People donating things to you that you don't even want, huge cemetery-looking stuff. They want you to put it in your playground. With names on it. In memory of . . . whatever. . . . We have a school to run."

One teacher who cared for the children at the blood-spattered shooting scene had her pay docked by the school for those days when she stayed home from teaching because she was too emotionally traumatized to face work. She looked into filing a worker's compensation claim, and was told to "forget it." The school board's attitude toward teachers trying to submit worker's comp claims in the aftermath of the shootings was "decisively negative and discouraging." She was misled by them into believing that the state of Arkansas didn't cover mental health claims. The school board president even told her, "It kind of seems to me like you've got some personal problems. You need to get yourself together."

Cruel and callous when on top, and afraid and smiling all the way to the grave when not—that pretty much sums up the post-Reagan *zeitgeist*. And if you're not just as cheerful as the rest, "you've got some personal problems." You're a weirdo if you complain. It's your own fault if you're traumatized by a massacre. It's your own fault if you're poor. It's your own fault if you get downsized, overworked, bullied, and fail. Get over it. This is how Americans have been taught from the Reagan era through today to deal with people who are vulnerable: blame them for their own suffering. Move on. And if they don't move on, that means they're weird. Tell them to get over it. Which is to say, "Get the fuck out of my face."

To recognize the essential meanness of modern American culture, caught so clearly in the example of Westside in how it was transmitted from adult to child, adult to adult, and child to child, is to attack the culture's DNA. If you admit that the callousness exhibited there is awful and yet as common as Home Depot outlets, then eventually, the context changes and the shootings make a lot of sense. The post-Reagan squeeze is even evident when the school administration, by reflex, tries to deny a teacher health care benefits that would have once been considered standard, docking her pay out of a deeply-ingrained reflex more than anything.

The whole country is infested with this meanness and coldness, and no one is allowed to admit it. Only the crazy ones sense that it is wrong—that what is "normal" is not at all normal—and some of them, adults and kids alike, fight back with everything they have.

POSTSCRIPT

RONALD REAGAN DIED just as I was completing this book. After all of the grue-some murders I studied, and all of the infuriating cultural-economic changes I researched and tracked, I started to assume, as one does when far too deep in his work, that everyone finally understood what a vicious old cannibal Reagan was.

Rage as we know it today did not exist when Ronald Reagan took power in 1981. Americans lived completely different lives then. The word stress had a far less lethal meaning then. The vise hadn't yet been applied so intensely and so broadly, from the middle-class employee's eighty-hour workweek down to the three-year-old's preschool exam prep course. Instead, malaise was the cultural toxin. Executives and shareholders earned a far smaller portion of the wealth and the middle class had a much larger chunk, not just of the economic pie, but of other scarce resources such as leisure and pleasure and cultural dignity and the sense of entitlement. That is gone now. No one wants to remember this part of the pre-Reagan past—because it's too depressing and speaks too obviously to the real decline in America. We went from the seventies malaise, which is just a euphe-mism for not feeling squeezed hard enough, to today's post-industrial slavery, where we have accepted, with a cheerful attitude, the notion that our master's interests—the constant transfer of wealth upward into the plutocratic class's pockets—are identical with our own interests. And we serve out their interests on our own initiative, rejecting any politics or ideology which might threaten our masters' pursuit of ever-increasing wealth and pleasure.

Before Reagan, there was no such thing as "going postal" or schoolyard ram-page murders. It all started with his reign and his revolution—specifically, with his reckless mass-firing of the striking air traffic controllers in 1981. In a sign of the sucker-collaboration which was soon to become the norm, PATCO, the air traffic controllers' union, was one of the very few unions to support Reagan's run for pres-ident in 1980. In 2004, after Reagan's death, newspapers reported on members of that destroyed union who are today still unemployed and impoverished, including one former Vietnam War veteran who lamented that he had been "shafted twice" by his country and another former controller who had been made homeless.

When Reagan fired the striking air traffic controllers in 1981, he told America he was literally willing to kill us all if we didn't give in to his wealth-transfer plan.

It was so shocking that it worked. The air controller's union broke—and so did a whole way of life. Thanks to Ronald Reagan, we are all miserable wage slaves, or schoolyard wretches being pressed and prepared for life in the office world. There is no other choice but that, or death.

The way this country supplicated before Reagan's corpse, elevating him to a kind of Khomeini status with the seven-day funeral and the endless orations about his humanity, intelligence, and how wonderfully simple life was under his reign, only reinforced the most disturbing conclusions that I was reaching as I wrote this book: that Americans have become perfect slaves, fools and suckers, while a small elite is cackling all the way to the offshore bank.

Take this example from *National Review* editor Stanley Kurtz, posted just after Reagan's death: "[T]he president bit the bullet and fired the striking controllers. That set the tone for labor negotiations with national, and even municipal, governments for years to come. More important, the whole world was watching Regan's conduct during the strike. This was obviously a man who would hang tough under pressure, and risk serious costs to back up a decision he believed to be necessary and right. The Soviet's took note." Firing the controllers wasn't about smashing a union and destroying workers' lives; it was a test of the master's character, or a collective tribal battle against the Soviet Union and "big government." You expect to get this kind of toe-sucking propaganda from high-paid right-wing mandarins like the *National Review* or Fred Barnes or William Kristol—it's the countless nobodies who prostrated themselves before Reagan's corpse that is most galling. Take this posting on a blog, www.gutrumbles.com, posted by JMFlynny at June 5, 2004 09:43 PM:

> I was at the Reagan Library yesterday. What a coincidence, my daughter's class was there competing in a "We the People" constitutional debate. I walked by a display commemerating his stand against the air traffic controllers union during their strike early in his first Presidency. His exact words, upon firing all striking controllers for breaking the law: "now people know what to expect from me; I say what I mean, and I mean what I say." I believe the world came to know the truth of those words, and was better for it.

At least JMFlynny was right about one thing: we learned that Reagan and the plutocrats meant business. Why do we need to love our own wretchedness? What stake did JMFlynny have in kissing Reagan's dead feet? Why do we need to celebrate, with a kind of malicious pride, our worsening condition? What the hell is wrong with us? Have we lost all of our dignity? Why is it that in those rare, exceptional cases when Americans take up arms against the malice that Ronald Reagan bequeathed to us we only turn on each other, in our workplaces, our post offices, and schools, rather than turning on the real villains in this tale? Why did we let Ronald Reagan die calmly in his sleep, at age ninety-three, almost a quarter century after he destroyed everything decent in America? This book is an attempt to dig up Reagan's remains, hang them upside down from the nearest palm tree, and subject him, at last, to a proper trial.

ENDNOTES

PART I: IF HE'D JUST GOT THE RIGHT PEOPLE

1: I told them I'd be back

p. 7–10: On September 14, 1989, Joseph Wesbecker . . . Seven were killed, twenty wounded.
Leslie Scanlon and Andrew Wolfson, "Disturbed worker kills 7 and wounds 13 in rampage with AK-47 at Louisville plant," *Louisville Courier-Journal*, September 15, 1989. Many of the details from section 1, part I, are drawn from accounts in the *Louisville Courier-Journal*'s post-murder issue, September 15, 1989.

p. 8: Bowman had given birth a few months earlier . . .
Morgan Atkinson ,*A Pain in the Innards*, BetaSP, Louisville, KY, 1998. In the documentary, Bowman, speaking from a wheelchair, expressed resentment toward those unscathed survivors of the shooting who said that the reason they weren't killed or injured was because God had saved them or that it was "meant to be," an apparently widespread sentiment. Bowman asked the interviewer of the documentary if that meant that God or Jesus had meant to paralyze her.

p. 9: It seems that Wesbecker . . .
Fentress v. Shea Communications, vol. 38, 23 (Ky. 1994).

2: Pow! Pow! Pow!

p. 11: There were two presses running . . .
Michael Campbell, in an interview with the author at Campbell's home in Brandenberg, Kentucky, August 30, 2001. Hereafter cited as Campbell Interview

p. 13: In an earlier interview . . . like a gun.
Gerald Ryan, "Standard Gravure victims recall horror of Sept. 14," *Louisville Courier-Journal*, October 3, 1989.

3: Little Doughboy

p. 14: "tormented by mental illness . . . persecution complex . . ."
Jim Adams, "Tormented man driven by his secret stresses," *Louisville Courier-Journal*, September 15, 1989.

p. 14 : "Wesbecker's first job . . . the money was better."
Adams, "Tormented man driven by his secret stresses."

p. 15: His first nickname at Standard Gravure was "Little Doughboy" . . . started calling

Wesbecker "Rocky."
Campbell interview, 2001.
p. 16: It all started in the early eighties . . . and had been working without a contract for months.
Ben Hershberg, "Shootings shook an already tense company," *Louisville Courier-Journal*, September 15, 1989; Campbell Interview, 2001.
p. 16: "Don Frazier . . . started to build."
Hershberg, "Shootings shook an already tense company."
p. 16: In 1986, the Binghams . . . stressful place to work.
Hershberg, "Shootings shook an already tense company"; Campbell interview, 2001.
p. 17: In pro-management author of New Arenas For Violence . . .
From "About The Author" for the book on amazon.com (http://www.amazon.com/exec/obidos/tg/detailed//0275956520/qid=1114275521/sr1-1/ref=sr_1_1/002-1210986-0931251?v=glance&s=books), "Kelleher specializes in strategic management, human resource management, staff education, and in threat assessment and management crisis resolution for organizations in the public and private sectors."
p. 17: "This tragedy should have been avoided . . . no option but to take revenge."
Michael D. Kelleher, *New Arenas for Violence: Homicide in the American Workplace* (Westport, CT: Praeger Publishers, 1996), 91.
p. 18: After the massacre, news reports told . . . wasn't a stressful place to work.
Scanlon and Wolfson, "Disturbed worker kills 7 and wounds 13 in rampage with AK-47 at Louisville plant"; Hershberg, "Shootings shook an already tense company"; Campbell interview, 2001.
p. 18: "It's miserable."
Hershberg, "Shootings shook an already tense company"; Campbell interview, 2001.
p. 18: "Oh, Joe? He was pushed into it! ... Still does, as it is!"
Earl Gardner, in an interview with the author, September 2, 2001.
p. 19: "that would obviously not be the case today."
Larry VonderHarr, interview with the Howland Group, *Anger in the Workplace*, spring 1999. http://www.howlandgroup.com/workplacetrends/vonderhaar.htm.
p. 19: "I think he was looking for the Supervisor...that's who he intended to get revenge on."
ibid.

4: Just Tough it Out

p. 19-20: Well, he came in complaining . . . at Standard Gravure you were exposed to this.
Fentress v. Shea Communications, vol. 38, 23
p. 20: "Toluene may affect . . . and hearing and color vision loss."
Agency for Toxic Substances and Disease Registry, "ToxFAQs for Toluene," http://www.atsdr.cdc.gov/tfacts56.html.
p. 21: "changes such as memory loss, sleep disturbances, loss of ability to concentrate, or incoordination ..."
Canada's National Occupational Health & Safety Resource, "What are the main

health hazards associated with breathing in toluene?"
http://www.bostikfindley.com.au/pdf/msds/bostik_craft_glue.pdf.
p. 21: Q. Did he make any . . . That was his attitude.
Fentress v. Shea Communications, vol. 38, 35

5: "Your request is . . . irrelevant"
p. 22: Well, the clearest memory that I have . . . in that stressful condition.
Fentress v. Shea Communications, vol. 38, 38
p. 23: "It is the company's contention that manic depression . . . we cannot totally exempt him from this duty permanently."
Ibid., 42–3
p. 23: "Pursuant to your letter of August the 7th . . . the following information and items."
Ibid., 43–44.
p. 24: "discrimination had occurred"
Ibid., 45.

6: Rocky's Best Friends
p. 24: (as one in six Americans do at some point in their lives)
Alison McCook, "Millions of U.S. adults depressed, few treated well," Reuters, June 17, 2003.
p. 25: "named three or four other workers . . . capable of doing that."
Atkinson, A Pain in the Innards, 1998.
p. 25: "Joe Wesbecker had a wonderful sense of humor . . . have me laughing."
Fentress v. Shea Communications, vol. 38, 52
p. 26: "No employer would ever admit to . . . she did not excel."
David Shipler, "A Poor Cousin of the Middle Class," New York Times Magazine, January 18, 2004.
p. 26: "He seemed like he was happy."
Jim Adams, "Tormented man driven by his secret stresses," Louisville Courier-Journal, September 15, 1989.
p. 26: [Mattingly]: Mr. Ganote had been involved. . .That's all I have.
Fentress v. Shea Communications, vol. 38, 63 (Ky. 1994).
p. 26: "He didn't fire at me . . . friends too."
Scanlon and Wolfson, "Disturbed worker kills 7 and wounds 13 in rampage with AK-47 at Louisville plant."
p. 27: "[S]omeone put something up . . . no one in authority had taken it down."
Fentress v. Shea Communications, vol. 38, 61
p. 27: "suicide more than once."
Fentress v. Shea Communications, vol. 38, 62

PART II: THE BANALITY OF SLAVERY

p. 29: "Our slave population . . . and harmless one."
Joseph C. Robert, The Road from Monticello: A Study of the Virginia Slavery Debate of 1832 (Durham, NC: 1941), 87

1: The Heart of Submissiveness

p. 29: The number of documented slave rebellions . . . number under a dozen.
Winthrop Jordan, *White Over Black: American Attitudes Towards the Negro,*
1550–1812 (Raleigh: University of North Carolina Press, 1995), 113. Blassingame, in
The Slave Community (216), counts only nine slave revolts between 1691 and 1865.
p. 30: Over a period of four centuries . . . barracoons or slave warehouses.
Daniel Mannix and Malcolm Cowley, *Black Cargoes* (New York: Penguin, 1977), 287.
p. 30: In 1800, the U.S. population was . . . made up 70 to 90 percent of the inhabitants.
Vincent Harding, *There Is a River: The Black Struggle for Freedom in America* (New
York: Harvest/HBJ Books, 1993), 53.
p. 30: "Whenever slaves offered violent resistance . . . raised against white."
Jordan, *White Over Black*, 112.
p. 31: Frederick Douglass explained that slaves . . . knew not of . . .
Frederick Douglass, *Narrative of the Life of Frederick Douglass: An American Slave,*
Written By Himself (New York: Pocket Books, 2004), 110.
p. 31: "During the Revolution, British armies . . . uprisings took place."
Jordan, *White Over Black*, 391.
p. 31: "A quarter of them [the American army] are Negroes, merry, confident, and sturdy."
Benjamin Quarles, *The Negro in the American Revolution* (Raleigh: University of
North Carolina Press, 1961), 78.
p. 32: There are stories of British agents . . . and taking their land).
Elizabeth Anne Fenn, *Pox Americana: The Great Smallpox Epidemic of 1775–82* (New
York: Hill & Wang, 2002), 131.
p. 32: "Many thousands of African Americans . . . from following them."
Africans in America, PBS series, 1998, http://www.pbs.org/wgbh/aia/
part2/2narr4.html.
p. 32: In Washington's Virginia, where chronic . . . moved to condemn it.
Robert A. Selig, "The Revolution's Black Soldiers: They Fought for Both Sides in
Their Quest for Freedom" *Colonial Williamsburg: The Journal of the Colonial
Williamsburg Foundation* 19, no. 4 (Summer 1997), 15-22.
p. 32: "Naturally, many slaves did remain . . . the large Negro population of the time."
Melville Jean Herskovits *The Myth of the Negro Past, Rev. Ed.* (1941; repr., Boston:
Beacon Press, 1990), 105. From the description of the book, "Originally published
in 1941, his unprecedented study of black history and culture recovered a rich
African heritage in religious and secular life, the language and arts of the
Americas."
p. 33: It is estimated that up to one million Europeans . . . than slaves elsewhere.
John Blassingame, *The Slave Community: Plantation Life in the Antebellum South,*
Second Ed. (New York: Oxford University Press, 1979), 50.
p. 33: "Within a few years after their capture . . . adopt new behavioral patterns."
Ibid., 61.
p. 33: "Occasionally old slaves made fun of new captives. . . favor with their masters."
Ibid., 61.
p. 33: "length of enslavement, treatment . . . and the proselytizing zeal of their masters."
Ibid., 63.

p. 33: "A peasant only knoweth how to . . . custom of the country."
Michael Mullet, *Popular Culture and Popular Protest in Late Medieval and Early Modern Europe* (London: Croom Helm, 1987), 50.
p. 33: Historian K. R. Bradley, author . . . the famous one led by Spartacus.
K. R. Bradley, *Slaves and Masters in the Roman Empire: A Study in Social Control* (New York: Oxford University Press, 1987), 31.
p. 33: "Slavery was such a fact of life . . . the greatest philosophers of their age."
Richard Donkin, *Blood Sweat & Tears: The Evolution of Work* (New York: Texere, 2001), 25.

2: Inanimate African Cargo
p. 35: According to Black Cargoes . . . on slave ships between 1699 and 1845 . . .
Mannix and Cowley, *Black Cargoes*, 32.

3: Slave Management
p. 36: One of the most frequent reasons . . . if they labored faithfully.
Blassingame, *Slave Community*, 292.
p. 36: As Lunsford Lane, "[M]y condition as a slave was comparatively a happy, indeed a highly favored one . . ."
Lunsford Lane, *The Narrative of Lunsford Lane* (Boston, 1842), iii.
p. 36–37: "The planters generally had little concern . . . before the day's labor commenced."
Blassingame, *Slave Community*, 107.
p. 37: "[Our master] allowed us generally to do . . . the privilege granted to us."
Elijah Marrs, *Life and History of the Rev. Elijah P. Marrs* (Louisville: The Bradley & Gilbert Company, 1885), 11.
p. 37: "unlimited juice to squeeze. . . all they were worth)."
Jill Fraser, *White Collar Sweatshop: The Deterioration of Work and Its Rewards in Corporate America* (New York: W. W. Norton, 2001), 40, 155, 159.
p. 37: "In order to obtain the maximum labor . . . you respect his feelings and wants.'"
Blassingame, *Slave Community*, 239.
p. 37–38: "Such justice and consideration . . . the increase of his estate."
Donkin, *Blood Sweat & Tears*, 18.
p. 38: "Is this what many hundreds of years . . . as we know it?"
Ibid.
p. 38: "Maybe not."
Ibid.
p. 38: "It is quite clear that Columella's . . . prelude to work efficiency and general loyalty."
Bradley, *Slaves and Masters*, 22.
p. 38: "[T]his has parallels . . . an atmosphere of mutual distrust."
Donkin, *Blood Sweat & Tears*, 19.
p. 38: "The institutionally defined role of the slave . . . ordered to do so."
Blassingame, *Slave Community*, 242.
p. 39: "The master should make it his business . . . act as becomes them."
Ibid, 245.
p. 39: "By means of this [pension plan] . . . reputation and continuing success."

Fraser, *White Collar Sweatshop*, 112.

p. 39: "the first principle and foundation . . . sets every wheel in motion."
Mannix, Cowley, *Black Cargoes*, 73–4.

p. 40: This irrational yet perhaps instinctual. . . Develop "habit of perfect dependence"
Harding, *There Is a River*, 105.

p. 41: "Middle managers in general . . . from the managers themselves."
Charles Heckscher, *White Collar Blues: Management Loyalties in an Age of Corporate Restructuring* (New York: Basic Books, 1994), 34. Quote sourced in *White Collar Sweatshop*, 232n.

p. 41: "had great confidence in me . . . or deceive him in any way."
Lucius Holsey, *Autobiography, Sermons, Addresses and Essays of Bishop L. H. Holsey* (Atlanta: Franklin Printing and Publishing Company, 1898), 10.

4: A Normal and Inevitable Aspect of Their Affairs

p. 42: "Throughout the colonial period . . . aspect of their affairs."
Louis Filler, *The Crusade Against Slavery 1830–1860* (New York: HarperCollins College Division, 1960), 1.

p. 42: "that it would be of Advantage . . . than when they were heathens."
Jordan, *White Over Black*, 191.

p. 43: "Argument against globalization were considered . . . would incite so much sixties-esque rage."
As another example, when my Moscow newspaper, the *eXile*, criticized corruption in one World Bank program in Russia, the World Bank's former Moscow representative, Charles Blitzer, accused my former co-editor Matt Taibbi of "helping the Communists." In other words, one who argued against the going paradigm was by design an enemy of the people, and most American correspondents in Moscow at the time completely agreed with Blitzer's view without even questioning it.

p. 43: When Parliament met in the early months . . . the colonists were talking about.
Thomas Slaughter, *The Whiskey Rebellion: Frontier Epilogue to the American Revolution* (New York: Oxford University Press, 1986), 17.

p. 43: "West Indian planters and Liverpool merchants . . . civilizing the primitive Africans."
Mannix and Cowley, *Black Cargoes*, 184.

p. 43: "Mayor Walton H. Bachrach declared . . . Negroes in the ghetto."
Kerner Commission, *Report of the National Advisory Commission on the Civil Disorders of 1967* (New York: Viking Press, 1969), 50.

5: Realists and Madmen

p. 44: "The only reason we can give . . . on board the ship."
Harding, *There is a River*, 20.

p. 44: "disease—a monomania, to which the negro race is peculiarly subject"
Herskovits, *Myth of the Negro Past*, 102.

p. 45: "It's not a postal problem . . . have a percentage of irrational people."
Don Lasseter, *Going Postal* (New York: Pinnacle Books, 1997), 270–71.

p. 45: "harassment, intimidation, [and] cruelty."
Ibid., 165.
p. 45: "That this slave should run away . . . no kind of provocation to go off."
Blassingame, *Slave Community*, 205.
p. 45: "The flight of one woman from Tuscaloosa . . . as supposed, contented and happy.'"
Harding, *There Is a River*, 114.
p. 45: "He was not somebody you would say . . . and start killing people.'"
Lasseter, *Going Postal*, 189.
p. 45: "I still cannot believe that Mitchell . . . wanted to be helpful."
Katherine Newman, *Rampage: The Social Roots of School Shootings* (New York: Basic Books, 2004), 78.
p. 46: described by then-governor James Monroe as "strange . . ."
Jordan, *White Over Black*, 4.
p. 46: "despised minority . . . [marked by] deep divisions among themselves."
Harding, *There Is a River*, 128.
p. 46: "You are not certain of heaven . . . will be glad to let you go free."
Deirdre Mullane, *Crossing the Danger Water: Three Hundred Years of African-American Writing* (New York: Anchor, 1993), 115–120.
p. 47: William Lloyd Garrison, . . . "practical reformers" or "realists."
Filler, Crusade Against Slavery, 58–9.
p. 47: "preferred to deal with problems . . . Van Buren's sub-treasury plan."
Ibid., 112–114.
p. 47: "It now seems clear that. . . in the way of rationality on either side."
Jordan, *White Over Black*, 113.
p. 47–48: ". . . recurring instances of masters, mistresses . . . in the role of a slave."
Ibid.
p. 48: As Blassingame . . . in the United States territory.
Blassingame, *Slave Community*, 195.

6: A Roman Catholic Plot

p. 49: "a crude rebellion that could have been . . . better planned."
Douglas Harper, "Slavery in the North," 2003. http://www.slavenorth.com/newyork.htm.
p. 50: "The reaction of New Yorkers to what seemed . . . baseness of Negroes in general."
Jordan, *White Over Black*, 118.

7: The Battle of Negro Fort

p. 51: "The American delegation reported that . . . much abuse on the Americans.'"
Harding, *There Is a River*, 65.

8: A Talent for Concerted Action

p. 52: "A chief source of danger . . . the Negro who was not a slave."
Jordan, *White Over Black*, 122.

p. 52: "Vesey's example must be regarded . . . to bow down in fear."
http://www.africawithin.com/bios/denmark_vesey.htm.
p. 52: In Charleston in 1822, . . . and 12,652 slaves.
Robert Starobin, "Terror in South Carolina 1822: An Introduction to Denmark
Vesey & the Slave Conspiracy in Charleston," *ChickenBones: A Journal*
http://www.nathanielturner.com/introductiontodenmarkvesey.htm.
p. 52–53: "I was struck with the appearance of the slaves . . . enjoying a holiday."
James Stirling, *Letters From the Slave States* (New York: Kraus Reprint, 1969), 287-
91.
p. 53: George Wilson, "a favorite and confidential slave"
Africans in America, PBS series, 1998.
p. 53: "I fear nothing so much as the Effects . . . in this Place [Charleston]."
Robert L. Paquette, "Jacobins of the Lowcountry: The Vesey Plot on Trial,"
William and Mary Quarterly 59, no. 1 (2002): 16,
http://www.historycooperative.org/cgi-bin/justtop.cgi?act=justtop&url=
http://www.historycooperative.org/journals/wm/59.1/paquette.html.
p. 53: A recent study by Johns Hopkins . . . monumentally absurd proportions.
Michael Johnson, "Denmark Vesey and His Co-Conspirators," *William and Mary
Quarterly* 58, no. 4 (2001): 915-76.
p. 54: "We want to believe in the revolt . . . their lives to fight injustice."
Glenn Small Homewood, "Sleuthing Prof Debunks Slave Plot," *Johns Hopkins
University Gazette Online* 31, no. 8 (2001): http://www.jhu.edu/~gazette/2001/
22oct01/22sleuth.html.
p. 54: Johnson's revisionist findings were praised, for example, in The Nation...
Jon Wiener, "Denmark Vesey: A New Verdict," *Nation*, February 21, 2002,
http://www.thenation.com/doc/mhtml%3Fi=2-2-311&s=wiener.
p. 54: "Let it never be forgotten, that our negroes . . . the DESTROYERS of our race."
Paquette, "Jacobins of the Lowcountry."
p. 55: She was led, handcuffed, by Wildshaw's assistant . . . effects of this infernal torture.
John Hawkins Simpson, *Horrors of the Virginian Slave Trade and of the Slave-Rearing
Plantations* (London: A. W. Bennett, 1863), 14–15.

9: "Without any cause or provocation"
p. 58: "What strikes us as the most . . . Southampton appeals to us in vain."
Africans in America, PBS series, 1998. http://www.pbs.org/wgbh/aia/part3/
3h499t.html.
*p. 58: "[Eric Harris] was a brilliant killer without a conscience . . . something even
worse."*
David Cullen, "The Depressive and the Psychopath: At last we know why the
Columbine killers did it," *Slate*, April 20, 2004. http://slate.msn.com/id/2099203/
p. 58: "Evil, not rage."
Joanne Jacobs, "Evil, not rage, drove teen killers," *San Jose Mercury News*,
December 20, 1999, 7B.
p. 59: "But it deserves to be said to the credit . . . and gratitude on that of the slaves."
Africans in America, PBS series, 1998. http://www.pbs.org/wgbh/aia/part3/
3h499t.html.

10: His Soul Is Marching On!

p. 60: but at the last minute she "fell ill and could not make it."
Karen Whitman, "Re-evaluating John Brown's Raid at Harper Ferry," *West Virginia Quarterly* 34, no. 1 (1972), 46–84.

p. 60: "murderers, traitors, robbers, insurrectionists...wandering, malicious, unprovoked, felons."
"Message of Gov. Wise—The Harper's Ferry Outrage Fully and Freely Discussed," *Valley Spirit* (Franklin, PA), December 14, 1859, 4.

p. 60–61: "John Brown, leader of the insurrection . . . under close restraint."
The Life, Trial and Execution of Captain John Brown (New York: Robert M De Witt, 1859), http://www.yale.edu/lawweb/avalon/treatise/john_brown/john_brown.htm.

11: Our Founding Fleecers
Much of the narrative in this section is derived from Thomas Slaughter's excellent study, *The Whiskey Rebellion*.

p. 61: "a party of madmen . . . "knaves," "thieves" and "madmen,"
Slaughter, *Whiskey Rebellion*, 48.

p. 61: Chief Justice William Cushing . . . desperate individuals."
Stephen C. O'Neill, "Shays' Rebellion," *Supreme Judicial Court Historical Society, Hampshire Gazette*, June 6, 1787, 1998.

p. 61: "Rebellion against a king may be pardoned . . . ought to suffer death."
Carol Berkin, *A Brilliant Solution: Inventing the American Constitution* (New York: Harcourt, 2002), 28.

p. 61: The coastal elite loathed the rebellious frontiersmen . . . "like so many pigs in a sty."
Slaughter, *Whiskey Rebellion*, 64.

p. 62–63: Several years before independence . . . offering as little as ten pounds for every two thousand acres
Ibid., 75.

p. 63 "in a joking way," . . . "Do not let it be known that I have any concern therein,"
Ibid., 73.

p. 63: "Washington's methods for acquiring . . . were machine-like in their efficiency."
Ibid., 74.

p. 63: In 1780, just one-third of western Pennsylvania's . . . and kept the remainder for themselves.
Ibid., 65.

p. 64–5: Alexander Hamilton enlisted the comical figure of George Clymer . . .
Ibid., 117–19.

p. 65: "an actual state of insurgency against . . . an honorable chance in an Indian War."
Ibid., 118.

PART III: RAGENOMICS

1: Rage Against the Gipper

p. 68: He pulled into the parking lot in his blue automobile . . . even though it should have been empty.
David Maraniss, "When the Post Office Became a Killing Field," *Washington Post*, February 20, 1987.

p. 68-69. Shortly before 7 AM, Sherrill entered . . . ". . . screaming as they were shot."
Lasseter, *Going Postal*, 80–91.

p. 69: meaning at least one Rockne lost on account of the Gipper.
To add to the irony, grandfather Knute worked as a postal clerk at a young age to help pay his way through college.

p. 69: "I heard two quick shots and then . . . someone screamed, 'Oh, my God!'"
S. Anthony Baron, *Violence in the Workplace* (Ventura, CA: Pathfinder Publishing, 1993), 58.

p. 69: One witness said that Sherrill "shot anything that moved,"
Baron, *Violence in the Workplace*, 58.

p. 69: Hubert Hammond, a postal employee . . . "Then there were three more shots. He got her."
Lasseter, *Going Postal*, 80–91.

p. 70: "A couple of minutes [after we arrived] . . . sound of a muffled gunshot."
Ibid., 88–9.

p. 70: "Probably more than any other . . . workplace into the media spotlight."
Baron, *Violence in the Workplace*, 55.

p. 70: investigators found numerous copies . . . A Family Doctor Tells His Story.
Ibid ., 57.

p. 71: "I just got the impression, you know, he's a weird guy,"
Lasseter, *Going Postal*, 66.

p. 71: "pants that people wore back in the 'fifties."
Ibid ., 68.

p. 71: "overweight bachelor who always expressed . . . I have ever known."
Ibid ., 71.

p. 71: A neighbor, Charles Thigpen, told Newsweek, *". . . to be the right answers."*
Daniel Pedersen, "Ten Minutes of Madness," *Newsweek*, September 1, 1986.

p. 71: When Sherrill's cremated remains were buried . . . he was pushed to do what he did."
Baron, *Violence in the Workplace*, 60.

p. 71: A postal union official blamed management . . . was an act of revenge.
Kelleher, *New Arenas*, 17.

P. 71: About nine months before the massacre, Bland . . . entrusted to your care."
Lasseter, *Going Postal*, 76.

p. 72: "Although I could not hear, it was obvious . . . as being very strange, eerie."
Ibid., 79.

2: "This has put a damper on our day"

p. 73: "the most extensive reorganization of a federal agency."
Rick Geddes, *Saving the Mail* (Washington: AEI Press, 2003), 2.

p. 73: Today, even with competition, USPS employees . . . criticized for by reformers.
Murray Comarow, "The Demise of the Postal Service?" *Cosmos*
www.cosmos-club.org/journals/2002/comarow.html, 2002.

p. 73–74: Perry Smith worked for the USPS for twenty-five years . . . to rise up against these forces of evil."
Lasseter, *Going Postal*, 13–21.

p. 74–75: A few months later, a fifty-three-year-old . . . gunshot wounds to the head.
Ibid., 22–29.

p. 75: Just over a year later, in Atlanta . . ."I don't think it was random."
Ibid ., 36–45.

p. 75: In December 1988, Warren Murphy shot . . . Murphy's work efficiency to slip.
Ibid ., 120–127.

p. 75: In March 1989, Don Mace became . . . had a "disciplinary history."
Ibid ., 128–131.

p. 76: "[S]omeone wondered what could have . . . John laughed too."
Baron, *Violence in the Workplace*, 38.

p. 76: "He was always unfailingly friendly . . . you'd come up with John Taylor."
Ibid ., 33.

p. 76: "John, he never voiced a complaint . . . My God, John Taylor? Who's next?"
Ibid ., 37.

p. 76: "I figured he was just being sarcastic because there was a ton of mail in there."
Ibid ., 38.

p. 76: Just a few months later, in November 1991. . . promotions and demotions.
Ibid , p. 164–198.

p. 76–77: In spite of the report and its recommendations . . . suspended and transferred.
Ibid ., 199–205.

p. 77: And then in May 1993, . . . a prehistoric era there, really."
Ibid ., 206–216.

p. 77: After the Royal Oak shooting . . . against supervisors and coworkers.
Baron, *Violence in the Workplace*, 65.

p. 77: A report issued in 1994 decried . . . I could have reported for work."
"Labor Management, Problems Persist on the Workroom Floor," *General Accounting Office Report*, September 1994, 10.
http://archive.gao.gov/t2pbat2/152801.pdf

p. 77: However, as Gloria Moore, a shop steward . . . are assaulting each other."
Michael Diamond, "Strained Relations," *Asbury Park Press*, January 21, 2001.

3: Disgruntled Employees

p. 81: "Everybody's in shock. how this could even happen or why."
"Ohio shooter a stranger to victims," Associated Press, November 6, 2003.

p. 82: "You always hear about the post office . . . never think it will happen to you."
Michele Abbott, "Shooting at Hendersonville, NC., employment office sparks security debate," Knight Ridder/*Tribune Business News*, April 13, 2004.

4: It Permeates the Entire Culture

p. 84: "Sometimes they just want to kill the company."
Tanya Bricking, "Workplace Murderers Rarely Just 'Snap,' Psychologists Say," *Honolulu Advertiser*, November 14, 1999.

p. 84: not the generally accepted profile ... white male aged twenty-five to forty.
See for example *New Arenas*, p. 42–3, which lists different profiles, all of which are broad and contradictory.

p. 85: "as though it was a disgruntled ... violence permeates the entire culture."
Bruce Dunford, "Xerox shooting suspect arrested," Associated Press, November 3, 1999.

p. 85: "He didn't seem weird," ... Rainbows lost to Texas Christian.
Bricking, "Friends say Uyesugi gave hints of an inner torment"

p. 85: "by far the worst tragedy in the history ... Hopefully we will."
Dunford, "Xerox shooting suspect arrested"

p. 85: Harry Friel, an office manager at ... didn't want to talk about it."
Bricking, "Friends say Uyesugi gave hints of an inner torment"

p. 86: "He continued to stress that he did what he had to do because he had to make a point."
Ken Kobayashi, "Uyesugi told police he felt like an outcast," Honolulu *Advertiser*, May 20, 2000.

5: Let Them Eat Prozac

p. 87: "Why don't they get new jobs if they're unhappy—or go on Prozac?"
"Unhappy Workers Should Take Prozac—Bush Campaigner," Reuters, July 29, 2004.

p. 87: "What income growth there was ..."
Fraser, *White Collar*, 119.

p. 88: "Frustration with increasing numbers ... building heights and lot coverage."
Patrick McMahon, "Mega-mansion upsets tiny town," *USA Today*, May 22, 2001.

p. 89: the Bureau of Labor Statistics, ... to 14.4 million from 19.3 million
Stephen Kinzer, "Treading Carefully, Wal-Mart Enters Labor's Turf," *New York Times*, July 6, 2004.

p. 89: In 1981, when Ronald Reagan took office... to just 70.4 percent of the poverty line.
Woodrow L. Ginsburg, "Minimum Wage: It ain't what it used to be," *Campaign for a Fair Minimum Wage*, 1998. http://www.adaction.org/mwbook.html.

p. 89: To put this into modern terms, 1981's $3.35 ... soar by triple-digit percentages!
Ibid.

p. 89: There are some eighty million white-collar workers in America.
Fraser, *White Collar*, 8.

p. 89: in 1997 white collar males earned just six cents more ... than they earned in 1973.
Ibid ., 43.

p. 89: Since President George W. Bush came to office.. .paid less what they made in their previous jobs.
Edmund Andrews, "It's not just the jobs lost but the pay in the new ones," *New York Times*, August 9, 2004.

p. 89-90: According to a study by Harvard Law Professor . . . has doubled since 1975.
Amelia Warren Tyagi and Elizabeth Warren, *Two Income Trap: Why Middle Class Mothers & Fathers Are Going Broke* (New York: Basic Books, 2003), 133.

p. 90: Between 1990 and 2000, CEO pay skyrocketed . . . grew only 34 percent.
Jennifer Gill, "We're back to serfs and royalty," *Businessweek*, April 9, 2001.

p. 90: In 1978, CEOs earned just under 30 times . . . earned 531 times their average workers' salaries.
Fraser, *White Collar*, 188; Gill, "We're back to serfs and royalty"

p. 90: One leading economist, Robert Frank. . .since the mid-1970s.
Molly Lanzarotta, "Across the Great Divide," *Impact Press* (August/September 2001), no. 34,
http://www.impactpress.com/articles/augsep01/divide80901.html.

p. 90: In just the period since Bush took office . . . barely registered a 0.3 percent blip.
Daniel Gross, "Are profits too high? Wall Street's unlikely worry," *Slate*, November 12, 2004, http://slate.msn.com/id/2109617/.

p. 90: And the Congressional Budget Office estimated . . . of the top 1 percent of Americans.
Paul Krugman, "Bush's own goal," *New York Times*, August 13, 2004.

p. 90: "We're back to serfs and royalty in the Middle Ages."
Jennifer Gill, "We're back to serfs and royalty," *Businessweek*, April 9, 2001.

p. 90: The moves to eliminate taxes on inheritance . . . and registered Republican.
Michelle Goldberg, "More Relief for Struggling Millionaires," *Salon*, November 20, 2004, http://salon.com/news/feature/2004/11/20/tax/index.html

p. 90: From 1979 to 1998, those who earned ...distribution of any first world nation.
Lanzarotta, "Across the great divide: America's growing wealth gap"
http://www.impactpress.com/articles/augsep01/divide80901.html.

p. 90: A Businessweek article published in early 2000. . .the same period.
Gene Koretz, "Not enough is trickling down," *Businessweek*, January 31, 2000.

p. 90: "The booming late 1990s appear to have . . . up from 18 times."
Janny Scott, "Boom of the 1990's missed many in middle class, data suggests," *New York Times*, August 31, 2001.

p. 91: "This year we almost fell out of our chairs. . . the emergence of two Americas."
"Exploring the Gap," *McNeil-Lehrer News Hour*, September 3, 1999,
http://www.pbs.org/newshour/bb/economy/july-dec99/wages_9-3.html.

p. 91: In Silicon Valley, executive pay for the top 150 . . . to the tune of $2.25 billion.
Hal Plotkin, "Kick 'em when they're down: Silicon Valley's usual CEO excuses don't tell the real story," *San Francisco Chronicle*, August 23, 2001.

p. 91: "In a San Jose Mercury News study of insider . . . of Silicon Valley's biggest losers."
Chris O'Brien and Jack Davis, "Rich man, poor company, How some Silicon Valley executives made fortunes while the value of their companies plunged," *San Jose Mercury News* , December 7, 2002.

p. 91-92: Lucent Technologies' former chairman . . . un-catastrophic for this lucky gal.
Ben Klayman, "Lucent reveals severance deals," Reuters, August 13, 2001.

p. 92: As the New York Times *reported in early 2004 . . . "retiree health care"*
Milt Freudenheim, "Companies limit health coverage of many retirees," *New York Times*, February 3, 2004.

p. 92: At the end of the 1970s, on the eve of the Reagan . . . of large businesses.
Fraser, *White Collar*, 60.
p. 92: By 1993, the number of private-sector workers . . . that number fell to 45 percent.
Kimberly Blanton, "Fewer get workplace health plans," *Boston Globe*, September 19, 2003.
p. 92: Over a two year period from 2003 to 2004, over 85 million . . . some period of time.
Ceci Connolly, "Higher costs, less care, data show crisis in health insurance," *Washington Post*, September 28, 2004.
p. 92: Put another way, from 1981, the year . . . illness multiplied by 2,000 percent.
Tyagi and Warren, *Two Income Trap*, 84.
p. 92: Even in 1991, two-thirds of all full-time . . . some kind of managed care.
Fraser, *White Collar*, 60.
p. 92: Meanwhile, the average employee . . . rocketed 75 percent in the last ten years.
Kimberly Blanton, "Fewer get workplace health plans," *Boston Globe*, September 19, 2003.
p. 92: Along with the poor, unemployed and retired . . . more than 20 percent of the workforce.
Milt Freudenheim, "Record level of americans not insured on health," *New York Times*, August 27, 2004.
p. 93: "[L]ow status translates into insecurity, stress . . . susceptibility to disease."
Dan Seligman, "Why the rich live longer," *Forbes*, May 20, 2004.
p. 93: Companies contributed sixty-three cents per hour for pension ...down to forty-five cents.
Fraser, *White Collar*, 68.
p. 93: In 1950, almost half of corporate employees . . . decline occurring in the 1990s.
Ibid., 44.
p. 93: After thirty years of steadily-increasing ...vacations are now weekend vacations.
Ibid ., 28.
p. 93: It takes the average American fifteen years . . . European worker's vacation-time.
Tim Munson, "Re-Envisioning Work," *Enough!*, no. 17 (Fall 2001): 2.
http://www.newdream.org/newsletter/pdf/reenvisioning.pdf.
p. 93: That's if an American even gets paid vacation . . . up from 5 percent in 1998.
Christine Romero, "Worker burnout costs companies productivity, experts say," Gannett, January 29, 2004.
p. 94: According to a 2003 study by Boston College. . .all in the previous year.
"Economic Indicators," *Progressive Review*, http://prorev.com/statsec.htm.
p. 94: "E.J. Borghetti [is] a Pitt employee . . . doesn't bother me in the least.'"
Gary Rotstein, "Who needs a vacation? Not these happy workers," *Pittsburgh Post-Gazette*, August 24, 2003.
p. 94: "Those slaves who have kind masters . . . I don't know as it can..."
William Grimes, *The Life of William Grimes the Runaway Slave, Brought Down to the Present Time* (N.P., New Haven: 1855), 81.
p. 94: the traditional one-hour lunch break has fallen now to an average of twenty-nine minutes.
Fraser, *White Collar*, 24.

p. 95: In 1801, 100,000 bales of cotton were . . . to 4.5 million bales in 1860.
Kwame Somburu, "Africans in America," *Socialist Action*, January 1999.

6: Making an Empire State Building Out of an Anthill
p. 95: "When I see someone who is making . . . that's middle class."
"Give 'em enough rope," *Salon*, June 9, 2004. http://www.salon.com/books/feature/2004/06/09/at_their_words/
p. 95: Over the past three decades, the average American's . . . European counterparts.
Kevin Phillips, *Wealth and Democracy: A Political History of the American Rich* (New York: Broadway, 2002), 113.
p. 95: Today nearly forty percent of American employees work more than fifty hours per week.
Diane E. Lewis , "Stress, interrupted: Taking vacations can cut burnout, increase creativity," *Boston Globe*, November 14, 2004.
p. 95: Eileen Appelbaum of the Economic . . . hours in 2000 that they did in 1990.
Joel Robinson, "How the Weekend Was Won," *Livelyhood* (PBS), 1998.
p. 96: Just over a ten-year period . . . office-enclosed executive supervisors.
Fraser, *White Collar*, 35.
p. 96. As Dr. Paul Rosch, president of . . . it's very frustrating."
Steve James, "Work stress taking a larger financial toll," Reuters, August 9, 2003.
p. 96: Fortune magazine named Plante & Moran . . . a computer for each staff member.
Donkin, *Blood, Sweat, & Tears*, 274.
p. 96: Well, nowadays Americans work . . . according to an International Labor Organization study.
David Goll, "America's global-leading workaholism gets worse," *East Bay Business Times*, June 4, 2004.
p. 97: In his autobiography Straight From the Gut . . . "A Short Reflection on Golf."
Jack Welch, *Straight From the Gut* (New York: Warner Business Books, 2001), 401–6
p. 97–98: "Sure I'm one of the fat cats . . . $83.6 million in 1998 alone.
Fraser, *White Collar*, 188.
p. 98 "If Mr. Welch's $83 million total compensation . . . smaller than an anthill."
"Shareholders press GE on "out of control" CEO pay, threaten to bring bad things to light," *United for a Fair Economy*, April 20, 1999.
p. 98–99: "I shouted 'yeah!' to myself over and over as I read a couple chapters . . .
http://www.amazon.com/gp/product/customerreviews/B0000E697T/ref=cm_rev_next/002-1210986-0931251?%5Fencoding=UT8&customer-reviews.sort%5Fby=%2BsubmissionDate&n=283155&customer-reviews.start=31&me=ATVPDKIKX0DER (viewed April 20, 2005).

7: What Human Flesh Tastes Like
p. 100: "The quality guru W. Edwards Denning . . . if we feel it ourselves."
Andrew Grove, *Only the Paranoid Survive* (New York: Doubleday, 1999), 109.
p. 100: Grove, who became famous for such personal management innovations as the "Scrooge Memo"
Scott Rosenberg, "Silicon Valley's power cults," *Salon*, http://archive.salon.com/21st/books/1997/12/cov_18books.html, December 18, 1997.

p. 100: "It's fear that gets you out of comfortable . . . warns your body that something is wrong."
David Lewis, "Living paranoid after September 11: the management philosophy of Andy Grove," *Financial Times (Mastering Management)*, 2001.
p. 102: "You can take the boy off the farm, but you can't take the farm out of the boy."
Edward Wong, "A stinging office memo boomerangs," *New York Times*, April 5, 2001.
p. 103: Jeffrey Pfeffer, "It's the corporate equivalent of whips and ropes and chains."
Ibid.
p. 103: Stephen Barley, author of The New World of Work *. . . role of coordination.*
Donkin, *Blood, Sweat, & Tears*, 277.
p. 103: "The half-life of an engineer, software, hardware engineer, is only a few years."
Fraser, *White Collar*, 159.
p. 103: Corporate layoffs increased . . . have tripled since the mid-1980s.
Ibid., 53–4.
p. 103: Shipping off American jobs to cheap labor markets . . . according to a bipartisan congressional commission.
Kimberly Blanton, "Outsourcing of jobs is accelerating in U.S., study shows," *International Herald Tribune*, November 18, 2004.
p. 104: He took over Scott Paper Co. in 1994 . . . with $100 million in just nineteen months.
Fraser, *White Collar*, 183.
p. 104: When his first wife divorced . . . infant hobbled away crying."
Christopher Bryon, *Testosterone Inc: Tales of CEOs Gone Wild* (Hoboken, NJ: Wiley, 2004), 25.
p. 104: "His people are living in fear of him—absolute fear."
Ibid., 147.
p. 104: When he took over as general manager at Sterling Pulp & Paper in 1967 and applied his "mean business" philosophy of bullying and firing, he soon began receiving death threats.
Ibid., 71.
p. 105: In 1998, Citigroup CEO Sandy Weill earned $167 million, at the same time that he cut 5 percent of his workforce and reduced 401(k), pensions, and other benefits.
Fraser, *White Collar*, 188.
p. 105: Another example, . . . no healthcare, no vacation, and no retirement.
Ibid., 162.
p. 105: 2002 report by the Institute for Policy . . . pay rocket 59 percent over the median.
"CEOs profit from layoffs, pension shortfalls, and tax dodges," *United for a Fair Economy & Institute for Policy Studies*, August 21, 2003.
p. 105: Between 1995 and 1997, AT&T's stock . . . himself a hefty $3.8 million reward.
Fraser, *White Collar*, 189.

8: Putting Their Heads on Pikes

p. 105: "They tell you, 'You're too old. There's no way we can help you.' It was very tough."
Fraser, *White Collar*, 55.
p. 107: According to an American Management Survey, more than three-quarters of

major companies spy on their employees, double the number just seven years ago.
Stephanie Armour, "More workplaces keep eye, and ear, on employees," *USA Today*, February 27, 2003.

p. 107: Nearly half of all companies pay someone to monitor their employees' e-mails and Web surfing habits, and about the same number audit their employees' e-mails on a regular basis.
Jo Best," Companies step up e-mail surveillance," Special to *ZDNet*, July 20, 2004.
http://news.zdnet.com/2100-1009_22-5276512.html

p. 107: Companies are increasingly hiring actors to pose as new employees whose job is to report to management what the other employees are saying or doing.
Stephanie Armour, "More workplaces keep eye, and ear, on employees," *USA Today*, February 27, 2003.

9: Workers Complain, But They Don't Quit

p. 108–09: My significant other works for Electronic Arts . . . And the answer is that in all likelihood we won't.
Anonymous livejournal posting at http://www.livejournal.com/users/ea_spouse/274.html?thread=9746#t9746 (viewed April 20, 2005).

p. 109: "Well, I know this doesn't help . . . following the same plans..."
Ibid.

p. 109: "A union just for Game Developers . . . every day of the week most of the time."
Ibid.

p. 109: In a private interview, Pastreich was not optimistic . . . EA is making money they don't see a problem."
Josh Pastreich, e-mail messages to author, December 4, 2004, and November 29, 2004.

p. 110: Earl S. Willlis, the manager of employee benefits . . . employer's most productive asset."
Fraser, *White Collar*, 100.

p. 111: "Loyalty to a company, it's nonsense," he told the Wall Street Journal.
Byron, *Testosterone, Inc.*, 164.

p. 111: In 1941, an AT&T employee handbook stated, . . . inside of our walls."
Fraser, *White Collar*, 112.

p. 111: Across America, temp employment quadrupled from 1986-1996.
Ibid., 140.

p. 111: "Until the 1970s, temps and contract workers hardly . . . of its manpower needs.
Louis Uchitelle, "Now, the pink slip is all in a day's work," *New York Times*, August 5, 2001.

p. 112: "The master who treated his slaves humanely . . . his interest in view always."
Henry Clay Bruce, *The New Man. Twenty-nine Years as a Slave. Twenty-nine Years as a Free Man. Recollections of H.C. Bruce* (York, PA: P. Anstadt & Sons, 1895), 88.

p. 183: "If you be not suspicious, and induce . . . useful, and affectionate creatures."
Blassingame, *Slave Community*, 246.

10: The Cost of Stress

p. 112: to "smile more often so that people would know just how grateful she was to still have her job."
Fraser, *White Collar*, 15.

p. 112: One study estimates . . . employee turnover, and insurance.
John Schwartz, "Always on the job, employees pay with health," *New York Times*, September 5, 2004.

p. 112: The European Agency for Safety and Health . . . a colleague becoming violent.
Steve James, "Work stress taking larger financial toll," Reuters, August 9, 2003.

p. 112:: According to the National Institute . . . "the number one stress" in their lives, according to the NIOSH.
Jane Weaver, "Job stress, burnout on the rise," MSNBC, September 1, 2003, http://www.msnbc.msn.com/id/3072410/

p. 113: Princeton Survey Research . . .
"Stress at work," National Institute for Occupation Health and Safety, last updated January 7, 1999, http://www.cdc.gov/niosh/stresswk.html (viewed April 20, 2005).

p. 113: the University of Chicago's National Opinion . . . social survey started in 1972.
Dan Seligman, "New Crisis—Junk Statistics," *Forbes*, October 18, 2004, http://www.forbes.com/forbes/2004/1018/118_print.html.

p. 113: "presenteeism," which describes the increasingly common phenomenon ...
Weaver, "Job stress, burnout on the rise."

p. 113: A study by Harvard Law School Professor Elizabeth Warren . . . than single-income families a generation ago.
Tyagi and Warren, *Two Income Trap*, 51–52.

p. 113: Based on current trends, one of every seven families with children, or more than five million households, will file for bankruptcy.
Ibid., 6.

p. 113: Home foreclosures in 2002 . . . family income from 1973 to 2000.
Tyagi and Warren, *Two Income Trap*, 32, 78.

p. 113: Car repossessions doubled between 1998 and 2002.
Ibid., 7.

p. 113: In fact, more than 90 percent of bankruptcies are declared by people who would be described as middle-class.
Ibid .

p. 113: Republican Senator Orrin Hatch said . . . first stop for some rather than a last resort."
Ibid ., 71–72.

p. 114: today's homeowners are three times more likely to foreclose than before deregulation.
Ibid ., 78.

p. 114: Meanwhile, to keep up, credit card debt rocketed 570 percent between 1981 and 1999.
Ibid ., 20.

p. 114: Today an American is 49 percent more . . . soared more than twenty times, or 2,000 percent.
Ibid., 84.

PART IV: WAGE RAGE

1: Hire One Bourgeois to Alienate the Other

p. 117: "One of the most universally popular . . . so dear by a property-based system..."
Harding, *There is a River*, 49.

p. 117-8: One downsized IT manager . . . strike back against their former companies.
Eve Tahmincioglu, "Vigilance in the face of layoff rage," *New York Times*, August 1, 2001.

p. 192: Indeed, the percentage of private-sector employees who belong to unions in 2003 was half of what it was in 1983, according to the US Labor Bureau.
US Department of Labor, "Union Members Summary," last modified January 27, 2005, http://www.bls.gov/news.release/union2.nro.htm (viewed April 25, 2005).

2: Profiling Anyone

p. 120: For instance, one study profiles potential office rage murderers . . . lethal violence in the workplace.
Kelleher, *New Arenas*, 42.

4: A Mom and Pop Operation

p. 121-23: This chapter on Larry Hansel's murder relies heavily on material from Baron, *Violence in the Workplace*, 7–14.

p. 123 "Management agreed with the need for improved . . . visitors now wear badges."
Ibid., 116.

5: Termination! Termination!

p. 124-29. This account of Robert Mack's murder, including interviews, is drawn from Michael Mantell, *Ticking Bombs: Defusing Violence in the Workplace* (New York: Irwin, 1994), 93–134.

p. 127: According to a PBS documentary . . . stripped down and on the cheap.
Hendrick Smith, *Surviving the Bottom Line*, PBS, 1998.

p. 209: "It was necessary," Rouke said . . . company's behavior brought this to a crisis point."
Ibid.

6: A Mellow Guy

p. 130: This account of Willie Wood's murder spree is drawn from Janet Gilmore, "Ex-city worker handed life term," *Los Angeles Daily News*, February 8, 1997; Kelleher, *Arenas*, 68; www.mayhem.net/Crime/murder3.html (viewed April 25, 2005).

7: Tuan & Song

p. 130-31: This account of Tuan Nguyen's murder spree is drawn mostly from "Murder They Wrought," *GoldenSea.com*, http://goldsea.com/Features2/Murders/murders.html (viewed April 25, 2005).

8: "I'm Not Gay!"

p. 132: Warren D. Adkins, "Crazed Killer—Shoots 6 & Self—Screaming 'I'm Not Gay!'" *Gay Today*, June 10, 1997, http://gaytoday.badpuppy.com/garchive/world/061097wo.htm.

9: A Nondescript Warren of Offices

p. 133-38: This chapter on Matthew Beck's murder is drawn largely from these sources: Blaine Harden, "Worker Kills Four at Conn. Lottery," *Washington Post*, March 7, 1998; "Angry lottery worker kills 4, self in Connecticut," CNN, March 6, 1998; Mike McIntire, Al Lara, and Matthew Hay Brown, "Special Report: The lottery shootings: Horrified workers witness killing in parking lot," *Hartford Courant*, March 7, 1998; Brigitte Greenberg, "Killer of four believed Connecticut lottery cheated people," Associated Press, March 8, 1998; Jim Yardley, "Madman turned place for dreams into a nightmare," *New York Times*, March 8, 1998; Doreen Iudica Vigue and Brian MacQuarrie, "Five die as Conn. lottery worker goes on rampage," *Boston Globe*, March 7, 1998; Lisa Chedekel, "New Britain mourns loss of former mayor," *Hartford Courant*, March 7, 1998.

p. 134: *"I loved my job. That's all I lived for, was to go to work and come home."*
Baron, *Violence in the Workplace*, 44.

p. 135: *"I saw no prospect that my condition would . . . how I might be free."*
Lane, *Narrative of Lunsford Lane*, 8.

p. 136: *"The slaves on a plantation could get together . . . the work on the plantation."*
Blassingame, *Slave Community*, 108.

10: The Summer of Rage

p. 139: *In 1998, there were nine recorded workplace massacres; in 2003, there were forty-five, leaving sixty-nine dead and forty-six wounded.*
"Terror Nine-to-five: Guns in the workplace 1994–2003," *Common Dreams*, May 12, 2004, http://www.commondreams.org/news2004/0512-11.htm, viewed April 21, 2005.

p. 140: *The bloodbath began promptly on July 1st, when an employee at Modine Manufacturing . . . a good customer who "hit none of the triggers" of a problem-gambler.*
Paul Sloca, "Three killed in Missouri plant shooting," Associated Press, July 2, 2003; David Walsh, "Latest workplace shooting in US," *World Socialist*, August 20, 2003. http://www.wsws.org/articles/2003/aug2003/chic-a29.shtml

p. 141: *I heard an employee in Texas went postal . . . have never worked for VZ!*
Anonymous message board posting on http://www.verizoneatspoop.com/COMMENTS.asp?submit=2&comment_id=3487.

p. 232: *In 2002, Verizon cut 18,000 jobs and earned $1.6 billion in profit.*
Light Reading, http://www.lightreading.com/document.asp?doc_id=51760&site=lightreading.

p. 141-142: *The downsizing worked so well that in 2003, . . . wage freezes, health care and retirement benefit cuts, and so on and so on.*
Steven Greenhouse, "Verizon and unions agree on tentative 5-year contract," *New York Times*, September 5, 2003.

p. 142: *Meanwhile their executives were paid . . . earned more than $58.4 million.*
Samuel Davidson, "78,000 workers face contract expiration," *World Socialist*, July

31, 2003. http://www.wsws.og/articles/2003/jul2003/tele-j31.shtml.

p. 142-143: July 8, a worker at a Lockheed-Martin plant in Meridian . . . Then, according to CS, "Several people attending the service stood up and applauded." The following sources were used in this account: Laura Houston, "Lockheed Martin gunman fired at close range," *Daily Mississippian*, July 10, 2003; "Girlfriend: Plant Shooter a Victim," CBS/Associated Press, July 11,2003, http://www.cbsnews.com/stories/2003/07/08/national/main562172.shtml; David Halbfinger with Ariel Hart, "Man guns down 5 co-workers, then shoots himself," *New York Times*, July 8, 2003; "Miss. Shooter was 'mad at the world,'" Associated Press, July 8, 2003; Deborah Sharp, "Gunman 'just hated a lot of people,'" *USA Today*, July 9, 2003; "Investigators search for motive in deadly plant shooting in Mississippi," Associated Press, July 9, 2003; Jeremy Hudson, "Why were 6 killed?" *Jackson (Miss.) Clarion-Ledger*, November 17, 2003; Fredie Carmichael, "Anatomy of a nightmare," *Meridian (Miss.) Star*, July 13, 2003.

p. 143: The long hot Summer of Rage . . . rage-surrender a rare exception.
"Barricaded gunman gives up; no one hurt," *Lansing State-Journal*, July 22, 2003, http://www.lsj.com/news/local/p_030722copbeat__3b.html.

p. 143: Two days later, on July 23, a Century 21 real estate salesman, Ron Thomas, . . . Walker Robinson, "Suit filed nearly a year after deadly office shooting," WOAI.com, June 11, 2004. http://www.woai.com/news/local/story.aspx? content_id=db6a7c4c-d6ce-4085-a4f764ce84afbc75; David McLemore, "Man kills 2 in workplace, fatally shoots self while driving," *Dallas Morning News*, July 23, 2003; Susan Romero, "Realty agent kills two co-workers: Did 'lousy' referral or racial tension trigger rampage?" *Inman News*, August 8, 2003; Maro Robbins, "Tension in office detailed," *San Antonio Express-News*, July 27, 2003.

p. 145–146: On August 19th, a 32-year-old factory worker named Ricky Shadle . . . talking to people or something like that."
For the account of Ricky Shadle's murder, the following sources were used: Dennis B. Roddy, "Two dead, two wounded as Ohio worker opens fire at auto parts plant," *Pittsburgh Post-Gazette*, August 20, 2003; M. R. Kropko, "Gunman kills self, co-worker," Associated Press, August 20, 2003; Jodi Wilgoren, "Man fired by warehouse in Chicago kills 6 of its 9 employees," *New York Times*, August 27, 2003; Bennie Currie, "7 killed in Chicago warehouse shooting," Associated Press, August 27, 2003; Nathaniel Hernandez, "Sole survivor recalls Chicago shooting," Associated Press, August 28. 2003; "Seven die in Chicago warehouse shooting," CNN, August 28, 2003. http:/www.cnn.com/2003/US/Midwest/08/28/chicago.shooting/.

11: "Evil, not rage"

p. 147: "The end of my junior year [1998], school shootings were making their way into the news."
Brooks Brown and Rob Merritt, *No Easy Answers: The Truth Behind Death at Columbine* (New York: Lantern Books, 2002), 97.

p. 247: "The School Stopper's Textbook: A Guide to Disruptive Revolutionary . . . Many of Carneal's school essays resembled the Unabomber Manifesto."
Newman, *Rampage*, 143.

p. 149: *He had bullied and brutalized, call "gay" and a "faggot."*
Ibid., 26–7.
p. 149: *"I am not insane, I am angry. I killed . . . I will do it with a bullet."*
Ibid ., 249.
p. 149: *"We're going to kick-start a revolution, a revolution of the dispossessed!"*
Eliot Aronson, *Nobody Left to Hate* (New York: Owl Books, 2001), 85.
p. 149: *"I want to leave a lasting impression on the world."*
Alan Prendergast, "I'm full of hate and I love it," *Westworld.com*, December 6,
2001, http://www.westword.com/issues/2001-12-06/news.html.
p. 150: *In a* Rocky Mountain News *article titled "Surfers Worship Heroes of Hate,"* ...
Holly Kurtz, "Surfers worship heroes of hate," *Rocky Mountain News*, February 6,
2000.
p. 151: *"They wanted cult-hero status. And they got it."*
Kirsten Go, "Web sites worship teen killers," *Denver Post*, December 14, 1999.
p. 151: *As this* New York Times *article, . . . help him control his anger.*
Michael Janofsky, "Desert boot camp shut down after suspicious death of boy,"
New York Times, July 4, 2001.
p. 153: "Evil, not rage, drove these killers."
Joanne Jacobs, "Evil, not rage, drove teen killers," *San Jose Mercury News*,
December 20, 1999, 7B.

12: A Rebellion of One
p. 155: *Boris Nemtsov, claimed that some 2,000 . . . putting the figure at 2,070.*
Yulia Latynina, "Dedovschina sure beats a coup d'etat," *Moscow Times*, March 26,
2003.

PART V: MORE RAGE. MORE RAGE.

1: I Don't Like Mondays
p. 158: *Brenda Spencer, a tiny, bespectacled sixteen-year-old high school student . . .*
*Brenda Spencer has consistently failed in her attempts at parole, the last denial coming
in 2001.* The account of Brenda Spencer's murder was taken largely from:
"'I Don't Like Mondays" killer refused parole," *TCM Archives* (Ireland),
http://archives.tcm.ie/breakingnews/2001/04/18/story10201.asp (viewed April 21,
2005); Anne Kreuger, "No parole for sniper who hated Mondays," *San Diego
Union-Tribune*, January 22, 1993.

2: This Place Is the Pits!
p. 159: *San Diego County was also the site of several . . . in El Cajon, the inland suburb
adjacent to Santee.*
Lasseter, *Going Postal*, 128–31.
p. 264: *In Dana Point, a mostly white, overwhelmingly Republican coastal town of
35,000 . . .*
According to 2000 statistics, population more than 2:1 registered Republicans, 75

percent white, http://www.orangecounty.net/cities/pdf/danapointstats.pdf.

p. 159–161: USPS employee Mark Hilbun joined the Dana Point Post Office in 1988 . . . his attorney agreed to plead guilty in exchange for ruling out the death penalty; Lasseter, *Going Postal,* 217-239; "Some start with family before taking violence to the office," *USA Today,* July 14, 2004.

p. 161: Dana Point, incidentally, was only incorporated in 1988 . . . "the only romantic spot in California.
http://www.orangecounty.net/cities/DanaPoint.html#history.

p. 161–162: But perhaps the most original rage attack . . . many residents criticized as unnecessarily brutal.
Virginia Association of Driver Education and Traffic Safety, "General Public," (no date), http://www.adtsea.iup.edu/vadets/GeneralPublic.htm.

p. 162: "The largest military complex" . . . 20 percent of San Diego County's GDP, according to the San Diego Chamber of Commerce's 2003 report.
"Forecast 2003," *San Diego Economic Bulletin,* 51: 1 http://www.sdchamber.org/economic/forecast2003.pdf.

p. 162: The county's twelve major military installations . . . one-fifth of the US Marine Corps and Navy are stationed there,
"San Diego," *GlobalSecurity.org,* last updated October 28, 2003, http://www.globalsecurity.org/military/facility/san_diego.htm.

p. 162: Revenues from defense spending directly for some 20 percent . . . San Diego Chamber of Commerce's 2003 report.
"Defense and Transportation Manufacturing,"San Diego Regional Economic Development Corporation, updated July, 2004, http://www.sandiegobusiness.org/industry_defense.htm.

p. 162: 260,000 retirees
Maureen Magee, "Fleet week takes off from Gillespie Field," *San Diego Union-Tribune,* September 26, 2004.

p. 162: "Apparently Mark Ames is under the illusion . . . Let's rock and roll."
Jack Truman, "The Mail", *New York Press,* June 15, 2004.

3: "It's only me"

p. 163: 85 percent white
http://santee.areaconnect.com/statistics.htm.

p. 163 : In 1998, a black Marine at a party in Santee was attacked by five whites and left paralyzed in what authorities descried as a hate crime.
"Beaten Black marine will face attackers," Associated Press, February 19, 1999.

p. 163 : As Santee Mayor Randy Voepel declared in 2001, "We are America."
Nancy Gibbs, "It's only me," *Time,* March 19, 2001.

p. 163 : It is the home of the Institute for Creation Research . . . promoting creationism in schools.
Raja Mishra, "Evolution foes see opening to press fight in schools," *Boston Globe,* November 16, 2004.

p. 163 : Coastal San Diegans call East County residents goat ropers, trailer trash, and haze suckers
Rich Gibson, "Lonely privilege in despair: Aiming for unfeigned hope," *Rich*

Gibson's Education Page For a Democratic Society, March 2001, http://www.geocities.com/elethinker/RG/Santee.htm.

p. 164: In 1999, Andy and his father moved to Twentynine Palms in the California desert...

David Hasemyer, David Washburn, and Joe Cantlupe, "Once cheerful and charming, the boy took on a darker side in recent months, pals say," *San Diego Union-Tribune*, March 7, 2001.

p. 165: According to one account, . . . and anti-abortion placards.

Gibson, "Lonely privilege in despair: Aiming for unfeigned hope."

p. 165: . . . along with a Beanie Baby doll . . . of happier times, he later explained).

Greg Moran, "Teen's explanation given in interviews with psychiatrist," *San Diego Union-Tribune*, August 16, 2002.

p. 165: egging him on

"Williams: '5,000 bullies in one place,'" *San Diego Union-Tribune*, October 11, 2002.

p. 165: Joshua Stevens, who held the sleepover . . . take part in the shooting.

Jeff McDonald, "Two killed, 13 wounded in rampage; suspect smiled as he fired, witnesses say," *San Diego Union-Tribune*, March 6, 2001.

p. 165: That same day, his father took him to nearby Lakeside . . . interest in the condo and his room.

Alex Roth, "Andy Williams harbors hope of someday being released," *San Diego Union-Tribune*, September 6, 2001.

p. 166: Before class, he got stoned with his "friends" . . . they missed checking his backpack . . .

Jeff McDonald, "Two killed, 13 wounded in rampage."

p. 166: "He seemed carefree. I asked him he if was gong to school he shook his head and said, 'Yeah.'"

Ibid.

p. 166: "...egging me on and egging me on."

"Williams: '5,000 bullies in one place,'" *San Diego Union-Tribune*, October 11, 2002.

p. 166: "You can't go back, everybody will think you're nothing..."

Newman, *Rampage*, 151.

p. 166: When Edwards, lying on the floor, asked Andy why he shot him, Andy told him to shut up.

Jason Anthony, "Affidavit: Suspect angry at new school," CNN, March 14, 2001.

p. 166: Richard Geske . . . and fled for safety.

Jeff McDonald, "Two killed, 13 wounded in rampage."

p. 166: "All I know is he turned around . . . and I wasn't on fire."

Ibid.

p. 167: One of those, Zuckor . . . her son was pronounced dead.

Greg Moran, "Williams reluctant to discuss past, future," *San Diego Union-Tribune*, August 18, 2002.

p. 167: Andy was interrogated just three and a half hours . . . "Yeah," Williams responded.

Ibid.

4: Sympathy Rage

p. 167: In the first seventy-two hours after . . . or for carrying weapons to school.
"An epidemic of violence: Incidents in schools rise sharply since Santee shooting," CNN, March 8, 2001. http://archives.cnn.com/2001/US/03/08/
alarming.incidents/

p. 168: As reported on March 8 by CNN and ABC News kids all across America rose up in rebellion: . . .
Bryan Robinson, "Unflattering imitation, experts explain alleged copycat incidents after Santana shooting," ABC News, March 8, 2001.

p. 169: . . . an eighteen-year-old high school student . . . finish what Andy started."
Greg Moran, "Man admits sending post-Santana threats," *San Diego Union-Tribune*, July 7, 2001.

p. 169-71 The account of Elizabeth Bush's attempted murder is taken from these sources:
Ovetta Wiggins, Barbara Boyer, John Way Jennings, and Ralph Vigoda, "In schools, a day of gunfire and anger," *Philadelphia Inquirer*, March 8, 2001; "'A cry for help' victim, students express sympathy for Pennsylvania shooting suspect," ABC News, March 9, 2001; David Morgan, "Pennsylvania girl admits school shooting," Reuters, April 4, 2001; Jodie Morse, "Girlhoods Interrupted," *Time*, March 19, 2001.

p. 170: "To me, high school is like Hell. You get up and go to Hell every day."
Alex Frost, interview, *Elephant*, DVD, Gus Van Sant, dir., (Burbank, CA: Warner Home Video, , 2004).

p. 171-2: The account of Jason Hoffman's shooting is taken from these sources:
Bryan Robinson, "Decoding the 'ethic of violence'" *ABC News*, March 26, 2001; Greg Moran, "Similarities can be seen locally, nationwide," *San Diego Union-Tribune*, June 22, 2002; Jeff McDonald, "Five injured in teen's rampage at Granite Hills," *San Diego Union-Tribune*, March 23, 2001.

p. 172: On March 27, all six public schools . . . Larry Marshall, a Harrison police lieutenant told CNN.
"'Vague' phone threats close 7 N.Y. schools," CNN, March 27, 2001, http://archives.
cnn.com/2001/US/03/27/school.threat/index.html.

p. 172: In the days and weeks after the massacre of April 20, 1999, schoolyard incidents included:
Thomas Capozzoli and R. Steve McVey, *Kids Killing Kids: Managing Violence and Gangs in Schools* (Boca Raton: Saint Lucie Press, 2000), 3.

5: Frog-Marching Across the Quad

p. 173-4: The account of the Laguna High school shooting plot was taken from these sources:
Charlie Goodyear, Chuck Squatriglia, and Mark Martin, "Columbine-style attack averted—2 students arrested in Elk Grove," *San Francisco Chronicle*, February 11, 2004; Mark Marti, John Hubbell, and Matthew Stannard, "Plot to attack school a 'fantasy,'" *San Francisco Chronicle*, February 12, 2004.

p. 175: nine students at Cupertino Middle School, aged twelve to fourteen . . .
Sandra Gonzales, "Plot foiled to burn school, cops say," *San Jose Mercury News*, February 15, 2004.

p. 175: two Dutchtown, Louisiana students, Christopher Levins, seventeen . . .
"Two students arrested in Columbine-style plot," CNN, January 13, 2004.
http://www.cnn.com/2004/US/South/01/13/creating.columbine.ap/.
p. 175: A few months later, on May 14, 2004, two middle school students in Winder,
Georgia . . .
Lori Johnston, "Ga. teens tried for alleged school plot," Associated Press, June 7,
2004; "Students ordered held without bail until trial," Associated Press, May 28,
2004; "Winder students accused of planning violent attack," Associated Press,
May 17, 2004; "Georgia students held in school killing plot," Associated Press,
May 26, 2004.
p. 176: Just six months before that, in Lovejoy, Georgia, a fourteen-year-old student . . .
"North Georgia teen jailed in Columbine-style plot," WJXT News, October 1,
2003. http://www.news4jax.com/news4georgia/2523910/detail.html/.
p. 176: One of the most widely reported of these school plots took place in New Bedford . . .
"Mass. teen pleads guilty in school plot," Associated Press, March 10, 2003.
p. 176: A USA Today editorial, "Columbine's Lessons Learned,". . .
"Columbine's Lessons Learned," *USA Today*, November 28. 2001.
p. 176: An initial rising in 1649 . . . repression to be taken.
Herskovits, *The Myth of the Negro Past*, 94.
p. 176: A third-grader in Pontiac, Michigan, brought a 1-1/2 inch by 1-1/2 inch medallion . . .
John Wisely, "State law dictates school officials take action even if weapons are
toys," *Oakland Press*, January 12, 2001.
p. 176: Two days after the Santee shootings, a fifteen-year-old student at a high school in
Belmont, California...
Matthew B. Stannard, "Threats in creative school work taken seriously," *San*
Francisco Chronicle, March 9, 2001.
p. 176: In May 2004, a fourteen-year-old boy at a middle-class intermediate school in
Walnut Creek, ...
"Walnut Creek student arrested for cartoon," *Bay City News*, May 27, 2004,
http://abclocal.go.com/kgo/news/052704_nw_student_cartoon.html.

6: Copycats on Copycats
p. 177: "Kids see this . . . brought to the forefront."
Bryan Robinson, "Unflattering imitation, experts explain alleged copycat incidents after Santana shooting," ABC News, March 8, 2001.
p. 177: "Maybe these are copycat cases, maybe there has always in violence in schools . . .
Ibid.
p. 177-78: "The copycat phenomenon is out there, and it is particularly damaging ...
Ovetta Wiggins, Barbara Boyer, John Way Jennings, and Ralph Vigoda, "In
schools, a day of gunfire and anger," *Philadelphia Inquirer*, March 8, 2001.
p. 178: "There is clearly a copy-cat contagion effect at work," James Allen Fox...
Fox Butterfield, "Tips by students result in arrests at five schools," *New York*
Times, March 8, 2001
p. 178: During the successful slave revolution in Hispaniola in 1797, newspapers...
Jordan, *White Over Black*, 384.

7: An Entirely New Phenomenon

p. 181: 1927, in Bath, Michigan, where a "demented farmer" killed his wife, then planted dynamite
Capozzoli and McVey, *Kids Killing Kids*, 4.

p. 181: In the 1980s, there were five school attacks ... one security guard, one student, and wounded four others.
Newman, *Rampage*, 236–7.

p. 181-82: ... until 1996, when fourteen-year-old Barry Loukaitis' attack ... Loukaitis was sentenced to two life terms plus 205 years in jail.
Ibid., 248, 252; Capozzoli and McVey, *Kids Killing Kids*, 8; Alex Tizon, "Scarred by killings, Moses Lake asks: What has this town become?" *Seattle Times*, February 23, 1997.

p. 182: A year later, in Bethel, Alaska, another ... and I'll be considered yesterday's news."
"Rage: A look at a teen killer: Alaskan shooter suffered from depression, anger," *60 Minutes II*, March 7, 2001.

p. 182: Woodham was sentenced to three life terms, and one of the plotters was sentenced to six months in a boot camp and five years probation.
Collin Johnson, "'Not enough,' say some of punishment," *Clarion-Ledger*, February 12, 2000.

p. 182: Michael Carneal opened fire on a prayer circle ... well-to-do two-parent home in an upscale section of the otherwise dreary, dying riverport town.
Newman, *Rampage*, 3–7.

p. 182: Joseph "Colt" Todd, a fourteen-year-old, ... cause pain on someone else."
"Teen arrested for shooting Arkansas classmates," CNN, December 19, 1997, http://www.cnn.com/US/9712/19/school.shooting/.

p. 182: ...was accused of being gay in a rumor column published in his 8th grade school newspaper.
Newman, *Rampage*, 94.

p. 182: "Please, just shoot me."
Ibid., 7.

p. 182: The following morning, a small group ... "We forgive you Mike."
Ibid., 179

p. 182: Vicky Whitman, Michael Carneal's former girlfriend ... strange for someone not to like school."
Ibid., 365–66.

p. 182: Exactly one month later, Andrew Wurst, ... None of this is real."
Ibid., 247.

p. 183: On March 24, 1998, Mitchell Johnson ... they brought it on themselves ..."
Ibid., 97

p. 183: A few weeks later, on May 21, 1998, Kip Kinkel ... his trench coat, and opened fire.
Ibid., 246, 259; "Bullets littered home of suspect in Oregon school shooting, documents say," Associated Press, October 2, 1998.

p. 183–184: The Justice Policy Institute noted in a report that seven in ten Americans believed a shooting was likely in their school.
Lori Dorfman and Vincent Schiraldi, "Off Balance: Youth, Race, & Crime in the

News," *Justice Policy Insitute*, April 2001.

8: Culturally Normative Behavior

p. 184: Devon Adams told the Governor's Columbine Review Commission that the ...
Holly Kurtz, "Columbine bully talk persists," *Rocky Mountain News*, August 26, 2000.

p. 184-185: As one member of the Columbine High School football . . . call them homos."
Aronson, *Nobody Left*, 71.

p. 185: Harris got it worse than most . . . giving the jocks more ammo to attack him.
Brown and Merritt, *No Easy Answers*, 51.

p. 185: "I was smoking cigarettes with . . . Dylan said. 'It happens all the time.'"
Ibid., 108.

p. 185: Once, a student reported them to the administration . . . the damage was done.
Ibid .

p. 185: Another time, according to a report, students surrounded them in the cafeteria and threw ketchup at them.
Newman, *Rampage*, 247.

p. 185: They were so marked for abuse that even talking ...wouldn't do anything about it"
Brown and Merritt, *No Easy Answers*, 54–55.

p. 185: Debra Spears, whose stepsons attended Columbine . . . essentially destroyed their lives.
Kurtz, "Columbine bully talk persists."

p. 185: One favorite bullying game for the seniors was to "go bowling" ...
Brown and Merritt, *No Easy Answers*, 50.

p. 185: Regina Huerter, Director of Juvenile Diversion . . . because they were afraid for their jobs.
Ibid ., 52-54.

p. 186: Bullying was so deeply ingrained that, . . . apparently such behaviors were culturally normative."
Patricia Marks Greenfield and Jaana Juvonen, "A developmental look at Columbine," *APA Monitor Online*, 30, no. 7 (July/August 1999), http://www.apa.org/monitor/julaug99/vp.html/

p. 186: DeAngelis, along with district officials, disagreed . . . How can things be so rosy?'"
Kurtz, "Columbine bully talk persists."

p. 186: . . . a poll taken five years after the Columbine massacre showed that 83 percent of Americans now blame the boys' parents.
David Brooks, "Columbine: Parents of a Killer," *New York Times*, May 15, 2004.

p. 186: Just three years before that, 81 percent of Americans blamed the Internet.
"After Columbine: geek profiling," http://slashdot.org/features/01/01/23/2341238.shtml.

p. 186: "My parents are the best fucking parents . . . They will never forget it."
Dan Luzadder, Kevin Vaughan, and Karen Abbott, "Chilling goodbye from killers, Harris, Klebold apologize, brag in videos made days, minutes before attack on Columbine," *Rocky Mountain News*, December 13, 1999.

p. 186-187: Slate's Dave Cullen, commenting on Harris's Web . . . entire race for its

appalling inferiority."
Dave Cullen, "The Depressive." *Slate*, April 20, 2004, http://slate.msn.com/id/
2099203/.
p. 187: "Research indicates that chronic targets . . . school culture at Columbine High."
Greenfield and Juvonen, "A developmental look at Columbine."
p. 187: Susan Klebold, Dylan's mother, told New York Times columnist David Brooks...
Brooks, "Columbine: Parents of a Killer."

9: Anorexic Andy

p. 187: "There's a lot of hate around here."
Terry McCarthy, "Society warning: Andy Williams here," *Time*, March 19, 2001.
*p. 187: Andy's appointed lawyer, Deputy Public Defender . . . "Some of the stuff basically
borders on torture."*
Alex Roth, "Dad says bullying drove son to act," *San Diego Union-Tribune*,
September 6, 2001.
*p. 188: When he visited, old school friends in rural Maryland . . . egged his father's apart-
ment or stole his homework and threw it into garbage bins.*
David Hasemyer, David Washburn, and Joe Cantlupe, "Once cheerful and charming, the boy took on a darker side in recent months, pals say," *San Diego Union-
Tribune*, March 7, 2001.
*p. 188: They called him "faggot" and "bitch" and "gay" and taunted him for not fighting
back when he was bullied.*
"Williams: '5,000 bullies in one place,'" *San Diego Union-Tribune*, October 11, 2002.
p. 188: "His ears stuck out, he was small, skinny, had a high voice . . . said Scott Bryan.
Rose Arce, "Study: Kids rate bullying and teasing 'big problem,'" CNN, March 8,
2001.
*p. 188: "He was picked on all the time," student Jessica Moore . . . freak, dork, nerd, stuff
like that."*
Scott Bowles and Martin Kasindorf, "Friends tell of picked-on but 'normal' kid,"
USA Today, June 19, 2001.
*p. 188: Laura Kennamer, a friend, said "They'd walk up to him and sock . . . wouldn't do
anything about it."*
McCarthy, "Society warning: Andy Williams here."
*p. 188: Even Andy's fifty-nine year-old neighbor, Jim Crider, . . . didn't always pay atten-
tion."*
Gregory Alan Gross, "People sketch different sides to teen suspect," *San Diego
Union-Tribune*, March 6, 2001.
p. 188: Anthony Schneider, . . . stole his skateboard [about a month ago]."
Ibid.
p. 188: While visiting friends in Maryland a . . . "My school is horrible. I hate it there."
David Washburn and David Hasemyer, "Violence study shows Williams 'fits the
pattern,'" *San Diego Union-Tribune*, March 9, 2001.
p. 189: "I was trying to prove a point."
"Williams: '5,000 bullies in one place.'"
p. 189: Prosecutor Kristin Anton told the San . . . continue to associated with each other."
Roth, "Dad says bullying drove son to act."

p. 189-190: District Superintendent Granger Ward also denied . . . same percentage of parents felt that the school was unsafe for their kids.
Jill Spielvogel, "Study shows bullying old problem at Santana High," *San Diego Union-Tribune*, February 2, 2002.
p. 190: A national survey on bullying conducted by the National Institute of Child Health and Human Development in mid-2001...
Erica Goode, "School bullying is common, mostly by boys, study finds," *New York Times*, April 25, 2001.
p. 190: A national survey on bullying conducted by the Kaiser Family Foundation ..."
Rose Arce, "Study: Kids rate bullying and teasing 'big problem,'" CNN, March 8, 2001.
p. 190: As one man in upper-middle-class suburban Iowa . . . he does not feel safe."
Marc Hansen, "Bullying of kids isn't just one town's problem," *Des Moines Register*, June 8, 2004.
p. 191: Research has shown that bullies are not the anti-social . . . behind those described as friendly, outgoing, and self-confident.
Natalie Angier, "Bully for you: Why push comes to shove," *New York Times*, May 20, 2001.

10: I Would Have Done It Too

p. 191: As recently as 1999, just a few months after Columbine, Time published . . . learned elsewhere.
Gibbs, "A week in the life of a high school."
p. 192: Dr. Tonja Nansel, who worked on a 1998 World Health Organization survey . . .
Goode, "School bullying is common, mostly by boys, study finds."
p. 193: As Dr. Nansel said, "In the past, bullying has simply been . . . normal part of growing up."
Ibid.
p. 193: One of the best of these post-Santee confessions was this brave op-ed . . .
Emily Stivers, "Young voices: Stop the teasing, or more kids may die," *Detroit Free Press*, March 20, 2001.
p. 193: As Carol Miller Lieber of Educators for Social Responsibility. . ."The winners . . .
Aronson, *Nobody Left*, 81.
p. 194: A few weeks after Stivers' op-ed, the Detroit Free Press published this article, "Mom's Group Tries to End Taunting," . . .
Lori Higgins, "Mom's group tries to end taunting," *Detroit Free Press*, April 11, 2001.
p. 194-195: At around the same time as the above op-ed was published, another heart-breaking account, this by an Asian-American parent named Chi-Dooh Li...
Chi-Dooh Li, "School bullying is rooted in a teenage caste system," *Seattle Post-Intelligencer*, March 29, 2001.

11: A Problem Overlooked

p. 195: In January 2004, a Eugene, Oregon school paid $10,000 for allowing the...
Heather Hollingsworth, "Parents turn to courts to stop bullying," Associated Press, May 21, 2004.

p. 195: By 2004, seventeen states had enacted anti-bullying legislation . . . ignoring this problem are very serious."
"Congresswoman Linda Sánchez introduces federal anti-bullying legislation," ABC News, December 12, 2003.

p. 196: As a New York Times article, "Fear in the Workplace," "It got to where I was twitching, literally, on the way to work."
Benedict Carey, "Fear in the Workplace," *New York Times*, June 22, 2004.

p. 196: Long before this, the 1994 US Postal Service commission . . . confrontational relations on the workroom floor."
"Labor management problems persist on the workroom floor," *General Accounting Office Report*, September 1994, 10, http://archive.gao.gov/t2pbat2/152801.pdf.

p. 196: For Andy Williams personally, the rebellion . . . parole when he turns sixty-five.
"Williams: '5,000 bullies in one place.'"

12: No Profile Possible

p. 197: Today, according to the book Kids Killing Kids, *as many as one of every four...*
Capozzoli and McVey, *Kids Killing Kids*, 25.

p. 198: The number of children and adolescents who take various psychiatric drugs more than doubled from 1987 to 1996 . . .
Erica Goode, "Study finds jump in children taking psychiatric drugs," *New York Times*, January 14, 2003.

p. 198: Today, 20 percent of high school students are on anti-depressants or medicines . . .
Aronson, *Nobody Left*, 38.

p. 198: Another study done by University of Texas physicians estimates that Ritalin . . .
Dr. John Breeding, "Texans for Safe Education: An estimate of current psychiatric drug use with school-age children in the United States," *Wildcolts.com* (no date), http://www.wildestcolts.com/safeEducation/estimate.html.

p. 198: However, according to a government study conducted in 1999, one in five . . .
Aronson, *Nobody Left*, 65.

p. 198: Secret Service "Safe School Initiative"
U.S. Secret Service National Threat Assessment Center, "Safe School Initiative," 2002, http://www.secretservice.org/ntac/ntac_ssi_report.pdf.

p. 198: The FBI in 2000 issue a study in which they cautioned . . .
Pierre Thomas, "FBI report to detail 'warning signs' that could lead to school shootings," CNN, September 6, 2000.

p. 199: In Eric Harris's diary, he writes, "You know what I hate? Racism . . .
Dave Cullen, "Kill mankind. No one should survive," *Salon*, September 23, 1999, http://www.salon.com/news/feature/1999/09/23/journal/.

p. 199: James P. McGee, chief psychologist for the Baltimore Police Department . . .
Washburn and Hasemyer, "Violence study shows Williams 'fits the pattern.'"

p. 199: As for "average intelligence," Andy Williams was an honor roll student . . .
Hasemyer, Washburn, and Cantlupe, "Once cheerful and charming, the boy took on a darker side in recent months, pals say."

p. 199: In a video diary, Eric Harris quoted Shakespeare's Tempest to apologize . . .
Aronson, *Nobody Left*, 40.

p. 200: The thirteen-year-old boy who shot and wounded five fellow students . . .
"4 Oklahoma middle schoolers wounded," CNN, December 6, 1999; "Four students shot at Oklahoma school," Associated Press, December 7, 1999.
p. 200: The Secret Service study found that two-thirds of the kids who launched rage . . .
Newman, *Rampage*, 244.
p. 200: "Sorry Dad, I love you."
Moran, "Teen's explanation."
p. 201: According to one survey, 63 percent of suburban teenagers either own a gun . . .
Aronson, *Nobody Left*, 47.
p. 201: "Eric is a very bright young man who is likely to succeed in life . . . hard work is part of it."
Ibid., 39–40.

13: Kids 4 Snitching

p. 201–203: DeGuzman . . .
Alex Ionides, "This boy's play," *Silicon Valley Metro*, February 28, 2002; Matthew P. Stannard, Alan Gathright, Stacy Finz, and Maria Alicia Gaura, "'Walking hate . . . ready to snap,' Suspect held in De Anza massacre plot," *San Francisco Chronicle*, January 31, 2001.
p. 204: WAVE Program
"After Columbine: geek profiling," http://slashdot.org/features/01/01/23/2341238.shtml; Lynn Burke, "A chilling wave hits schools," *Wired*, April 17, 2000; Nick Mamatas, "High school confidential," *In These Times*, October 1, 2001; Jim Redden, *Snitch Culture: How Citizens are Turned into the Eyes and Ears of the State* (Los Angeles: Feral House, 2000), 137.

14: St. Eric and St. Dylan

p. 205–206: DeGuzman
Jason Bennert and May Wong, "Massacre plot alleged, Filipino American Al DeGuzman pleads not guilty," *Asianweek*, February 9 – 15, 2001; Stannard, Gathright, Finz, and Gaura, "'Walking hate . . . ready to snap'"; Alex Ionides, "This boy's play."
p. 206: On November 7, 2001, just seven months after Andy Williams' shooting spree . . .
Jill Spielvogel and Chris Moran, "New shooting threat limits attendance at Santana High School," *San Diego Union-Tribune*, November 10, 2001.
p. 206: At Westside Middle School in Jonesboro, Arkansas, three days after . . . he was escorted out.
Newman, *Rampage*, 278.
p. 206: 'Things were better at Columbine, as far as how people treated one another . . . but others hadn't changed at all."
Brown and Merritt, *No Easy Answers*, 195.
p. 206: Six months after the massacre, Carla Hochhalter . . . in an interview later as "amazing."
Lynn Bartels, "A story of healing and hope," *Rocky Mountain News*, April 20, 2004.

p. 201: *More recently, in early 2002, two Columbine High students were suspended ...*
Jeff Kass, "Sheriff to seek felony charges for Columbine 'hit list' teens," *Rocky Mountain News*, February 23, 2002.

15: Target: America

p. 210: *Katherine Newman notes, "[J]ust about everyone at school—often a shooter's ...*
Newman, *Rampage*, 250.

p. 210: *Along with their guns, a TEC-9, a Hi-Point 9-millimetere ... spark an explosion failed.*
Peggy Lowe and Kevin Vaughan, "Sheriff's final report traces killers' steps," *Rocky Mountain News*, May 14, 2000.

p. 210: *As Eric Harris explained in a diary entry dated April 26, 1998, "We use bombs ...*
Brown and Merritt, *No Easy Answers*, 5–6.

p. 210: *The slaves destroyed tirelessly. Like the peasants in the Jacquerie or the ...*
C. L. R. James, *The Black Jacobins* (New York: Vintage, 1989), 88.

p. 210: *"I live in Denver, and dammit, I would love to kill almost all its residents," Eric Harris wrote ...*
Cullen, "Kill mankind. No one should survive."

p. 210-211: *"They explain over and over why they want to kill as many people ... their rage grew."*
Karen Abbott and Dan Luzadder, "I really am sorry ... but war's war.'" *Rocky Mountain News*, December 13, 1999.

p. 211: *...their rage was so great that according to CNN, had they survived the massacre, ... away as we go down."*
"Columbine killer envisioned crashing plane into NYC," CNN, December 6, 2001. http://archives.cnn.com/2001/US/12/05/columbine.diary/

p. 211: *Reuters got evangelical in their account: "One group came to the parking lot ...*
Maureen Harrington, "Two Columbine high school sweethearts murdered," Reuters, February 16, 2000.

p. 211: *Tom Galland, a pastor in Jonesboro where ... now everyone is suing each other.*
Newman, *Rampage*, 210–11.

PART VI: WELCOME TO THE DOLLHOUSE

1: Bad Intentions

p. 213-215: The account of the cheating scandal was drawn from personal interviews and from the following sources:
"Saratoga cheating blamed on competitive environment," NBC11, January 26, 2004; Lisa Toth, "District expels two Saratoga High School students for cheating," *Saratoga News*, February 11, 2004; "Saratoga High student believed to have plotted to blow up school," Associated Press, January 31, 2004. http://www.kget.com /news/state/story.aspx?content_id=2608b2f9-1b23-42ba-92bf-e7257b2774b9; Elisa Banducci and Maya Suryaraman, "Sheriff defends teen's release," *San Jose Mercury News*, February 2, 2004; Crystal Carreon, "Another Saratoga High student arrested for alleged threats," *San Jose Mercury News*, February 3, 2004; Elisa Banducci, Crystal Carreon, and Maya Suryaraman, "Student to face bomb plot charges,"

San Jose Mercury News, February 4, 2004; Sandra Gonzales and Elise Banducci, "High school bomb plot alleged," *San Jose Mercury News*, January 31, 2004; Maria Alicia Gaura and Alan Gathright, "Saratoga High cheating scandal gets uglier," *San Francisco Chronicle*, February 5, 2004.

2: The Maze

p. 216: Steven Spielberg was a student at Saratoga for one year in the 1960s . . .
Ronald Grover, "Steven Spielberg: The Storyteller," *Businessweek*, July 13, 1998.
p. 216–217: In 1982, the year before I graduated, a sophomore student at neighboring Los Gatos High . . .
Gloria I. Wang, "Arrest made in '82 murder of Los Gatos High student," *Los Gatos Weekly Times*, May 14, 2003; Hong Dao Nguyen, "No bail for man accused in '82 Los Gatos death," *San Jose Mercury News*, October 24, 2003; Ryan Kim, "CA coroner can't find remains of '82 teen victim," *San Francisco Chronicle*, March 15, 2004.
p. 217: On April 30, 1999, three fourteen and fifteen-year-old boys at Willow Glen High in west San Jose...
Jessica Lyons, "SJPD calls 'copy-cat' bomb scare at WG High a hoax," *Saratoga News*, May 12, 1999.
p. 218: On March 16, 2001, a couple of weeks after Andy Williams's shooting in Santee, a fifteen-year-old boy at Westmont High in Campbell...
Erin Mayes, "Westmont and Prospect both report threats of violence," *Silicon Valley Metro*, March 28, 2001.

3: A 4.0 Failure

p. 218: Saratoga High School holds a top rank in the state of California for . . . SAT average score of 1272.
Kamika Dunlap, "200 parents pack meeting on cheating at Saratoga High," *San Jose Mercury News*, January 30, 2004.
p. 219: "If you're just a 4.0, you're perceived by your family as a failure."
Wendy Shieu and Kalvin Wang, "Parents seek roots of cheating," *Saratoga Falcon*, February 13, 2004.
p. 219: A graduate from the class of 1999, Ankur Luthra, became Saratoga's first-ever . . .
Mandy Major, "Hard work has helped Saratoga's Ankur Luthra earn a trip to Oxford University as a Rhodes Scholar," *Saratoga News*, January 15, 2003; Linh Tat, "Saratoga High Schools' Allan Chu has made amazing acheivements," *Saratoga News*, June 11, 2003.
p. 219: A teacher at the Princeton Review SAT course said, "I've had parents and . . .
Melinda Sacks, "High anxiety: Silicon Valley families devote time and money to help kids ace the SAT," *San Jose Mercury News*, February 11, 2004.
p. 220: As a New York Times article about these prep camps described it, "No campfires."
Tamar Lewin, "How I spent summer vacation: At getting-into-college camp," *New York Times*, April 18, 2004.
p. 220: In March 2002, the Securities and Exchange Commission filed a civil fraud . . . "sick of people thinking GAAP was important."
Securities and Exchange Commission v. Dale Peterson (United States District Court for the Northern District of California C.A. No. C02-01467), http://www.sec.gov/

litigation/litreleases/lr17439.htm.

p. 220: Roughly a year later, another wealthy Saratoga resident, Reza Mikaillia, was convicted on ten counts of securities . . .

"Software executive convicted," *Silicon Valley Business Journal*, November 21, 2003, http://houston.bizjournals.com/sanjose/stories/2003/11/17/daily64.html.

p. 220: A Rutgers study of 4,500 high school students in 2001 revealed that 76 percent . . .

Davina Pruitt-Mentle, "Plagiarism in the 21st century: Paper mills, cybercheating, and internet detectives in the electronic age," July 16, 2002. Cyberethics, Cybersafety, & Cybersecurity Conference, University of Maryland, June 18, 2004, http://edtechoutreach.umd.edu/SeminarHandouts/CyberSeminar_Plagiarism_2.ppt.

4: A Kind and Caring Stranger

p. 221: Several of the students who committed violent acts in school were thought to be . . .

Capozzoli and McVey, *Kids Killing Kids*, 129.

p. 221: "Sleep schedules just get insane," Saratoga High senior Gene Wang . . .

Maya Suryaraman and Becky Bartindale, "School takes action, but pressure to excel remains," *San Jose Mercury News*, May 30, 2004.

p. 221: The problem is so bad that the school newspaper . . . Not enough sleep causes more stress," she said.

Dora Chua and Elaine Ho, "Sufficient sleep soothes stress, researchers say," *Saratoga Falcon*, May 24, 2004.

p. 221: a personal homepage of a former Saratoga student, nineteen-year-old Daniel Walter Yang

Daniel Walter Yang's "About Me" page, http://www.danielyang.com/propaganda.

p. 222: Philip Sung's life became much easier after entering MIT . . . competitive than Saratoga High.

"Students grapple with changes, ethics after cheating incidents," *Saratoga Falcon*, February 13, 2004.

p. 222: In May 2000, Lancy Chui, a seventeen-year-old student, committed suicide . . .

Kara Chalmers, "Students continue to cope with grief as tragedy dogs high school," *Saratoga News*, March 28, 2001.

5: The Post-Diaper Rat Race & Testing for Caldwell Brokers

p. 222: "Pressure is pushing kids to the limit."

Suryaraman and Bartindale, "School takes action, but pressure to excel remains."

p. 223: In the 1960s, only 4 percent of children were enrolled . . . are placed in pre-schools.

Tyagi and Warren, *Two-Income Trap*, 37.

p. 223: Chicago public school district pre-school tuition was $6,500 per year, more than the tuition at the University of Illinois.

Ibid., 38–9.

p. 223: . . .the recent securities fraud case of Citigroup chairman Sandy Weill and star telecoms analyst Jack Grubman . . .

Dan Ackman, "Weill-Grubman dealings were child's play," *Forbes*, November 14, 2002.

p. 224: . . .a New York magazine article about an ambitious couple and their four-year-old boy named Andrew . . .

Ralph Gardner, Jr., "Four and failing," *New York*, November 15, 1999.

6: Globalization High

p. 225–226: Kim Mohnike, an English teacher at Saratoga . . . students is the grade."
Suryaraman and Bartindale, "School takes action, but pressure to excel remains."
p. 384: As Todd Dwyer, a popular economics teacher at Saratoga High . . . under a bridge.
Todd Dwyer, "San Jose cheating was an aberration," *San Jose Mercury News*, June 4, 2004.

7: The Groaning Horde

p. 227–228: S. Muthiah, writing for an Indian newspaper . . . Their focus is the classroom —and exams."
S. Muthiah, "Silicon Valley sojourn: Get SAT, Go!" *Hindu*, April 25, 2004.

8: Every Child Left Behind

p. 229: "It wasn't just Grandma Millie who had money stolen, it was our children."
Bryan Corliss, "Enron case tied to school costs," *Everett (Wash.) Daily Herald*, July 2, 2004.
p. 230: "When this election [in 2000] comes Bush will fucking whack this shit, man."
"Enron traders caught on tape," KUTV.com, June 1, 2004.
p. 230: "We will not take any action that makes California's problems . . . President George W. Bush
Ibid.
p. 230: some three thousand schools and four million children were dropped from the school lunch program . . .
"School Lunch Programs," *American Federation of State, County, and Municipal Employees Federation Resolution*, Resolution No. 38, June 21, 1982, http://www.afscme.org/about/resolute/1982/r25-038.htm.
p. 230: In 1999, one in every six children lived in poverty . . . France, Belgium, and Austria.
Sue Pleming, "Report: One in six U.S. children lives in poverty," Reuters, April 19, 2001.

10: From Columbine to Bin Laden

p. 232-230: On February 9, 2004, just as the Saratoga school district was debating what to do about their crisis, Jon Romano . . .
Danielle Furfaro and Brendan Lyons, "A warning, then gunfire. Student, 16, charged in shooting that wounded high school teacher," *Albany Times-Union*, February 10, 2004; Kate Perry, "District, students seeking answers: Columbia High classes resume in wake of Monday's shooting incident," *Troy Record*, February 11, 2004.
p. 233: The following day, Tuesday, February 10, police were called into nearby Corinth High School . . .
Jim Kinney, "Corinth police check out suspicious writing at school," *Saratogan*, February 11, 2004.
p. 233: As of early February, 2004, there were twenty-one shootings with thirty-six school-related deaths, according to Kenneth Trump . . .

Rick Carlin, "School-related violence on rise in U.S.," *Albany Union-Tribune*, February 10, 2004.

p. 233–235: Charles Bishop, piloted a small plane into an office high-rise in Tampa ... nuclear bomb left over from the 1967 Israeli-Syrian war."

Brad Hunter and Malcolm Balfour, "Kamikaze teen 'Was no loner,'" *New York Post*, January 8, 2002; "Teachers: 'Sweet boy' showed no signs of suicide flight, Flyer's family 'appalled and devastated,'" CNN, January 7, 2002. http://archives.ccn.com/2002/US/01/07/plane.crash.suicide/; "Teen pilot was prescribed drug linked to suicide," *USA Today*, January 8, 2002; Shankar Vedantam, "Plane crash reinforces that Accutane can cause suicide," *Washington Post*, January 11, 2002.

11: Move On or Get Over It!

p. 236: "We'd like to think that [Superintendent Cynthia Hall Ranii is] sincere in helping the family move on."

Elisa Banducci, Crystal Carreon, and Maya Suryaraman, "Student to face bomb plot charges," *San Jose Mercury News*, February 4, 2004.

p. 237: "You start hearing talk about 'moving beyond this.'"

Newman, *Rampage*, 217.

p. 237: Beverly Ashford, a Westside teacher, told the interviewers ..."

Ibid., 224.

p. 237: Mary Curtis, a teacher caught in the crossfire, told the Harvard team, "I heard secretaries ..."

Ibid ., 216.

p. 237: The mother of one Jonesboro victim said, "The people I work with avoid me ..."

Larry Furgate, "Westside shooting survivors reflect as anniversary nears," *Jonesboro Sun*, March 22, 2003.

p. 237: Betsy Woods, a Jonesboro counselor, told the Harvard interviewers ..."

Newman, *Rampage*, 215.

p. 237: "The kids who continued to attend were sometimes mocked by classmates ..."

Ibid ., 217.

p. 237: "Some students complained to their teachers that their parents would not listen to them, saying instead, 'It's time to get over it.'"

Ibid ., 224.

p. 237: On the messageboard of Techrepublic.com linking to an article titled "Lost your job? Don't look overseas."

http://techrepublic.com.com/5208-6230-0.html?forumID=10&threadID=153619&start=0&tag=search.

p. 238: Britt Hume of FoxNews attacked the soldier's families, saying "[Y]ou have to feel like saying to people, 'Just get over it.'"

"Fox News pundit Brit Hume tells families of dead American soldiers to 'Just Get Over it,'" *Counterbias.com*, March 28, 2004, http://www.counterbias.com/news004.html

p. 238: Paul O'Rear wrote, "Several months after Dad's death ..."

Paul O'Rear, "Get Over it?" *Waxahackie Daily Light*, October 23, 1997.

p. 238: Nancy Ruhe, executive director of Parents of Murdered Children in Cincinnati, told CNN ...

"Killer taunts victim's family over the Internet," Associated Press, January 13, 2004.
p. 238: *"That is a telling illustration of where we are as a community . . .*
Newman, *Rampage*, 225.
p. 238: *"Just when is it going to end?" Susan Miller, a Westside administrator . . .*
Ibid., 226.
p. 239: *One teacher who cared for the children at the blood-spattered shooting scene . . .*
Ibid., 226, 372.

POST SCRIPT:
p. 242: *Take this example from* National Review *editor Stanley Kurtz . . . Soviet's took note."*
Stanley Kurtz, "A Lesson in Backbone," *National Review*, June 7, 2004,
http://www.nationalreview.com/kurtz/kurtz200406070917.asp.

LaVergne, TN USA
26 August 2009

155959LV00001B/185/A